WORLD REPORT

2013

EVENTS OF 2012

www.hrw.org

Human Rights Watch is dedicated to protecting the human rights of people around the world.

We stand with victims and activists to prevent discrimination, to uphold political freedom, to protect people from inhumane conduct in wartime, and to bring offenders to justice.

We investigate and expose human rights violations and hold abusers accountable.

We challenge governments and those who hold power to end abusive practices and respect international human rights law.

We enlist the public and the international community to support the cause of human rights for all.

HUMAN RIGHTS WATCH

Human Rights Watch is one of the world's leading independent organizations dedicated to defending and protecting human rights. By focusing international attention where human rights are violated, we give voice to the oppressed and hold oppressors accountable for their crimes. Our rigorous, objective investigations and strategic, targeted advocacy build intense pressure for action and raise the cost of human rights abuse. For over 30 years, Human Rights Watch has worked tenaciously to lay the legal and moral groundwork for deep-rooted change and has fought to bring greater justice and security to people around the world.

Human Rights Watch began in 1978 with the founding of its Europe and Central Asia division (then known as Helsinki Watch). Today, it also includes divisions covering Africa; the Americas; Asia; and the Middle East and North Africa; a United States program; thematic divisions or programs on arms; business and human rights; children's rights; health and human rights; international justice; lesbian, gay, bisexual, and transgender rights, refugees, terrorism/counterterrorism; and women's rights; and an emergencies program. It maintains offices in Amsterdam, Beirut, Berlin, Brussels, Cairo, Chicago, Geneva, Johannesburg, London, Los Angeles, Moscow, New York, Paris, San Francisco, Tokyo, Toronto, Washington DC, and Zurich, and field presences in 20 other locations globally. Human Rights Watch is an independent, nongovernmental organization, supported by contributions from private individuals and foundations worldwide. It accepts no government funds, directly or indirectly.

The staff includes Kenneth Roth, Executive Director; Michele Alexander, Deputy Executive Director, Development and Global Initiatives; Carroll Bogert, Deputy Executive Director, External Relations; Jan Egeland, Deputy Executive Director, Europe; Iain Levine, Deputy Executive Director, Program; Chuck Lustig, Deputy Executive Director, Operations; Walid Ayoub, Information Technology Director; Pierre Bairin, Media Director; Clive Baldwin, Senior Legal Advisor; Emma Daly, Communications Director; Alan Feldstein, Associate General Counsel; Barbara Guglielmo, Acting Operations Director; Peggy Hicks, Global Advocacy Director; Babatunde Olugboji, Deputy Program Director; Dinah PoKempner, General Counsel; Tom Porteous, Deputy Program Director; Aisling Reidy, Senior Legal Advisor; James Ross, Legal and Policy Director; Joe Saunders, Deputy Program Director; Frances Sinha, Global Human Resources Director; and Minky Worden, Director of Global Initiatives.

The division directors of Human Rights Watch are Brad Adams, Asia; Joseph Amon, Health and Human Rights; Daniel Bekele, Africa; John Biaggi, International Film Festival; Peter Bouckaert, Emergencies; Richard Dicker, International Justice; Bill Frelick, Refugees; Arvind Ganesan, Business and Human Rights; Liesl Gerntholtz, Women's Rights; Steve Goose, Arms; Alison Parker, United States; Graeme Reid, Lesbian, Gay, Bisexual, and Transgender Rights; José Miguel Vivanco, Americas; Zama Coursen-Neff, Children's Rights; Sarah Leah Whitson, Middle East and North Africa; and Hugh Williamson, Europe and Central Asia.

The advocacy directors of Human Rights Watch are Philippe Bolopion, United Nations–New York; Juliette De Rivero, United Nations–Geneva; Kanae Doi, Japan; Jean-Marie Fardeau, Paris; Meenakshi Ganguly, South Asia; Lotte Leicht, European Union; Tom Malinowski, Washington DC; and Wenzel Michalski, Berlin.

Acknowledgments

A compilation of this magnitude requires contribution from a large number of people, including most of the Human Rights Watch staff. The contributors were:

Arwa Abdelmoula, Fred Abrahams, Brad Adams, Tamara Alrifai,
Cressida Arkwright, Chris Albin-Lackey, Laetitia Bader, Pierre Bairin,
Amanda Bailly, Jayshree Bajoria, Clive Baldwin, Heather Barr, Noah Beaudette,
Jo Becker, Daniel Bekele, Eleanor Blatchley, Carroll Bogert, Philippe Bolopion,
Jana Boulus, Nick Bourland, Amy Braunschweiger, Sebastian Brett, Reed Brody,
Jane Buchanan, Wolfgang Buettner, Maria Burnett, Inga Butefisch,
Elizabeth Calvin, Anna Chaplin, Grace Choi, Jane Cohen, Carlos Conde,
Adam Coogle, Eva Cosse, Zama Coursen-Neff, Emma Daly, Philippe Dam,
Mariana Dambolena, Kiran D'Amico, Juliette Delay, Juliette de Rivero,
Rachel Denber, Yasemin Derviscemallioglu, Boris Dittrich, Corinne Dufka,
Mariam Dwedar, Brahim Elansari, Marianna Enamoneta, Jessica Evans,
Elizabeth Evenson, Erin Evers, Lama Fakih, Jean-Marie Fardeau, Alice Farmer,
Jamie Fellner, Bill Frelick, Lydia Gall, Arvind Ganesan, Meenakshi Ganguly,
Liesl Gerntholtz, Alex Gertner, Neela Ghoshal, Giorgi Gogia, Vugar Gojayev,
Eric Goldstein, Steve Goose, Yulia Gorbunova, Jessie Graham, Amna Guellali,
Eric Guttschuss, Danielle Haas, Mariwan Hama, Andreas Harsono, Ali Hasan,
Jehanne Henry, José Luis Hernández, Peggy Hicks, Nadim Houry, Kyle Hunter,
Lindsey Hutchison, Peter Huvos, Claire Ivers, Cameron Jacobs, Balkees Jarrah,
Rafael Jimenez, Ahmed Kaaniche, Tiseke Kasambala, Aruna Kashyap,
Scout Katovich, Elise Keppler, Amr Khairy, Viktoriya Kim, Phelim Kine,
uliane Kippenberg, Anna Kirey, Mariam Kirollos, Boukje Kistemaker,

Natalie Kiwajko, Amanda Klasing, Adrian Klocke, Kyle Knight, Adrianne Lapar, Lucie Lecarpentier, Leslie Lefkow, Lotte Leicht, Iain Levine, Diederik Lohman, Tanya Lokshina, Anna Lopriore, Drake Lucas, Tom Malinowski, Kaitlin Martin, Sarah Margon, Veronica Matushaj, Géraldine Mattioli-Zeltner, Andrea Mazzarino, Maria McFarland, Nicholas McGeehan, Ola McLees, Megan McLemore, Amanda McRae, Grace Meng, David Mepham, Lianna Merner, Wenzel Michalski, Darcy Milburn, Kathy Mills, Lisa Misol, Alba Morales, Heba Morayef, Stephanie Morin, Priyanka Motaparthy, Rasha Moumneh, Lewis Mudge, Jim Murphy, Samer Muscati, Otsieno Namwaya, Agnes Odhiambo, Babatunde Olugboji, Shaivalini Parmar, Richard Pearshouse, Rona Peligal, Sunai Phasuk, Camille Pifteau, Laura Pitter, Dinah PoKempner, Tom Porteous, Andrea Prasow, Youssef Ramez, Ben Rawlence, Graeme Reid, Aisling Reidy, Samantha Reiser, Meghan Rhoad, Sophie Richardson, Lisa Rimli, Mihra Rittmann, Phil Robertson, Kathy Rose, James Ross, Kenneth Roth, Hanan Salah, Katya Salmi, Ricardo Sandoval-Palos, Faraz Sanei, Joe Saunders, Ida Sawyer, Lea Scarpel, Rebecca Schleifer, Max Schoening, Laura Schulke, Birgit Schwarz, Jake Scobey-Thal, Diana Semaan, Anna Sevortian, Kriti Sharma, Ivy Shen, Bede Sheppard, John Sifton, Gerry Simpson, Emma Sinclair-Webb, Param-Preet Singh, Jillian Slutzker, Mickey Spiegel, Nik Steinberg, Joe Stork, Zaman Sultani, Judith Sunderland, Steve Swerdlow, Sylvie Stein, Veronika Szente Goldston, Letta Tayler, Carina Tertsakian, Elena Testi, Tej Thapa, Storm Tiv, Katherine Todrys, Annkatrin Tritschoks, Bill van Esveld, Gauri van Gulik, Elena Vanko, Nisha Varia, Jamie Vernaelde, José Miguel Vivanco, Janet Walsh, Benjamin Ward, Matt Wells, Sarah Leah Whitson, Daniel Wilkinson, Hugh Williamson, Cynthia Wong, Minky Worden, Marina Yalon, and Yasmin Yonis.

Senior Editor Danielle Haas edited the report with assistance from Deputy Program Directors Tom Porteous and Babatunde Olugboji. Publications Director Grace Choi and Graphic Designer Rafael Jiménez oversaw layout and production, in coordination with Multimedia Producer Anna Lopriore, Creative Director Veronica Matushaj, Senior Online Editor Jim Murphy, and Publications Specialist Kathy Mills. Program Office Project Coordinator Marina Yalon coordinated editing and production.

The report was proofread by Grant writer Leeam Azulay, Coordinator Adrianne Lapar, and Associates Noah Beaudette, José Luis Hernández, Kyle Hunter, Lindsey Hutchison, Scout Katovich, Kaitlin Martin, Darcy Millburn, Shaivalini Palmer, Jake Scobey-Thal, Annkatrin Tritschoks, Matthew Rullo, Sylvie Stein, and Elena Vanko.

Table of Contents

Foreword

The World Report is Human Rights Watch's twenty-third annual review of human rights practices around the globe. It summarizes key human rights issues in more than 90 countries and territories worldwide, drawing on events from the end of 2011 through November 2012.

The book is divided into three main parts: an essay section, photo essays, and country-specific chapters.

 In the introductory essay, Human Rights Watch Executive Director Ken Roth considers the "day after" the end of abusive rule in countries. As the euphoria of the Arab Spring gives way to frustration over the slow pace of change, he notes that toppling dictators may yet prove easier than the messy and complicated process of building a rights-respecting democracy. But while the future may be uncertain, he warns against pining for the predictability of author- itarian rule, and cautions those now in power not to restrict the rights of others based on so-called morals, cherished values, or whatever restrictions a majority of voters will support. In this crucial, norm-building period, he says, effective courts, accountable public officials, and institutions of governance are needed to ensure that rights are upheld and the promise of the Arab Spring is realized.

Next, Graeme Reid sounds a warning about countries evoking tradition and traditional values to undermine human rights, especially for women and members of the lesbian, gay, bisexual, and transgender community ("The Trouble With Tradition: When "Values" Trample Over Rights"). He argues that far from being benign, as its language suggests, a recently passed United Nations Human Rights Council resolution "promoting human rights and fundamental freedoms" via "a better understanding of traditional values of humankind" tramples over diversity, and fails to acknowledge just how fluid traditional practice and customary law can be.

As year one of the UN-backed Guiding Principles on Business and Human Rights, 2012 was supposed to mark a big step forward in addressing the failure of many global businesses to operate with sufficient regard for human rights. But as Chris Albin-Lackey notes, efforts to promote respect for human rights by

1

businesses remain hobbled by the failure of governments to oversee and regulate their human rights practices ("Without Rules: A Failed Approach to Corporate Accountability"). A "workable balance" is needed, he writes, which limits human rights abuses while acknowledging that companies can face real difficulties in addressing human rights problems linked to their operations.

Finally, Juliane Kippenberg and Jane Cohen criticize the failure of governments, international agencies, and nongovernmental organizations to see environmental issues through the prism of human rights and address them together in laws or institutions ("Lives in the Balance: The Human Cost of Environmental Neglect"). They argue that the environmental and human rights movements must work together to ensure that those who damage the environment and trample on human rights are held accountable, and that those who suffer environmental degradation can be heard, participate in debate about environmental issues, and seek redress when needed.

The photo essays that follow focus on the experiences of three very different groups: migrants and asylum seekers in Greece; people with disabilities in Russia; and children and adults living in, and working around, gold mines in Nigeria's Zamfara State. Yet all suffer from lack of legal protections and a range of abuses that impact their health, ability to fully participate in society, and other human rights.

Each country entry identifies significant human rights issues, examines the freedom of local human rights defenders to conduct their work, and surveys the response of key international actors, such as the United Nations, European Union, the United States, and various regional and international organizations and institutions.

The report reflects extensive investigative work that Human Rights Watch staff undertook in 2012, usually in close partnership with human rights activists in the country in question. It also reflects the work of our advocacy team, which monitors policy developments and strives to persuade governments and international institutions to curb abuses and promote human rights. Human Rights Watch publications, issued throughout the year, contain more detailed accounts of many of the issues addressed in the brief summaries in this volume. They can be found on the Human Rights Watch website, www.hrw.org.

As in past years, this report does not include a chapter on every country where Human Rights Watch works, nor does it discuss every issue of importance. The absence of a particular country or issue often simply reflects staffing limitations and should not be taken as commentary on the significance of the problem. There are many serious human rights violations that Human Rights Watch simply lacks the capacity to address.

The factors we considered in determining the focus of our work in 2012 (and hence the content of this volume) include the number of people affected and the severity of abuse, access to the country and the availability of information about it, the susceptibility of abusive forces to influence, and the importance of addressing certain thematic concerns and of reinforcing the work of local rights organizations.

The World Report does not have separate chapters addressing our thematic work but instead incorporates such material directly into the country entries. Please consult the Human Rights Watch website for more detailed treatment of our work on children's rights, women's rights, arms and military issues, business and human rights, health and human rights, international justice, terrorism and counterterrorism, refugees and displaced people, and lesbian, gay, bisexual, and transgender people's rights, and for information about our international film festivals.

The Day After

By Kenneth Roth

Two years into the Arab Spring, euphoria seems a thing of the past. The heady days of protest and triumph have been replaced by outrage at the atrocities in Syria, frustration that the region's monarchs remain largely immune to pressure for reform, fear that the uprisings' biggest winners are Islamists who might limit the rights of women, minorities, and dissidents, and disappointment that even in countries that have experienced a change of regime, fundamental change has been slow and unsteady. Difficult as it is to end abusive rule, the hardest part may well be the day after.

It should be no surprise that building a rights-respecting democracy on a legacy of repression is not easy. The transitions from communism in Eastern Europe and the former Soviet Union yielded many democracies, but also many dictatorships. Latin America's democratic evolution over the past two decades has been anything but linear. Progress in Asia and Africa has been uneven and sporadic. Even the European Union, which has successfully made democratic reform and respect for human rights conditions of membership, has had a harder time curbing authoritarian impulses once countries—most recently Hungary and Romania—became members.

Moreover, those who excelled at overthrowing the autocrat are often not best placed to build a governing majority. The art of protest does not necessarily match the skills needed for governing. And allies in ousting a despot are sometimes not the best partners for replacing despotism.

But those who pine for the familiar days of dictatorship should remember that the uncertainties of freedom are no reason to revert to the enforced predictability of authoritarian rule. The path ahead may be treacherous, but the unthinkable alternative is to consign entire peoples to a grim future of oppression.

Building a rights-respecting state may not be as exhilarating as toppling an abusive regime. It can be painstaking work to construct effective institutions of governance, establish independent courts, create professional police units, and

4

train public officials to uphold human rights and the rule of law. But these tasks are essential if revolution is not to become a byway to repression by another name.

The past year offers some key lessons for success in this venture—as valid globally as they are for the states at the heart of the Arab Spring. There are lessons for both the nations undergoing revolutionary change and the international community. Here are a few.

Avoid Majoritarian Hubris

Any revolution risks excesses, and a revolution in the name of democracy is no exception. It is no surprise that a revolution's victors, long repressed by the old regime, do not want to hear about new restraints once they have finally found their way to power. But a rights-respecting democracy is different from unrestrained majority rule. Frustrating as it can be, majority preferences in any democracy worthy of its name must be constrained by respect for the rights of individuals and the rule of law. Majoritarian hubris can be the greatest risk to the emergence of true democracy.

As the region's fledgling governments set about drafting new constitutions, no major political actor is proposing to jettison rights altogether. But unlike, say, Bosnia, Kenya, South Sudan, and many Latin American states, none of the region's constitutions simply incorporates international human rights treaties—the surest way to resist back-sliding because it avoids watered-down formulations and helps to insulate the interpretation of rights from the perceived exigencies of the moment. Many of the region's constitutions continue to make at least some allusion to Sharia (Islamic law)—a reference that need not substantially conflict with international human rights law but often is interpreted in a manner that threatens the rights of women and religious or sexual minorities.

For example, the controversial new constitution of the region's most influential nation, Egypt—which was being put to a national referendum at this writing—seems a study in ambiguity, affirming rights in general terms as it introduces clauses or procedures that might compromise them. It has some positive elements, including clear prohibitions on torture and arbitrary detention—abuses that, perhaps not coincidentally, members of the governing Muslim Brotherhood regularly suffered under the ousted government of former President Hosni Mubarak. In article 2, it affirms the "principles" of Sharia, a clause copied from Egypt's prior constitution, which is broadly understood to correspond with basic notions of justice, rather than the proposed alternative "rulings" of Sharia, which would impose strict rules and leave no room for progressive interpretation.

However, the new document contains dangerous loopholes that could cause problems down the line. All rights are conditioned on the requirement that they not undermine "ethics and morals and public order"—elastic caveats that are found in rights treaties but are susceptible to interpretations that compromise rights. The principles of Sharia are to be interpreted in consultation with religious scholars and in accordance with a certain school of Islam, potentially opening the door to interpretations that run afoul of international human rights law. The right to freedom of expression is qualified by a proscription against undefined "insults" to "the individual person" or the Prophet Muhammad. Freedom of religion is limited to the Abrahamic religions, which would appear to exclude those who practice other religions, such as the Baha'i, or no religion at all. Military trials of civilians appear to be allowed for "crimes that harm the armed forces," which leaves intact the military's broad discretion to try civilians. Gender discrimination is not explicitly prohibited, and the state is asked to "balance between a women's obligations toward the family and public work"—a possible invitation for future restrictions on women's liberties. A proposed ban on human trafficking was rejected because some drafters feared it would block the shipment of Egyptian children to the Persian Gulf for early marriage. And efforts to exert civilian control over the interests of the military, whether its impunity, budget, or businesses, appear to have been abandoned.

So for the foreseeable future, rights in Egypt will remain precarious. That would have been true even if even a less qualified document emerged, since every constitution requires interpretation and implementation. But it is all the more risky because of this constitution's limits on many rights.

Despite these disappointments, it is essential that electoral losers not give up on democracy. That is a dangerous tactic, premised on the view that Islamists, once having taken power by electoral victory, can never be trusted to cede it by electoral loss. When Algeria's military acted on that rationale by halting elections that Islamists were poised to win, the result was not democracy but a decade of civil war with massive loss of life. It is a perspective that undervalues the potent combination of domestic protest and international pressure that would coalesce to challenge new attempts to monopolize power. Its proponents have a high burden to meet before they can convincingly contend that the prognosis for elected government under an Islamic party is so bleak that a return to the dark days of the past is warranted.

By the same token, electoral victors must resist the temptation to impose whatever restrictions on rights a majority of legislators will support. That is important as a matter of principle: unbridled majority rule is not democracy. It is important for reasons of pragmatism: today's electoral victor can be tomorrow's loser. And it is important for reasons of compassion: even those unable to conceive electoral loss should have sufficient empathy to recognize the defeated as deserving of their own freedom and aspirations.

Defend Women's Rights

As the Islamist-dominated governments of the Arab Spring take root, perhaps no issue will define their records more than their treatment of women. International human rights law prohibits the subordination of people on the basis of not only race, ethnicity, religion, and political views, but also gender. That is, it prohibits forcing women to assume a submissive, secondary status, and similarly rejects a "complementary" role for women as a substitute for gender equality. As noted, the Egyptian constitution contains troubling language on this subject, and while Egypt's Supreme Constitutional Court has historically interpreted the "principles of Sharia" progressively, many fear that more conservative interpretations may now prevail.

Some opponents of women's rights portray them as a Western imposition, at odds with Muslim religion or Arab culture. But rights do not prevent women from leading a conservative lifestyle if they choose. Rather, the imposition involved is when national or local authorities—inevitably dominated by men—insist that women who want equality and autonomy cannot have it. Calling such rights a Western imposition does nothing to disguise the domestic oppression involved when women are compelled to assume a subservient role.

The need for vigilance is highlighted by the Middle Eastern government that is most notorious for subordinating women in the name of Islam: Saudi Arabia. Once discrimination is entrenched in law, progress becomes extraordinarily difficult, as demonstrated in 2012 by the kingdom's grudging progress toward recognizing women's rights by allowing (under pressure) two women to compete on its Olympic team, even though women and girls may not participate in most sports at home. Saudi Arabia did announce that for the first time, it would allow women to obtain licenses to practice law and represent clients in court, as well as the right to work in four new industries, but it did so in the context of a male guardianship system that forbids women from traveling abroad, studying at university, seeking a job, operating a business, or undergoing certain medical procedures without a male guardian's consent. Strict gender segregation prevails in all educational institutions and most offices, restaurants, and public buildings, and women still may not drive.

A small group of Saudi women have made clear in social media that they see these restrictions as unwelcome impositions by male authorities. The Saudi and other governments should recognize that a desire for autonomy, fairness, and equality is shared by many women in all parts of the world—including their own countries—and that the invocation of culture, tradition, and religion cannot justify denying them these rights.

Protect Freedom of Speech

Electoral majorities are also tempted to restrict others' rights when speech is seen to transgress certain bounds, such as by criticizing government leaders, disparaging ethnic or racial groups, or offending religious sentiments. Some restrictions on speech are, of course, justified: for example, speech that incites violence should be suppressed through the justice system. Hate speech should also be challenged through rebuttal and education. Politicians especially should refrain from language that fosters intolerance.

The line between speech that incites violence and speech that is merely controversial varies with local conditions, such as the degree of risk that speech will lead people to violence and the ability of the police to prevent a violent turn. But it is also important to distinguish between those who incite violence, and those who oppose free speech and use violence to suppress or punish it. And while international law permits restrictions on speech that incites hatred and hostility, they must be enshrined in law, strictly necessary for reasons of national security or public order, and proportionate.

Those who seek to suppress controversial speech typically claim the moral high ground by suggesting they are guarding cherished values or preventing national discord. But that is not how such restrictions tend to play out because it is usually the strong who repress the speech of the weak. When Pakistani authorities charged a 12-year-old Christian girl with a mental disability with blasphemy, the values of the Quran that she was (falsely) accused of desecrating were never in jeopardy, but the girl was a conveniently weak figure for unscrupulous adherents of the dominant religion to exploit. When Indonesian officials prosecuted members of the minority Ahmadiyah religious community for blasphemy, the country's dominant religion was never at risk, but a Muslim sect that many Islamic countries declare to be deviant was persecuted. The same could be said of the Saudi youth facing the death penalty for apostasy because of a Tweet questioning his own faith.

Governments sometimes justify prosecuting a contentious speaker by arguing that he or she "provoked" a violent reaction. That is a dangerous concept. It is easy to imagine governments seeking to suppress dissenters by suggesting they provoked a violent response from government forces or their allies. Security forces in Bahrain, for example, attacked and rounded up peaceful activists on the grounds that they were disturbing public order. Even the early Tahrir Square demonstrations in Egypt might have been shut down under such a robust concept of provocation. When people react violently to non-violent speech because they object to its content, they—not the speaker—are the offender. The state has a duty to stop their violence, not give them an effective veto over the speech by censoring it.

Respect Minority Rights: The Case of Burma

The problem of unbridled majority rule is not limited to the Arab world. In the past year, the most vivid demonstration of the problem could be found in Burma, a long-entrenched military dictatorship that is giving way at a surprising pace to at least signs of limited democracy. Many of the outstanding issues concern the military: Will it give up its constitutionally guaranteed quarter of the seats in parliament? Will it countenance civilian oversight of its conduct and business interests? Will it release all political prisoners still languishing in prison and permit unfettered competition in the 2015 elections? The leading opposition political party, the National League for Democracy (NLD), headed by Nobel laureate Aung San Suu Kyi, is understandably preoccupied with these questions of power and political rights.

But the NLD has been disappointing in its reluctance to look beyond a quest for power to secure the rights of less popular, more marginal ethnic groups. For example, it has not pressed the military to curtail, let alone prosecute, war crimes being committed against the ethnic Kachin population as part of continuing counterinsurgency operations in the north. Most dramatically, the NLD has refused to speak out against severe and violent persecution of the Muslim Rohingya in the west, many of whom are stateless as a result of a discriminatory nationality law, despite coming from families who have lived in Burma for generations. Suu Kyi has disappointed an otherwise admiring global audience by failing to stand up for a minority against whom many Burmese harbor deep prejudice.

Western sanctions played a key role in convincing the Burmese military that, without reform, it would never match the economic development of its Association of Southeast Asian (ASEAN) neighbors (let alone escape economic dependence on China). However, European nations and the United States rushed to suspend sanctions and to undertake high-profile visits to Burma before genuine reforms—including protections for persecuted minorities—were implemented, losing considerable leverage in the process to protect minority and other rights.

Bolster Weak States that Lack the Rule of Law: The Case of Libya

As much as strong states can be dangerous when unrestrained by basic rights protections, so are weak and disintegrating ones. Paradoxically, the state can not only be a threat to human rights, but is also a necessity for their realization. To avoid the plight of Afghanistan or Somalia, the alternative to a repressive state should be a reformed, not a dismantled, one.

Among the Arab Spring states, Libya best illustrates the problem of a weak state. No longer plagued by the dictatorship of Muammar Gaddafi and its repressive grip, Libya suffers foremost from a lack of government—one that is dedicated to respecting rights and incapable of enforcing them.

That void is partly Gaddafi's design: he deliberately kept governmental institutions weak to reduce threats to his reign. But it is also due in part to the NATO powers' eagerness, having overthrown Gaddafi, to declare victory and move on, rather than commit serious effort and resources to the less dramatic but essential work of institution building.

The problem is particularly acute with respect to the rule of law. The Libyan government still does not have anywhere near a monopoly on the use of force. Militias operating autonomously continue to dominate many parts of the country and in some places commit serious abuses with impunity, such as widespread torture, occasionally resulting in death. Thousands remain in detention, including many accused Gaddafi supporters—held sometimes by the government, sometimes by militias—with little immediate prospect of being charged, let alone of confronting in court whatever evidence exists against them. The problem is illustrated by the case of Saif al-Islam Gaddafi, the late dictator's son. Libya resists surrendering him to the International Criminal Court (ICC), promising instead to provide a fair trial itself, but the government cannot even secure custody of him from the militia that is holding him.

11

Address the Atrocities in Syria

Syrians do not yet have the luxury of erecting a rights-respecting democracy. At this writing, opposition forces are fighting the brutal dictatorship of President Bashar al-Assad, and the world has been at once preoccupied with stopping the slaughter of civilians by Assad's forces and ineffective at doing so. Tens of thousands have been killed. The leading Western countries and several Arab states imposed sanctions in an effort to curb the government's atrocities, but Russia and China have blocked a unified international response with their multiple vetoes in the United Nations Security Council.

Russia and China deserve blame for their obstructionism, yet other governments have not put enough pressure on them to make them end their indifference to countless atrocities. For example, the United Kingdom and France allowed Rosoboronexport, the principal Russian arms exporter that has been a major supplier to Syria, to continue to display its wares at sales exhibitions outside London and Paris. For much of 2012, the US continued to purchase helicopters from Rosoboronexport for service in Afghanistan.

The UN Security Council's referral of Syria to the ICC would have provided a measure of justice for the victims and helped to deter further atrocities. But even though many Western governments said they supported such action, they have not exerted the kind of strong, sustained, public pressure that could have moved Russia and China to allow the referral to go forward in the Security Council. For example, only in December 2012 did the EU adopt a formal common position on the matter; at this writing, it was unclear if that would yield a strong diplomatic effort to build a global coalition in favor of referral. So far, Switzerland has been left to spearhead such an effort.

The Arab League, for its part, announced various sanctions against Syria but appeared unable to build a consensus among its member states to implement them, or even to stop its member Iraq from enabling the transfer of weapons to Syria from Iran.

The leading powers of the Global South were also disappointingly complacent. Many have been preoccupied with their belief that NATO went beyond protecting civilians in Libya to deliver regime change—a belief facilitated by NATO's refusal to debate its actions. Seemingly determined to avoid this overreach in Syria, leading members of the UN Security Council from the Global South, such as Brazil, India, Pakistan, and South Africa, never used their positions to press for an end to atrocities in that nation. All abstained on at least one of the key Security Council votes, providing political cover for the Russian and Chinese vetoes. Rather than also press the world to uphold its responsibility to protect people facing crimes against humanity, Brazil devoted its energies to promoting the important but distinct concept of "responsibility while protecting," which focuses on the actions and duties of forces assigned the task of protecting.

The experience of Libya shows that, even while armed conflict continues, it is not too early to work toward a new government that upholds rights. The international community can start by pressing the Syrian rebels to respect rights now—to refrain from torturing or executing prisoners, or fomenting sectarian strife. Yet the principal arms suppliers to the rebels—Qatar and Saudi Arabia—handed out weapons without any apparent effort to exclude forces that violate the laws of war.

The international community should be particularly attentive to atrocities and actions that exacerbate sectarian tensions—the greatest threat of sustained violence after the Assad government. Rebel groups should be urged to promote a vision for their country that has a place for all Syrians and to subscribe to and promote codes of conduct that reinforce their forces' obligations under the laws of armed conflict. And when ICC member states press to bring Syria's atrocities before the international court, they should remind rebel leaders that the court would look at atrocities committed by both sides.

Prescriptions for the International Community

The transition from revolution to rights-respecting democracy is foremost a task for the people of the country undergoing change. But the international community can and should exert significant influence to ensure its success. Too often, however, global powers sell their influence short—or settle for less than they should—because of competing priorities. For example, the US and European governments, as noted, in their eagerness to wrest Burma from China's influence have been tempted to embrace the new government before genuine reforms are adopted. A similar temptation exists for Washington to downplay domestic threats to rights in Egypt so long as Cairo supports US policy toward Israel. A more constructive international response would include the following:

Be principled

Fortunately, we have come a long way since the Western powers abandoned democracy promotion in the region once Islamists did unexpectedly well in elections in Egypt and Gaza. This time around, the international reaction to the victory of Islamic parties has been more principled: accepting their electoral triumphs while encouraging them to uphold internationally recognized rights. That is as it should be, since elections are an essential, if insufficient, part of democracy.

However, Western support for human rights and democracy throughout the region has been inconsistent. It was easy for the West to support popular aspirations for reform in the case of governments that were traditionally adversaries, such as Gaddafi's Libya and Assad's Syria. Western support for protest movements in countries led by friendly autocrats, such as Egypt and Tunisia, was belated but, in the end, principled. Yet Western support for democratic change has fallen short when interests in oil, military bases, or Israel are at stake.

For example, the West gave only lukewarm support to Bahraini protesters facing killings, detention, and torture amid worries that the US Fifth Fleet naval base in Bahrain was at risk, and Saudi fears about the emergence of a democracy so close to its own shores, especially given the Shia majorities in Bahrain and in Saudi Arabia's own oil-producing Eastern Province. There has been virtually no international pressure to reform the other monarchies of the region. At this writing, the United Arab Emirates held more than 60 peaceful Islamist activists in arbitrary detention with nary a peep of international protest. There is much hand-wringing about the dangers to women and minorities from newly elected Islamists in Egypt and Tunisia, but Saudi Arabia's institutional oppression of women and discrimination against religious minorities warrant at most a shrug. Much is made of Morocco's modest reforms rather than pressing its monarchy to do more. The message sent is that the West is willing to tolerate Arab autocrats who support Western interests and will jump on the reform bandwagon only when it is about to arrive at its destination.

That lack of principle is noticed. The Arab uprisings have created a new solidarity among the people of the Middle East and North Africa that is more genuine than the worn rhetoric of Arab nationalism sometimes invoked by the Mubaraks and Gaddafis of the region. Double standards are sniffed out and resented, more readily.

Don't forget justice

New governments must subject officials to the rule of law if they are to break from the impunity that fueled their predecessors' abuses. Yet international support for that effort has been uneven, fueling protests against selective justice from many repressive governments. And by reducing the certainty of justice being done, inconsistency undermines its deterrent value.

For example, the UN Security Council accepted an impunity deal for former Yemeni president Ali Abdullah Saleh. It seemed to lose interest in justice in Libya once Gaddafi fell, failing to condemn an amnesty for abuses committed by Libyans in the course of toppling the dictatorship. As the UN General Assembly prepared to grant Palestine observer-state status, the United Kingdom pressed Palestinian leaders to promise not to access the ICC, evidently fearful that it might be used against Israeli settlements on the West Bank or war crimes in Gaza (even though it might also address Hamas' rocket attacks on Israeli civilians).

Elsewhere, the US and the EU provided financial and political backing to the International Criminal Tribunal for the former Yugoslavia (ICTY), a notable success. But the UN Security Council still has not launched a commission of inquiry to examine war crimes by Sri Lankan government forces and the separatist Tamil Tigers that resulted in up to 40,000 civilian deaths in the final months of the armed conflict in 2008 and 2009. There was little international concern expressed about the ICC's sole focus to date on atrocities committed by forces allied with ousted Côte d'Ivoire President Laurent Gbagbo, which left the impression that the world was ignoring abuses of forces loyal to sitting President Alassane Ouattara. The US went out of its way to prevent the UN Security Council from naming Rwanda as the main military supporter of the abusive M23 rebel movement in eastern Congo, let alone imposing sanctions against Rwandan officials complicit in the rebel group's war crimes or encouraging their prosecution (the way former Liberian president Charles Taylor was convicted for aiding and abetting rebels in neighboring Sierra Leone). Western governments (particularly the US) backed President Hamid Karzai's efforts to suppress a report by Afghanistan's independent human rights commission on past atrocities by warlords, many of whom are now Karzai's allies or in his government.

Speak to the people

An important lesson of the Arab Spring is that a mobilized public can be an agent of positive change. Yet many governments in their foreign policies still frequently prefer quiet diplomacy and backroom dialogue to the exclusion of public commentary that all can hear. Social media has proven a powerful new tool, giving each individual the potential to report repression and mobilize against it. To enlist this newly empowered public in reform efforts, the international community must speak to it. Talking privately with governments about reform has its place, but it is no substitute for engaging the public.

Respect rights yourself

It is difficult to preach what one does not practice, yet the rights records of the major powers have fallen short in areas of relevance to Arab Spring states, reducing their influence. The US, for example, remains handicapped in efforts to bring torturers to justice—a major issue in Egypt, for example—because President Barack Obama refuses to allow investigation of officials in former president George W. Bush's administration who are implicated in torture. The US government's failure to prosecute or release most detainees at Guantanamo hamstrings its ability to oppose detention without trial. And US efforts to rein in the arbitrary use of deadly force bump up against its deployment of aerial drones to target individuals abroad without articulating clear limits to their use under the laws of war and law-enforcement standards, and a process beyond the executive branch's unilateral determinations to guard against misuse.

The problem is not only the US. No UK official has been held accountable for helping to send Gaddafi's opponents to endure torture in Libya, and the UK has yet to convene a credible inquiry into wider allegations of its complicity in overseas torture. Europe's efforts to oppose sectarian tensions are hurt by its own difficulties securing Roma, immigrant, and minority rights. Its laws on insulting religion and Holocaust denial undermine its attempts to promote free speech. Some European states' restrictions on religious dress that target women, and on building mosques and minarets impede their promotion of religious freedom.

Turkey's ability to serve as a model for blending democracy with an Islamic governing party, as many people wish, is marred by its persecution of journalists, continuing restrictions on its Kurdish minority, prolonged imprisonment of Kurdish political activists, and serious concerns about unfair trials and the lack of judicial independence.

Similarly, Indonesia, a country often cited as successfully blending democracy and Islam, has a rights record plagued by discrimination against religious minorities and impunity for military abuses. Its constitution protects freedom of religion, but regulations against blasphemy and proselytizing are routinely used to prosecute atheists, Baha'is, Christians, Shiites, and Ahmadiyah. Some 150 regulations restrict the rights of religious minorities. More than 500 Christian churches have been closed since President Susilo Bambang Yudhoyono took office in 2004. The government has cracked down on Jemaah Islamiyah, the al Qaeda affiliate that has bombed hotels, bars, and embassies, but because the governing coalition includes intolerant Islamist political parties, the government has not intervened to stop other Islamist militants who regularly commit less publicized crimes against religious minorities. Meanwhile, there is no civilian jurisdiction over soldiers who commit serious human rights abuses, leaving only military tribunals that rarely convene, lack transparency, and often treat major crimes as mere disciplinary measures.

Help springtime wherever it takes root

Russia and China do not pretend to set a democratic example. Rather, they are preoccupied with preventing the inspiration of the Arab Spring from catching on at home. Despite their power, the international community should regularly speak out against their repression, both for the sake of the Russian and Chinese people, and because these highly visible examples of repression embolden authoritarian leaders worldwide who seek to resist the same currents in their own countries.

The Kremlin was clearly alarmed when large numbers of Russians began protesting in late 2011 against alleged fraud in parliamentary elections and Vladimir Putin's decision to seek a new term as president. The protests at the time sparked hope for change and greater space for free expression, but Putin's return to the presidency has sent the country into a steep authoritarian backslide. The result is a spate of repressive laws and practices designed to induce fear—to discourage public dissent and continuing protests. Participants in protests face massive new fines; human rights groups that receive foreign funding are now required to wear the demonizing label of "foreign agent;" criminal penalties for defamation have been restored; and the crime of treason has been amended so broadly that it now could easily be used to ensnare human rights activists engaged in international advocacy.

As China underwent a highly controlled leadership transition to the presidency of Xi Jinping, it responded to threats of a "Jasmine Spring" and a growing dissident movement with its own crackdown. It has paid particular attention to social media, to which the Chinese people have taken in enormous numbers— an estimated 80 to 90 percent of China's 500 million internet users. Beijing's notorious "Great Firewall" is of little use to this effort, because the source of dissident ideas is not foreign websites, but the Chinese people's own thoughts. The government is devoting massive resources to preventing discussion of issues that it deems sensitive, but many people in China have come to excel at using circumlocutions to evade the censor. That social media users are winning this cat-and-mouse game is suggested by the government's need to climb down from several controversial actions because they had become the subject of mass critical commentary.

Even China, with its extensive resources, depends on private internet companies to hold the frontline in censorship efforts. In the Arab world, governments have used powerful internet surveillance technologies sold by Western companies to target human rights defenders and suspected dissidents. The absence of enforceable standards against corporate complicity in such censorship and surveillance efforts makes them more likely to succeed, undermining the potential of online technologies to facilitate political reform.

Conclusion

The Arab Spring continues to give rise to hope for an improved human rights environment in one of the regions of the world that has been most resistant to democratic change. Yet it also spotlights the tension between majority rule and respect for rights. It is of enormous importance to the people of the region–and the world–that this tension be resolved with respect for international standards. A positive resolution will require acts of great statesmanship among the region's new leaders. But it will also require consistent, principled support from the most influential outsiders. No one pretends it will be easy to get this right. But no one can doubt the importance of doing so.

The Arab Spring has inspired people the world over, encouraging many to stand up to their own autocratic rulers. As its leaders act at home, they also set an example for the world. Much is riding on making this precedent positive—one that succeeds in building elected governments that live by the constraints of rights and the rule of law.

Kenneth Roth is the executive director of Human Rights Watch.

The Trouble With Tradition:

When "Values" Trample Over Rights

By Graeme Reid

"Tradition!" proclaims Tevye the milkman, in his foot-stomping opening to the musical Fiddler on the Roof. "Tradition!"

Tevye's invocation of the familiar as a buffer against the vagaries of his hardscrabble life rings true—after all, what is more reassuring, more innocuous, than the beliefs and practices of the past?

Which is why the resolution passed by the United Nations Human Rights Council (HRC) in September 2012 seems, at first blush, to be so benign.

Spearheaded by Russia, it calls for "promoting human rights and fundamental freedoms through a better understanding of traditional values of humankind." It warns that traditions cannot be invoked to contravene rights, and even mentions such bedrock human rights instruments as the Universal Declaration of Human Rights and the 1993 Vienna Declaration, while calling for a survey of "best practices"—all in the name of "promoting and protecting human rights and upholding human dignity."

By the sound of it, the resolution deserves a standing ovation.

But a close look at the context from which this resolution arose reveals that traditional values are often deployed as an excuse to undermine human rights. And in declaring that "all cultures and civilizations in their traditions, customs, religions and beliefs share a common set of values," the resolution invokes a single, supposedly agreed-upon value system that steamrolls over diversity, ignores the dynamic nature of traditional practice and customary laws, and undermines decades of rights-respecting progress for women and members of the lesbian, gay, bisexual, and transgender (LGBT) communities, among others.

In countries around the world, Human Rights Watch has documented how discriminatory elements of traditions and customs have impeded, rather than enhanced, people's social, political, civil, cultural, and economic rights.

In Saudi Arabia, authorities cite cultural norms and religious teachings in denying women and girls the right to participate in sporting activities—"steps of the devil" on the path to immorality, as one religious leader called them (Steps of the Devil, 2012). In the United States in the early 1990s, "traditional values" was the rallying cry for evangelist Pat Robertson's "Culture War"—code for opposition to LGBT and women's rights that he claimed undermined so-called family values. Today, it is familiar rhetoric of the US religious right, which has used the same language to oppose gay marriage and to accuse political opponents of undermining tradition and "Western civilization." And in Kenya, the customary laws of some ethnic communities discriminate against women when it comes to property ownership and inheritance; while some traditional leaders have supported transforming these laws, many others defend them as embodying "tradition" (Double Standards, 2003). As one woman told us, "They talk about African traditions, but there is no tradition you can speak of—just double standards."

International human rights law—including the Convention on the Elimination of All Forms of Discrimination against Women, and the Protocol to the African Charter of Human and Peoples' Rights on the Rights of Women in Africa—calls for customary and traditional practices that violate human rights to be transformed to remove discriminatory elements.

United Nations treaty monitoring committees, such as the Committee on the Rights of the Child (CRC) and the Committee Against Torture (CAT), have also stated that customs and traditions cannot be put forward as a justification for violating rights. UN Secretary-General Ban Ki-moon in June 2012 told the New York Human Rights Watch Film Festival, "In all regions of the world, LGBT people suffer discrimination—at work, at home, at school, in all aspects of daily life…. No custom or tradition, no cultural values or religious beliefs, can justify depriving a human being of his or her rights."

But such authoritative statements have done little to dampen growing support among UN member states for resolutions that support "traditional values." Not only did September's HRC resolution pass easily—with 25 votes for, 15 against, and 7 abstentions—it was the latest in a series of efforts that Russia has championed in an effort to formalize an abstract set of universal moral values as a lodestar for human rights. In October 2009, for example, the HRC passed a resolution calling for the UN high commissioner for human rights to convene an expert workshop "on how a better understanding of traditional values of humankind ... can contribute to the promotion and protection of human rights." And in March 2011, the council adopted a second resolution requesting a study of how "better understanding and appreciation of traditional values" can promote and protect these rights.

Tradition need not be out of step with international human rights norms and standards. For many people living in rural areas, such as parts of sub-Saharan Africa, traditional values interpreted in customary law may be the only recourse to any form of justice. Nor is the substance of the HRC resolution all bad. It does not, for example, necessarily indicate a global consensus (many countries, including some from the developing world, did not support it), and its text specifically states that "traditions shall not be invoked to justify practices contrary to human dignity and that violate international human rights law."

But unfortunately, such language can seem out of touch with a reality in which "tradition" is indeed often used to justify discrimination and crackdowns on rights—especially those of women and members of the LGBT community, among others—and is easily hijacked by nations determined to flout the rights of particular groups and to quash broader social, political, and legal freedoms.

In such environments, "tradition" subordinates human rights. It should be the other way around.

Rights Curtailed, Rights Ignored

There are potentially negative implications for many groups when traditional values trample on human rights—but they are not always the same.

For women, upon whose shoulders the burden of upholding cultural norms and values often falls, traditional values can be a tool that curtails their human rights. Human Rights Watch has shown that such "values" are sometimes used to justify forced marriages in Afghanistan, virginity testing in Indonesia, "honor crimes" in Iraq, and marital rape in Kyrgyzstan. In Yemen, the abolition of the minimum marriage age on religious grounds in 1999 means that girls as young as eight are married off to much older men, some of whom rape their prepubescent girl brides without legal consequence (How Come You Allow Little Girls to Get Married?, 2011). In Bangladesh, unlike in neighboring India, even the most reasonable demands of Hindu women and women's rights activists—such as divorce on a few grounds that include cruelty and abandonment—have been stalled for decades by critics of such moves, who cite "religion" (Will I Get My Dues ... Before I Die?, 2012).

While many representatives in Yemen's parliament agree that a minimum marriage age is vital to safeguarding young girls' rights, they have been held hostage by a small but powerful group of parliamentarians who oppose any minimum age restriction on the grounds that it would lead to "spreading of immorality" and undermine "family values."

For LGBT people, the traditional values argument may not just be used to limit human rights, it may be used to entirely negate them. That's because the language of traditional values tends to cast homosexuality as a moral issue, and not a rights issue—as a social blight that must be contained and even eradicated for the good of public morality.

Public morality narrowly invoked, as the International Covenant on Civil and Political Rights (ICCPR) recognizes, may provide a legitimate reason to temporarily restrict some rights. But it should not be a smokescreen for prejudice or conflated with majority opinion, and it may never be used as an excuse to violate the covenant's non-discrimination provisions.

It often is.

In 2008, for example, Human Rights Watch showed how vague and ill-defined "offenses against public morality" laws are used in Turkey to censor or close LGBT organizations and to harass and persecute LGBT people (We Need a Law For Liberation). A year later, the Philippine Commission on Elections invoked "morality," "mores," "good customs," and "public morals" when it rejected an LGBT group's application to register as a political organization. The Supreme Court of the Philippines rejected this argument in 2010, holding that the country's democracy precluded "using the religious or moral views of part of the community to exclude from consideration the values of other members of the community."

Similarly, several former British colonies, including Nigeria and Malaysia, use moral terms such as "gross indecency" and "carnal knowledge against the order of nature" in rejecting homosexuality, citing so-called traditional values embodied in laws that in fact only date to the relatively recent, and otherwise derided, colonial era. In the 2008 report This Alien Legacy, for example, Human Rights Watch highlighted the irony of foreign laws being exalted as "citadels of nationhood and cultural authenticity." "Homosexuality, they [judges, public figures, and political leaders] now claim, comes from the colonizing West," the report states. "They forget the West brought in the first laws enabling governments to forbid and repress it."

In Uganda, Malaysia, Moldova, and Jamaica, where the state rejects LGBT rights, claims that homosexuality is simply "not in our culture" are ubiquitous. "All countries are ruled by principles," Alexandru Corduneanu, the deputy mayor of Chisinau, said in 2007, after the Moldovan capital city banned a demonstration by LGBT activists for the third year running. "Moldova is ruled by Christian principles, and that is why we cannot allow you to go against morality and Christianity by permitting this parade."

A Tool of Repression

Traditional values need not be at odds with human rights; indeed, they may even bolster them.

In Iraqi Kurdistan, for example, where tradition, custom, morality, and Islam have been invoked to justify continuing female genital mutilation (FGM) from one generation to the next, the highest Muslim authority issued a fatwa in July 2012, signed by 33 imams and scholars, saying that Islam does not require FGM (They Took Me and Told Me Nothing, June 2010). Disappointingly, implementation of the Family Violence Law that went into effect on August 11, 2011, and includes several provisions to eradicate FGM, has been lackluster.

There has also been some progress in adapting or banning "traditional" practices that fail to respect human rights. The 2009 Elimination of Violence Against Women Law in Afghanistan, for example, outlawed baad—the practice by which disputes are settled in the community by giving up women or girls as compensation for crimes—although implementation of the law has been poor.

Several countries have also amended their laws related to family—the conduit of many traditions—to different degrees, illustrating the space for negotiation and constant change to improve women's rights rather than place them within a static framework of unchanging "traditional values."

Several recent legal cases, including in South Africa, Kenya, and Botswana (which voted against the HRC resolution), also show that rights-limiting traditional practices need not hold sway over inclusive, rights-respecting national law.

In 2008, for example, South Africa's Constitutional Court found in favor of a daughter inheriting her father's chieftaincy—in line with the country's constitution and against a male rival's claim that the Valoyi people's tradition of male leadership meant he was the rightful hosi, or chief, of the 70,000-strong group. In issuing its ruling, the court noted that tradition is never static, and should adhere to human rights standards laid out in a rights-based constitution.

Kenyan courts ruled in 2005 and 2008 that, despite customary laws of particular ethnic groups favoring sons for inheritance purposes, daughters must have an equal right to inherit a father's property. The courts noted that where discrimination is at stake, human rights must prevail. Kenya has since amended its constitution, enshrining women's equal rights to land and property.

Meanwhile, Botswana's High Court in October 2012 ruled in favor of four sisters who had fought a five-year battle with a nephew who claimed rightful ownership of the family home. The court ruled that the customary law upon which the nephew based his case contravened constitutional guarantees of equality for men and women. The attorney general had reportedly agreed that customary law was discriminatory, but argued that Botswana was not ready to change it. "Culture changes with time," the court observed

But such examples are rare.

Too often, "traditional values" are corrupted, serving as a handy tool for governments in the business of repression. For Russia, which spearheaded the HRC resolution, the insertion of traditional values into the realm of human rights comes amid intensifying government repression of civil society and the media, and is part of a concerted effort to roll back the gains made by women and LGBT people in Russia.

In 2012, St. Petersburg became one of nine Russian regions to date to adopt so-called homosexual propaganda laws that outlaw creating "distorted perceptions" about the "social equality of traditional and non-traditional family relationships." Russian Foreign Minister Sergei Lavrov justified the laws—which Russia's Supreme Court upheld in restricted form in October—by arguing that LGBT human rights were merely an "appendage" to universal values. There is active debate about introducing similar legislation that cynically links homosexuality and child abuse, in Moscow and on a federal level.

And in 2010, the Constitutional Court of the Russian Federation upheld the conviction of lesbian activist Irina Fedotova for an administrative offense under provincial law after she displayed posters near a school in the city of Ryazan, southeast of Moscow, declaring, "Homosexuality is normal" and "I am proud of my homosexuality." The court ruled that the "homosexual propaganda law," which the city adopted in 2006, did not interfere with Fedotova's freedom of expression, since "traditional understandings of family, motherhood and childhood" were values necessitating "special protection from the State."

The UN Human Rights Committee, the international expert body that monitors implementation of the ICCPR, begged to differ, ruling in November 2012 that the federation was in violation of the covenant's freedom of expression provisions. "[T]he purpose of protecting morals," the committee stated, "must be based on principles not deriving exclusively from a single tradition."

A Comforting Ideal

It's no coincidence that traditional values—and the related push against LGBT rights—are finding an eager and broadening international audience at this time.

In some cases there's a specific context, as in Russia with President Vladimir Putin's broader clampdown on civil society and Russia's efforts to roll back the mandates of the international human rights machinery while encouraging like-minded allies to do the same. In sub-Saharan countries, such as Zimbabwe and Uganda, the devastation of AIDS, economic crisis, and political instability have lawmakers scrambling to pass increasingly repressive legislation against homosexuality on the grounds that doing so is necessary to protect African culture and tradition in the face of encroaching foreign values.

More broadly, the current climate of political uncertainty, social upheaval, and economic crisis in much of the world has enhanced the appeal of the timeless universal essence that tradition is claimed to embody. In Uganda, as Human Rights Watch showed in 2012 (Curtailing Criticism), the government's clampdown on civil society organizations is in part justified by an appeal to homophobia, amid increased political tension, escalating public criticism, and President Yoweri Museveni's own political ambitions to serve another term after the 2016 elections.

Blaming one group for the ills befalling society is easy and appealing in the face of such instability. Gays and lesbians, who often live in secret due to laws and social prohibitions against homosexuality, are particularly easy targets for the moral panics that can erupt at a time of social crisis. In Jamaica, gay men in particular are seen as harbingers of moral decay, leading to public vitriol which often ends in violence, including a June 2004 mob attack on a man perceived to be gay in Montego Bay. The mob chased and reportedly "chopped, stabbed and stoned" him to death with the encouragement of the police (Hated to Death, 2004).

In Zimbabwe, where gays and lesbians frequently find themselves playing the role of "folk devils," gay-bashing follows the election cycle all too predictably, with President Robert Mugabe raising the specter of homosexuality as a way to deflect attention from the country's more pressing social, political, and economic problems. In 1995, as his regional stature was diminishing, Mugabe unleashed a vitriolic attack on gays, whom he said "offend against the law of nature and the morals of religious beliefs espoused by our society." In 2012, Mulikat Akande-Adeola, the majority leader of Nigeria's House of Representatives, was equally unequivocal when she supported a sweeping anti-LGBT bill when it passed its second reading: "It is alien to our society and culture and it must not be imported," she said. "Religion abhors it and our culture has no place for it."

Transformation, Not Rejection

The human rights movement is not opposed to the existence of customary law, religious law, and tradition; it is opposed to those aspects of them that violate rights.

As a result, the task at hand is one of transformation, not rejection—as reflected in international human rights law that calls for customary and traditional practices that violate human rights to develop in order to remove discriminatory elements. As the Convention on the Elimination of All Forms of Discrimination against Women stipulates, states should "modify" the social and cultural patterns of conduct of men and women to eliminate "prejudices and customary and all other practices which are based on the idea of the inferiority or the superiority of either of the sexes or on stereotyped roles for men and women."

"Culture changes with time," Botswana's High Court stated in its October 2012 ruling in favor of the four sisters battling for their family home in the face of customary law. And that is precisely the point. Culture does change with time.

Evoking a static and vague concept of "tradition" not only fails to account for these shifts, it fossilizes society. The risk is that instead of advancing human rights and basic freedoms, the HRC resolution and its call for a "better understanding of traditional values" could be used as an excuse to bury rights under a mound of cultural relativism—threatening to roll back women's rights and exclude LGBT people from a human rights framework in the process.

Graeme Reid is director of the LGBT Rights division at Human Rights Watch.

Without Rules:
A Failed Approach to Corporate Accountability
By Chris Albin-Lackey

Some of the most powerful and sophisticated actors on the world stage are companies, not governments. In 2011 alone, oil and gas behemoth ExxonMobil generated revenues of US$467 billion—the size of Norway's entire economy. Walmart, the world's third-largest employer with more than 2 million workers, has a workforce that trails only the militaries of the United States and China in size.

Many global businesses are run with consideration for the well-being of the people whose lives they touch. But others—whether through incompetence or by design—seriously harm the communities around them, their workers, and even the governments under which they work.

Much of the problem lies with companies themselves—even those that think of themselves as ethical. Too many still deal with human rights problems on the fly, without forethought and often in a de facto regulatory vacuum that they lobby vigorously to maintain. In many parts of the world, company human rights practices are shaped by self-created policies, voluntary initiatives, and unenforceable "commitments"—not by binding laws and regulations. History's long and growing catalogue of corporate human rights disasters shows how badly companies can go astray without proper regulation. Yet many companies fight to keep themselves free of oversight, as though it were an existential threat.

But the lion's share of the responsibility to prevent and address company-driven human rights abuse lies with governments. As companies continue to extend their global reach, their actions affect the human rights of more and more people in profoundly important ways. Governments have failed to keep pace.

Most, if not all, countries have laws on the books requiring that companies adhere to basic human rights standards. Some governments take these responsibilities more seriously than others, while others are so weak that the task of regulating multinational corporations running vast and highly complex operations on their soil is hopelessly beyond them.

Governments of countries that are home to the world's biggest and most powerful corporations—including the US, European nations, and emerging powers like Brazil and China—have consistently and inexcusably failed to scrutinize the actions of their companies when they go abroad. Most governments fall somewhere in between the extremes; few, if any, do all that they should.

These combined failures cause real and lasting harm to vulnerable people in communities all over the world. In 2012, Human Rights Watch showed how government regulators in India stand idle while out-of-control mining operations fuel corruption and harm entire communities (*Out of Control, 2012*). Farmers in Goa, initially hopeful that mining would improve the local economy, instead watched as pollution poisoned groundwater and withered their crops. We also investigated how government regulators in Bangladesh avert their eyes as the country's $650 million tannery industry runs roughshod over environmental, health, and safety laws—poisoning and maiming its workers and spewing pollutants into nearby communities (*Toxic Tanneries, 2012*). And in Qatar, we documented concerns that, unless reforms are undertaken now, the country's hugely expensive preparations to host the 2022 World Cup could be marred by abuses against migrant laborers doing much of the construction on state-of-the-art stadiums, sleek new hotels, and other cup-related projects (*Building a Better World Cup, 2012*).

We have nearly reached the paltry limits of what can be achieved with the current enforcement-free approach to the human rights problems of global companies. It is time for governments to pull their heads out of the sand, look the problem they face in the eye, and accept their responsibility to oversee and regulate company human rights practices.

The Guiding Principles

As year one of the UN-backed Guiding Principles on Business and Human Rights, 2012 was supposed to mark a huge step forward for efforts to address these problems. But while the Guiding Principles do mark progress in some areas, they also underscore the failures of the current approach to business and human rights issues—one that is driven by weak government action and undue deference to the prerogatives of businesses.

The Guiding Principles were supposed to "operationalize" the UN's "Protect, Respect, Remedy" framework, which stresses the responsibility of governments to protect individuals from human rights abuses tied to business operations, the responsibility of companies to respect human rights, and the need for abuse victims to be able to access effective remedies.

The principles mark a real step forward in some ways, not least because they have secured remarkably strong buy-in from companies that just a decade ago would have disputed the idea they even *have* human rights responsibilities. A potentially useful and practical guide to companies that want to behave responsibly, they bring us closer than we have ever been to a shared understanding of how businesses should think about at least *some* of their core human rights responsibilities.

The principles also emphasize a crucial point that could prevent many real-world human rights problems if companies take it up *effectively* and in good faith: the importance of human rights due diligence. This is the idea that companies should design and implement effective policies and procedures to identify any risk of causing human rights abuse, act to avoid that harm, and position themselves to respond appropriately to abuses that occur in spite of those safeguards.

Last year, for example, Human Rights Watch found evidence that Nevsun Resources, a Canadian mining firm, might be implicated in the use of forced labor—absolutely prohibited under international law—via a local contractor in Eritrea (*Hear No Evil: Forced Labor and Corporate Responsibility in Eritrea's Mining Industry*, January 2013). It was a foreseeable problem: Eritrea's government mobilizes and exploits forced labor on a massive scale and assigns some of its conscripts to work for state-affiliated companies, including the one Nevsun hired. Conscripts are often subjected to appalling conditions—and to imprisonment and torture if they try to flee from their "jobs." In this case,

Nevsun initially failed to take adequate steps to prevent its contractor from using forced labor at its project site, and the company's belated efforts to investigate and address the allegations have floundered. Other companies developing mines in Eritrea now seem in danger of falling into the same trap. This is precisely the sort of situation that human rights due diligence is meant to help companies avoid.

But the Guiding Principles are no panacea. Human Rights Watch and others have criticized the principles for setting a lower bar than international human rights standards in some areas, like ensuring a victim's right to redress and accountability. This is especially problematic because many companies now see the principles—incorrectly—as the world's definitive, one-stop standard for good human rights practice. There is a risk that many companies will simply ignore standards the Guiding Principles do not echo.

Most important, while the principles provide some useful guidance to businesses interested in behaving responsibly they also represent a woefully inadequate approach to business and human rights issues. That is because without any mechanism to ensure compliance or to measure implementation, they cannot actually *require* companies to do anything at all. Companies can reject the principles altogether without consequence—or publicly embrace them while doing absolutely nothing to put them into practice. The principles do not explicitly insist that governments regulate companies with the requisite scope and rigor; they also fail to push governments hard enough to ensure that companies respect human rights.

For all the progress they represent in some areas, the Guiding Principles may actually help entrench a dominant paradigm among companies and many governments, which derides the rules and regulations that companies need in favor of voluntary and largely unenforceable commitments that simply don't do nearly enough to protect human rights.

Voluntary Initiatives and their Shortcomings

The last decade has seen a proliferation of voluntary initiatives that bring together multinational corporations, civil society actors, and governments to address the human rights concerns of particular global industries. They aim to provide crucial guidance to companies that want to operate responsibly, while allowing member companies to cast themselves as responsible and ethical.

For example, the Voluntary Principles on Security and Human Rights brings together major oil, mining, and gas companies around standards requiring them to prevent and address abuses by security forces that protect their operations. The Global Network Initiative includes companies in the information and communications technology sector that have pledged to avoid complicity in censorship or surveillance by repressive governments. There are many others of varying strength and effectiveness.

These voluntary initiatives have a useful role to play. Human Rights Watch helped found the two described above, and we regularly work through those and other voluntary initiatives to try and secure better human rights practice by companies.

But they are not enough.

Voluntary initiatives all face the same crucial limitations: they are only as strong as their corporate members choose to make them, and they don't apply to companies that don't want to join. They often do a good job of helping to define good company human rights practice, but enforceable rules are the only way of ensuring real, systematic change.

The world's dearth of binding human rights rules for companies has consequences. When companies stand in for absentee governments, in whatever role, things tend to end badly. Decades of failed development efforts led by oil companies in Nigeria's oil-rich Niger Delta have proven that point with brutal eloquence, and it holds equally true in other contexts.

In 2010, we interviewed women who described being gang-raped at the hands of private security guards employed by Canadian-owned Barrick Gold at a Papua New Guinea mine (*Gold's Costly Dividend*, 2011). Crucial lapses in oversight meant that Barrick—the world's largest gold company—did not take the allegations seriously or do anything to address them until we went into the field to get the evidence ourselves.

That should have been the government's job, not ours. But Papua New Guinea's government is hobbled by corruption, poverty, and remarkably low institutional capacity. Instead of overseeing Barrick's activities, it effectively left the company to do the job itself. Barrick has since pursued reforms aimed at preventing future abuse and has promised to compensate victims. But that doesn't change the fact that even a sophisticated and well-resourced company proved unable to bridge the gap left by missing government oversight.

It wasn't only the government of Papua New Guinea that left Barrick to its own devices, but also the government of Canada, where Barrick—and indeed most of the world's mining and exploration companies—are based. Canada's government probably has as much experience overseeing complex mining operations as any other on earth. Allegations of human rights abuse by Canadian firms surface regularly in countries around the globe, but authorities in Ottawa do not know how many of these are credible. In fact, they have steadfastly refused to give themselves a mandate to find out.

This failure of high-capacity governments to scrutinize the human rights practices of their own corporate citizens when they operate abroad is a problem that urgently needs solving.

Need for Extraterritorial Oversight and Regulation

Governments worldwide have consistently failed to oversee or regulate the extraterritorial human rights practices of their companies. The only way forward is to change this.

Multinational companies operate all around the world in countries that cannot or will not provide enough oversight or regulation of their human rights practices. The trend is only increasing. Weakly governed developing countries like Papua New Guinea, Bangladesh, Mozambique, and Guinea continue to welcome massive new foreign investment in industries with an immense potential for environmental destruction and human rights abuse.

If companies are not going to get meaningful human rights oversight from the governments of the countries in which they operate, they need to get it somewhere else. At a minimum, governments should take it upon themselves to proactively monitor the conduct of their companies when they work in other countries and to investigate credible allegations of human rights abuse linked to those operations.

Doing so would still leave hard questions on the table—like how governments should articulate and enforce extraterritorial human rights obligations for companies. But it would at least end an indefensible status quo where governments *refuse to find out* whether their corporate citizens are credibly implicated in serious human rights abuses abroad.

Beyond this, Human Rights Watch and others have argued that governments should regulate the human rights practices of their businesses, including by requiring them to carry out human rights due diligence activity and fulfill their human rights responsibilities under international law. Not only is this responsible policy, but it is supported by emerging norms of international law.

In 2011, a meeting of international and human rights law experts adopted the Maastricht Principles on Extraterritorial Obligations of States in the area of Economic, Social and Cultural Rights. Among other things the Maastricht Principles describe the obligation of states to regulate non-state actors such as transnational corporations and other business enterprises that are domiciled or closely linked in other ways to their territories.

The path from here to there is reasonably clear. The real question is whether governments will find the courage to take steps in the right direction, and whether businesses will stand in their way or act as partners. So far, both have disappointed, and vulnerable people have suffered as a result.

Red Herrings

Companies have their reasons for opposing extraterritorial human rights oversight or regulation by home governments, but they don't stand up well to scrutiny.

One of the most common arguments is that such oversight would put them at a competitive disadvantage against unscrupulous firms from countries with less progressive governments. But frankly, companies should not invest in markets where they cannot effectively compete without being complicit in serious human rights abuses that they need to hide from their own governments and shareholders.

Plus, there is ample reason to think these concerns are overblown. In recent years, governments around the world have passed increasingly tough laws that criminalize overseas corruption by their citizens and companies. Corruption is far trickier for businesses to stay clear of than complicity in serious human rights abuses. Yet while tougher anti-corruption laws may have made companies more honest, there is no real evidence they have made them less competitive.

The only legitimate fear companies have about responsible, measured steps in the direction of extraterritorial oversight and regulation is that "responsible" and "measured" might in some cases be code for "extreme" and "anti-business." Some worry that opening the door even a crack would lead to stifling overregulation and the criminalization of honest, understandable mistakes.

Compounding this is suspicion among some business leaders that nongovernmental advocates of oversight and regulation are inherently hostile toward their industries. And those fears are somewhat understandable—while many nongovernmental organizations are pushing for reasonable rules, there are also activists who probably would like nothing better than to see the mining industry, for instance, crushed by excessive regulation.

But those voices shouldn't dictate the terms of this discussion or be used as an excuse to avoid having it.

Companies may never end up liking the kind of oversight and regulation that they need, and they may be correct in calculating that it is not in their narrow self-interest to see it come about. But extraterritorial oversight and regulation of company human rights practices can be done in a way that businesses can live with and profit under. Government action need not be unduly burdensome in order to be effective, and there is far too much avoidable human suffering on the other side of the scale to justify inaction.

First Steps and Useful Models

We already have at least some useful models that show us what responsible, measured government action on these issues ought to look like.

Under section 1504 of the Dodd-Frank financial overhaul bill, all US-listed oil, mining, and gas companies will be required to publish the payments they make to foreign governments. This essentially makes mandatory the core requirement of a multi-stakeholder initiative called the Extractive Industry Transparency Initiative (EITI).

EITI was born of an understanding that the vast revenues extractive industries produce have often fueled corruption and abuse rather than development and progress. EITI tries to combat this by promoting greater transparency. Section 1504 is a modest but potentially transformative step in the right direction.

Incredibly a powerful coalition of industry groups led by the American Petroleum Institute has sued to gut the rules that would put the law into force. They are effectively demanding the right to keep the public and even their own shareholders in the dark about their payments to foreign governments. Industry groups have also sued to obstruct implementation of another key component of Dodd-Frank—a provision that would require companies to ensure that their mineral supply chains do not fuel conflict and abuse in the Democratic Republic of Congo.

In spite of all the acrimony (or perhaps underlying it), Dodd-Frank's transparency requirement speaks to a controversial but important truth: most of what has been achieved through the hodgepodge of voluntary initiatives that dominate the global business and human rights landscape could be done more effectively and even-handedly via binding laws and regulations.

The core requirements of many voluntary initiatives could be translated into relatively straightforward regulatory mandates. As models for regulation, those standards have the advantage of having already been accepted as legitimate benchmarks for corporate behavior by leading global companies. Their implementation has also been proved feasible and useful for the many companies who have taken them up voluntarily. Of course, most companies fiercely oppose the idea that their voluntary human rights commitments should be transformed into the basis for binding human rights regulation.

But that doesn't mean it wouldn't work.

Similarly, as Human Rights Watch has argued, human rights due diligence would be a stronger tool if governments make it mandatory. The US government recently took a narrow but positive step in this direction, requiring companies that invest in Burma to publicly report any due diligence activities they undertake on a variety of issues including human rights and to report to it any human rights risks, impacts, and mitigation efforts the company identifies.

Yet another useful model for government action in this area lies in international efforts to combat corruption. A steadily growing number of governments have moved to criminalize bribery of foreign public officials, no matter where in the world it occurs. In fact, the UN Convention against Corruption and the Organisation for Economic Co-operation and Development's (OECD) Anti-Bribery Convention both require this. Companies have responded to tough anti-bribery laws by implementing rigorous due diligence programs that are not altogether different from the human rights due diligence activity that the Guiding Principles promote.

Governments should also look at how they can push companies towards better human rights practices through existing multilateral institutions, which should in turn examine how they can better help the governments they lend to address these issues. For instance, governments could work through the World Bank's International Finance Corporation (IFC) to better tie the international financing that private companies receive to robust human rights safeguards and require independent monitoring of company compliance.

This would not only help push IFC-funded projects towards better human rights performance, it would likely influence other lenders too. In 2012, the IFC began implementing new performance standards that go some way toward considering human rights in international financing—a small but important step.

Other existing institutions could also be made stronger and more useful. The OECD Guidelines for Multinational Enterprises set out baseline standards for corporate performance in human rights, environmental protection, and a range of other issues. They also call on member countries to establish "contact points"—forums that are able to hear complaints regarding the overseas activities of companies. However, these contact points are generally quite weak and strictly non-adjudicatory. In 2012, Denmark revamped its contact point to allow it to undertake proactive, independent investigations of companies—a real step forward.

Finally, governments should examine the positive precedents that international labor standards set regarding private, transnational employment agencies. As our research in countries such as Bahrain and the United Arab Emirates has documented, many migrant workers suffer serious abuses after being placed in overseas employment by these agencies and many are deliberately misled about the conditions they can expect in their new jobs.

Governments that have ratified International Labour Organization (ILO) Convention 181 must take measures to protect and prevent abuse of migrant workers recruited for work abroad by private employment agencies based on their own soil. That convention also calls for penalties for agencies that engage in abuses or fraudulent practices. ILO Convention 189 on Domestic Workers sets out similar obligations for private employment agencies recruiting domestic workers, including those migrating for overseas employment.

***

Ultimately what's needed is a workable balance that reduces serious human rights abuses while acknowledging the reality of a complex world where companies do not always have full control over the local environments in which they operate.

Getting there will require something from all sides.

Governments need to find the courage to make respect for human rights by powerful corporations mandatory wherever they operate, rather than treating it as just a nice idea. Human rights activists should help design workable regulatory frameworks that are fair to companies. And businesses should welcome, rather than reject, efforts to provide them with the kind of rules and oversight they need to be responsible actors who respect the fundamental human rights of the people they impact.

Chris Albin-Lackey is a senior researcher in the Business and Human Rights division at Human Rights Watch.

Lives in the Balance:
The Human Cost of Environmental Neglect

By Juliane Kippenberg and Jane Cohen

Every year, environmental crises affect millions of people around the world causing sickness and decimating lives and livelihoods.

When environmental degradation garners international attention its impact is often framed in terms of harm to nature. But another, often overlooked, way to understand a toxic spill or a mining disaster is in terms of its impact on human rights—not least the right to life, to health, and to safe food and water.

In 2011, in Henan province, eastern China, for example, rivers ran blood-red from pollution, and thick smoke choked the air around the lead smelters and battery factories that power the local economy—a deeply worrying situation in terms of environmental pollution. But as the Human Rights Watch 2011 report My Children Have Been Poisoned showed, Henan's health and environmental crisis has also led to human rights violations that have robbed citizens of a host of internationally recognized rights—such as those to health and to protest peacefully—and have jeopardized the physical and intellectual development of thousands of children.

Unfortunately, in practice, governments and international agencies do not often enough analyze environmental issues through the prism of human rights or address them together in laws or institutions. But they should, and they should do so without fear that doing so will compromise efforts to achieve sustainability and environmental protection.

Indeed, rather than undermine these important goals, a human rights perspective brings an important and complementary principle to the fore—namely that governments must be accountable for their actions. And it provides advocacy tools for those affected by environmental degradation to carve out space to be heard, meaningfully participate in public debate on environmental problems, and where necessary, use independent courts to achieve accountability and redress. As the old legal maxim goes, there can be no right without a remedy.

Regional human rights instruments—such as the Additional Protocol to the American Convention on Human Rights in the Area of Economic, Social and Cultural Rights, the African Charter on Human and Peoples' Rights, and its Additional Protocol on the Rights of Women—recognize a right to a healthy environment (or a "general satisfactory" environment in the case of the African Charter, adopted in 1981). And it has been over two decades since the United Nations General Assembly in a resolution recognized that all individuals are entitled to live in an environment adequate for their health and well-being.

In a 2001 groundbreaking ruling, the African Commission on Human and Peoples' Rights demonstrated that regional accountability for violations of human rights, including the right to a healthy environment, was possible. The commission found that, through a consortium with Shell Petroleum Development Corporation, the former military government in Nigeria had caused environmental damage to the Ogoni People in the Niger Delta region, in violation of the right protected by African Charter. The commission found that the government had not taken the necessary steps to protect the Ogoni population from harms done by the oil production and had not "provided nor permitted studies of potential or actual environmental and health risks caused by oil operations in Ogoni Communities." Strikingly, the commission also found that the right to life had been violated by the level of "humanly unacceptable" pollution and environmental degradation that had destroyed the lands and farms upon which the Ogonis' survival depended.

Yet despite such decisions, there is still insufficient human rights accountability for environmental issues, as illustrated by the scope of environmental harm that occurs globally without apparent redress. The international human rights community needs to help strengthen both the content and framework for the right to a healthy environment, and to institutionalize the link between human rights and the environment. Such steps would include developing accountability mechanisms that could offer an effective remedy for the millions of people impacted by environmental crises.

The Right to Life and to Health

Under international human rights law, governments have numerous obligations to protect their citizens' right to life and to health. The Universal Declaration of Human Rights, the International Covenant on Economic and Social and Cultural Rights (ICESCR), and the Convention on the Rights of the Child (CRC) all establish the right to the highest attainable standard of health. Under the ICESCR, the right to health includes an obligation to improve environmental health, to protect citizens from environmental health hazards, to guarantee healthy working conditions, and to protect the right to safe food and safe water.

Yet, many governments regularly fail to protect and uphold these commitments.

Human Rights Watch has documented the devastating impact of such neglect by authorities in many parts of the world.In the state of Zamfara, northern Nigeria, for example, over 400 children have died of lead poisoning since 2010—one of the worst recorded outbreaks in history—due to exposure to lead-contaminated dust produced during small-scale gold mining. Nigeria's government has dragged its feet in the face of this unprecedented disaster, despite many signs of an impending crisis. In the short film A Heavy Price (2012), Human Rights Watch documented how children continue to live and play in contaminated homes and face exposure to lead at life-threatening levels that can cause life-long disabilities, if not death.

Unfortunately, Nigeria is not a unique case: governments often respond to environmental problems with denial, or offer weak and disjointed responses that fail to clean up environmental damage, impose or enforce regulations, or prevent and treat resulting health conditions.

The Right to Know, Protest, and Seek Justice

International law also obligates governments to guarantee people's right to know, participate in political processes, peacefully protest, and seek justice. These rights, enshrined in the International Covenant on Civil and Political Rights (ICCPR), ensure that citizens can actively and meaningfully participate in decisions that affect their lives.

In practice, governments frequently fail to inform citizens about the most basic facts regarding environmental health, violating their right to information. In Japan, for example, the government failed to provide residents of Fukushima with basic information about the level of radiation in their food and environment after the prefecture's March 2011 nuclear disaster, leaving local newspapers, as one local doctor told Human Rights Watch, "to accept whatever the prefecture says on faith."

Even in countries that have elaborate safeguards to ensure transparency and participation of affected populations, the reality is often bleak. In many countries, governments not only fail to provide information to their citizens, they also clamp down on those who demand transparency and official remedies. Human Rights Watch has documented a range of government actions against those who protest—and even those who merely seek information— including threats, arrests, imprisonment, and even murder.

Our 2010 research in four Chinese provinces, for example, found that the government detained people protesting lead pollution from factories, and even parents seeking medical treatment for their poisoned children (My Children Have Been Poisoned). In the Philippines, Human Rights Watch has documented the murder of three environmental activists since October 2011: the men had vocally opposed mining and energy operations that they said threatened the environment and would displace local communities in Bukidnon and North Cotabato provinces from their land. No one has been punished, and evidence points to the involvement of paramilitary forces under military control. And in Kenya—which in 2010 included the right to a healthy environment in its consti- tution—Human Rights Watch has been working with an environmental activist who has repeatedly faced threats and arrest for seeking information and redress from a local factory that has polluted the air and water near the city of Mombasa.

Regulating Business

Businesses are at the heart of environmental problems today. Whether multina- tional corporations or small, local operations, they have a responsibility to ensure that their operations do not cause or contribute to human rights violations, as reflected in the United Nations Guiding Principles on Business and Human Rights. It is a responsibility they frequently fail to fulfill (see also "Without Rules: A Failed Approach to Corporate Accountability" in this volume).

For example, the Porgera mine of Barrick Gold in Papua New Guinea dumps 14,000 tons of liquid mining waste daily into a nearby river, causing potential environmental and ill-health to local communities (Gold's Costly Dividend, 2011). In Bangladesh's capital Dhaka, around 150 tanneries expose local residents to untreated effluent that contains chromium, sulphur, ammonium, and other chemicals that cause skin diseases, rashes, and diarrhea, among other health problems (Toxic Tanneries, 2012).

Companies, including foreign investors, international buyers, and retailers, have a responsibility to ensure that they are not contributing to human rights abuses, either directly or indirectly. The store that sells a belt made from leather tanned and cured in acid-filled pits in Dhaka should have due diligence procedures in place to ensure it does not indirectly contribute to rights abuses; so should international buyers to ensure their suppliers are not violating health and safety laws or poisoning the environment. And governments should ensure they adequately regulate the private sector—something they are often reluctant to do because environmental regulations interfere with private sector interests and are seen as burdening economic development and growth.

For example, in October 2010, Canada's House of Commons voted down a bill that would have allowed the government to monitor the environmental and human rights impacts of Canadian extractive industries operating globally. In doing so, an important opportunity was lost: Canada is home to most of the world's mining and exploration companies. The industry accounted for 21 percent of Canadian exports in 2010 and derived about US$36 billion dollars from its mining practices that year.

In Bangladesh, where tanneries contaminate air, water, and soil, our research found that the government has failed to enforce environmental or labor laws, and for a decade has ignored a court ruling ordering the government to ensure that the tanneries install adequate waste treatment systems. A government official told Human Rights Watch that the tannery sector is not properly regulated because "tannery owners are very rich and politically powerful."

And in India, for example, a 2012 Human Rights Watch investigation in the southern states of Goa and Karnataka (Out of Control) found that the supposedly independent and accurate environmental impact assessments of potential mining projects are often flawed and commissioned by the same, largely domestic, mining companies that seek permission from the Indian government to operate.

Corruption also sometimes undermines environmental regulations and safeguards. In Indonesia, Human Rights Watch has shown how blatant corruption has undermined environmental policies on logging (Wild Money, 2009); as a result, much of Indonesian timber has been logged illegally, violating policies intended to protect local communities and the environment.

The Hardest Hit

Environmental degradation often disproportionately impacts vulnerable and discriminated against populations—including poor rural populations, displaced people, women, ethnic minorities, and indigenous people—which rarely have access or political clout to be able to critique governments or hold them to account.

Indigenous peoples are particularly susceptible to serious rights violations when governments or multinational corporations clear their land and ecosystems in the name of "economic development." According to the UN Declaration on the Rights of Indigenous Peoples, indigenous peoples can only be relocated with their free, prior, and informed consent, after agreement on just and fair compensation of land, property, and livelihood. Yet as Human Rights Watch has shown, this is often not the case.

In Ethiopia, for example, Human Rights Watch research in 2011 found that indigenous people are being forcibly removed from the Omo Valley, which provides their primary source of livelihood, to make way for large-scale commercial sugar plantations. The government has used harassment, violence, and arbitrary arrests to impose its plans, leaving members of local indigenous groups, including one man from the Mursi tribe, to wonder, "[w]hat will happen if hunger comes" when the river has dried and land has been seized? (What Will Happen If Hunger Comes? 2012)

Another group vulnerable to the effects of environmental pollution is children—even though protecting child health is a core obligation in international law. Toxic chemicals have particularly harmful consequences for children, whose developing bodies absorb them more easily than those of adults, leading in some cases to irreversible long-term damage, disability, or even death.

Children from poor, disadvantaged, or marginalized backgrounds can be particularly at risk as their communities lack political influence and information. For example, Human Rights Watch research on child labor in artisanal gold mining in Mail—an industry that involves an estimated 15 million artisanal gold miners globally—has found that children's exposure to mercury, a toxic metal, has hardly been addressed on national or global levels (A Poisonous Mix, 2011).

Human Rights Watch has also documented how children and adults from the marginalized Roma minority, who were displaced after the 1999 war in Kosovo, were housed for years in a lead-contaminated displaced camps in northern Kosovo (Kosovo: Poisoned by Lead, 2009). Children were particularly vulnerable to lead poisoning. The UN—the effective civil authority at the time—knew about the contamination, but failed to move them to a safer location for over five years. It lacked a comprehensive health plan and stopped treatment for children without any medical reason.

Children in wealthy countries are also not immune to the impacts of a toxic environment. In the United States agriculture industry, child laborers—many from migrant families—work in or near fields that are regularly sprayed with pesticides. Yet the US government has failed to outlaw hazardous child labor in agriculture, prioritizing the interests of agribusiness over stricter regulations on pesticide exposure for children (Fields of Peril, 2010).

Global Challenges and Opportunities

The government response to environmental degradation is often weak and disconnected, and oblivious to the critical impact that climate change, pollution, and other environmental problems have on human rights.

In June 2012, the Rio+20 Summit brought together more than 100 heads of state or government and 45,000 people in the biggest UN conference to date. However, the scale of the gathering far exceeded its efficacy. World leaders missed the chance to bridge the false divide between development and environmental protection and almost completely whittled down rights language in the final document, "The Future We Want."

International laws and regulations are important tools for protecting the environment, but they tend to focus on technical aspects of regulation, emissions, and processes, and—like the 2004 Stockholm Convention on Persistent Organic Pollutants—often fail to comprehensively address the health and human rights impact of environmental degradation, if they address them at all.

And while international financial institutions aim to promote development, their actions sometimes violate human rights and result in further environmental degradation. The World Bank's safeguard policies, which are designed to prevent social and environmental harm in its projects, require governments to analyze the environmental impact of certain projects but do not require a comprehensive analysis of human rights impacts. The bank's review and update of these policies is an important opportunity to remedy this major shortfall.

But the news is not all bad.

Environmental NGOs, other civil society groups, and affected communities have scored some notable successes in their efforts to push for accountability. In Burma, open protest by civil society groups against the potentially devastating consequences of the Myitsone Dam project on the Irawaddy River prompted the Burmese government in 2011 to suspend its plans for what would have been the one of the world's largest hydroelectric power stations.

And in 2012, the UN Human Rights Council (HRC) appointed its first independent expert on human rights obligations relating to the enjoyment of a safe, clean, healthy, and sustainable environment. One of the expert's most important tasks will be to help define the content of the human right to a healthy environment, and to seek broad buy-in and support for ensuring full respect, protection, and fulfillment of this right.

Another positive move is the November 2012 road map by Latin American governments towards a regional treaty on rights of access to environmental information, participation, and justice. Such an instrument already exists in Europe: many European and Central Asian governments have ratified the 2001 Aarhus Convention on access to information, public participation, and access to justice in environmental matters, which is the first of its kind to codify these civil rights in relation to the environment.

There are also some future opportunities for pressing a human rights approach when it comes to environmental issues—including negotiations for the global mercury treaty.

Human Rights Watch has participated in these negotiations, in Kenya in 2011 and Uruguay in 2012, as well in regional meetings in Latin America and Africa. Throughout our advocacy we have urged a stronger focus on human rights, in particular the right to health and protection from hazardous child labor. During negotiations in Uruguay, governments agreed to include special measures in the treaty for children affected by mercury in artisanal gold mining. It was also agreed that governments must devise health strategies on mercury for affected artisanal mining communities. While the treaty still lacks references to human rights and a strong overall health strategy on mercury, the specific measures on gold mining are a step in the right direction.

What Next?

Even when governments do enforce environmental regulations and safeguards, they often disregard the harmful impact of environmental problems on human rights, and the disproportionate impact on vulnerable and marginalized populations.

What is lacking is a broader framework that analyzes human rights impacts and protects the right to health, food, water, and livelihoods—core economic rights—as well as civil and political rights, such as the rights to information, participation, free expression, and remedy for all citizens. When governments are not held accountable, they are less likely to remediate contaminated sites and ensure full access to justice to those whose rights have been violated.

Strong systems of accountability—in which governments, international financial institutions, businesses, and other private actors must account for their actions using the principles of transparency and full information, participation, and free expression—are needed to address the human rights impact of environmental damage. And there needs to be rigorous regulation processes, including government oversight, to prevent environmentally damaging projects from operating in the first place. When harm is done, those responsible must account for their actions, remediate the situation, and face justice.

The HRC, and those governments which have not done so yet, should recognize the right to a healthy environment as a freestanding right, which would help to strengthen accountability and understanding of the consequences for human rights of environmental damage. International treaties on the environment and universally agreed development goals should be grounded in international human rights law and monitored on the international and national level.

Cooperation between the environmental and the human rights movements will be crucial to help advance these goals. For it is only by working together— locally and globally—that true progress can be made in standing up to those who damage the environment, cause harm to others, and violate fundamental human rights.

Juliane Kippenberg is a senior researcher in the Children's Rights division; and Jane Cohen is a researcher in the Health and Human Rights division at Human Rights Watch.

WORLD REPORT 2013
PHOTO ESSAYS

The photo essays that follow focus on the experiences of
what appear to be three very different groups of people—
migrants and asylum seekers in Greece, people with
disabilities in Russia, and adults and children living in, and
working around, gold mines in Nigeria's Zamfara State. Yet all
suffer from lack of legal protections and from a range of
abuses that impact their health, their full participation in
society, and other fundamental human rights.

A child works in the processing site at a gold mine in

A HEAVY PRICE
LEAD POISONING AND GOLD MINING IN NIGERIA'S ZAMFARA STATE

BY MARCUS BLEASDALE/VII
FOR HUMAN RIGHTS WATCH

Since 2010, ongoing, widespread, acute lead poisoning has killed at least 400 children in Nigeria's Zamfara State. The lead poisoning is a result of artisanal gold mining: small scale mining with rudimentary tools. It is considered the worst outbreak of lead poisoning in modern history, with more than 3,500 children requiring urgent, life-saving treatment. Fewer than half are receiving it. Zamfara has significant gold deposits of gold. Miners crush and grind ore to extract gold, and in the process release dust that is highly contaminated with lead. Children in affected areas are exposed to this dust when they work in the processing site, when their relatives return home covered with the dust, and when the processing occurs at home. Children are also exposed to toxic lead in contaminated water and food sources.

Amina Murtala, a Bagega resident, told
Human Rights Watch that three of her six
children died from lead poisoning. Lead
levels were measured at 23,000 parts per
million in Amina's family compound. A safe
level is under 400 parts per million.

A mine worker crushes rocks in a flour grinder in the process of extracting gold. The dust is highly toxic and many adults suffer the effects of lead poisoning, ranging from swelling, dizziness and vomiting to organ failure, infertility, and death.

Children work in the processing site at a gold mine in Bagega.

A man holds a piece of gold mined
and processed in Zamfara State.

BREAKING BARRIERS
THE DISABILITY RIGHTS MOVEMENT IN RUSSIA

BY PLATON FOR HUMAN RIGHTS WATCH

Although people with disabilities in Russia have seen improvements since the end of the Soviet era, they remain largely cut-off from society. Public attitudes and a lack of legal protections create barriers to equality that prevent them from fully participating in public life. Human rights advocates hope that Russia's ratification of the Convention on the Rights of Persons with Disabilities (CRPD) in May 2012 will hasten the end of widespread discrimination against 13 million Russian citizens with mental and physical disabilities. The 2014 Sochi Olympics will certainly be a major test, as Russia will host a large number of people with disabilities as guests of the winter games and the subsequent Paralympics.

Yulia Simonova

Yulia is a co-program director of the inclusive education program at Perspektiva, Russia's leading disability capacity-building and advocacy organization, holding training sessions on disability issues; inclusive education workshops for teachers, parents and activists; and disabilities awareness classes for school-children. Yulia has taught 1,000 young people to be trainers on disability issues for Russian schools. She swims, rides horseback, and loves driving.

Vanya (Ivan) Alexeev

Vanya's mother is an active member of the Parents' Group at Perspektiva. Since early childhood, Vanya has taken part in many public actions organized by Perspektiva to support people with disabilities. Vanya has read all of the Harry Potter books and hopes to write a sequel someday. He loves to play with his younger brother and sister.

Yulia Averyanova

For two years, Yulia ran Perspektiva's sports programs and now remains a consultant with the organization. Yulia enjoys skiing, ice-skating, and paragliding. She recently introduced a blind friend of hers to the delight of downhill skiing.

Alexei Krykin

Alexei is an active participant in Best Buddies Russia, a volunteer movement that creates one-to-one friendships for persons with intellectual and developmental disabilities. Together with his buddy Ruslan, a university student, he goes out to the movies, theater, and soccer games. Alexei is active in the "Theater of the Naïve," an acting program engaging people with disabilities, and in an artisan workshop making all sorts of arts and crafts, including ceramics. He plays the flute, enjoys listening to music, and likes table tennis.

Vera Kocheshkova
and her mother Tatiana

In 2011, Vera graduated from a high school for children with disabilities. She is also active in Best Buddies Russia. She enjoys helping her mother around the house; they are best friends. "A daughter's smile makes a happy mother," says Tatiana. "Nothing is more important in life."

GREECE
HATE ON
THE STREETS

BY ZALMAÏ
FOR HUMAN RIGHTS WATCH

Greece prides itself on its hospitality.
But while tourists are welcome, the country
has become decidedly inhospitable for
many foreigners over the past decade.
Migrants and asylum seekers may be
subject to detention in inhuman and
degrading conditions, risk destitution, and
suffer xenophobic violence at the hands of
gangs of Greeks who attack them in central
Athens and elsewhere in the country with
frightening regularity. Human Rights Watch
found that despite clear patterns to the
violence, and evidence that it is increasing
amid deep economic crisis and after years
of mismanaged migration and asylum
policies, the police have failed to respond
effectively to protect victims and hold
perpetrators to account.

103 قهوه‌خانه سنتی

They asked me first, 'Where are you from?' I said, 'Somalia.' When I answered they tried to take my daughter away.... They hit me on my head with a wooden stick.... I fell down bleeding. When I fell down and they saw I was bleeding they ran away. My daughter was crying. All the people [around at the time of the attack] they were watching but nobody helped me. I didn't go to the hospital.... It didn't matter if I was hurt. I just thought about the baby and my daughter.

Mina Ahmad, a 20-year-old Somali woman, was attacked by a group of men near the Aghios Panteleimonas church in Athens in October 2011. She was with her infant daughter and was six-months pregnant at the time.

73

The Lord's Resistance Army (LRA) and Insecurity in Central Africa

Outcomes from a Workshop Held in Dungu, DR Congo, October 2011

DOCUMENTS RELATED TO THE CENTRAL AFRICAN REPUBLIC

March 2012

WORLD REPORT
2013

AFRICA

Angola

Angola held general elections on August 31, 2012, reaffirming the ruling Popular Movement for the Liberation of Angola (Movimento Popular de Libertação de Angola, MPLA) party's position in power and for the first time awarding incumbent José Eduardo dos Santos, in power for 33 years, the presidency through a vote.

The MPLA, which has ruled Angola since 1975, secured the two-thirds majority in parliament—175 out of 220 seats—sufficient to amend the constitution without opposition support. Forty percent of eligible voters did not vote. The constitutional court rejected fraud complaints from three opposition parties for lack of evidence. The main opposition party, National Union for the Total Independence of Angola (União Nacional para a Independência Total de Angola, UNITA), filed an additional complaint at the constitutional court challenging the constitutionality of acts by the national electoral commission (NCE) during the preparations of the elections. At this writing, the complaint remained pending.

The elections were generally peaceful during the campaign and on polling day, yet fell short of international and regional standards. The playing field for political parties was uneven, with unequal access to state resources; the media was overwhelmingly dominated by the MPLA and the elections oversight body sided with the ruling party by not taking any action when the ruling party violated electoral laws. As during the last national elections in 2008, independent observation of the elections was seriously hampered by massive delays and restrictions in the accreditation of domestic and international observers and international journalists.

The elections took place in a more restricted environment for the media, free expression and peaceful assembly than in 2008. Numerous incidents of violence by apparent police in plain clothes against peaceful protesters and activists in the months before the elections contributed to a climate of fear.

Elections

The CNE, despite a more balanced composition than in 2008, was not able or willing to fulfill its role as an impartial oversight body. The CNE failed to address major violations of electoral laws, including unequal access of parties to the public media and ruling party abuse of state resources and facilities. Moreover, the CNE hampered independent observation through the massively delayed, restrictive, and selective accreditation of domestic and international observers. The CNE also obstructed the accreditation of opposition officials at the polling stations, leaving up to half of opposition representatives without credentials on polling day.

The police did not act impartially during the election campaign, on several occasions arbitrarily arresting opposition activists. Most were released without charges. On the eve of the elections, police arbitrarily detained at least 19 opposition activists and others, including polling station officials and opposition representatives, as well as passersby during two protests in front of the CNE's headquarters in Luanda, the capital. While five were released without charges, fourteen people including activists of the opposition coalition Broad Convergence for Angola's Salvation–Electoral Coalition (Convêrgencia Ampla de Salvação de Angola- Coligação Eleitoral, CASA-CE), polling station officials, and passersby at a protest were jailed for three days and may face charges for allegedly having organized an illegal campaign rally.

Freedom of Media

The media face a broad range of restrictions that hamper the right to free expression and encourage self-censorship. The state media and a number of private media owned by senior officials are ruling party mouthpieces in which censorship and self-censorship are common.

In addition, the 2006 press law and the criminal code provide criminal penalties for defamation and similar offenses, such as "abuse against press freedom." At this writing, the necessary by-laws and other complementary laws to the 2006 press law that would at least partially lift excessive administrative restrictions on private radio and television stations and allow community radio broadcasting were yet to be passed in parliament.

Journalists have been regularly arrested, detained, harassed and questioned by the authorities while trying to cover protests in Luanda and elsewhere, and have been targeted with both threats and official offers to cooperate with the ruling party. Some journalists who have criticized the government are facing criminal charges, some pending for years. In October 2011, a court imposed a one-year suspended sentence and US$100,000 in damages on William Tonet, the director of the private weekly newspaper *Folha 8*. Tonet's appeal was pending at this writing. On March 12, police raided *Folha 8*'s office and confiscated the paper's equipment, presenting a search warrant on charges of alleged "outrage against the president," an offense under the 2010 crimes against the law, Crimes Against the Security of the State.

Freedom of Assembly

The 2010 constitution guarantees the rights to freedom of assembly and peaceful demonstration, and Angolan laws explicitly allow public demonstrations without government authorization. However, since 2009, the government has banned a number of anti-government demonstrations and the police have prevented the majority of peaceful demonstrations from taking place.

Since early 2011, a youth movement unconnected to any political party and inspired by the pro-democracy Arab Spring movements, has organized a number of demonstrations in Luanda and in the city of Benguela calling for freedom of expression, social justice, and the president's resignation. Since May 2012, another set of protests has gained momentum, staged by former soldiers from all the former armed movements in Angola. The protesters were protesting unpaid pensions and other benefits.

The authorities have responded to protests, even small-scale protests, with excessive force, arbitrary arrests, unfair trials and intimidation of journalists and other observers. Since February 2011, the ruling party has spread fear among the population by alleging that the protests could result in civil war. Such messages have an intimidating effect on the majority of the Angolan population, as a result of a decade-long civil war that ended 10 years ago.

The main perpetrators of violence during demonstrations have been groups of armed individuals who act in complete impunity and appear to be security agents in civilian clothes. In the months preceding the elections campaign, the threats and attacks against youth protest leaders and opposition activists by these plainclothes security agents increased, appeared systematic, and included attacks against protesters in their private homes, abductions, and forced disappearances.

In one of the most violent crackdowns on peaceful protests in 2012, on March 10, a dozen plainclothes security agents armed with wooden and metal clubs, knives, and pistols, attacked a crowd of 40 demonstrators in Luanda's Cazenga neighborhood, severely injuring 3 protest organizers. On the same day, plainclothes security agents attacked two senior politicians of the opposition party Democratic Bloc (Bloco Democrático) in Luanda's city center.

In another particularly serious case, two organizers of a May 27 protest for former presidential guards who were claiming unpaid salaries, Isaias Cassule and Antonio Alves Kamulingue, were both abducted by unidentified assailants. Their whereabouts remain unknown. The police have rejected the requests of their families to investigate the abductions. In September, the local lawyer's organization Maos Livres filed a complaint with the attorney-general's office. Human Rights Watch is not aware of the attorney-general taking any action since then.

Protesters who became victims of violence, threats and abductions have since 2011 filed numerous complaints with the police against their aggressors. At this writing, Human Rights Watch was not aware of any credible police investigation into any of those cases.

Human Rights Defenders

Human rights defenders have for many years been targets for threats, intimidation, co-option attempts, censorship, and alleged defamation in state-owned or ruling party-controlled media.

Officials have also used defamation laws to deter human rights reporting in the country. In January 2012, Manuel Helder Vieira Dias "Kopelipa," minister of state and long-term head of the president's Military Office (recently renamed Security Office), and six other generals and senior officials, all shareholders of the private security company Teleservice and the diamond company Sociedade Mineira do Cuango, filed a defamation lawsuit in Portugal against anti-corruption campaigner and human rights activist Rafael Marques.

The lawsuit was in response to a complaint filed by Marques in November 2011 at the Angolan attorney-general's office in Luanda against 17 Angolan officials, including nine generals of the Angolan Armed Forces, alleging they were responsible for over 100 documented serious human rights abuses, including killings, rape and torture, in the diamond-rich Lunda Norte province. A Luanda court only heard four victims of abuses who testified on cases documented by Marques; the court case against the officials remained pending at this writing.

Rafael Marques has been regularly threatened for documenting cases of high-level corruption in Angola involving the presidency and a broad range of senior officials. His anti-corruption blog *www.makaangola.org* has suffered a series of apparently targeted "denial of service" attacks in 2011, which effectively undermined public access to the website, even if temporarily.

Mass Expulsions of Migrants

In a positive step, the government has undertaken efforts to build new transit prisons with more humane conditions for migrants. However, Human Rights Watch is not aware of any credible and thorough investigation and prosecution of those security forces officials who were responsible for serious human rights violations against Congolese migrants during expulsions from Angola. Expulsions from the diamond-rich Lunda Norte province have been frequent, but also from other areas bordering the Democratic Republic of the Congo, such as the enclave of Cabinda. Corroborated abuses include targeting women and girls for rape, sexual coercion, beatings, deprivation of food and water and—in some cases—sexual abuse in the presence of children and other inmates.

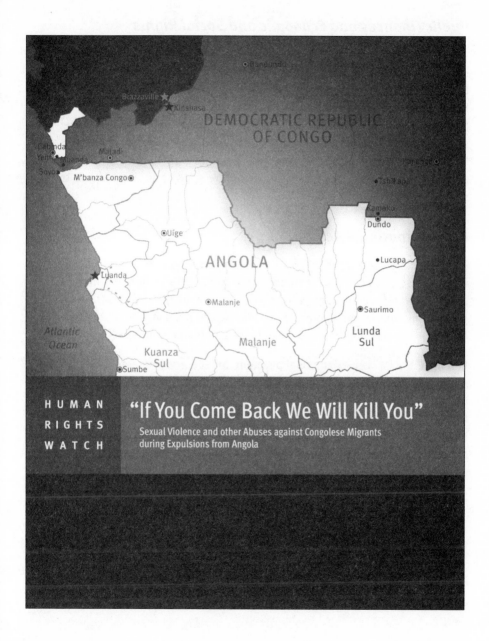

HUMAN
RIGHTS
WATCH

"If You Come Back We Will Kill You"

Sexual Violence and other Abuses against Congolese Migrants
during Expulsions from Angola

Public Finances and Economic and Social Rights

Longstanding concerns about mismanagement of Angola's oil revenues as a key impediment to the realization of economic and social rights resurfaced in 2012. Despite high oil revenues, Angola's development indicators remain low, with high poverty levels and limited access to social services. The International Monetary Fund (IMF) revealed in December 2011 that Angolan government spending, between 2007 and 2010, of US$32 billion in oil revenues bypassed budget processes, audits, and other forms of public accountability. This amount, equivalent to 25 percent of the country's GDP, was spent largely by the state oil company, Sonangol.

Key International Actors

Angola remains one of Africa's largest oil producers and China's second most important source of oil and most important commercial partner in Africa. This oil wealth, soaring economic growth, and Angola's military power in Africa have greatly limited leverage of other governments and regional and international organizations pushing for good governance and human rights.

In March, the IMF issued the final payment under a 2009 emergency loan to Angola. Civil society groups had urged the IMF to withhold the financing until the government adequately explained the $32 billion in off-budget spending from oil revenues during the loan period. They argued that making the final payment may give the impression that the IMF was not concerned about the Angolan government's lack of accountability to its citizens.

Burundi

Human rights in Burundi in 2012 present both progress and serious concerns. For example, the number of political killings decreased in 2012 after a sharp escalation in 2011, but political space remains restricted. The Burundian government failed to address widespread impunity, especially for members of the security forces and the youth league of the ruling National Council for the Defense of Democracy-Forces for the Defense of Democracy (CNDD-FDD). The report of a commission of inquiry, set up by the prosecutor general to investigate cases of extrajudicial executions and torture, acknowledged that killings had occurred, but concluded that they did not constitute extrajudicial executions.

There were very few arrests or prosecutions for politically motivated killings, and in the incident that claimed the largest number of victims in 2011—the attack at Gatumba resulting in 39 deaths—the trial of the alleged perpetrators was seriously flawed. Several leading opposition figures remained outside the country, and the CNDD-FDD continued to dominate the political scene.

Civil society organizations and media continued to investigate and publicly denounce human rights abuses; however, freedom of expression was constantly under threat. State pressure on journalists and civil society activists continued, as the government counted them among the political opposition. Draft legislation placing new restrictions on media freedoms was tabled before parliament in October.

The National Independent Human Rights Commission continued to work in an independent manner, expanding its representation in several provinces and investigating reports of human rights abuses.

Political Killings

Political killings diminished significantly in 2012, but there were sporadic attacks by armed groups as well as killings of members or former members of the opposition National Liberation Forces (FNL). Despite repeated promises to deliver justice for these crimes, the government failed to take effective action to

HUMAN RIGHTS WATCH

"YOU WILL NOT HAVE PEACE WHILE YOU ARE LIVING"

The Escalation of Political Violence in Burundi

do so. In the vast majority of politically motivated killings, thorough investigations were not carried out, and there were no arrests or prosecutions. Impunity was particularly pronounced in cases where the perpetrators were suspected to be state agents or members of the Imbonerakure, the youth league of the CNDD-FDD.

The Gatumba attack, which claimed 39 lives in September 2011, was one of the rare cases that resulted in prosecution. However, the trial of 21 people accused of involvement in the attack, which concluded in December 2011, was seriously flawed. Despite the complexity of the case, the trial only lasted a few days and was marked by irregularities, with several aspects of proceedings casting doubt on the fairness of the trial and the reliability of the judges' ruling. In January, 16 of the 21 defendants were found guilty; seven were sentenced to life imprisonment. At this writing, their appeal was pending. The report of a commission of inquiry investigating the Gatumba attack, which was completed in October 2011, has still not been published.

In June, the prosecutor general set up a commission of inquiry into cases of torture and extrajudicial killings, including cases reported by Human Rights Watch, Amnesty International, and the Burundian human rights organization, Association for the Protection of Human Rights and Detained Persons (APRODH).

In August, the commission published its report, recognizing that killings had occurred, but concluded that they did not constitute extrajudicial executions. The report stated that casefiles had been opened on a number of these incidents and that investigations were underway. It attempted to discredit the findings of Human Rights Watch, APRODH, and the human rights section of the United Nations Office in Burundi (BNUB). BNUB issued a press release challenging the commission's conclusions, and reiterated the state's responsibility for human rights abuses by its agents.

The commission's work resulted in the arrest of about eight people, including policemen, alleged to have been involved in cases of killings or torture. At this writing, they were in preventive detention.

However, in the majority of other cases documented by Human Rights Watch, even when prosecutors had opened a file, judicial authorities made little effort to conduct in-depth investigations and rarely questioned witnesses or victims' relatives. Many family members of victims were often too afraid to demand justice. Several faced threats for speaking out about the deaths of their relatives.

Transitional Justice

In December 2011, the government published a draft law establishing a Truth and Reconciliation Commission to cover crimes committed since 1962. While long overdue and broadly welcomed by Burundian civil society, the law did not provide for the establishment of a special tribunal to prosecute individuals accused of committing the most serious offenses, including war crimes, crimes against humanity, and genocide. The Truth and Reconciliation Commission is yet to be established, despite promises by President Pierre Nkurunziza that it would be set up by the end of 2012.

Pressure on Civil Society Activists and Journalists

State authorities repeatedly threatened human rights activists, journalists, and other members of civil society. In February, Pierre Claver Mbonimpa, president of APRODH, received a letter from the minister of interior accusing his organization of launching a "campaign of disinformation" against the state after APRODH alleged that state security forces were arming youth. The minister threatened "severe sanctions" if Mbonimpa did not produce evidence of the state arming youths within 10 days.

On February 7, Faustin Ndikumana, president of the nongovernmental organization, Words and Action for Awakening Consciences and Changing Mentalities (PARCEM), was arrested after denouncing alleged corruption in the ministry of justice in relation to procedures for recruiting magistrates. He was detained for two weeks, released on bail, tried by the Anti-Corruption Court, and sentenced in July to five years' imprisonment for making false statements. The court also fined him and PARCEM for defaming the minister of justice. Ndikumana remains free pending his appeal.

Minister of Interior Edouard Nduwimana ordered Human Rights Watch to cancel a May 2 press conference and report launch in Bujumbura, and to stop distributing copies of its report on political killings in Burundi. The government spokesperson issued a public statement on May 7 describing the Human Rights Watch report as a "declaration of war" against the people of Burundi.

After long delays, the trial of those accused of involvement in the murder of anti-corruption campaigner Ernest Manirumva in 2009 concluded in May 2012. Fourteen people were sentenced to prison terms ranging from 10 years to life imprisonment. The Burundian government had established three successive commissions of inquiry to investigate Manirumva's death and had accepted assistance from the FBI. However, the prosecution disregarded leads and recommendations from the third commission and from the FBI, which might have uncovered the possible involvement of Burundian officials in Manirumva's death. Appeal hearings began in November.

State agents, including high-ranking members of the intelligence services, repeatedly threatened journalists, accusing them of siding with the opposition, and warning them to stop criticizing the government.

The National Assembly was considering a new draft law on the press at this writing. If adopted without being amended, this law would drastically curtail free speech. The draft law contains several provisions that would restrict the ability of journalists to operate independently. Journalists would not be able to protect their sources in cases deemed to threaten state security or public order or cases involving defense secrets, among others. The draft law requires journalists to only broadcast or publish "balanced information from sources that have been rigorously verified." One improvement compared to the existing law is that offenses would no longer be punishable by imprisonment; however, new heavy fines would restrict the ability of media organizations to operate.

In June, Hassan Ruvakuki, of Radio France Internationale and Bonesha FM, was sentenced to life imprisonment for alleged participation in terrorist acts after interviewing a new rebel group in the eastern province of Cankuzo in late 2011. Twenty-two co-accused persons were also found guilty. Ruvakuki maintained that he was interviewing the group in his capacity as a journalist and that he was not a member of the group or spreading its propaganda. His lawyers walked out of the trial, citing procedural irregularities and bias on the part of the judges. Appeal hearings concluded in November.

Prisoner Releases

The Ministry of Justice launched an initiative to address overcrowding and irregular detentions in Burundi's prisons by reviewing prisoner case files and provisionally releasing certain prisoners, including those who had served at least a quarter of their sentence. In addition, a presidential decree in June announced that several categories of prisoners, including those sentenced to five years' imprisonment or less (except those convicted of rape, armed robbery, illegal possession of weapons, and endangering state security), pregnant women, prisoners suffering from incurable diseases, prisoners over the age of 60, and those under the age of 18 would benefit from presidential grace; other prisoners' sentences would be halved. Several thousand prisoners could be released thanks to these two initiatives, which began to be implemented during the year.

Key International Actors

Foreign diplomats in Bujumbura continued to follow high-profile trials, including those of Ndikumana and Ruvakuki, the individuals accused of killing Ernest Manirumva, and the Gatumba trial. The European Union issued two statements, one in February expressing concern about flawed procedures in the Gatumba trial and delay in delivering justice for the killing of Manirumva, and another in August regretting the verdict in the trial of Ndikumana, and expressing concern about difficulties facing Burundian civil society activists.

The Dutch government suspended part of its training program for the Burundian police following the report of the prosecutor general's commission of inquiry into extrajudicial executions and the lack of progress in bringing perpetrators to justice.

Côte d'Ivoire

Ongoing socio-political insecurity, failure to deliver impartial justice for past crimes, and inadequate progress in addressing the root causes of recent political and ethnic violence—notably the lack of an independent judiciary and impunity for government forces—undermined Côte d'Ivoire's emergence from a decade of grave human rights abuses.

A wave of attacks on villages and military installations launched within Côte d'Ivoire and from neighboring Liberia and Ghana—many, if not all, likely planned and carried out by militant supporters of former President Laurent Gbagbo—fostered insecurity, reversed trends of demilitarization, and led to widespread rights abuses by the Ivorian military.

The first parliamentary elections in 11 years took place in December 2011. The Ivorian government also made meaningful progress in rebuilding rule of law institutions, particularly in the north, where state institutions were reestablished after a decade-long absence. Longstanding deficiencies within the judiciary, particularly corruption and the influence of political pressure, continued to undermine rights.

Eighteen months after the end of the 2010-2011 post-election crisis, justice for the grave crimes committed remained disturbingly one-sided. Ivorian authorities and the International Criminal Court (ICC) have yet to arrest and prosecute any member of President Alassane Ouattara's camp for post-election crimes, reinforcing dangerous communal divisions.

Côte d'Ivoire's international partners supplied significant assistance for justice and security sector reform, but remained reluctant to criticize the government publicly for its lack of progress on ensuring impartial justice and an end to security force abuses.

Insecurity and Lack of Disarmament Progress

Progress in restoring security was marred by attacks throughout the year that Ouattara's government blamed on pro-Gbagbo militants intent on destabilizing the country, a claim that an October report from the United Nations Panel of Experts on Côte d'Ivoire generally supported. Attackers killed at least 25 civilians during cross-border raids from Liberia between April and June, including a June 8 attack in which seven UN peacekeepers were killed.

Insecurity intensified in August and September, when armed men launched nine strikes, many of them seemingly coordinated and well-organized, against military installations in Côte d'Ivoire. In the most daring raid, attackers killed six soldiers on August 6 at the Akouédo military camp near Abidjan and absconded with a substantial cache of weapons.

There was scant progress in disarming tens of thousands of youth who fought on opposing sides during the armed conflict. In August, President Ouattara created a single agency responsible for disarmament, demobilization, and reintegration in an attempt to improve a previously uncoordinated and disorganized disarmament effort. The new agency effectively started anew, beginning a census of ex-combatants in late August.

Security Force Abuses

The Ivorian military, known as the Republican Forces, committed numerous human rights violations when responding to security threats, particularly the August attacks on the military. Soldiers rounded up hundreds of youth perceived to be Gbagbo supporters in mass arbitrary arrests and detained and interrogated them illegally at military camps. Cruel and inhuman treatment was common, as soldiers regularly beat detainees, who were forced to stay in extremely overcrowded cells and deprived of food and water.

In at least some cases in Abidjan and San Pedro, the mistreatment rose to the level of torture—with military personnel inflicting extreme physical abuse in pressuring detainees to sign confessions or divulge information. Several commanders who oversaw these crimes were previously implicated in grave crimes during the post-election crisis.

The security forces were also implicated in criminal acts, including theft and extortion, perpetrated during neighborhood sweeps when some soldiers stole cash and valuables from homes and people, and at detention sites where some

HUMAN
RIGHTS
WATCH

"A LONG WAY
FROM RECONCILIATION"

Abusive Military Crackdown in Response to Security Threats in Côte d'Ivoire

soldiers demanded money to release people from illegal detention. The military hierarchy made little effort to stop the abuses or to discipline the soldiers involved.

National Accountability for Post-Election Crimes

While Ivorian authorities have charged more than 140 civilian and military leaders linked to the Gbagbo camp with crimes related to the post-election crisis, no member of the pro-Ouattara forces has been arrested, much less charged, for such crimes. There was growing impatience among Ivorian civil society and some diplomats to see tangible progress made toward impartial justice.

In August, a national commission of inquiry that President Ouattara established in June 2011 published a report on crimes committed during the post-election crisis. Although lacking in details on specific incidents, the report's balance in situating responsibility was noteworthy—documenting 1,009 summary executions by pro-Gbagbo forces and 545 summary executions by the Republican Forces. At this writing, the commission's work had not prompted more serious judicial investigations into crimes by pro-Ouattara forces.

The special investigative cell in the Ministry of Justice continued investigations into crimes committed during the post-election crisis. The absence of a prosecutorial strategy and lack of proactive efforts to reach pro-Gbagbo victims—many of whom remain too afraid of reprisals to bring complaints—hampered progress toward impartial justice. The government's decision in September to assign more judges and prosecutors to the special cell was positive, but the continued lack of concrete action fuels concerns about the political will to prosecute pro-Ouattara forces.

On October 2, the first trial for post-election crimes opened in a military court against four officers from pro-Gbagbo forces, including the former head of the Republican Guard, Brunot Dogbo Blé, who was sentenced to 15 years for kidnapping, illegal detention, and murder. Ivorian justice officials indicated that trials in civilian courts, including against high-level officials like former First Lady Simone Gbagbo, would begin in late November.

International Criminal Court

On November 29, 2011, the Ivorian government surrendered Laurent Gbagbo to the ICC, where he was charged as an indirect co-perpetrator with four counts of crimes against humanity. On November 2, the court ruled that Gbagbo was fit to stand trial, following a closed hearing in late September on the issue.

On November 22, the ICC unsealed an arrest warrant against Simone Gbagbo and asked Ivorian authorities to surrender her to the court. Diplomats and civil society had previously voiced concern over whether the Ivorian government would cooperate with the ICC in executing additional arrest warrants, as the government increasingly asserted that it could handle all cases going forward. Many perceived this as an effort by the Ouattara government to protect its military commanders from potential prosecution for their own serious crimes between 2002 and 2011.

The office of the prosecutor continued to stress that additional investigations were ongoing, including against pro-Ouattara forces. However, frustration grew among Ivorian civil society and human rights groups over the ICC's significant delay in issuing an arrest warrant against someone from the Ouattara side, reinforcing the problem of one-sided justice within Côte d'Ivoire.

Reestablishing Rule of Law

In December 2011, legislative elections took place for the first time in 11 years, and the new National Assembly sat for its first session on April 24. For the first time in nine years, state authority—including judges, customs officials, and other civil servants—was restored throughout northern Côte d'Ivoire. The Ivorian government also made significant progress in rehabilitating courthouses and prisons, many of which were seriously damaged during the conflict. However, the judiciary's lack of independence remained a concern.

The police, gendarmerie, and judicial police remained poorly equipped and marginalized. In early 2012, there was gradual progress in ensuring that these forces, not the military, took the lead in day-to-day internal security. However, after the August attacks, the military again hijacked responsibilities far outside its mandate, including by conducting neighborhood searches and arresting, detaining, and interrogating people.

Key International Actors

Côte d'Ivoire's international partners, including the European Union, France, the United States, and the UN, supported justice and security sector reform initiatives but were reluctant to pressure the government publicly on the lack of accountability for past crimes and ongoing abuses by the military. However, several made notable statements on press freedom after the national press council suspended pro-Gbagbo newspapers from publishing in September. The press council promptly lifted the suspensions.

During the first half of 2012, Liberian authorities failed to respond adequately to pro-Gbagbo militants' use of Liberia as a staging ground to recruit and launch attacks into Côte d'Ivoire. Several Liberian mercenaries implicated in grave crimes during the Ivorian crisis were quietly released on bail in February, and authorities made no progress in these prosecutions during the year. However, after the June 8 attack in which UN peacekeepers were killed, Liberian authorities increased their border presence, arrested individuals involved in cross-border attacks, and extradited 41 Ivorians allegedly involved in post-election crimes.

Ghana appeared to serve as a base where pro-Gbagbo militants planned attacks on Côte d'Ivoire, as Ghanaian authorities failed to extradite pro-Gbagbo leaders who lived in Ghana and were subject to Ivorian and international arrest warrants. Following the August attacks in Abidjan, Ghanaian authorities arrested Justin Kone Katinan, Gbagbo's former budget minister, but the extradition hearing was repeatedly postponed.

In January, the UN Human Rights Council's (HRC) independent expert on human rights in Côte d'Ivoire published his first report, highlighting the state's failure to prevent human rights abuses and slow progress in security sector reform. In May, the UN Security Council visited Côte d'Ivoire to assess rule of law, security, and reconciliation challenges. In October, a panel of experts under the Security Council's authority reported that the government may have violated the council's arms embargo, and that pro-Gbagbo militants had established a "strategic command" in Ghana in their efforts to destabilize Côte d'Ivoire.

The UN Operation in Côte d'Ivoire (UNOCI) actively documented human rights violations and visited detention sites, though it rarely published reports or publicly criticized the Ivorian government, including on issues such as one-sided justice. The Security Council has still not published the findings of the 2004 commission of inquiry that investigated serious human rights and international humanitarian law violations during the 2002-2003 armed conflict.

Democratic Republic of Congo

State security forces and Congolese and foreign armed groups committed numerous and widespread violations of the laws of war against civilians in eastern and northern Democratic Republic of Congo (Congo).

In late 2011, opposition party members and supporters, human rights activists, and journalists were threatened, arbitrarily arrested, and killed during presidential and legislative election periods.

Gen. Bosco Ntaganda, sought on arrest warrants from the International Criminal Court (ICC) for war crimes and crimes against humanity, defected from the army in March and started a new rebellion with other former members of the National Congress for the Defense of the People (CNDP), a rebel group integrated into the army in early 2009. The new M23 rebel group received significant support from Rwandan military officials. Its fighters were responsible for widespread war crimes, including summary executions, rapes, and child recruitment.

As the government and military focused attention on defeating the M23, other armed groups became more active in other parts of North and South Kivu, attacking civilians.

Abuses during National Elections

Presidential and legislative elections in November 2011 were characterized by targeted attacks by state security forces on opposition party members and supporters, the use of force to quell political demonstrations, and threats or attacks on journalists and human rights activists. President Joseph Kabila was declared winner of the November 28, 2011 election, which international and national election observers criticized as lacking credibility and transparency.

The worst election-related violence was in the capital, Kinshasa, where at least 57 opposition party supporters or suspected supporters were killed by security forces—mostly Kabila's Republican Guard—between November 26 and December 31.

Human Rights Watch received credible reports of nearly 150 other people killed in this period, their bodies reportedly dumped in the Congo River, in mass graves on Kinshasa's outskirts, or in morgues far from the city center. Scores of people accused of opposing Kabila were arbitrarily detained by Republican Guard soldiers and the police. Many were held in illegal detention centers where they were mistreated and some were killed.

Abuses against opposition supporters also occurred in other areas, including North and South Kivu, Katanga, and the Kasai provinces. In some areas, soldiers and militia members backing Kabila used intimidation and force to compel voters to vote for certain candidates.

War Crimes by M23 Rebels

In March, General Ntaganda, the former rebel who had become a general in the Congolese army, defected from the army with several hundred former members of the National Congress for the Defense of the People (CNDP) rebel group. Ntaganda's troops forcibly recruited at least 149 people, including at least 48 children, in Masisi, North Kivu, in April and May. The mutiny began soon after the government indicated that it was planning to deploy ex-CNDP soldiers outside of the Kivus. A parallel military structure had been established in the Kivus with troops loyal to Ntaganda responsible for targeted killings, mass rapes, abductions, robberies, and resource plundering.

Soon after Ntaganda's mutiny was defeated by the Congolese army in April, other former CNDP members led by Col. Sultani Makenga launched another mutiny in Rutshuru territory, North Kivu. Ntaganda and troops loyal to him joined this new rebellion, which called itself the M23 after the March 23, 2009 peace agreement between the Congolese government and the CNDP.

From its start, the M23 rebellion received significant support from Rwandan military officials, including in the planning and command of military operations and the supply of weapons and ammunition. At least 600 young men and boys were recruited by force or under false pretenses in Rwanda to join the rebellion. Demobilized fighters, Congolese refugees, and other men and boys were recruited by neighborhood chiefs and Rwandan army officers. Rwandan soldiers then escorted them across the border to Congo, where they were trained to fight in camps led by Rwandan military officers. Several hundred Rwandan soldiers were deployed to Congo to support the M23 in their military offensives, helping the rebels gain control of much of Rutshuru territory.

In mid-November, M23 rebels launched another offensive with support from the Rwandan military and took control of Goma, the provincial capital, and the town of Sake. On December 1, M23 withdrew most of its forces from Goma and Sake, after the Congolese government said it would negotiate with them.

M23 fighters were responsible for widespread war crimes, including summary executions, rapes, and child recruitment. At least 33 new recruits and other M23 fighters were executed when they attempted to flee. Journalists and human rights activists who documented or spoke out against the M23's abuses received death threats. M23 fighters attempted to rape a human rights activist in Rutshuru and told her they were targeting her because of her work. When she tried to flee, they shot her in the leg.

Attacks on Civilians by Other Armed Groups

The Democratic Forces for the Liberation of Rwanda (FDLR), a predominately Rwandan Hutu rebel group some of whose members took part in the 1994 genocide in Rwanda, and other Congolese armed groups increased their military activities, taking advantage of rising ethnic tensions and the security vacuum created by the army's focus on the M23.

Some of the most intense fighting was between the Congolese armed group Raia Mutomboki (meaning "outraged citizens" in Swahili), the FDLR, and their allies. Hundreds of civilians were killed in Masisi, Walikale, Kalehe, and Shabunda territories in North and South Kivu, as each side accused the local population of supporting its enemies.

The M23 sought to ally with some of the other armed groups, providing them with periodic or sustained support, including weapons and ammunition, and on occasion organizing coordinated attacks.

The Lord's Resistance Army (LRA) and Insecurity in Central Africa

Outcomes from a Workshop Held in Dungu, DR Congo, October 2011

DOCUMENTS RELATED TO THE DEMOCRATIC REPUBLIC OF CONGO

April 2012

Abuses by the Lord's Resistance Army

The Lord's Resistance Army (LRA), a Ugandan rebel group with a long record of atrocities, continued to attack civilians in northern Congo and eastern Central African Republic. Local activists reported 273 LRA attacks between October 2011 and October 2012, in which at least 52 civilians were killed and 741 others abducted. About half of those abducted were released after three days. The LRA's three senior leaders sought on arrest warrants from the ICC—Joseph Kony, Odhok Odhiambo, and Dominic Ongwen—remain at large.

Justice and Accountability

Appeal hearings began in the trial of those accused of the assassination of human rights activist Floribert Chebeya and the disappearance of his driver Fidèle Bazana in Kinshasa in June 2010. In June 2011, the deputy head of special police services Colonel Daniel Mukalay, and three fugitive police officers were sentenced to death. Another defendant was sentenced to life imprisonment. General John Numbi, the former police chief who was implicated in the murder, has not been arrested and apparently not seriously investigated.

On October 4, 2011, seven humanitarian workers of the Banyamulenge ethnic group were killed near Fizi, South Kivu province, in an ethnically motivated attack by Mai Mai Yakutumba fighters. Despite pledges from the authorities to bring to justice those responsible, one year later no one had been arrested in connection with the attack.

On December 2, 2011, judicial authorities opened an investigation into election-related violence on November 26 and 28, 2011. One year later, the investigation has made little progress. In late 2011 and early 2012, government officials and security forces attempted to cover up evidence, denied access to hospitals and morgues to human rights activists, and intimidated witnesses and family members of the victims.

The ICC issued its first-ever conviction and sentenced, in July, Congolese armed group leader Thomas Lubanga to 14 years in prison for recruiting and using child soldiers in Ituri district in eastern Congo in 2002 and 2003. The evidence phase of the trial of Mathieu Ngudjolo and Germain Katanga, leaders of an armed group that opposed Lubanga's group in Ituri, was completed in May.

Ntaganda, Lubanga's co-accused at the ICC, remained at large at this writing. Ntaganda has been wanted by the ICC since 2006 for recruiting and using child soldiers, crimes which he continued to commit in 2012. In July, the court issued a second warrant against him for war crimes and crimes against humanity, also in connection with his activities in Ituri.

In July, the ICC indicted Sylvestre Mudacumura, the FDLR's military commander, for war crimes; he remained at large at this writing. Two FDLR political leaders, Ignace Murwanashyaka and Straton Musoni, were on trial in Germany on charges of war crimes and crimes against humanity.

There was little progress on the government's proposal to establish a specialized mixed court with jurisdiction over war crimes and crimes against humanity committed since 1990 and on the adoption of legislation implementing the ICC statute. In September, the justice minister pledged to adopt the ICC implementing legislation promptly. In October, she took initial steps to revive draft legislation on the specialized mixed court.

Key International Actors

In late 2011, the United States deployed 100 special forces personnel to the LRA-affected region as military advisers to regional armed forces carrying out operations against the LRA. In March, the African Union announced a regional cooperation initiative to strengthen efforts to combat the LRA, including deploying a 5,000-member regional task force.

In August 2012, the US Security and Exchange Commission (SEC) adopted a rule mandated by the Dodd-Frank Wall Street Reform and Consumer Protection Act requiring companies to publicly disclose their use of conflict minerals originating from Congo or neighboring countries. On October 19, the US Chamber of Commerce and National Association of Manufacturers sued to have the rule modified or set aside in US federal court.

In September, US President Barack Obama announced that the US was with-holding foreign military financing from Congo for a second year because of the army's continued recruitment and use of child soldiers. The administration also announced that the US would not train a second army battalion until Congo signed a UN action plan to end its use of child soldiers. The Congolese govern-ment signed the plan on October 4.

Several foreign governments and intergovernmental organizations, including the UN Security Council, denounced M23 abuses and called for those responsi-ble to be brought to justice. In June, the UN high commissioner for human rights identified five senior M23 leaders as "among the worst perpetrators of human rights violations in the DRC, or in the world."

A UN group of experts monitoring the arms embargo and sanctions violations in Congo presented detailed evidence of Rwandan military support to the M23 rebels in an addendum to its interim report in June and in its final report in November. Its final report also included evidence that Uganda's security forces were supporting M23.

Equatorial Guinea

Corruption, poverty, and repression continue to plague Equatorial Guinea under President Teodoro Obiang Nguema Mbasogo, who has been in power since 1979. Vast oil revenues fund lavish lifestyles for the small elite surrounding the president, while most of the population lives in poverty. Those who question this disparity are branded "enemies." Despite some areas of relative progress, human rights conditions remain very poor. Arbitrary detention and unfair trials continue to take place, mistreatment of detainees remains commonplace, sometimes rising to the level of torture.

While access to Equatorial Guinea improved somewhat for international journalists attending major events in the country, several reported being harassed or intimidated. Government repression of local journalists, civil society groups, and members of the political opposition continues.

President Obiang seeks to enhance his international standing and reputation. To that end, Equatorial Guinea hosted the Africa Cup of Nations and other prominent events in 2012 to present a new image of both the president and the country. The United Nations Educational, Scientific and Cultural Organization (UNESCO) issued a long-stalled prize sponsored by the president after earlier dropping his name from the controversial award.

Obiang also continues to defend the reputation of Teodorín, his eldest son and presumed successor, whom he elevated to be the country's second vice president—a position not contemplated in the new constitution. The government strongly objected when France seized Teodorín's Paris mansion and issued an international arrest warrant against him on money-laundering charges, claiming the son's post granted him immunity from prosecution abroad. The government also asked the International Court of Justice to order France to halt the case.

Economic and Social Rights

Fulfillment of key socio-economic rights, such as the right to education and basic healthcare, remains poor, despite significant oil revenues and the country's small population, which make Equatorial Guinea's per capita gross domestic product—at approximately US$30,000 according to UN figures—among the highest in Africa and the world.

Government social spending has increased relative to prior years since the adoption of the Horizon 2020 development plan in 2007, and was supplemented by projects financed largely by foreign oil companies. However, such spending remains low in relation to need and available resources. The country has reduced alarmingly high maternal mortality rates by 81 percent over 20 years, and the child mortality rate also fell from 1990 to 2010. Much of the population lacks access to adequate sanitation, potable water, and reliable electricity.

The government continued a massive building spree, financed by oil revenues, which raises questions about its spending priorities. Beyond infrastructure such as roads and power plants, much of the construction is for the enjoyment of the country's tiny elite and foreign guests. Projects include a new city being built in a remote rainforest and a planned $77 million presidential guesthouse.

Foreign investigations into high levels of corruption involving President Obiang and his close associates gathered further momentum in France, Spain, and the United States. In June, a legal filing in the US government's asset seizure case alleged extortion and embezzlement of public funds by Teodorín on a grand scale. The complaint details more than $300 million in spending from 2000 to 2011, including on art by master painters and mansions on four continents, allegedly with the use of illicitly obtained funds. In July, after a French judge issued an arrest warrant against Teodorín, French authorities also seized his luxurious Paris mansion, whose contents they had earlier claimed.

Freedom of Expression and Association

Equatorial Guinea remains notorious for its lack of press freedom. Journalists from state-owned media outlets remain unable to criticize the government without risk of censorship or reprisal. The few private media outlets that exist are generally owned by persons close to President Obiang; self-censorship is common. *El Lector*, a private, infrequently-published newspaper whose editor is simultaneously a Ministry of Information official, has at times run articles featuring members of the opposition.

The government remains intolerant of critical views from abroad. A greater number of foreign journalists were permitted to travel to cover events in the country, but several who attended the Cup of Nations in early 2012 reported being subjected to surveillance and harassment while they worked.

Human Rights Defenders

The country has no legally registered independent human rights groups. The few local activists who seek to address human rights related issues are vulnerable to intimidation, harassment, and reprisals.

Fabián Nsue Nguema, a lawyer who has handled sensitive cases involving political prisoners and those accused of coup plots, "disappeared" after visiting a client in prison. He was illegally arrested and kept in secret and incommunicado detention for several days before being allowed to see his family. He was released without charge after eight days, following international pressure.

In another case, Dr. Wenceslao Mansogo Alo, a human rights defender and opposition figure, was jailed in February and convicted in May for professional negligence in a trial widely regarded as unjust. He was harassed in detention, and there were restrictions on his visitors, contrary to a court order. Mansogo and 21 other prisoners were pardoned on the president's birthday in June. He filed an appeal against court orders to close his private health clinic, pay $13,000 in fines, and cease practicing medicine for five years.

The government inhibited the careers of other human rights defenders throughout the year. In April, Ponciano Mbomio Nvó, one of Mansogo's lawyers and a frequent defender of jailed political opponents, was suspended from legal practice for two years for arguing in Mansogo's trial that the case was politically motivated. In January, government officials allegedly pressured a private company to rescind a job offer made to Alfredo Okenve, the head of a local NGO who was sacked in 2010 by the National University after criticizing the government.

Political Parties and Opposition

The ruling Democratic Party of Equatorial Guinea (PDGE) maintains a monopoly over the country's political life. It orchestrated a constitutional referendum that was approved in November 2011 with 97.7 percent approval in a vote marred by irregularities. The opposition was deterred from observing the voting and protested efforts to prevent some opposition members from monitoring the polling places and from speaking out against voting fraud. A year later, none of the "independent" oversight bodies created under the new constitution had been established and the president declared that new presidential term limits would not apply retroactively.

Most political parties are aligned with PDGE, which benefits from a virtual monopoly on power, funding, and access to national media. Political opponents are pressured through various means, including arbitrary arrest and harassment, as well as inducements—such as employment opportunities—if they join the PDGE. Breakaway factions of the two political parties that maintain independence—the Convergence for Social Democracy (CPDS) and the People's Union (UP)—joined the ruling party.

Torture, Arbitrary Detention, and Unfair Trials

Due process rights continue to be flouted in Equatorial Guinea and prisoner mistreatment remains common. Lawyers and others who have visited prisons and jails indicate that serious abuses continue, including beatings in detention that amount to torture. Fabián Nsue Nguema reported that the client he sought to visit when he was himself arrested in October, Agustín Esono Nsogo, was tortured. The International Committee of the Red Cross (ICRC) visited some detention centers but did not have full access to others in 2012.

President Obiang exercises inordinate control over the judiciary, which lacks independence. Lawyers have reported that judges say they need to consult with the office of the president regarding their decisions in sensitive cases. The president is designated as the country's "chief magistrate." Among other powers, he chairs the body that oversees judges and appoints the body's remaining members.

Florentino Manguire, who spent over two years in prison on unsubstantiated theft charges filed by his former business associate, Obiang's son Teodorín, received a presidential pardon in June. In August, he was again arbitrarily arrested and held for 10 days, until his release without charge after receiving a stern warning not to reveal information about Teodorín.

Key International Actors

Following a contentious split vote in May 2012, UNESCO's governing board reinstated a prize established in 2008 at Obiang's request after renaming it the UNESCO-Equatorial Guinea prize. It did not resolve continued questions surrounding the source of the funding that was provided by Obiang. Neither UNESCO's director-general nor Obiang attended the award ceremony in July, which coincided with French judicial actions against Teodorín.

The Obiang government filed a case against France at the International Court of Justice in the Hague over its pursuit of Teodorín. Teodorín has railed against foreigners in speeches broadcast on state media. He filed a defamation case against the head of Transparency International (TI) France in March. The government of Equatorial Guinea then filed a domestic criminal defamation complaint against the head of TI France in September and requested that Interpol issue an international arrest warrant against him.

Spain, the former colonial power, applied some pressure on Equatorial Guinea to improve its human rights record. The Spanish government publicly opposed the UNESCO prize and criticized the imprisonment of Dr. Mansogo.

The US is Equatorial Guinea's main trading partner and source of investment in the oil sector. The US government credited the Obiang government for making some improvements in its human rights record, but expressed deep concern over the prosecution of Mansogo and strongly opposed the Obiang prize at UNESCO. It also co-organized an off-the-record June meeting between representatives of civil society, including Human Rights Watch, and President Obiang. The meeting was not followed by any decisive action to address the groups' calls for meaningful reform.

Eritrea

Torture, arbitrary detention, and severe restrictions on freedom of expression, association, and religious freedom remain routine in Eritrea. Elections have not been held since Eritrea gained independence in 1993, the constitution has never been implemented, and political parties are not allowed. There are no institutional constraints on President Isaias Afewerki, now in his twentieth year in power.

In addition to ongoing serious human rights abuses, forced labor and indefinite military service prompt thousands of Eritreans to flee the country every year.

Access to the country for international humanitarian and human rights organizations is almost impossible and the country has no independent media. In recognition of the "continued widespread and systematic violation of human rights," the United Nations Human Rights Council (HRC) in 2012 appointed a special rapporteur on Eritrea.

Forced Labor and Indefinite Military Service

National service keeps most young Eritreans in perpetual bondage. Although a decree mandating compulsory national service limits service to 18 months, in practice the government prolongs service indefinitely. National service conscripts are poorly fed and receive inadequate medical care. Eritrean refugees describe them as emaciated. Their pay (less than US$30 per month) is insufficient to provide sustenance for a family. Female conscripts report sexual abuse by commanding officers. In early 2012, President Isaias acknowledged that national service members and government employees are so poorly paid that they essentially "have been fulfilling their duties apparently without pay" for the past 20 years.

Conscripts allegedly provided forced labor to construct infrastructure at the Bisha gold mine, Eritrea's only operating mine and a major source of revenue. Although the Eritrean government had agreed with the mine's principal international owner that no national service conscripts would be allowed to work at Bisha, it required use of a ruling party-controlled contractor, Segen

Construction. Segen makes widespread use of conscript labor and there is evidence that it did so at Bisha as well. Escapees told Human Rights Watch in 2012 that they worked 12-hour shifts and endured dangerously inadequate food and housing conditions. They did not complain because, as one escapee told Human Rights Watch, "we were afraid for our lives."

Recent escapees report that conscripts are also involuntarily assigned to public works projects, the ruling party's commercial and agricultural enterprises, farms owned by high-tanking military officers, and the civil service.

On average, over 1,500 Eritreans flee the country monthly despite shoot-to-kill orders to border guards and immense dangers along escape routes. Unaccompanied minors also flee; the office of the United Nations High Commissioner for Refugees (UNHCR) reported over 1,100 unaccompanied minors living in one Ethiopian refugee camp in 2012. Not only are ordinary citizens defecting, so are those the government had privileged with authority, foreign travel, and publicity.

In October, two senior air force pilots defected to Saudi Arabia in the plane normally used by Isaias. Earlier, Eritrea's standard bearer at the 2012 Olympics asked for asylum along with three teammates. Repression in Eritrea, he said, "forces people to do things that may cost them their life, but at the end of the day sometimes there isn't a choice." Two prominent musicians were also reported to have fled abroad.

Torture, Death, and Prolonged Incarceration without Trial

Eritreans are routinely subject to imprisonment without explanation, trial, or any form of due process. Incarceration often lasts indefinitely. Senior government officials and journalists, arrested in 2001 after they raised questions about President Isaias' rule, remain jailed incommunicado. Defecting guards report that most of these officials have died.

According to accounts from those who have fled, conditions in Eritrea's detention facilities are abysmal, with minimal food and medical care. Prisoners are held in underground cells and shipping containers, subject to boiling and freezing temperatures. Many prisoners die from the harsh conditions.

Torture and other abuses during detention are routine. Punishments include mock drowning, being hung from trees by the arms, being tied up in the sun in contorted positions for hours or days, being doubled up inside a rolling tire, having handcuffs tightened to cut off circulation, as well as frequent beatings.

Restrictions on Freedoms of Expression and Association

The Isaias government closed the independent press in 2001 by revoking their licenses and arrested its editors and publishers. Based on former guards' testimony, Reporters without Borders reported that four journalists died in prison in 2012, including two imprisoned since 2001. Journalists working for government agencies, arrested since 2009 for allegedly providing information to Western nongovernmental organizations and governments, remain incarcerated incommunicado.

All domestic media are controlled by the government. Two of four internet service providers prohibit access to sites unapproved by the government and persons using internet cafes are subject to surveillance. Eritrea periodically jams satellite radio transmissions by opposition groups. For the sixth year, the Committee to Protect Journalists (CPJ) in 2012 named Eritrea "one of the world's most censored countries."

Defectors describe a climate of intense fear in the country. To question authority, much less criticize it, can result in imprisonment and worse. Gatherings of more than seven unrelated people are forbidden and formation of NGOs is prohibited. Political organization is restricted to the ruling party, the Peoples Front for Democracy and Justice (PFDJ). Unions are prohibited, except for PFDJ subsidiaries.

Interference with Religious Beliefs and Practices

The Isaias government controls all religious activity. The government acknowledges a right to exist only for four "recognized" religious groups, the Orthodox Church, Sunni Islam, Roman Catholicism, and the Evangelical (Lutheran) Church. Other religious groups have applied for recognition since 2002 but the government has never acted on their applications. It deposed the Eritrean

Orthodox Church patriarch in 2005, after he protested government interference in church affairs. He remains under house arrest in ill health. The government selected his successor and also appointed the current Sunni *mufti*, the chief Islamic legal authority.

Members of "unrecognized" religions are arrested, held in oppressive conditions, and sometimes tortured to compel them to recant their faith. Jehovah's Witnesses are especially victimized. Twelve were arrested in 2012 while attending a funeral, and one died in 2012 because of heat prostration in an underground cell. Currently, 56 Jehovah's Witnesses are incarcerated, including 11 in their 70s and 80s and 3 conscientious objectors held since 1994.

Retaliation against Family Members

Since at least 1995, Eritrea has imposed a 2 percent income tax on Eritrean expatriates (retroactive to 1992) to be eligible for consular services, such as notarizing powers of attorney, certifying educational decrees, and issuance of travel documents. Relatives in Eritrea of expatriates who refuse to pay the tax have been threatened with loss of business licenses or have been prevented from selling property because of a missing notarial. Canada and Germany prohibit collection of the tax, while the Netherlands and others are considering a ban.

Families of national service conscripts who abscond are fined 50,000 Nakfa (US$3,333), a crushing sum for many in a country where annual per capita income is 8,040 Nakfa (US$536).

Horn of Africa Relations

Eritrea is under UN sanctions for trying to destabilize neighboring states by arming rebel groups and for having attacked Djibouti.

Relations with Ethiopia remain strained 12 years after the end of a border war between the two countries. Ethiopia occupies territory that a Boundary Commission, established by the parties' armistice agreement, awarded to Eritrea, a decision that Ethiopia has ignored. A United Nations Security Council

(Security Council) Monitoring Group on Eritrea and Somalia reported in July 2012 that Eritrea continued to violate Security Council resolutions "by deploying Ethiopian armed opposition groups via Somali territory." Earlier in the year, Ethiopia launched brief cross-border raids against rebel groups that Ethiopia claimed Eritrea was training and arming. Eritrea mobilized but did not retaliate militarily. In October, Ethiopia released 75 Eritrean prisoners of war (POWs) captured in the raids; seven POWs asked for asylum.

Eritrea invaded Djibouti in 2008 but persistently denied it had done so until 2010 when, succumbing to international pressure, it pulled back its troops and agreed to Qatari mediation of border issues. Even so, Eritrea refused to address Djibouti's claims that it was holding 19 POWs. In 2012, three escaped POWs told the UN Monitoring Group they had been among eight POWs held by Eritrea. All suffered from malnutrition and denial of medical treatment for wounds. As a result, the other five prisoners were too weak to escape; two had gone blind, one had lost use of an arm.

The UN Monitoring Group reported it had found no evidence of direct Eritrean support for Al-Shabaab in Somalia in 2012.

Key International Actors

At the end of 2011, Eritrea expelled nearly all remaining foreign nongovernmental aid groups (a small UN aid mission remains). Although President Isaias asserts the expulsions promote his policy of self-reliance, they reinforce his policy of isolating the Eritrean population from foreigners. Earlier in 2011, Isaias accused international NGOs of having a "pathological compulsion for espionage."

In late 2011, Eritrea cancelled a multi-year European Union assistance program. No country that had previously provided loans or grants to Eritrea announced new financial assistance in 2012. Isaias repeatedly accuses the CIA of conspiring against Eritrea. The CIA, he said in 2012, "is preoccupied with targeting the key aspects of the Eritrean economy."

One source of foreign exchange comes from extensive smuggling of weapons and Eritrean refugees to Sudan and Egypt by Eritrean security forces, according to the UN Monitoring Group.

Ethiopia

The sudden death in August 2012 of Ethiopia's long-serving and powerful prime minister, Meles Zenawi, provoked uncertainty over the country's political transition, both domestically and among Ethiopia's international partners. Ethiopia's human rights record has sharply deteriorated, especially over the past few years, and although a new prime minister, Hailemariam Desalegn, took office in September, it remains to be seen whether the government under his leadership will undertake human rights reforms.

Ethiopian authorities continued to severely restrict basic rights of freedom of expression, association, and assembly in 2012. Thirty journalists and opposition members were convicted under the country's vague Anti-Terrorism Proclamation of 2009.The security forces responded to protests by the Muslim community in Oromia and Addis Ababa, the capital, with arbitrary arrests, detentions, and beatings.

The Ethiopian government continues to implement its "villagization" program: the resettlement of 1.5 million rural villagers in five regions of Ethiopia ostensibly to increase their access to basic services. Many villagers in Gambella region have been forcibly displaced, causing considerable hardship. The government is also forcibly displacing indigenous pastoral communities in Ethiopia's Lower Omo Valley to make way for state-run sugar plantations.

Freedom of Expression, Association, and Assembly

Since the promulgation in 2009 of the Charities and Societies Proclamation (CSO Law), which regulates nongovernmental organizations, and the Anti-Terrorism Proclamation, freedom of expression, assembly, and association have been increasingly restricted in Ethiopia. The effect of these two laws, coupled with the government's widespread and persistent harassment, threats, and intimidation of civil society activists, journalists, and others who comment on sensitive issues or express views critical of government policy, has been severe.

Ethiopia's most important human rights groups have been compelled to dramatically scale-down operations or remove human rights activities from their mandates, and an unknown number of organizations have closed entirely. Several of the country's most experienced and reputable human rights activists have fled the country due to threats. The environment is equally hostile for independent media: more journalists have fled Ethiopia than any other country in the world due to threats and intimidation in the last decade—at least 79, according to the Committee to Protect Journalists (CPJ).

The Anti-Terrorism Proclamation is being used to target perceived opponents, stifle dissent, and silence journalists. In 2012, 30 political activists, opposition party members, and journalists were convicted on vaguely defined terrorism offenses. Eleven journalists have been convicted under the law since 2011.

On January 26, a court in Addis Ababa sentenced both deputy editor Woubshet Taye and columnist Reeyot Alemu of the now-defunct weekly *Awramaba Times* to 14 years in prison. Reeyot's sentence was later reduced to five years upon appeal and most of the charges were dropped.

On July 13, veteran journalist and blogger Eskinder Nega, who won the prestigious PEN America Freedom to Write Award in April, was sentenced to 18 years in prison along with other journalists, opposition party members, and political activists. Exiled journalists Abiye Teklemariam and Mesfin Negash were sentenced to eight years each in absentia under a provision of the Anti-Terrorism Law that has so far only been used against journalists. Andualem Arage, a member of the registered opposition party Unity for Democracy and Justice (UDJ), was sentenced to life for espionage, "disrupting the constitutional order," and recruitment and training to commit terrorist acts.

In September, the Ethiopian Federal High Court ordered the property of Eskinder Nega, exiled journalist Abebe Belew, and opposition member Andualem Arage to be confiscated.

On July 20, after the government claimed that reports by the newspaper *Feteh* on Muslim protests and the prime minister's health would endanger national security, it seized the entire print run of the paper. On August 24, *Feteh*'s editor, Temesghen Desalegn was arrested and denied bail. He was released on August 28, and all the charges were withdrawn pending further investigation.

Police on July 20 raided the home of journalist Yesuf Getachew, editor-in-chief of the popular Muslim magazine *Yemuslimoche Guday* (Muslim Affairs), and arrested him that night. The magazine has not been published since, and at this writing, Yesuf remained in detention.

On December 27, 2011, two Swedish journalists, Martin Schibbye and Johan Persson, were found guilty of supporting a terrorist organization after being arrested while traveling in eastern Ethiopia with the Ogaden National Liberation Front (ONLF), an outlawed armed insurgent group. They were also convicted of entering the country illegally. The court sentenced them to 11 years in prison. On September 10, they were pardoned and released along with more than 1,950 other prisoners as part of Ethiopia's annual tradition of amnesty to celebrate the Ethiopian New Year.

On several occasions in July, federal police used excessive force, including beatings, to disperse largely Muslim protesters opposing the government's interference with the country's Supreme Council of Islamic Affairs. On July 13, police forcibly entered the Awalia mosque in Addis Ababa, smashing windows and firing tear gas inside the mosque. On July 21, they forcibly broke up a sit-in at the mosque. From July 19 to 21, dozens of people were rounded up and 17 prominent leaders were held without charge for over a week. Many of the detainees complained of mistreatment in detention.

Forced Displacement

The Ethiopian government plans to relocate up to 1.5 million people under its "villagization" program, purportedly designed to improve access to basic services by moving people to new villages in Ethiopia's five lowland regions: Gambella, Benishangul-Gumuz, Afar, Southern Nations Nationalities and Peoples' Region (SNNPR), and Somali Region.

In Gambella and in the South Omo Valley, forced displacement is taking place without adequate consultation and compensation. In Gambella, Human Rights Watch found that relocations were often forced and that villagers were being moved from fertile to unfertile areas. People sent to the new villages frequently have to clear the land and build their own huts under military supervision, while

HUMAN RIGHTS WATCH

"What Will Happen if Hunger Comes?"

Abuses against the Indigenous Peoples of Ethiopia's Lower Omo Valley

the promised services (schools, clinics, water pumps) often have not been put in place.

In South Omo, around 200,000 indigenous peoples are being relocated and their land expropriated to make way for state-run sugar plantations. Residents reported being moved by force, seeing their grazing lands flooded or ploughed up, and their access to the Omo River, essential for their survival and way of life, curtailed.

Extrajudicial Executions, Torture and other Abuses in Detention

An Ethiopian government-backed paramilitary force known as the "Liyu Police" executed at least 10 men who were in their custody and killed 9 other villagers in Ethiopia's Somali Region on March 16 and 17 following a confrontation over an incident in Raqda village, Gashaamo district.

In April, unknown gunmen attacked a commercial farm owned by the Saudi Star company in Gambella that was close to areas that had suffered a high proportion of abuses during the villagization process. In responding to the attack, Ethiopian soldiers went house to house looking for suspected perpetrators and threatening villagers to disclose the whereabouts of the "rebels." The military arbitrarily arrested many young men and committed torture, rape, and other abuses against scores of villagers while attempting to extract information.

Human Rights Watch continues to document torture at the federal police investigation center known as Maekelawi in Addis Ababa, as well as at regional detention centers and military barracks in Somali Region, Oromia, and Gambella. There is erratic access to legal counsel and insufficient respect for other due process guarantees during detention, pre-trial detention, and trial phases of politically sensitive cases, placing detainees at risk of abuse.

Treatment of Ethiopian Migrant Domestic Workers

The videotaped beating and subsequent suicide on March 14 of Alem Dechasa-Desisa, an Ethiopian domestic worker in Lebanon, brought increased scrutiny to

HUMAN
RIGHTS
WATCH

"WAITING HERE FOR DEATH"
Displacement and "Villagization" in Ethiopia's Gambella Region

the plight of tens of thousands of Ethiopian women working in the Middle East. Many migrant domestic workers incur heavy debts and face recruitment-related abuses in Ethiopia prior to employment abroad, where they risk a wide range of abuses from long hours of work to slavery-like conditions (see chapters on the United Arab Emirates, Saudi Arabia, and Lebanon).

Key International Actors

Under Meles Zenawi's leadership, Ethiopia played an important role in regional affairs: deploying UN peacekeepers to Sudan's disputed Abyei area, mediating between Sudan and South Sudan, and sending troops into Somalia as part of the international effort to combat al-Shabaab. Ethiopia's relations with its neighbor Eritrea remain poor following the costly border war of 1998-2000. Eritrea accepted the ruling of an independent boundary commission that awarded it disputed territory; Ethiopia did not.

Ethiopia is an important strategic and security ally for Western governments, and the biggest recipient of development aid in Africa. It now receives approximately US$3.5 billion in long-term development assistance each year. Donor policies do not appear to have been significantly affected by the deteriorating human rights situation in the country.

The World Bank approved a new Country Partnership Strategy in September that takes little account of the human rights or good governance principles that it and other development agencies say are essential for sustainable development. It also approved a third phase of the Protection of Basic Services program (PBS III) without triggering safeguards on involuntary resettlement and indigenous peoples.

Guinea

The government of President Alpha Condé, elected in largely free and fair elections in December 2010, took some steps to address the serious governance and human rights problems that have characterized Guinea for more than five decades. However, a full transition to democratic rule and greater respect for the rule of law were undermined by continued delays in organizing parliamentary elections, rising ethnic tension, endemic corruption, and inadequate gains in strengthening the chronically neglected judiciary.

The government in 2012 prioritized reform and ensuring better discipline within the security sector. There were fewer examples than in past years of excessive use of force in responding to demonstrations, and the government made strides in reducing the size of the 45,000-strong security sector, which has long been hampered by lack of discipline and impunity.

Guinea made some progress in ensuring accountability for past atrocities, particularly the 2009 massacre of unarmed demonstrators by security forces. However, the establishment of a reconciliation commission and independent human rights body made little progress. The year was marked by numerous arbitrary arrests, breaches of the freedoms of assembly and association, and the killing by men in military uniform of a high-level government official investigating corruption allegations.

International actors—including France, the United States, the European Union, the Economic Community of West African States (ECOWAS), and the African Union exerted pressure on President Condé to organize parliamentary elections, but rarely spoke out on the need for justice for past and recent crimes by state actors.

Accountability for the September 28, 2009 Massacre and Other Crimes

The government made some progress in holding accountable members of the security forces implicated in the September 2009 massacre of some 150 people and the rape of over 100 women during the military regime of Moussa Dadis

Camara. A 2009 report by the United Nations-led International Commission of Inquiry concluded that the abuses committed by security forces very likely constituted crimes against humanity. In 2010, the then-government committed to bringing the perpetrators to justice, and a Guinean prosecutor appointed three investigating judges to the case.

To date, the judges have interviewed over 200 victims and charged at least seven suspects in connection with the crimes. Two high-level suspects and military officers who have been charged are Col. Moussa Tiegboro Camara, Guinea's current minister in charge of fighting drug trafficking and organized crimes, and Col. Abdoulaye Cherif Diaby, Guinea's former health minister.

However, at this writing, the investigation had yet to be completed and some suspects had been detained longer than the two year limit under Guinean law. Meanwhile some 100 victims continued to wait to provide statements to the judges. Also, potential mass graves with bodies of those allegedly disposed of secretly by the security services have yet to be investigated, and the judges had yet to question members of the security forces who might have knowledge of the crimes.The government's refusal for much of the year to provide adequate financial support to the investigating judges, coupled with President Condé's failure to suspend men in his administration who are suspected of involvement in the massacre, brought into question the government's commitment to ensure justice for the crimes.

The International Criminal Court (ICC), which in October 2009 confirmed that the situation in Guinea was under preliminary examination, visited the country in April to assess progress made in national investigations, bringing the number of visits since 2010 to six.

Truth-Telling Mechanism and Independent Human Rights Institution

The "Reflection Commission," created by presidential decree in June 2011 to promote reconciliation, made no visible progress in defining, much less fulfilling, its mandate. Progress was undermined by inadequate consultation with victims and civil society about the goals, composition, or powers of the commis-

HUMAN
RIGHTS
WATCH

WAITING FOR JUSTICE

Accountability before Guinea's Courts for the September 28, 2009
Stadium Massacre, Rapes, and Other Abuses

sion, and inadequate financial support. The interim co-presidents appeared to limit its mandate to promoting reconciliation largely through prayer, while local human rights groups pushed for a commission that could meaningfully address impunity. Rising ethnic tensions, as well as concerns about corruption, demonstrated the urgent need for a truth-telling mechanism with the capacity to make recommendations to address Guinea's human rights challenges.

There has been no progress in setting up the independent human rights institution, as mandated by Guinea's 2010 constitution. However, during a cabinet reshuffle in October, President Condé created a Ministry for Human Rights and Civil Liberties.

Judiciary and Detention Conditions

Decades of neglect of the judiciary by successive regimes has led to striking deficiencies in the sector, and allowed perpetrators of abuses to enjoy impunity for crimes. The allocation for the judiciary, which for several years has stood at around 0.5 percent of the national budget, decreased in 2012 to 0.29 percent. As a result, there continued to be severe shortages of judicial personnel and insufficient infrastructure and resources, which when coupled with unprofessional conduct and poor record-keeping, contributed to widespread detention-related abuses.

Prison and detention centers in Guinea are severely overcrowded, and inmates and detainees lack adequate nutrition, sanitation, and medical care. Several inmates died from inadequate medical attention in 2012. The largest detention facility—designed for 300 detainees—accommodates over 1,000. An estimated 70 percent of prisoners in Guinea are held in prolonged pre-trial detention.

The government failed to establish the Superior Council of Judges, which is tasked with discipline, selection, and promotion of judges; and reviewing the outdated penal code.

But the justice sector did remove judges alleged to be unprofessional, created a secretariat to coordinate reform of the justice system, and brought about a slight reduction of those in pre-trial detention. International and Guinean legal aid groups helped ensure representation for the indigent, train paralegals, and assist victims of security sector abuses.

Conduct of the Security Forces

The government and military hierarchy made some progress in ensuring that their subordinates responded proportionately to civil unrest. The army largely remained in their barracks during marches, and there were fewer instances of the use of lethal fire than in past years by those mandated to address crowd control.

There were nevertheless numerous allegations of unprofessional conduct and several of excessive use of force: security forces killed at least three protesters in often-violent demonstrations, and arbitrarily detained and beat others. There were few attempts to investigate, discipline, or prosecute those implicated.

In August, alleged members of the security forces killed six men from the village of Zoghota in southeastern Guinea after a nearby international mining company had been vandalized. Also in August, security forces fired tear gas canisters and allegedly a few live rounds of bullets at a vehicle carrying several opposition leaders. The government denounced both incidents, and the Ministry of Justice launched investigations; however, at this writing, there had been no arrests.

The security forces were implicated in numerous cases of robbery and extortion, solicitation of bribes, mistreatment, torture, and in a few cases, deaths of detainees. Police and gendarme leadership made no effort to investigate the reported abuses.

Parliamentary Elections and Governance

Crucial parliamentary elections, which have not been held since 2002, were delayed over demands by the opposition to address the lack of parity between the ruling and opposition parties in the electoral commission, and because of technical concerns about the revision of the electoral list. The delay undermined the transition to democratic rule, deepened a concentration of power in the executive branch, and generated considerable frustration within Guinean civil society and the country's international partners.

Guinean authorities on several occasions undermined the right to freedom of assembly by denying demonstrators permission to protest the cost of living, labor conditions, and lack of progress on the legislative elections. On at least three occasions, the security forces attacked opposition leaders or their party headquarters. In August, the government closed a private radio station, allegedly for its reporting on demonstrations. Security forces responding to violent clashes between militants of opposing political parties appeared to disproportionately crack down on those from the opposition.

Aside from the removal of several ministers implicated in corrupt practices, there was little systematic effort to improve economic governance. The president or one of his ministers signed several large contracts for resource extraction, without competitive bidding and with virtually no oversight. There was little effort to implement a 2011 mining code envisioned to improve management of Guinea's extensive natural resources. On November 9, 2012, unidentified men in military uniform killed Aissatou Boiro, director of the Office of the Treasury, in the capital, Conakry. Boiro was investigating a high-level corruption case.

Key International Actors

Guinea's key international partners, notably the EU, ECOWAS, the UN Office in West Africa (UNOWA), France, and the US, remained largely focused on ensuring progress in the long-delayed parliamentary elections. However, they remained largely silent on the need for those responsible for the September 2009 violence or more recent killings by members of the security forces to be held accountable for their crimes.

The Office of the United Nations High Commissioner for Human Rights (OHCHR), the EU, and the UN Development Programme (UNDP) took the lead in strengthening Guinea's judicial system. However, much of the EU's support was conditioned on the conduct of transparent legislative elections. UNOWA led the other international partners in advising the government how to reform the security sector.

In January, President Condé asked for support from the UN Peace Building Commission (PBC), which has funded programs supporting security sector reform, reconciliation, and peacebuilding. In September, Guinea benefited from $2.1 billion in debt relief under the World Bank and International Monetary Fund (IMF) Heavily Indebted Poor Countries (HIPC) initiative, representing two-thirds of its $3.2 billion total external debt.

Kenya

Kenya continues to face serious challenges with implementing its new constitution and police reforms, as well as ending impunity for serious crimes by public officials and security forces. Kenya will hold general elections in March 2013, the first polls under the 2010 constitution. Four Kenyans, including three senior public officials—two of whom are running for the presidency in 2013—are facing charges of crimes against humanity at the International Criminal Court (ICC). This followed the post-election violence of 2007, which left 1300 people dead. There are concerns of further election-related violence around the 2013 elections.

Kenya's October 2011 military incursion into Somalia sparked a string of retaliatory attacks across the north of the country and in Mombasa and Nairobi in 2012. Dozens of civilians and security personnel were killed and injured in shootings and grenade attacks, allegedly by supporters of the armed Somali Islamist group al-Shabaab. Security forces often responded by arbitrarily arresting, detaining and beating civilians in Wajir, Mandera, Garissa, and the Dadaab refugee camps.

Election Campaigns, Ethnic Profiling, and Violence

Early campaigns around the country were characterized by mobilization along ethnic lines, ethnic profiling and violence. Some politicians instructed members of their communities to support certain presidential candidates, or face dire consequences. Others launched national campaigns that appeared to demonize specific candidates and their communities in advance of the 2013 elections, heightening ethnic tensions and the risk of election related violence in Coast, Central Kenya, Rift Valley and Nyanza regions. In July 2009, a new law prohibiting hate speech was promulgated. Under this law, which has been largely ineffectual, the National Cohesion and Integration Commission (NCIC) has taken four politicians to court, with no convictions. This raises concerns about the independence and capacity of the police, the NCIC and the office of the director of public prosecutions (DPP) to deal with ethnic profiling and hate speech.

HUMAN
RIGHTS
WATCH

CRIMINAL REPRISALS
Kenyan Police and Military Abuses against Ethnic Somalis

Politically instigated violence broke out in various parts of the country in 2012. In Isiolo and Moyale counties, at least 21 people were killed and at least 20,000 displaced in inter-clan violence that persisted for weeks without decisive government intervention. The government eventually arrested at least 26 people and charged them with participating in the violence. Police initially suggested that a member of parliament was implicated in the violence and would be apprehended. No such arrest had been made at this writing.

Between April and August, in Mandera, over 30 people were killed and thousands temporarily displaced over the border into Ethiopia in clashes between different clans competing for control of districts and constituencies ahead of the elections.

Ongoing tensions since January erupted in August in Tana River, when over 100 people were killed and 200,000 displaced following a series of retaliatory politically motivated attacks. Dhadho Godhana, a member of parliament, was charged with incitement, while other politicians were also believed to be involved in this particular violence.

Kenya's Incursion into Somalia

Since late 2011, unknown people believed to be sympathizers of al-Shabaab, the armed Islamist group fighting the Somali government and allied forces in Somalia, carried out terrorist attacks on civilian targets and security forces in North Eastern Province bordering Somalia, and in Mombasa and the capital, Nairobi.

In the most serious attack, gunmen opened fire and hurled grenades killing 17 and injuring 60 during services at two churches in Garissa on July 1. In Mombasa, gunmen opened fire on a restaurant, a church, and a bar in three separate attacks. Police posts, patrols, and vehicles belonging to government agencies, including the army, were attacked with landmines and improvised explosive devices across North Eastern province, in Wajir, Mandera, Dadaab refugee camps, and at the Liboi border. Two refugees in Dadaab were assassinated in separate attacks at the start of the year.

There were numerous cases where Kenyan security forces responded to the attacks by abusing civilians. Documented abuses included rape and attempted sexual assault; beatings; arbitrary detention; extortion; the looting and destruction of property; and various forms of physical mistreatment, including forcing victims to sit in water, to roll on the ground in baking temperatures, or to carry heavy loads while standing on one spot or while walking around for extended periods. Despite government promises to investigate, there have been no investigations and no security official has faced disciplinary action in relation to the abuses.

Extrajudicial Killings, Disappearances, and Police Reform

In August 2012, unknown gunmen shot dead Islamic preacher Sheikh Aboud Rogo. At the time of his killing, Rogo, who had complained of police threats and requested protection, was facing charges of illegal possession of weapons and recruiting for al-Shabaab. On July 24, he had reported to the police, the Kenyan National Commission on Human Rights, and the court in which he was being tried that unknown assailants had attempted to abduct him and his co-accused, Abubakar Shari Ahmed, when they arrived in Nairobi for the court hearing.

Rogo's killing followed the abductions and deaths earlier in 2012 of several other people charged with recruitment and other offenses related to al-Shabaab. In March, Samir Khan, who was also charged with possessing illegal firearms and recruiting for al-Shabaab, and his friend Mohammed Kassim, were pulled from a public bus in Mombasa by men who stopped the vehicle and identified themselves as police officers. Khan's mutilated body was found a few days later in Tsavo National Park. Kassim's whereabouts remain unknown.

Four other suspected al-Shabaab members facing charges in court disappeared in 2012 after being arrested by people who identified themselves as police, according to local human rights groups.

In response to allegations of police involvement, the DPP, the police, and the Kenya National Commission on Human Rights instituted a joint probe on to investigate Rogo's killing. The killing prompted renewed calls for police reforms that have stalled. No inspector general has been appointed in the five years since reforms were promised following electoral violence in 2007-2008. A National Police Service Commission that was supposed to vet all police officers ahead of the 2013 elections is not yet operational.

The ICC and Other Post-Election Violence Cases

The International Criminal Court (ICC) set April 2013 trial dates in cases against four prominent Kenyans charged with committing crimes against humanity during the post-election violence of 2007-2008.The ICC prosecutor raised concerns with the Kenyan government that the e-mail accounts of witnesses had been hacked and correspondence accessed, and warned publicly against witness tampering. In March, the Kenyan police arrested blogger Denis Itumbi on suspicion of hacking into the ICC email system, although he was never charged.

The Kenyan government has pledged to cooperate with the ICC, and has committed to national trials of additional perpetrators of the 2007-2008 violence. However, it has failed to create a special mechanism for prosecutions to overcome weaknesses in the existing judicial system. The DPP initially announced that his office would review up to 5000 cases with the view to prosecuting them ahead of the 2013 elections, but a committee appointed by the DPP to review the cases said in August 2012 it was finding it difficult to obtain evidence and the cases have not proceeded.

In April 2012, an extraordinary summit of East African heads of state attended by Kenya's President Mwai Kibaki, recommended that the mandate of the East African Court of Justice be expanded to include trials for crimes against humanity. The African Union Assembly in July 2012 deferred adoption of a protocol to expand the jurisdiction of the African Court of Justice and Human Rights (ACJHR) to include the prosecution of individuals for international crimes in order to study further the financial and structural implications of any such expansion. Kenya had supported these initiatives, apparently motivated by its interest in creating competing jurisdictions in order to derail the ICC's Kenyan investigations.

Migrant Domestic Workers

Thousands of Kenyan women have migrated to the Middle East as domestic workers in recent years. Many face deception during the poorly regulated recruitment process prior to employment abroad, where they risk a wide range of abuses from long hours of work to slavery-like conditions (see chapter on Saudi Arabia). After a number of high-profile abuse cases, Kenya banned further migration of domestic workers to the Middle East in June 2012. Similar bans enacted by other labor-sending countries have rarely been effective and have increased the risk of irregular migration and trafficking.

Key International Actors

The East African Legislative Assembly (EALA) passed a resolution allowing the expansion of the mandate of the East African Court of Justice (EACJ) to include crimes against humanity. Kenya also supported the decision by the AU to establish a committee to examine how to expand the mandate of the African Court on Human and People's Rights (AfCHPR) to include international crimes.

The United States and European governments have a growing relationship with the Kenyan military as it has become more involved in Somalia.

Mali

The Tuareg rebellion, Islamist occupation of the north, and political upheaval generated by a March military coup led to a drastic deterioration in respect for human rights in Mali. The insecurity led to the displacement of some 400,000 northern residents. The worsening human rights, security, and humanitarian situation country-wide generated considerable attention from the international community.

Several armed groups—which began operations in January 2012 and by April had consolidated control of the northern regions of Kidal, Gao and Timbuktu—committed often-widespread abuses against civilians. These included sexual abuse, looting and pillage, summary executions, child soldier recruitment, and amputations and other inhumane treatment associated with the application of Islamic law. Islamist groups destroyed numerous Muslim shrines and at least one Dogon cultural site. In January, rebel groups allegedly summarily executed at least 70 Malian soldiers in the town of Aguelhoc.

Malian soldiers arbitrarily detained and in many cases tortured and summarily executed alleged rebel collaborators and members of rival military units. There was no meaningful effort to investigate, much less hold accountable, members of the security forces implicated in these incidents.

Fears that the occupation of the north by Islamist groups linked to al Qaeda would destabilize West Africa and threaten international security led to considerable diplomatic efforts to resolve the crisis as well as a plan supported by the Economic Community of West Africa States (ECOWAS), African Union, United Nations, European Union, France, and the United States to militarily oust the Islamist groups from the north. While most of these actors widely criticized abuses by groups in the north, there was inadequate consideration of the potential for abuse by Malian security forces and pro-government militias, or the issues, including endemic corruption and ethnic tension, that had given rise to the crisis.

Political and Military Instability

On March 22, 2012, junior military officers led by Capt. Amadou Sanogo launched a coup against then-President Amadou Toumani Touré in protest of what they viewed as the government's inadequate response to the rebellion of the Tuareg National Movement for the Liberation of Azawad (MNLA), which began in January. The MNLA and Islamist armed groups swiftly occupied the north as they took advantage of the chaos created by the coup.

Following international pressure, notably from ECOWAS, Sanogo in April agreed to hand over power to a transitional government that would organize elections and return the country to democratic rule. However, with the backing of security forces loyal to him, he continued to exert considerable influence, meddle in political affairs, and undermine efforts by the transitional authorities and international community to address the political and security crisis.

The groups occupying the north included the separatist Tuareg MNLA; a local ethnic Arab militia, based in and around the city of Timbuktu; and three Islamist groups—Ansar Dine, the Movement for Unity and Jihad in West Africa (MUJAO), and Al Qaeda in the Islamic Maghreb (AQIM)—which seek to impose a strict interpretation of Sharia or Islamic law throughout Mali. MUJAO and AQIM are primarily made up of foreign fighters.

Abuses by Tuareg Separatist Rebels and Arab Militias

The majority of abuses committed during and immediately after the April offensive against the north were committed by the MNLA and, in Timbuktu, Arab militiamen allied to it. Abuses included the abduction and rape of women and girls; pillaging of hospitals, schools, aid agencies, warehouses, banks, and government buildings; and use of child soldiers. At least 30 women and girls were raped; the majority of assaults, including numerous gang rapes, took place within the Gao region.

Abuses by Islamist Groups

After largely driving the MNLA out of the north in June, the Islamist groups— Ansar Dine, MUJAO and AQIM— committed serious abuses against the local population while enforcing their interpretation of Sharia. These abuses included beatings, floggings, and arbitrary arrests against those engaging in behavior decreed as *haraam* (forbidden), including smoking or selling cigarettes; consuming or selling alcoholic beverages; listening to music on portable audio devices; and failing to attend daily prayers. They also punished women for failing to adhere to their dress code and for having contact with men other than family members.

Throughout the north, the punishments for these "infractions" as well as for those accused of theft and banditry, were meted out by the Islamic Police, often after a summary "trial" before a panel of judges handpicked by the Islamist authorities. Many of the punishments were carried out in public squares after the authorities had summoned the local population to attend. Islamist militants in Timbuktu destroyed numerous structures—including mausoleums, cemeteries, ritual masks, and shrines—which hold great religious, historical, and cultural significance for Malians. Islamists on several occasions intimidated and arbitrarily detained local journalists and in one case severely beat a local journalist; they forced the closure of numerous local Malian radio stations.

Citing adultery, Islamist authorities on July 30 stoned to death a married man and a woman to whom he was not married in Aguelhoc. Since April, the Islamist groups amputated the limbs of at least nine men accused of theft and robbery. On September 2, MUJAO claimed to have executed the Algerian vice-consul; the group had earlier claimed responsibility for the April 5 kidnapping of seven Algerian diplomats from their consulate in Gao; three of the diplomats were freed in July.

Recruitment of Children and Child Labor

Northern-based rebel groups and pro-government militias recruited and used child soldiers. The MNLA and Islamist groups recruited, trained, and used several hundred children, some as young as 11. The children manned checkpoints, conducted foot patrols, guarded prisoners, and gathered intelligence. The Ganda-Kio pro-government militia recruited and trained numerous children, although at this writing they had yet to be used in a military operation. Armed groups occupied and used numerous public and private schools in both the rebel-controlled north and government-controlled south.

Child labor in agriculture, domestic service, mining and other sectors remains common, and often includes dangerous work that Malian law prohibits for anyone under the age of 18. Tens of thousands of children continue to work in artisanal gold mining, facing risk of injury and of exposure to mercury. A government action plan on child labor remained largely unimplemented.

Abuses by Malian Army Soldiers

Malian government soldiers arbitrarily detained and in several cases executed men they accused of collaborating with the rebel groups in the north. The majority of victims were of Tuareg or Arab ethnicity or Mauritanian nationality. In April, four Tuareg members of the security services were detained and believed executed by the military in Mopti.

On September 8, 16 Islamic preachers on their way to a religious conference in the capital, Bamako, were detained and hours later executed within a military camp in Diabaly, some 270 miles (430 kilometers) from Bamako, for their alleged links with Islamist groups. Their driver, seen in military custody days after the killings, has since disappeared. The Malian government, under pressure from Mauritania, from which nine of the victims hailed, apologized for the incident and promised an investigation, but has made no arrests. On October 21, soldiers executed at least eight Tuareg herders, also in Diabaly.

In May, members of the security forces loyal to Captain Sanogo forcibly disappeared at least 21 soldiers allegedly linked to an April 30 counter-coup, and committed torture and other abuses against dozens of others. The soldiers were handcuffed and tied for days at a time; beaten with batons, sticks, and guns; kicked in the back, head, ribs, and genitals; stabbed in their extremities, and burned with cigarettes and lighters. Four men were forced at gunpoint to engage in anal sex with one another. The detainees were also subjected to psychologi-

cal abuse including death threats and mock executions. Several journalists critical of the coup leadership were detained, questioned, and intimidated; in July,
armed and masked gunmen abducted two journalists, severely beat them, and
dumped them on the outskirts of Bamako after warning them to stop criticizing
the military.

Accountability

In July, the government of Mali, as a state party to the International Criminal
Court (ICC), referred "the situation in Mali since January 2012" to the ICC prosecutor for investigation. The prosecutor's office visited Mali in August, October,
and November and will determine at a future date whether it can take jurisdiction of the situation. Meanwhile, there was no effort by the Malian government
to investigate or hold to account members of the security forces implicated in
serious abuses. Despite his direct implication in torture and enforced disappearances, Sanogo was in August put in charge of security sector reform of the
Malian army.

Key International Actors

Mali's international partners struggled to harmonize plans on how to address
the military and human rights crisis in the north. A plan by ECOWAS to send in
some 3,300 troops to oust the Islamists failed for much of the year to generate
support from either Mali or the international community. Meanwhile ECOWAS,
Algerian, and Malian efforts to negotiate with the northern groups made no
headway. On September 18, the Malian government formally requested a UN
Chapter VII mandate for an international military force to help it recover the
north.

France took the lead in pushing the plan and drafted UN Security Council
Resolution 2071, adopted on October 12, which tasked the UN Secretariat,
ECOWAS, and the AU to submit to the council "detailed and actionable recom-
mendations" in preparation for the deployment of an international military force
in Mali. On November 13, the AU's Peace and Security Council endorsed an
ECOWAS plan for a military intervention to regain occupied areas in northern

Mali. The Security Council will need to pass a second resolution to formally authorize the deployment.

The EU, France, and the US offered to provide logistical and training assistance, but the details of a military intervention, including who would provide troops, remained unclear. On November 19, foreign ministers from the EU agreed to send 250 military trainers to Mali to support African-led efforts to retake the north.

The Office of the UN High Commissioner for Human Rights (OHCHR) issued several statements denouncing the human rights situation in Mali, and in July, after a request from the UN Human Rights Council (HRC), dispatched a human rights officer to the country. In October, UN Assistant Secretary-General for Human Rights Ivan Simonovic visited Mali and reported concerns back to the Security Council. In November, an OHCHR team conducted a fact-finding mission to Mali; it will present its findings during the HRC's March 2013 session.

Nigeria

Attacks by the militant Islamist group Boko Haram and abuses by government security forces led to spiraling violence across northern and central Nigeria. This violence, which first erupted in 2009, has claimed more than 3,000 lives. The group, which seeks to impose a strict form of Sharia, or Islamic law, in northern Nigeria and end government corruption, launched hundreds of attacks in 2012 against police officers, Christians, and Muslims who cooperate with the government or oppose the group.

In the name of ending Boko Haram's threat to Nigeria's citizens, government security forces have responded with a heavy-hand. In 2012, security agents killed hundreds of suspected members of the group or residents of communities where attacks occurred. Nigerian authorities also arrested hundreds of people during raids across the north. Many of those detained were held incommunicado without charge or trial, in some cases in inhuman conditions. Some were physically abused; others disappeared or died in detention. These abuses in turn helped further fuel the group's campaign of violence.

The failure of Nigeria's government to address the widespread poverty, corruption, police abuse, and longstanding impunity for a range of crimes has created a fertile ground for violent militancy. Since the end of military rule in 1999, more than 18,000 people have died in inter-communal, political, and sectarian violence.

Episodes of deadly inter-communal violence, including in Plateau and Kaduna States, continued in 2012. Abuses by government security forces and the ruling elite's mismanagement and embezzlement of the country's vast oil wealth also continued largely unabated. Free speech and the independent media remained robust. Nigeria's judiciary continued to exercise a degree of independence, but many of the corruption cases against senior political figures remained stalled in the courts.

HUMAN
RIGHTS
WATCH

Spiraling Violence
Boko Haram Attacks and Security Force Abuses in Nigeria

Boko Haram Violence

Suspected Boko Haram members have carried out hundreds of attacks, including suicide bombings, across northern and central Nigerian since 2009, killing more than 1,600 people. The group has primarily targeted police and other government security agents, Christians, and Muslims working for or accused of cooperating with the government.

At this writing, suspected Boko Haram members had gunned down or bombed worshipers in at least 16 church services in 2012. The group also burned schools, bombed newspaper offices, and assassinated Muslim clerics, politicians, and traditional leaders. In the first 10 months of 2012 alone, more than 900 people died in suspected attacks by the group—more than in 2010 and 2011 combined.

Conduct of Security Forces

Government security forces have been implicated in serious human rights violations in response to the Boko Haram violence. During raids in communities where attacks have occurred in 2012, soldiers have allegedly burned homes and executed Boko Haram suspects or residents with no apparent links to the group. Nigerian authorities have rarely brought anyone to justice for these crimes.

Nigeria's police force continues to be implicated in frequent human rights violations, including extrajudicial killings, torture, arbitrary arrests, and extortion-related abuses. Despite promising public statements by the new inspector general of police, corruption in the police force remains a serious problem. The police routinely solicit bribes from victims to investigate crimes and from suspects to drop investigations. Senior police officials embezzle or mismanage police funds, often demanding monetary "returns" from money that their subordinates extort from the public.

Meanwhile, the authorities have still not prosecuted members of the police and military for the unlawful killing of more than 130 people during the 2008 sectarian violence in Jos, Plateau state, the soldiers who massacred more than 200 people in Benue State in 2001, or soldiers involved in the complete destruction of the town of Odi, Bayelsa State, in 1999.

Inter-Communal and Political Violence

Episodes of inter-communal violence continued in both Plateau and Kaduna States, in central Nigeria. At this writing more than 360 people had died in 2012 in these two states. Victims, including children, were hacked to death, shot, and burned alive—in many cases simply based on their ethnic or religious identity. Inter-communal clashes in 2012 in Adamawa, Bauchi, Benue, Ebonyi, Nasarawa, and Taraba States left more than 185 dead and hundreds more displaced. Federal and state authorities failed to break the cycle of violence by holding the perpetrators of these crimes accountable.

State and local government policies that discriminate against "non-indigenes" people who cannot trace their ancestry to what are said to be the original inhabitants of an area—also continue to exacerbate inter-communal tensions and perpetuate ethnic-based divisions.

Government Corruption

President Goodluck Jonathan sacked the chairperson of the leading anti-corruption agency, the Economic and Financial Crimes Commission (EFCC), in November 2011, but the EFCC, under its new head, Ibrahim Lamorde, has also made little progress in combating government corruption. At this writing, the EFCC had filed corruption charges in 2012 against a former governor of Bayelsa State, who had fallen out with President Jonathan, and oil marketers for their alleged role in a fraudulent fuel subsidy scheme, but executive interference with the EFCC, a weak and overburdened judiciary, and the agency's own failings have continued to undermine the effectiveness of its work.

The country's other prominent anti-corruption agency, the Independent Corrupt Practices and Other Related Offences Commission, filed charges in September against a former inspector general of police, Sunday Ehindero, and a former police commissioner for allegedly embezzling public funds. At this writing, not a single senior political figure in Nigeria was serving prison time for corruption.

Violence and Poverty in the Oil-Producing Niger Delta

The federal government's 2009 amnesty program—which saw some 26,000 militants, youth, and gang members surrender weapons in exchange for amnesty and monthly cash stipends— has reduced attacks on oil facilities in the Niger Delta. The government has doled out these financial incentives—some US$400 million annually—from the additional oil revenue, but it has still not addressed the underlying causes of violence and discontent in the region, such as poverty, government corruption, environmental degradation from oil spills, and impunity for politically sponsored violence. Meanwhile, others want part of the lucrative rewards, and in September the government announced that an additional 3,642 "ex-militants" would be added to the program.

Sexual Orientation and Gender Identity

Nigeria's criminal and penal codes punish consensual homosexual conduct with up to 14 years in prison. Sharia penal codes in many northern Nigerian states criminalize consensual homosexual conduct with caning, imprisonment, or death by stoning. In March, a court in Nasarawa State sentenced two men to two-year prison terms for having sexual intercourse, and in September an Abuja court sentenced a man to three months in prison for sodomy.

In November 2011, the Senate passed sweepingly discriminatory legislation that would criminalize anyone who enters into or assists a same-sex marriage, or supports lesbian, gay, bisexual, or transgender groups or meetings. At this writing, the House of Representatives had passed the second reading of the bill. Similar legislation has stalled at least twice in the past amid opposition from domestic and international human rights groups.

Health and Human Rights

Widespread lead poisoning from artisanal gold mining in Zamfara State has killed at least 400 children since 2010. At this writing 1,500 children were being treated for lead poisoning, but thousands of other affected children had not received any medical care. Funds were pledged by the federal government in May to clean up the environment but had not been released at this writing. The government has also failed to implement safer mining practices, which could reduce the rate of lead poisoning.

Freedom of Expression and Media

Civil society and the independent media openly criticize the government and its policies, allowing for robust public debate. Yet journalists are still subject to arrest and intimidation when reporting on issues implicating Nigeria's political and economic elite. In October, a High Court judge in Abuja awarded Desmond Utomwen, a journalist with the weekly *The News* magazine, more than $630,000 in damages after police officers in December 2009 severely assaulted him while covering a protest outside a bank in Abuja, the capital.

Several journalists were also killed in 2012. In January, Nansok Sallah, news editor for the federal government's *Highland FM*, was found dead under a bridge in Jos, and in April Ibrahim Mohammed, a film editor with Africa Independent Television, a private station, was found dead in a pool of blood in Kaduna. Chuks Ogu, a cameraman with a private television station in Edo State, Independent Television, was gunned down in April in Benin City.

On January 20, Enenche Akogwu, a journalist with Channels Television—also a private station—was killed during citywide attacks by Boko Haram on police facilities in Kano. Boko Haram bombed the offices of a private newspaper *ThisDay* in Abuja and Kaduna on April 26, killing at least seven people. The group also threatened to attack other media establishments.

Key International Actors

Nigeria's role as a regional power, Africa's leading oil exporter, and a major contributor of troops to United Nations peacekeeping missions, has led foreign governments to be reluctant to exert meaningful pressure on Nigeria over its poor human rights record.

The United States government in June designated three Boko Haram members as "Specially Designated Global Terrorists," and in August pledged to help Nigeria develop an "intelligence fusion cell." In November, the US State

Department expressed serious concerns about Nigerian security force abuses in combating the Boko Haram violence.

The United Kingdom continued to play a leading role in international efforts to combat money laundering by corrupt Nigerian officials. A London court in April sentenced powerful former Delta State governor James Ibori to a 13-year prison term for money laundering. However, the UK continues to provide substantial foreign aid to Nigeria, including security sector assistance, without demanding accountability for government officials or members of the security forces implicated in corruption or serious human rights abuses.

UN High Commissioner for Human Rights Navi Pillay warned in January and June that Boko Haram's attacks may constitute crimes against humanity. The International Criminal Court (ICC) continued its "preliminary examination" of the situation in Nigeria. The ICC prosecutor, Fatou Bensouda, visited Abuja in July and her office released a report in November stating that there is a reasonable basis to believe that Boko Haram has committed acts constituting crimes against humanity.

Rwanda

Rwanda has made important economic and development gains, but the government has continued to impose tight restrictions on freedom of expression and association. Opposition parties are unable to operate. Two opposition party leaders remain in prison and other members of their parties have been threatened. Two journalists arrested in 2010 also remain in prison, and several others have been arrested. Laws on "genocide ideology" and the media were revised, but had not been adopted at this writing.

Community-based *gacaca* courts set up to try cases related to the 1994 genocide closed in June 2012. The trial of Jean Bosco Uwinkindi, the first case transferred to Rwanda by the International Criminal Tribunal for Rwanda (ICTR), opened in Kigali.

Several governments have suspended part of their assistance to Rwanda in response to Rwandan military support for the M23 rebel group in the Democratic Republic of Congo (DRC).

Political Opponents

Bernard Ntaganda, founding president of the PS-Imberakuri opposition party, remained in prison after the Supreme Court in April upheld charges of endangering state security and divisionism, and confirmed his four-year sentence handed down in 2011. The charges related solely to his public criticisms of the government.

Several other PS-Imberakuri members were threatened, intimidated, and questioned by the police about their political activities. On September 5, Alexis Bakunzibake, the party's vice president, was abducted by armed men in the capital Kigali, blindfolded, and detained overnight in a location he could not identify. His abductors questioned him about the PS-Imberakuri's activities, its membership and funding, and its alleged links to other opposition groups. They tried to persuade him to abandon his party activities, then drove him to an undisclosed location before dumping him across the border in Uganda.

The trial of Victoire Ingabire, president of the FDU-Inkingi party, which began in September 2011, concluded in April. She was charged with six offenses, three of which were linked to "terrorist acts" and creating an armed group. The three others—"genocide ideology," divisionism, and spreading rumors intended to incite the public to rise up against the state—were linked to her public criticism of the government. On October 30, after a flawed trial, she was found guilty of conspiracy to undermine the government and genocide denial, and sentenced to eight years in prison. There were doubts about the reliability of some evidence after a witness called by the defense undermined the credibility of one of Ingabire's co-defendants. The co-defendant may have been coerced into incriminating Ingabire while in military detention. The witness (a prisoner) was subjected to intimidation after making his statement. Prison authorities searched his cell on the orders of the prosecution and seized his personal documents, including notes he had prepared for his court statement. In court, the prosecution confirmed the search by producing the notes.

In September, eight FDU-Inkingi members were arrested in Kibuye and accused of holding illegal meetings. They were charged with inciting insurrection or public disorder and held in preventive detention. Also in September, Sylvain Sibomana, secretary-general of the FDU-Inkingi, and Martin Ntavuka, FDU-Inkingi representative for Kigali, were detained overnight by police near Gitarama after they made critical comments about government policies during an informal conversation on a bus. They were released without charge.

Frank Habineza, president of the Democratic Green Party of Rwanda who had fled the country in 2010 following the murder of the party's vice president, returned to Rwanda in September to re-launch his party and register it before parliamentary elections in 2013. The party had to postpone its congress planned for November because the government did not grant the necessary authorization.

The trial of six men accused of attempting to assassinate Gen. Kayumba Nyamwasa, a former senior army official who became an outspoken government critic, in Johannesburg in 2010, continued in South Africa.

Journalists

Parliament approved new media laws, which in theory could increase the scope for independent journalism. The laws were awaiting adoption at this writing. In practice, journalists continue to be targeted for articles perceived to be critical of the government.

Agnès Uwimana and Saidati Mukakibibi, journalists writing for the newspaper *Umurabyo*, who were arrested in 2010, remained in prison. After being sentenced in 2011 to 17 years and 7 years, respectively, in connection with articles published in their newspaper, they appealed the verdict. On April 5, the Supreme Court reduced their sentences to four and three years, respectively. It upheld charges of endangering national security against both women, and a charge of defamation against Uwimana. It dropped charges of minimization of the 1994 genocide and divisionism against Uwimana.

In August, Stanley Gatera, editor of *Umusingi* newspaper, was arrested and charged with discrimination and sectarianism in connection with an opinion article published in his newspaper about marital stability and the problems posed, in the author's view, by the supposed allure of Tutsi women. He was sentenced to one year's imprisonment in November.

In April, Epaphrodite Habarugira, an announcer at Radio Huguka, was arrested and charged with genocide ideology after apparently mistakenly, during a news broadcast, mixing up words when referring to survivors of the genocide. He spent three months in prison before being acquitted in July. The state prosecutor appealed against his acquittal.

Idriss Gasana Byringiro, a journalist at *The Chronicles* newspaper, was abducted on June 15, questioned about his work and his newspaper, and released the next day. In the following days, he received anonymous threats, warning him to abandon journalism. He reported his abduction and threats to the police. On July 17, the police arrested him. Two days later, he was presented at a press conference where he retracted his earlier statements and claimed he had faked his own abduction. Initial information indicated he may have been coerced into making this "confession." He was released on bail and was at this writing awaiting trial for allegedly making a false statement to the police.

In June, Tusiime Annonciata of Flash FM radio was beaten unconscious by police and security personnel outside parliament after they accused him of trying to enter a parliamentary committee session without authorization.

Charles Ingabire, editor of the online newspaper *Inyenyeri News* and a vocal government critic, was shot dead in the Ugandan capital Kampala on November 30, 2011. He had been threatened in the months leading up to his death. Ugandan police stated they were investigating the case, but no one was prosecuted for Ingabire's murder.

Civil Society

Independent civil society organizations remained weak due to years of state intimidation. Few Rwandan organizations publicly denounced human rights violations. The Rwandan government and pro-government media reacted in a hostile manner towards international human rights organizations and attempted to discredit their work.

Genocide Ideology Law

In June, the Council of Ministers approved an amended version of the 2008 genocide ideology law, which has been used to silence critics. At this writing, the revised law was before parliament. The revised law contained improvements, in particular a narrower definition of the offense and a reduction in prison sentences. However, it retained the notion of "genocide ideology" as a criminal offense punishable by imprisonment and contained vague language that could be used to criminalize free speech.

Justice for the Genocide

Community-based *gacaca* courts, which were set up to try genocide-related cases, closed in June, after trying almost two million cases, according to government statistics.

In the first case to be transferred from the ICTR, Jean Bosco Uwinkindi was sent from Arusha, Tanzania, to Rwanda in April to stand trial for genocide.

Preliminary court hearings took place in Kigali. The ICTR agreed to transfer seven other cases to Rwanda.

In January, academic and former government official Léon Mugesera was sent back to Rwanda from Canada to face charges of planning of and incitement to genocide. Preliminary court hearings took place in Kigali.

Court proceedings against Rwandan genocide suspects took place in several other jurisdictions, including Canada, Norway, Sweden, Germany, and the Netherlands.

Unlawful Detention and Torture

On January 13, the High Court in Kigali, ruling in the trial of 30 people accused of involvement in grenade attacks in 2010, sentenced 22 defendants to prison terms ranging from five years to life imprisonment, and acquitted eight defendants. The judges did not take into account statements by several defendants that they had been detained incommunicado in military custody and tortured.

Gen. Kayumba Nyamwasa's brother, Lt-Col. Rugigana Ngabo, who was arrested in 2010 and held incommunicado in military custody for five months, was tried by a military court behind closed doors and sentenced in July to nine years' imprisonment for endangering state security and inciting violence. In response to a habeas corpus application by his sister in 2010, the East African Court of Justice (EACJ) ruled in December 2011 that Ngabo's incommunicado detention without trial had been illegal. The Rwandan government appealed this decision, but it was upheld by the EACJ's appellate division in June.

Rwandan Military Involvement in the DRC

The Rwandan military provided support to the Congolese rebel group M23, which launched a mutiny against the Congolese army in March. The M23 committed serious abuses in eastern Congo, including killings of civilians, summary executions, rape, and forced recruitment (see chapter on the DRC). In violation of the UN arms embargo on non-state actors in eastern Congo, Rwandan military officials supplied the M23 with weapons, ammunition, and new recruits, including children. Rwandan troops crossed into Congo to assist the M23 in military operations, including a November offensive in which the M23 took control of the town of Goma. The Rwandan government denied any involvement in supporting the M23.

Key International Actors

Several governments—including those of the United States, the United Kingdom, Germany, Sweden, the Netherlands, Belgium, and the European Union—suspended or delayed part of their assistance programs to Rwanda in response to Rwandan military support to the M23. In September, the UK government resumed half the aid it had suspended in July, despite continued Rwandan military backing for the M23. Expressions of diplomatic concern intensified in November as the M23 took control of Goma.

In October, Rwanda was elected to the United Nations Security Council, raising concerns about a conflict of interest in view of Rwanda's breaches of the UN arms embargo and the involvement of its troops in Congo.

Somalia

Somalia's long-running armed conflict continues to leave civilians dead, wounded, and displaced in large numbers. Although the Islamist armed group al-Shabaab lost ground in 2012, abandoning control of key towns such as Beletweyne, Baidoa, and the strategic port city of Kismayo, it continues to carry out attacks and targeted killings, including in the capital, Mogadishu.

Both al-Shabaab and the forces arrayed against it—a combination of Somali government security forces, troops with the African Union Mission in Somalia (AMISOM), Ethiopian government forces, and allied militias—committed abuses, including indiscriminate attacks harming civilians and arbitrary arrests and detentions. In areas under its control, al-Shabaab administered arbitrary justice and imposed harsh restrictions on basic rights. The transitional Somali government largely failed to protect the basic rights of the population in areas under its control; its forces and allied militia committed serious abuses against civilians.

In 2012, the situation in Mogadishu improved somewhat, with less open armed conflict. The mandate of the transitional government of Somalia ended on August 20 with the inauguration of a new administration with a new president, prime minister, and speaker of parliament. However, improving security remains a serious challenge for the new Somali National Government, highlighted by the increase in targeted killings of journalists and infighting between government forces and militias.

Abuses in Government Controlled Areas

Targeted killings of civilians, notably journalists, increased in areas controlled by the Somali authorities. Fifteen journalists were killed in 2012, which the Transitional Federal Government (TFG) failed to investigate. TFG forces and allied militias committed a range of abuses against internally displaced persons (IDPs) in Mogadishu, including rape, looting of food aid from IDP camps, and arbitrary arrests and detentions.

Civilians continue to be killed and wounded by crossfire, particularly during infighting between TFG forces over control of roadblocks, and by improvised explosive devices and grenade attacks primarily by al-Shabaab fighters. Al-Shabaab carried out several high-profile suicide attacks in Mogadishu including one on September 20 that killed at least 18 people, including three journalists. According to the World Health Organization (WHO), between January and late September, four hospitals in Mogadishu treated 5,219 casualties, with 118 dying from weapon-related injuries.

Government-affiliated forces and allied militias committed targeted killings and summary executions in towns recently vacated by al-Shabaab, and arbitrarily detained civilians, particularly men, during security operations. Between mid-January and mid-March in Beletweyne, the Shabelle Valley State (SVS) forces that are allied to the TFG and other militias committed at least seven summary executions. In late May, TFG forces including the National Security Agency (NSA) arbitrarily arrested and detained hundreds of men and boys following the takeover of Afgooye.

Civilians were killed and wounded as a result of indiscriminate fire by TFG forces and allied militias. On March 21, following a hand grenade attack on TFG-allied militia, the militia responded by opening fire on civilians in Baidoa, killing at least six.

The TFG military court continued to sentence to death and execute TFG personnel; at least six executions were carried out in 2012.

Abuses in Area Controlled by Al-Shabaab

Al-Shabaab committed serious abuses such as targeted killings, beheadings, and executions, and forcibly recruited adults and children in areas under its control. On July 22, 2012, in the coastal town of Merka, al-Shabaab publicly executed three men it accused of being Western spies. Al-Shabaab continued to apply an extreme form of Islamic law in areas under its control, restricting the movement of people in need of humanitarian assistance or seeking to flee fighting in Kismayo.

HUMAN RIGHTS WATCH

NO PLACE FOR CHILDREN
Child Recruitment, Forced Marriage, and Attacks on Schools in Somalia

Recruitment of Children and Other Abuses

All of the Somali parties to the conflict have continued to commit serious abuses against children, including recruiting children into their forces. Al-Shabaab has targeted children for recruitment, forced marriage, and rape, and has attacked teachers and schools.

In July 2012, the TFG signed a plan of action against child recruitment; yet the same month, 15 children were identified among a group of new recruits sent to a European Union-funded training in Uganda. The government has also detained children formerly associated with al-Shabaab, and used them as informants.

Abuses by Foreign Forces

Foreign forces have committed grave abuses in south-central Somalia, including indiscriminate shelling. Since October 2011, Kenyan air and naval forces have indiscriminately bombed and shelled populated areas, killing and wounding civilians and livestock. On August 11, a naval strike on Kismayo resulted in the deaths of at least three civilians, including two boys.

Ethiopian forces arbitrarily arrested, detained, and mistreated persons in their custody, notably in Beletweyne and Baidoa.

Restrictions on Humanitarian Assistance

In February 2012, the UN declared that the famine in Somalia was over, but stressed that at least two million people were still in need of emergency humanitarian assistance. Humanitarian access remains restricted due to ongoing conflict, insecurity, restrictions imposed by parties to the conflict, and diversion of aid.

Al-Shabaab maintains restrictions on humanitarian assistance and prohibits more than 16 humanitarian organizations, including the UN's Children Fund (UNICEF) and Action Contre la Faim (ACF), from working in areas under its control. On October 8, 2012, al-Shabaab banned one of the last remaining international aid organizations, Islamic Relief, from working in areas under its control.

In towns recently vacated by al-Shabaab, insecurity, including infighting between TFG-allied forces, has limited access by aid agencies. Targeted attacks on humanitarian workers persist throughout the country. On August 27, 2012, a Somali staff member working with the UN Food and Agriculture Organization (FAO) was killed in Merka.

The diversion of humanitarian aid within Mogadishu by government forces, allied militia, officials and others, and insecurity at food distribution sites have significantly limited the access that displaced persons have to assistance.

Somaliland

The Somaliland government frequently and arbitrarily arrested and detained journalists—mainly those reporting on sensitive political issues such as the self-proclaimed Khatumo State—and clamped down on opposition protests. In April 2012, the government responded to a series of protests that opposition party members organized after being disqualified from local elections by temporarily arresting and detaining supporters. On March 8, 2012, the police also arbitrarily detained 71 people, including children, from Las Anod for peacefully protesting in support of the Khatumo State. Due process violations, including lengthy remand detention and the detention of children, remain a concern. On May 17, 2012, the military court sentenced 17 civilians to death.

On at least two occasions, the Somaliland authorities deported large numbers of Ethiopians, including refugees and asylum seekers. On August 31, Somaliland forcibly sent up to 100 Ethiopians, mostly women and children, back to Ethiopia, including refugees and asylum-seekers. This followed police raids on August 30 and 31, 2012, on an informal settlement in Hargeisa. Police fired live ammunition during the raids, wounding at least six Ethiopians, and then arrested and detained 56 Ethiopians.

Key International Actors

The TFG's international partners, including the United States, United Kingdom, EU, and Turkey, have sought to build the capacity of Somalia's weak governmental institutions and some regional administrations. The main focus of foreign partners and neighboring countries in 2012 was on implementing the roadmap developed to guide the execution of priority transitional tasks, including the adoption of a constitution and parliamentary reform, before the end of the transitional period.

The other focus has been on military support to AMISOM and the TFG forces, notably by the US and the EU. The US acknowledged for the first time in 2012 that it had authorized aerial drone strikes and special forces' operations against al-Shabaab inside Somalia. The UK deployed a military liaison unit to Mogadishu.

On February 22, 2012, the UN Security Council authorized the African Union, with inadequate provisions on accountability, to increase the number of peacekeepers deployed in Somalia from 12,000 to 17,731.

In addition to their large military presence in Somalia, Kenya, and Ethiopia continue to train and offer military support to TFG-affiliated militia. They have a particular interest in the administrations in control of the areas that border their countries: Lower Juba and Gedo, including Kismayo.

The UN is undertaking a review process to examine its presence in the country and improve coordination in Somalia. The strengthening of UN human rights mechanisms will be crucial to the review's success.

While improving accountability at the national level is currently on the international agenda, much needs to be done to ensure that this renewed commitment leads to concrete improvements on the ground. Given the gravity of the crimes committed in Somalia, accountability at the international level, notably through establishing a UN commission of inquiry—or a comparable, appropriate mechanism—is critical to document serious crimes and recommend appropriate measures.

South Africa

The killing of 34 miners at the Lonmin Platinum Mine in Marikana, North West Province, on August 16, 2012, shocked South Africans and highlighted increasing concerns over police brutality and underlying grievances over the government's failure to fulfill basic economic and social rights.

Despite South Africa's strong constitutional protections for human rights and its relative success at providing basic services, the government is struggling to meet public demands for better realization of economic and social rights. In addition, financial mismanagement, corruption, and concerns about the capacity of leadership and administration—especially at the local government level— have contributed to further delaying the progressive realization of economic and social rights.

Concerns that the ruling African National Congress (ANC) is increasingly encroaching on civil and political rights are exemplified by the Protection of State Information Bill which the National Assembly passed in 2011, but has not yet become law. Debates over its constitutionality regarding its impact on freedom of expression continued in 2012. At this writing, the Traditional Courts Bill, which parliament was considering, may have negative implications for vulnerable groups such as women, children, and lesbian, gay, bisexual, and transgender (LGBT) persons to access justice and other rights.

The Killing of Mine Workers

The tragedy at Lonmin Platinum Mine, which resulted in the death of 34 miners when police opened fire on illegal strikers, is one of the worst death tolls in violent protests since 1994. The tragedy highlighted the poverty and the grievances of many in the mining industry, the historical bastion of South Africa's migrant labor system.

The government acted swiftly to respond to public outcry and established a judicial commission of inquiry to ascertain the facts and investigate the conduct of the mining company, the trade unions, and the police. The inquiry will investigate the nature, extent, and application of any standing orders by police that gave rise to the tragedy, as well as whether the use of force was reasonable and justified in the circumstances.

Freedom of Expression

The controversial Protection of State Information Bill aims to regulate the classification, protection, and dissemination of state information, weighing state interests against the importance of freedom of expression. The National Assembly passed the bill in November 2011 and amended it in 2012 in response to criticism from civil society organizations and state institutions, such as the South African Human Rights Commission (SAHRC). Following the amendment, section 49 of the bill was expunged. It had criminalized the disclosure of information relating to any state security matter, even if those responsible were unaware that the information was a matter of state security. Section 43, which pertains to the publication of classified information, was also amended to offer whistleblowers more protection.

However, some concerns remain, such as the bill's relation to the Promotion of Access to Information Act (PAIA), which is based on the constitutional right of access to information held by the state and private bodies. Early versions of the new law gave it precedence over the PAIA. And while amendments in 2012 deleted the clause that pertained to the bill superseding the PAIA, it remains unclear whether it trumps the right of access to information.

The amendments improved the balance in the law between the importance of the right to freedom of expression and the state's interest in classifying information. Given the bill's contentious nature, it is almost certain that the government itself will itself take the bill to the constitutional court for certification before it is signed into law. If it does not do so, civil society organizations will challenge the bill before the constitutional court.

Women's Rights

Section 9 of South Africa's Constitution provides strong protection for women, prohibiting discrimination on the grounds of gender, sex, pregnancy, sexual orientation, and marital status. In addition to legislation such as the Promotion of

Equality and Prevention Unfair Discrimination Act of 2000 and the establishment of the Commission for Gender Equality, the government in 2010 created the Department of Women, Children and People with Disabilities. This illustrated the government's commitment to promote and protect the rights of women and matters related to women's equality and empowerment.

However, the reintroduction of the Traditional Courts Bill in 2012, after the government withdrew it in 2008 following widespread criticism, may have dire consequences for the rights of women.

The bill aims to affirm the traditional justice system based on restorative justice and reconciliation. As such, it emphasizes the position of traditional leaders in the administration of justice, and effectively centralizes their power as the arbiters of customary law. As it stood at time of writing, the bill will give traditional leaders the authority to enforce controversial versions of customary law such as the practice of *ukutwala* (forced marriage), adjudicate compliance, and enforce penalties. The penalties are of particular concern as section 10 of the bill imposes sanctions including fines, forced labor, and the withdrawal of customary benefits, such as the enjoyment of communal land.

Section 4 provides for the minister of justice to appoint traditional leaders who are recognized in the Traditional Leadership and Governance Framework Act as presiding officers of traditional courts. Most traditional leaders are men, and the bill does not assign women any role in the courts. A significant concern with the traditional justice system is its entrenchment of patriarchy, as well as discriminatory social and economic practices, such as access to land, inheritance, and forced marriage.

South Africa was a leading advocate for the adoption of International Labour Organization (ILO) Convention on Decent Work for Domestic Workers in 2011, but has not yet itself ratified it. Moreover, the enforcement of its legislation covering the estimated 1 to 1.5 million domestic workers in South Africa remains weak.

Sexual Orientation and Gender Identity

South Africa continues to play a leading role on sexual orientation and gender identity at the United Nations Human Rights Council (HRC). A report by the Office of the UN High Commissioner on Human Rights (OHCHR), documenting violence and discrimination against LGBT people worldwide and compiled in accordance with a 2011 South Africa sponsored resolution on "Human Rights, Sexual Orientation and Gender Identity," was presented to the HRC in March 2012. This is the first time that any UN body approved a resolution affirming the rights of LGBT persons.

Farmworkers

Following the Human Rights Watch report on the living and working conditions of farmworkers in 2011, the government has shown a commitment to strengthening the rights of those in the farming community. As a result, during 2012, the government engaged extensively with civil society, academia, farmer associations, and trade unions about a draft document on land tenure security before it is submitted to parliament as a bill. The consultations have indicated that the document is vague on how the nature and content of rights of farmworkers and farm dwellers will be strengthened and protected, and will need to be more robust to protect the rights of workers.

Addressing the tenure insecurities of farmworkers is critical to South Africa's overall land reform agenda.

International Justice

South Africa continued to play a leadership role in affirming the need to uphold obligations to the International Criminal Court (ICC), although it has yet to block African Union decisions, which call for states not to cooperate with the court in the arrest of suspect Sudanese President Omar al-Bashir. The first domestic criminal case in South Africa for international crimes committed in Zimbabwe also commenced, although it was initially challenged by South's Africa's police and prosecuting authority.

Rights of Refugees

In defiance of court orders, the Department of Home Affairs closed three of its seven Refugee Reception Offices, which caused a crisis for asylum-seekers' and refugees' access to asylum and refugee procedures. The closures are part of the department's plan to move asylum-processing to the country's borders, which has limited access to work, adequate shelter, and assistance for asylum seekers.

Key International Actors

South Africa's role as a non-permanent member of the UN Security Council ended in December. Its tenure on the Security Council was marked by erratic stances on human rights concerns, particularly regarding UN engagement on Libya and Syria. South Africa abstained from voting on a draft UN security resolution threatening UN action in Syria in July 2012.

South Sudan

The first year of South Sudan's independence, declared on July 9, 2011, was marred by intense inter-communal fighting in Jonglei state, deteriorating relations with Sudan amid ongoing conflicts along their shared border, and the economic consequences of South Sudan's decision to shut down oil production.

The government took steps to develop its legal and institutional structure but has yet to ratify major human rights treaties, despite repeatedly saying it would do so. South Sudan is struggling to protect civilians from violence and human rights abuses—including abuses by its own security forces, especially while carrying out disarmament operations. Across the country, lack of capacity and inadequate training of police, prosecutors, and judges have resulted in numerous human rights violations in law enforcement and administering justice.

Legislative Developments

The National Legislative Assembly enacted several new laws, including a Political Parties Act and Elections Act, but has yet to pass laws governing the media and the National Security Service, including defining the security service's powers of arrest and detention.

The assembly also passed an austerity budget—significantly cutting operating costs and basic services—to mitigate the economic consequences of the February oil shutdown, which included inflation, fuel shortages, and price increases.

The National Constitutional Review Commission, appointed in November 2011, stalled over disagreements about political party and civil society representation. The transitional constitution, which entered into force on July 9, 2011, will remain in effect until a permanent constitution is adopted following national elections in 2015.

South Sudan has yet to formally ratify key international human rights treaties. In June, the president signed a Refugee Provisional Order containing international standards on refugee rights, and in July, the country acceded to the 1949 Geneva Conventions and their Additional Protocols.

North-South Tensions, Border Conflicts

Tensions between Sudan and South Sudan over unresolved post-secession issues increased steadily throughout 2011 and early 2012, exacerbated by South Sudan's decision to shut down oil production in February, followed by armed clashes between the two countries' armed forces at Heglig oil fields in April.

The African Union, Peace and Security Council, and the United Nations Security Council responded by adopting a roadmap for the two governments to cease hostilities, resume negotiations, and reach agreements by certain deadlines, or face penalties. In September, the two governments agreed to resume oil production and trade, among other things, but failed to agree on the final status of Abyei, a disputed border area claimed by both countries.

Clashes between northern and southern forces in Abyei in May 2011 displaced tens of thousands of civilians from the area, most of whom have yet to return.

The AU and UN roadmap also required Sudan and the Sudanese armed rebel group, the Sudan People's Liberation Army-North (SPLA-N), to stop fighting in Southern Kordofan and Blue Nile states. The conflicts, which began in June 2011, have caused massive displacement of more than 170,000 civilians to refugee camps in South Sudan's Unity and Upper Nile states.

Inter-Communal Violence

Retaliatory attacks between Lou Nuer and Murle ethnic groups in Jonglei state escalated into large-scale conflict in late December 2011, when more than 6,000 Lou Nuer armed youth attacked Murle communities. According to UN investigations, more than 800 people of both ethnicities were killed between December 2011 and February 2012. Women and children were abducted and property was looted and destroyed.

The South Sudanese military and UN peacekeepers stationed in the area had only limited success in protecting civilians from the mass violence, and were unable to prevent the attacks from spreading. The government launched a statewide peace process and a civilian disarmament campaign in March 2012.

Lack of accountability for the crimes is widely believed to contribute to the cycle of retaliatory violence. President Salva Kiir established an Investigation Committee with a mandate to investigate those responsible for the violence, but at this writing, the government has not released funds for the committee or sworn in its members.

Abuses by Security Forces

During the Jonglei disarmament operation, "Operation Restore Peace," which began in March 2012 and continued throughout the year, soldiers were responsible for extrajudicial killings, severe beatings, tying people up with rope, and submerging their heads in water to extract information about the location of weapons. Soldiers were also implicated in sexual violence against women and girls.

Although the military took some steps to address violations by soldiers, such as distributing the code of conduct to those involved in disarmament and deploying judge-advocates to bolster the military justice system, these steps were not sufficient to curb the abuses or hold soldiers accountable for human rights violations. The absence of civilian judicial personnel in Pibor also undermined efforts to ensure accountability.

South Sudanese security forces also detained and intimidated perceived critics and independent journalists. In February, security guards assaulted Mading Ngor, a radio journalist, while he was visiting the National Assembly in Juba. Police in Rumbek arrested and detained a radio host, Ayak Dhieu Apar, for two days over a radio call-in show perceived as critical of the police, while in Bentiu, the Sudan People's Liberation Army (SPLA) detained and questioned *Sudan Tribune* journalist Bonifacio Taban Kuich for three days over an article he wrote about the grievances of widows of SPLA soldiers.

The National Security Service also arrested and detained without charge numerous individuals, including journalists, without legal basis to do so. In December 2011, national security officials in Juba detained the editor of *The Destiny* news-

HUMAN
RIGHTS
WATCH

"Prison Is Not For Me"
Arbitrary Detention in South Sudan

paper for almost two weeks and did not allow him access to a lawyer or to his family. In September, security officials in Juba arrested and detained for three days without charge a *Citizen* newspaper reporter.

Media advocates say in the absence of laws that regulate the media, editors and reporters are especially vulnerable to harassment, arbitrary arrest, and censorship by security forces.

Rebel and Militia Activity

In December 2011, the SPLA killed George Athor, leader of the rebel South Sudan Democratic Movement/Army (SSDM/A). In early 2012, the SPLA reappointed Peter Gadet, a former leader of the South Sudan Liberation Army (SSLA) who signed a ceasefire agreement in August, to a high ranking position as General. Hundreds of the two groups' former militia members have been integrated into the SPLA pursuant to the president's 2011 amnesty.

Other groups, however, have not accepted the amnesty, and have clashed with SPLA in Upper Nile state in April and in Jonglei state from August onward, displacing thousands of civilians. On multiple occasions since 2010, both rebel groups and SPLA soldiers have been responsible for serious human rights abuses, including unlawful killings, destruction of property, and mass civilian displacements.

High-profile opposition and rebel leaders remain in military detention. Former militia leader Gabriel Tanginye, who had signed a peace agreement with the government, and opposition politician Peter Sule, accused of recruiting militia in Western Equatoria, have been in SPLA custody for more than a year without being formally charged with crimes.

Administration of Justice

Weaknesses in the justice system give rise to serious human rights violations, such as prolonged periods of pre-trial detention and poor detention conditions. Children are often detained with adults, while persons with mental disabilities languish in prison without any legal basis for their detention and do not receive treatment. Lack of legal aid, including for people accused of serious crimes punishable by death, also contributes to due process violations. South Sudan retains the death penalty and carried out two executions in August. More than 230 prisoners are on death row. In November, human rights groups called on the government to place a moratorium on the death penalty.

Women and Children

Child marriage is widespread, and many women and girls are deprived of the right to choose a spouse and do not enter into marriage with their full and free consent. Almost half (48.1 percent) of girls aged 15 to 19 years are currently married, out of which 17 percent were married before age 15. Women and girls are subjected to other practices that violate human rights law—such as wife-inheritance and the use of girls to pay debts—and also face the risk of domestic violence. They have few rights in marriage; for example, they do not have the right to own and inherit property. Domestic disputes are resolved by traditional courts that often apply discriminatory customs against women.

South Sudan signed a new action plan with the UN in March 2012 to end its use of child soldiers. It also issued military orders for the release of all children from the SPLA and allowed UN verification visits to SPLA barracks and training centers. In June, the UN reported that more than 150 children were found in SPLA barracks.

Key International Actors

The UN Security Council renewed the mandate of the UN Mission in South Sudan (UNMISS), with peacekeepers and civilian staff deployed in all 10 states. The mission continued to support the UN Interim Security Force for Abyei (UNISFA), established in June 2011 to monitor troop redeployments, facilitate humanitarian aid, and protect civilians from imminent threat, among other tasks.

The AU's High-Level Implementation Panel continued to play a key role in facilitating negotiations between South Sudan and Sudan, particularly after conflict between them in April. The outstanding post-secession issues, addressed in

September, included oil production arrangements, the status of Abyei, demarcation of the border, and citizenship.

The UN Human Rights Council (HRC) again requested that the UN high commissioner for human rights present a report on the human rights situation in the country. In October, South Sudan expelled, without warning or explanation, a senior UN human rights staff. Both the Office of the High Commissioner for Human Rights (OHCHR) and the UN peacekeeping mission denounced the expulsion.

In October, United States President Barack Obama waived the application of the Child Soldiers Prevention Act to South Sudan, citing US national interests. The law prohibits several categories of US military assistance to governments using child soldiers.

Sudan

Sudan's relations with newly independent South Sudan deteriorated in early 2012, leading to clashes along the shared border in April. Although the two governments signed an agreement in September, paving the way for resumption of oil production, fighting between Sudanese government forces and rebel movements continues in Darfur, as well as in Southern Kordofan and Blue Nile states where Sudan's indiscriminate bombardment and obstruction of humanitarian assistance forced more than 170,000 to flee to refugee camps in South Sudan.

Student-led protests in Sudan's university towns intensified in response to wide-ranging austerity measures and political grievances. From June through August, riot police and national security officials violently dispersed a wave of protests, with hundreds arrested, at least 12 protesters shot dead, and scores of others detained and subjected to harsh interrogations, ill-treatment, and torture.

Sudanese authorities also harassed, and arbitrarily arrested and detained other perceived opponents of the government, including suspected members of the Sudan People's Liberation Movement/North—which was banned in September 2011—members of other opposition parties, civil society leaders, and journalists. They also censored the press.

Protection Concerns on Border with South Sudan

Following South Sudan's independence in July 2011, Sudan's ruling National Congress Party (NCP) and the South's ruling Sudan People's Liberation Movement (SPLM) were deadlocked on a range of issues including oil production, debt, the status of the nationals of one country in the other, border security, resolution of border disputes, and the status of Abyei. Amid rising tensions, both countries accused the other of supporting or harboring rebel groups. South Sudan shut down oil production in February, seriously affecting the economies of both countries.

In early 2012, cross-border attacks, including aerial bombardments by Sudan into South Sudan, increased culminating in 10 days of armed conflict between the two nations in April at Heglig, an oil-producing area along the border. The armed clashes and bombing in and around Bentiu, Unity state, resulted in civilian casualties and displacement.

South Sudan withdrew under international pressure and both the African Union and the United Nations endorsed a roadmap for resumption of negotiations over post-secession issues. In the following months, though political tensions eased, sporadic clashes and bombing continued and caused injuries, and displaced civilians in Northern Bahr el Ghazal state, South Sudan.

In September, the two governments signed agreements on oil, borders, and citizenship among other issues, but did not agree on the status of Abyei or address the ongoing conflict in Southern Kordofan and Blue Nile, which has forced more than 200,000 people into refugee camps in South Sudan and Ethiopia.

Humanitarian Law Violations in the Southern Kordofan and Blue Nile Conflict

Fighting continued in Southern Kordofan and Blue Nile states between Sudan government forces and the armed opposition group, Sudan People's Liberation Army-North (SPLA-North), which grew out of the southern rebel SPLA's wartime presence in Sudan. In Southern Kordofan, ground clashes and government bombing forced hundreds of thousands of civilians to flee their homes. Many fled to caves and mountains where they lacked food, shelter, and hygiene. By November, more than 65,000 had fled to a refugee camp in South Sudan.

The conflict spread to Blue Nile state in September 2011, with ground fighting and government bombing forcing hundreds of thousands of people to flee their homes. As of November, more than 145,000, many of them travelling on foot for weeks or months, had fled to refugee camps in South Sudan and Ethiopia. The Sudanese government has refused to allow aid groups to access needy populations living in rebel-controlled areas in both states, effectively depriving civilians of essential food, medicine, and other basic services.

HUMAN
RIGHTS
WATCH

UNDER SIEGE
Indiscriminate Bombing and Abuses in Sudan's Southern Kordofan and Blue Nile States

Conflict in Darfur

The Doha Document for Peace in Darfur, signed in July 2011 by Sudan and a Darfur rebel group, Liberation and Justice Movement (LJM), has had little impact in improving security or human rights in Darfur. The parties set up the Darfur Regional Authority, a body to implement the agreement, and appointed some LJM members to government positions. Donors, particularly Qatar, promise to fund early recovery and development activities.

Non-signatory rebel groups including Sudan Liberation Army (SLA) and Justice and Equality Movement (JEM) have joined with SPLA-North in a national coalition, known as the Sudan Revolutionary Front (SRF). Clashes between rebels and government forces, and government bombing of rebel-held areas, continued particularly in North Darfur and East Jebel Mara areas. In September, fighting between government-aligned militia groups and rebels near Hashaba, North Darfur led to the death of dozens of civilians. On November 2, government forces attacked Sigili village in North Darfur, killing 13 civilians.

The Sudanese government continued to deny peacekeepers from the United Nations-African Union Mission in Darfur (UNAMID) access to much of Darfur. Despite such restrictions, UNAMID reported on the government's arbitrary arrests and detentions of real and perceived opponents, and on patterns of sexual violence. A state of emergency, empowering governors to detain people indefinitely without judicial review, remains in place throughout Darfur.

Lawlessness and insecurity hampered the work of the peacekeepers and aid groups. Armed gunmen attacked and killed peacekeepers, including four Nigerians in October, abducted UNAMID and humanitarian staff and carjacked dozens of vehicles. The vast majority of Darfur's displaced population, estimated around 2.5 million people, remain in camps in Darfur and Chad.

Justice and Accountability

Seven years after the International Criminal Court (ICC) issued arrest warrants or summons to appear against six individuals, Sudan continued to refuse to cooperate with the ICC or to meaningfully prosecute the crimes in its own courts. The UN Security Council had in 2005 referred the situation in Darfur to the ICC, which issued the warrants or summons to appear against President Omar al-Bashir and five others, on charges of war crimes, crimes against humanity, and genocide, although the charges were not confirmed against one of the suspects, Bahar Idriss Abu Garda.

Despite the appointment of a fifth special prosecutor for Darfur in June, Sudan has done little to promote accountability. It has made none of the justice reforms recommended in the 2009 report from the AU's High-level Panel on Darfur, headed by former South African President Thabo Mbeki.

Crackdown on Protests

In late 2011 and early 2012, security forces violently dispersed peaceful protests across the country, often at universities. Students protested against price increases student elections, and in solidarity with the Manaseer community's demands for compensation for their forced displacement from land in Red Sea state by the construction of the Merowe Dam in 2008.

In June and July, as the economic consequences of the oil-shut down surfaced, student and youth-led protests increased in number and size. The protests were larger than the Arab Spring-inspired protests in early 2011, despite the lack of official backing from major opposition parties. Starting June 16 at Khartoum University, protests were staged on a near daily basis in dozens of towns against the government's austerity measures and other policies.

Riot police and national security forces used batons, sticks, rubber bullets and in some cases live ammunition to disperse the gatherings. Many protesters were wounded and required medical care. In South Darfur, on July 31, the security forces killed 12 protesters including several children under 18 years old. National security forces, often in pick-up trucks, arrested hundreds of protesters and people who did not participate directly in the protests, such as suspected organizers, political activists and prominent members of the opposition.

While many were released within days, a large number remained in National Security Service (NSS) custody for several weeks or months. Members of the activist group *Girifna* (We are fed up) were particularly targeted for arrest and detention. One Darfuri member, Rudwan Daoud, was charged with espionage and crimes against the state, punishable by death. Following international pressure, charges were dropped and he was released. Most of the student protesters were released in mid-August before the end of Ramadan.

Dozens of released detainees reported being subjected by national security officers to severe beatings, sleep deprivation, and other forms of torture during interrogations. Many were forced to provide their Facebook and email addresses passwords, and to reveal the names and whereabouts of political activists. Upon their release, detainees were made to renounce their political activism, promise not to engage in political activity, or agree to work as informants for NSS.

Political Repression and Media Restrictions

In addition to protest-related harassment, the NSS targeted opposition party members, particularly SPLM-North, which was banned in September 2011. Security officials also targeted human rights workers, civil society members, and perceived opponents for harassment, arrest and detention, particularly during the period that protests were being held. For example, in July, a group of more than 13 women activists were held for more than a month in Omdurman women's prison, in poor conditions.

Many people were detained because of their real or perceived links to the SPLM-North, which was banned in September 2011 when war broke out in Blue Nile state, or as a result of their human rights activism. Abdelmonim Rahama, a poet and former adviser to the Blue Nile state government, spent 11 months in detention in Sennar state. Nuba human rights activist, Bushra Gammar, was released after more than one year in detention without charge, while Jalila Khamees, a Nuba schoolteacher and human rights defender, was arrested from her home in Khartoum in March 2012 by national security officials, and in July was charged with crimes against the state that could carry the death sentence.

In the wake of fighting with South Sudan's army at Heglig in April, Sudanese authorities stepped up hostile rhetoric and political repression. NSS summoned prominent Sudanese journalist and human rights defender, Faisal Mohamed Salih, for several hours of questioning and ordered him to report back daily for nearly two weeks in connection with his comments critical of the government on Al Jazeera Arabic television.

Authorities censored articles, confiscated newspaper editions, and blacklisted more than 15 journalists for reporting on sensitive topics, including a church-burning incident in April prompted by a radical imam's hostile rhetoric. National security officials also routinely instructed editors to refrain from publishing criticisms of the president or the armed forces, the economic impact of the oil shutdown, or the conflicts in Southern Kordofan and Blue Nile.

In May, the Humanitarian Aid Commission (HAC) suspended or expelled seven humanitarian organizations from working in Eastern Sudan. In September, HAC began summoning local organizations that receive foreign funding, in an apparent effort to cut off foreign funding of civil society groups.

Key International Actors

Following the armed hostilities at Heglig in April, the AU and UN, through Security Council Resolution 2046, endorsed a roadmap for cessation of hostilities and resumption of negotiations on post-secession issues. The AU's High-Level Implementation Panel continued to facilitate the negotiations. Ethiopia remains an important actor in these negotiations despite the death of Prime Minister Meles Zenawi in August.

In September, Sudan and South Sudan reached a deal on oil production arrangements, border management and citizenship, but remained deadlocked on the status of Abyei. Sudan and SPLM-North did not enter into direct negotiations. While the parties did accept the tri-partite proposal submitted by the AU, UN, and League of Arab States to permit humanitarian access to the affected populations in the two states, Sudan has refused to implement it.

The UN extended the mandate of UNAMID for a fifth year, while adopting plans to downsize its military and police components. Its Joint Special Representative, Ibrahim Gambari, finished his term July 31 and has yet to be replaced. In the contested territory of Abyei, the UN Interim Security Force for Abyei (UNISFA) continued to deploy and prepare for its role in wider border management, pursuant to 2011 agreements.

Sudan did not grant the UN's Independent Expert on the situation of human rights in the Sudan access to Darfur and he was therefore only allowed to hold meetings in Khartoum. In September, the UN Human Rights Council strengthened the mandate and called on Sudan to allow the expert to access to the entire country including conflict zones in Darfur, Southern Kordofan and Blue Nile.

While al-Bashir was welcomed in Egypt and Libya this year, ICC member Malawi indicated it would arrest al-Bashir if he entered that country to attend the AU summit scheduled to take place there in June 2012. As a result, the summit was moved to Addis Ababa, Ethiopia.

Uganda

After 26 years of President Yoweri Museveni's rule, increasing threats to freedom of expression, assembly, and association raise serious concerns about Uganda's respect for the rule of law. The security forces continue to enjoy impunity for torture, extrajudicial killings, and the deaths of at least 49 people during protests in 2009 and 2011.

The government banned a political pressure group calling for peaceful change, stopped opposition groups from holding rallies, and harassed and intimidated journalists and civil society activists in 2012. Organizations monitoring governance, accountability of public resources, land rights, oil revenue, and the rights of lesbian, gay, bisexual, and transgender (LGBT) people face increased obstructions. The notorious draft Anti-Homosexuality Bill, which proposes the death penalty for some consensual same-sex activities, remains tabled in parliament, threatening the rights of Uganda's LGBT people.

After an eight-year civil society campaign supporting the bill, parliament unanimously passed a law defining and criminalizing torture that the president signed, bringing it into force in July.

Freedom of Assembly and Expression

Police interference in, and unlawful obstruction of, public gatherings remains a significant problem, often accompanied by arrests and detentions of organizers and participants. In March, police stopped opposition leaders from touring a public works project in Kampala, the capital. In the resulting melee, a policeman, John Bosco Ariong, was hit by an object and died. Police closed off the area, arrested over 50 people, and beat them in detention. One person was charged with Ariong's murder and is awaiting trial. The mayor of Kampala and an opposition leader were charged with organizing an unlawful assembly with the purpose of inciting members of the public against the police.

In April, the attorney general banned the political pressure group Activists for Change, which orchestrated the April 2011 "Walk to Work" protests, labeling the group an unlawful society under the penal code. The ban came a day before a planned rally to call attention to police abuse of opposition supporters. Police placed opposition leader Kizza Besigye under house arrest without a court order in April during the international assembly of the Inter-Parliamentary Union (IPU) in Kampala, arguing that he would disrupt the meeting.

In October, as Uganda marked 50 years of independence, celebrations were marred by protests and widespread arrests as the government stopped opposition rallies, a "Walk to Freedom" protest organized by 4GC (For God and Country, formerly Activists for Change), and house arrests of prominent political figures, including Besigye and the mayor of Kampala.

Police restricted public debate and expression of concerns over governance throughout 2012. For example, two authors of a book critical of President Museveni—Doreen Nyanjura and Ibrahim Bagaya Kisubi—were arrested at the Kampala book launch in April. Nyanjura was charged with participating in unlawful society and inciting violence and detained for two weeks. In August, Barbara Allimadi, a member of another pressure group, Concerned Citizens, was arrested and briefly detained after staging a demonstration in parliament. Police confiscated Allimadi's t-shirts, which had anti-corruption slogans.

Journalists continue to be physically attacked and harassed by police in the course of their work. Between January and June, a media watchdog organization registered 50 attacks on journalists, despite multiple police pledges to respect media freedom.

Restrictions on Nongovernmental Organizations

The government is deploying hostile rhetoric and an array of tactics to intimidate and obstruct the work of nongovernmental organizations on sensitive issues such as governance, human rights, land, oil, and the rights of LGBT people. Tactics include closing meetings, forcing NGO representatives to issue apologies, occasional physical violence, threats, harassment, and heavy-handed bureaucratic interference in NGO registration and operations. NGOs are required to register to work in Uganda, but due to government hostility, organizations working on the rights of LGBT people cannot register to operate legally

HUMAN
RIGHTS
WATCH

JUSTICE FOR SERIOUS CRIMES
BEFORE NATIONAL COURTS
Uganda's International Crimes Division

as is required under law. Senior government officials and police have unlawfully tried to stifle discussion of LGBT rights.

In February, the minister of ethics and integrity closed down a meeting organized by Sexual Minorities Uganda; in June, police broke up a meeting organized by the East and Horn of Africa Human Rights Defenders; and in August, police shut down a gay pride march in Entebbe. In September, a British producer was arrested and charged for staging a play about homosexuality, though he was later released, and on November 8, police blocked another local theatre production about the rights of LGBT people.

Torture, Extrajudicial Killings, and Lack of Accountability

Police leadership disbanded the Police's Rapid Response Unit (RRU) in December 2011 explicitly because of its poor human rights record, renaming it the Special Investigations Unit (SIU). However the police have failed to investigate abuses committed by RRU officers or ad hoc operatives, some of whom continue to work with the SIU. In September, four members of the opposition Forum for Democratic Change (FDC) appeared before court charged with treason. They complained of torture in detention after having been detained by the SIU for 14 days.

The government failed to investigate the killing of over 40 people by security forces during the September 2009 riots, and the deaths of nine people during the "Walk to Work" demonstrations in April 2011.

No charges were filed against the police officer who in April assaulted Ingrid Turinawe, head of the FDC's Women's League, as police prevented her from attending a rally.

Electoral violence marred six of the nine parliamentary by-elections held between February and September. In Bukoto South, armed paramilitary groups travelling in unmarked cars beat supporters of the Democratic Party candidate on election day, despite a heavy police presence. Incidents of election-related violence also occurred in other parts of the country.

There have been no arrests for the killings of three Muslim leaders this year. On April 20, prominent Muslim scholar Abdu Karim Senatmu was shot by unknown assailants and on August 18, Sheikh Yunus Abubakari was shot and killed after leading night prayers. President Museveni claimed Sentamu's death was due to his connections with the Allied Democratic Forces (ADF), a rebel group operating in the Democratic Republic of Congo (DRC). In September, Imam Abdul Jowadi Sentuga was also shot and killed. Police spokespeople said that the killings are related to the ADF and promised to release a report, but it was not completed at the time of writing.

The Lord's Resistance Army

The Ugandan armed rebel group, the Lord's Resistance Army (LRA), continued to kill and abduct people across Central African Republic, southern Sudan, and northern DRC though at a reduced scale from previous years (see DRC chapter).

Warrants issued by the International Criminal Court (ICC) for LRA leaders in 2005 remain outstanding. The War Crimes Division of the High Court did not begin its first trial of the only defendant in custody, former LRA fighter Thomas Kwoyelo, who has been charged with willful killing, taking hostages, and extensive destruction of property. Kwoyelo had previously applied for amnesty. In January, the High Court ordered the prosecutors to grant amnesty and release him, but the state has appealed and the case was, at this writing, pending before the Supreme Court.

Uganda's parliament permitted key provisions of the amnesty law to lapse, meaning that for the first time since 2000, LRA fighters who end up in custody could face criminal trial.

Bills Violating Human Rights Law

The Anti-Homosexuality Bill, which proposes the death penalty for some con-sensual same-sex activities, and the HIV/AIDS Prevention and Control Act, which criminalizes intentional or attempted transmission of HIV, are before par-liamentary committees and could still come up for debate and vote. The Public Order Management Bill, which grants police overly broad discretionary powers in the management of all public meetings, was also presented in parliament and was pending at this writing.

Key International Actors

On October 19, Uganda's auditor general reported extensive fraud regarding €22.9 million, prompting the governments of Denmark, Ireland, Norway, Sweden, and the United Kingdom to suspend development aid. No one has been held accountable for the loss of US$44 million which disappeared in the lead-up to the 2007 Commonwealth meeting, despite multi-year donor efforts to recover the funds. Three ministers who were to face prosecution returned to office.

International bilateral donors continue to press the government to respect LGBT rights. United States Secretary of State Hillary Clinton presented the State Department's 2011 Human Rights Defenders Award to the Civil Society Coalition on Human Rights and Constitutional Law, for its efforts to defeat the Anti-Homosexuality Bill.

In contrast to donor pressure on LGBT rights, there has been minimal criticism of security force conduct. US reliance on the Ugandan military for regional counterterrorism operations may explain the diminished criticism of Uganda's deteriorating domestic human rights record. The army continues to receive logistical support and training from the US for counterterrorism, its leading role in the African Union Mission in Somalia (AMISOM), and counter-LRA operations in the Central African Republic (CAR). One hundred US military advisors are supporting anti-LRA efforts. Accused by United Nations experts of backing the M23 rebels in the DRC in October, Uganda claimed it could potentially suspend its involvement in Somalia and LRA operations.

Zimbabwe

Human rights developments in Zimbabwe in 2012 were dominated by the drafting of a new constitution and the implementation of the Global Political Agreement (GPA), signed in 2008, which created the power-sharing coalition between the former ruling party, the Zimbabwe African National Union-Patriotic Front (ZANU-PF), and the opposition party Movement for Democratic Change (MDC) following the 2008 elections. There has been little progress in implementing key aspects of the GPA, notably the need for institutional and legal reforms, ending political violence, and ensuring accountability for past human rights abuses.

The Global Political Agreement and the Constitution

More than four years after ZANU-PF and the MDC signed the GPA, few of the reforms outlined in the agreement have been fully implemented. Reforms needed to improve the human rights environment and to create conditions for democratic elections include: a parliament-led process to write a new constitution; police training; prioritizing a legislative agenda to enshrine the agreement's provisions; renouncing the use of violence; and ensuring that the government fully and impartially enforces domestic laws in bringing all perpetrators of politically motivated violence to justice. The GPA also guarantees free political activity whereby all political parties are able to propagate their views and canvass for support, free of harassment and intimidation, and calls for respect for the rule of law. It also commits the unity government to ensure the full implementation and realization of the rights to freedom of association and assembly, and the promotion of freedom of expression and communication.

After 36 months of discussions, the Constitutional Select Committee of Parliament produced a final draft of the constitution on July 18, 2012. ZANU-PF and the MDC engaged in long debates over key provisions. The MDC endorsed the final draft, but ZANU-PF called for further amendments, including questioning limits to presidential powers and references to devolution. After some pressure from the regional body, the Southern African Development Community (SADC), ZANU-PF backed down and a stakeholder's conference to discuss the constitution was held from October 21 to October 23. A date for a referendum on the new constitution has yet to be set and elections must be held by June 2013, as prescribed by the GPA.

While legislation to establish an independent and credible human rights commission and electoral commission has been passed, there are significant concerns with the two commissions. The law establishing the human rights commission states that it can only investigate alleged human rights abuses since the formation of the power-sharing government in February 2009. This prevents the commission from investigating other serious crimes, including election-related violence in 2002, 2005 and 2008; the massacre of an estimated 20,000 people in Matabeleland North and South in the 1980s, as well as the government-led mass demolitions of homes and business structures, and evictions of several thousand people from their homes in 2005.

Concerns persist over the composition of the Zimbabwe Electoral Commission, many of whose members are regarded as highly partisan supporters of ZANU-PF.

Freedom of Expression, Association, and Assembly

The power-sharing government has either failed to amend or come to agreement on amending repressive laws such as the Access to Information and Protection of Privacy Act (AIPPA), the Public Order and Security Act (POSA), and the Criminal Law (Codification and Reform) Act, which severely curtail basic rights through vague defamation clauses and draconian penalties. The failure to amend or repeal these laws, and to develop mechanisms to address the partisan conduct of the police, limits the rights to freedom of association and assembly ahead of and during the coming elections.

Provisions in AIPPA and POSA that provide criminal penalties for defamation, undermining the authority of, or insulting the president, have routinely been used against journalists and human rights defenders. ZANU-PF has repeatedly blocked attempts by the MDC to amend POSA and bring it in line with commitments in the GPA. Police often deliberately interpret provisions of POSA to ban lawful public meetings and gatherings. Prosecutors have often used section 121 of the Criminal Procedure and Evidence Act against opposition and civil society activists to overturn judicial rulings granting bail and extend detention by seven days.

Activists continue to be wrongly prosecuted and charged under these laws. On March 19, 2012, six civil society activists, arrested in 2011 for watching a video of Arab Spring protests, were convicted under section 188 of the Criminal Law (Codification and Reform Act) of conspiracy to commit violence. On March 21, a Harare magistrate gave the activists two-year suspended sentences, US$500 fines, and 420 hours of community service. Lawyers representing the activists appealed the verdict at the Harare High Court, and called for an investigation into allegations by the activists that police and security agents tortured them in efforts to extract confessions that they were planning an uprising against the government.

On September 12, 2012, the minister of media, information and publicity, Webster Shamu, threatened to use the AIPPA to revoke the operating licenses of media organizations, accusing them of abusing their media freedoms by denouncing the country and its leadership.

In February 2012, the ZANU-PF governor of Mazvingo province threatened to deregister 29 nongovernmental organizations involved in providing various social services—including providing food, clothing, and assisting people with disabilities—for failing to register with his office. Although he had no legal authority to deregister NGOs, fears that such threats might spread to other provinces became a reality when on August 23, a similar threat was issued against the director of Gays and Lesbians of Zimbabwe (GALZ) for operating an "unregistered" organization, after he and other GALZ members were arrested.

Human Rights Defenders

Attacks on human rights defenders continued in 2012. Police repeatedly arrested members of Women of Zimbabwe Arise (WOZA) as they conducted peaceful protests related to human rights and the economic situation.

Police also regularly harassed the director of the Zimbabwe Human Rights NGO Forum, Abel Chikomo. He was arrested and released on bail in 2011 after police accused him of running an unregistered organization. Chikomo was required to report to the Harare police station on numerous occasions throughout the year and was eventually summoned to stand trial on July 3, 2012. The state withdrew the summons on July 25, but reiterated its intentions to serve fresh summons at a future date. In the meantime, police have continued to harass Chikomo by repeatedly visiting the offices of the NGO Forum.

Sexual Orientation and Gender Identity

The government intensified its attacks against lesbian, gay, bisexual, and transgender (LGBT) rights activists despite statements by Prime Minister Morgan Tsvangirai that LGBT rights should be enshrined in the new constitution.

On August 20, 2012, police occupied the Harare offices of GALZ for six hours. They confiscated documents, advocacy materials, and computers. Earlier on August 11, police raided the group's offices without a warrant after the group issued its 2011 LGBTI Rights Violations Report and a briefing on the draft constitution. During the raid, police briefly detained 44 GALZ members, punching and slapping them, and assaulting them with batons. Police took the names of all 44 members before releasing them without charge. The following week, police went to some of the members' homes and took them to police headquarters for further questioning.

In July 2012, police summoned the director of GALZ and informed him that they would prosecute him for continuing to display in GALZ's offices a letter from the mayor of San Francisco criticizing President Robert Mugabe for being homophobic.

Key International Actors

Led by the South African government, SADC continued to mediate efforts to ensure the implementation of the GPA and a road map towards free, fair, and peaceful elections in Zimbabwe. At an annual summit on August 18, 2012, SADC leaders urged the power-sharing government to create conditions for free and fair elections, and called for the implementation of reforms under the GPA.

Human rights activists and other critics have considered these statements to be inadequate and have questioned SADC's ability to robustly address the slow pace of human rights reforms and ZANU-PF's blocking of the rigorous implementation of the GPA.

In February 2012, the European Union renewed restrictions on development assistance to Zimbabwe for six months instead of one year, as it had done in the past. The EU eased restrictions against ZANU-PF members and party allies by removing 51 people and 20 companies from its sanctions list. Some human rights activists expressed concerns that some of those removed from the list had links to illicit diamond mining in Marange and should not have been taken off it.

On July 23, 2012, in response to what it considered encouraging progress in implementing the GPA, the EU announced an immediate suspension of restrictions on development assistance and pledged that it would suspend the rest of its restrictive measures if a credible and peaceful referendum was held on a new constitution. This came after the UN high commissioner for human rights, Navi Pillay, called for the suspension of sanctions in a visit to Zimbabwe in May.

Australia also took similar steps in 2012 to remove people and entities from its list of restrictive measures.

The United States government was appropriately more cautious in lifting its own restrictive measures against ZANU-PF. It held its position to continue such measures until "substantial and irreversible progress" has been made towards implementation of the GPA.

Tightening the Grip

Concentration and Abuse of Power in Chávez's Venezuela

WORLD REPORT
2013

AMERICAS

Argentina

Argentina continues to make significant progress in prosecuting military and police personnel for enforced disappearances, killings, and torture during the country's "Dirty War" between 1976 and 1983, although trials have been subject to delays.

Comprehensive legislation was adopted in 2009 to regulate broadcast media, but a 2010 court injunction obtained by Argentina's largest media company suspended the implementation of provisions in the law that limit the ownership of radio and television outlets. In November 2012, the director of the regulatory body responsible for the law's implementation indicated that a major media company would lose some of its media licenses in December, when the court injunction was set to expire.

In recent years, the Supreme Court has defended the right of pre-trial detainees to be held in adequate conditions, the right of critical print media not to face discrimination in allocating official advertising because of their editorial position, and, in 2012, the right to legal abortions.

Significant ongoing human rights concerns in 2012 include poor prison conditions, torture, and arbitrary restrictions on reproductive rights.

Confronting Past Abuses

Several important human rights cases from Argentina's last military dictatorship (1976-1983) were reopened in 2003 after Congress annulled the 1986 "Full Stop" law, which had stopped prosecution of such cases, and the 1987 "Due Obedience" law, which granted immunity to all members of the military, except those in positions of command. In 2005, the Supreme Court upheld the unconstitutionality of the amnesty laws, originally decided by a judge in 2001 in a case brought by the Center for Legal and Social Studies (CELS)and Abuelas de Plaza de Mayo. Starting in 2005, federal judges struck down pardons that then-President Carlos Menem issued between 1989 and 1990 to former officials convicted of, or facing trial for, human rights violations.

As of August 2012, the number of persons accused of crimes against humanity had increased to 1,926, from 922 in 2007, according to CELS. There were 799 people facing charges for these crimes, and 262 who had been convicted and sentenced.

Trials have been subject to delays at the appellate level, with appeals normally taking more than two years to be heard after the sentence of the trial court. As of August 2012, the Supreme Court had confirmed final sentences in only eight of the cases reactivated after the annulment of the Full Stop and Due Obedience laws.

In July 2012, a federal court sentenced Jorge Videla, de facto president from 1976 to 1981, to 50 years in prison for implementing a plan to steal babies from women who gave birth while they were being held in torture centers before they were killed, and to hand them over to military families for adoption. More than 400 babies are estimated to have been affected. Other officers, including the head of the last military junta, Reynaldo Bignone (1982-1983), also received prison sentences. The court concluded that the theft of babies was a "systematic and generalized practice." Videla had been convicted in 1985 for crimes against humanity and was already serving a life sentence.

The "mega-trial" of state agents responsible for crimes committed at the Navy Mechanics School (ESMA) continued in 2012. In October 2011, a federal court sentenced 12 of the perpetrators to life imprisonment for the illegal arrest, torture, and murder of detainees held at the center. A second trial commenced in November 2012, in which 67 state agents faced similar charges. Seven of them were being tried for their alleged participation in "flights of death," in which prisoners held at ESMA were drugged and dropped from planes into the Atlantic.

The security of witnesses in human rights trials is a concern. After Jorge Julio López, a former torture victim, disappeared from his home in September 2006—a day before he was due to attend one of the final days of a trial—the government implemented measures to protect witnesses. The fate or whereabouts of López have still not been clarified.

Freedom of Expression

A law to regulate the broadcast media, which Congress approved in 2009, aims to promote diversity of views by limiting the ability of corporations to own large portions of the broadcasting frequency spectrum. The law contains vague definitions of what "faults" could lead to sanctions, including the revocation of broadcasting licenses. The Federal Authority for Audiovisual Communication Services (AFCSA), the regulatory body responsible for implementing and enforcing the law, issued repeated decisions in 2011 and 2012 against Cablevision, the cable TV division of the Clarín Group—Argentina's largest media corporation and a prominent government critic—for failing to reorganize its channels according to AFCSA regulations.

In October 2010, the Supreme Court upheld an injunction in favor of Clarín and suspended application of an article of the law that would oblige the company to sell within a year its outlets that exceed the new legal limits. In May 2012, the court ruled that the suspension would finally be lifted on December 7, 2012, even though a lower court was still considering the law's constitutionality. AFCSA's director, Martín Sabbatella, stated in November that only one media group had not agreed to present proposals to restructure its holdings before the December 7 deadline—a clear reference to Clarín— and that AFCSA would begin procedures for reassigning its excess licenses if it failed to do so.

In March 2011, the Supreme Court unanimously upheld an administrative court ruling in favor of Perfil publications, which had filed for an injunction against the government of President Néstor Kirchner for refusing to allocate official advertising to *Noticias* and *Fortuna* magazines, and to the *Perfil* newspaper, because of their critical editorial positions. The current administration of President Cristina Fernández has failed to comply with the court's ruling that it must provide advertising to Perfil's publications in "reasonable balance" with that provided to similar outlets without reference to their editorial positions. In August 2012, an administrative appeals court ordered the government to comply with the Supreme Court ruling within 15 days. Following a successful government appeal against this order, the Supreme Court was expected to give a final decision on the case.

Argentina does not have a national law ensuring public access to information held by state bodies. A bill to this effect has been stalled in the Chamber of Deputies since it received Senate approval in September 2010.

Prison Conditions

Overcrowding, inadequate physical conditions, and inmate violence continue to be serious problems in prisons. In the province of Buenos Aires, inmates continue to be confined in police lock ups not designed or equipped to hold detainees for long periods, although their number has declined significantly since 2010 when the provincial authorities began relocating detainees after expressions of concern by national and international human rights bodies. Detention cells in 138 police stations in the province were closed in 2011 and detainees transferred to the already-overcrowded Buenos Aires prison system, according to CELS. According to the Committee against Torture of the Provincial Commission for Memory, 127 prisoners in Buenos Aires prisons died in attacks by other inmates, suicides, and accidents in 2011, the last year for which figures were available.

Torture and ill-treatment by prison guards are common problems. In its 2011 annual report, the National Register of Torture and Ill-Treatment reported 584 cases of physical violence by prison guards. The group is a monitoring organization set up by the National Penitentiary Procurator (*ProcuraciónPenitenciaria de la Nación*), an official body created by the legislature.

Counterterrorism Legislation

In December 2011, Congress approved additions to Argentina's criminal code that double the penalties for crimes committed with the aim of "terrorizing the population," or of obliging the authorities to take an action or refrain from doing so. The broadness of this language—and its applicability to any crime in the criminal code— raises concerns about possible misuse of the law against those responsible for actions that fall short of terrorism, such as violence during public protests.

Transnational Justice

At this writing, no one had been convicted for the 1994 bombing of the Jewish Argentine Mutual Association (AMIA) in Buenos Aires in which 85 people died and over 300 were injured. Judicial corruption and political cover-ups hindered criminal investigations and prosecutions from the outset. Iran, which is suspected of ordering the attack, has refused Argentina's requests for the extradition of former Iranian President Ali Akbar Hashemi-Rafsanjani and six Iranian officials. In September 2012, in a joint statement following a meeting at the United Nations, the Argentine and Iranian foreign ministers said they would continue to search for "a legal mechanism that is not in contradiction with the legal systems of Argentina and Iran" until a "mutually agreed" solution was found.

Reproductive Rights

Abortion is illegal in Argentina, with limited exceptions, and women and girls face numerous obstacles to reproductive health products and services, such as contraception, voluntary sterilization procedures, and abortion after rape (one of the circumstances in which abortion is permitted). As a result of these barriers, women and girls may face unwanted or unhealthy pregnancies.

In a landmark ruling in March 2012, the Supreme Court determined that prior judicial authorization was unnecessary for abortion after rape. The court urged provincial governments to adopt protocols to ensure access to legal abortions. As of September, 10 out of Argentina's 23 provinces had taken steps to do so, and 5 had announced that they were in the process of doing so.

Also in September, the legislature for the city of Buenos Aires legislature passed a law implementing the ruling in its jurisdiction. However, the city's governor, Mauricio Macri, vetoed the law, claiming that it went beyond what the court required. The local ministry of health's protocols implementing the court's ruling—which contained requirements that could serve as obstacles for access to legal abortion—remained in effect. In October, after anti-choice groups won a court order that would have prevented the victim of a sex trafficking ring from obtaining an abortion, the Supreme Court intervened to allow the abortion to be performed.

Sexual Orientation and Gender Identity

In May 2012, a law entered force establishing the right of individuals over the age of 18 to choose their gender identity and their right to undergo sex-change operations and hormonal treatment without need for administrative or legal authorization.

Key International Actors

In his report on his November 2011 visit to Argentina, the UN special rapporteur on the rights of indigenous peoples, James Anaya, expressed concern at the large number of evictions of indigenous communities due to "the grave situation of legal uncertainty over indigenous land." The special rapporteur also observedthat those who resist eviction or protest against it may be subject to a "disproportionate use of force by police" and criminal prosecution.

At the Organization of American States (OAS) General Assembly in June 2012, Argentina's foreign minister publicly questionedthe role of the Inter-American Commission on Human Rights (IACHR), suggesting that it should not be critical of the region's "democracies" today in the same way it had been critical of "dictatorships" in the past.

Bolivia

Judicial investigations and adjudication of human rights cases are subject to long delays that continued to hinder accountability in 2012. The fate of scores who "disappeared" before democracy was reestablished in 1982 has still not been clarified, and most perpetrators of disappearances and extrajudicial executions have escaped justice. The insistence of military courts on trying military accused of abuses has continued to obstruct justice in the case of an army recruit killed in suspicious circumstances during a training exercise in 2011.

In 2012, government officials used legislation that prohibits the expression of racist ideas in the media to seek criminal charges against private media and journalists because of reporting to which they objected.

Accountability for Abuses

Long delays in the conduct of trials continue to obstruct justice for human rights violations under earlier governments. The only notable advance in recent years was the sentencing in August 2011 of five generals to 10 to 15 years imprisonment each for killing at least 60 people during anti-government protests in September and October 2003, when the army used lethal force to quell violent demonstrations in the highland city of El Alto. Two members of former President Gonzalo Sánchez de Lozada's cabinet received three-year suspended sentences for their part in the events, often referred to as "Black October."

The armed forces have failed to turn over files that might clarify the fate or whereabouts of people who were killed or "disappeared" before democracy was restored in 1982. In July 2012, in response to protestors who were demanding that files from the government of Luis García Meza (1980-1981) be declassified, Vice President Alvaro García stated that only one filing cabinet had been found and the rest had been stolen "years ago."

In April 2012, Congress approved a law reducing the compensation to be paid to victims of political violence and their relatives that had been provided for under legislation dating from 2004. Many alleged that they were denied access to compensation because they had to produce documentary evidence to support their claims, such as medical proof of torture, death certificates, and other documents.

Trials of opposition leaders, local government officials, and others accused of killings during violent clashes between supporters and opponents of President Evo Morales in 2008 have been subject to long delays. For example, as of September 2012, a La Paz court was still hearing evidence against eight defendants in connection with a September 2008 massacre in Porvenir, Pando department, in which 13 people were killed. The proceedings were subject to numerous suspensions.

The former prefect of Pando department, Leopoldo Fernández, who was indicted in October 2009 on charges of homicide, terrorism, and conspiracy in the Porvenir case, had been held in pre-trial detention for four years in a maximum security prison, a year more than the maximum that Bolivian law allows. Justice officials, witnesses, and victims in the case have reported receiving threats or "undue pressures," according to the United Nations Office of the High Commissioner for Human Rights (OHCHR).

Military Jurisdiction

The military justice system's assertion of jurisdiction over human rights abuses committed by armed forces members has been an obstacle to accountability for many years. Such courts lack essential guarantees of independence and impartiality, and their continuing jurisdiction in such cases is inconsistent with rulings of the Inter-American Court of Human Rights (IACtHR). Competition between civilian and military courts creates additional delays in judicial investigations.

There has been little progress in the investigation of the death in February 2011 of a 26-year-old conscript, Gróver Poma, following a hand-to-hand combat training exercise—allegedly after instructors beat him on the head and chest. The military disregarded the ombudsman's requests to hand the case to a civilian court, as well as a Senate resolution recommending it to do so.

In April 2012, an official from the human rights ombudsman's office alleged that the military had not cooperated in detaining three suspects who were fugitives from justice. The civilian court submitted the jurisdictional dispute to the

Constitutional Court, which by November had not issued a ruling. In another case involving the torture of a military recruit in September 2009, the army turned the suspects over to a civilian court only at President Morales' insistence.

Freedom of Expression

Under a law against racism and other forms of discrimination passed in October 2010 (Law 045), media that "endorse or publish racist or discriminatory ideas" can be fined and have their broadcasting licenses suspended. Journalists "spreading ideas based on racial superiority or hatred" could face up to five years in prison.

In August 2012, the government filed a criminal complaint under the anti-racism law against the Fides News Agency (ANF) and the *Página Siete* and *El Diario* newspapers, objecting to their coverage of a speech by Morales about food shortages. Morales had remarked that in the east—the lowland part of Bolivia that enjoys a warm climate favorable to agriculture—only "laziness" could explain people going hungry.

His remarks provoked an angry reaction from authorities in the eastern city of Santa Cruz, traditionally opponents of the Morales administration. The government accused the three media outlets of disseminating and inciting racism by asserting in their headlines that Morales had accused people from eastern Bolivia of being lazy. As of November, a prosecutor continued to investigate the charge, which could carry a penalty of up to four years' imprisonment.

In July 2012, the mayor of Oruro, a highland city that hosts a popular religious carnival, filed a criminal complaint of inciting racism against TV presenter Milena Fernández for calling the city "fetid" in a program on tourism for the Red PAT television network. Fernández was criticizing the sanitary facilities of the city, which receives thousands of visitors every year. Although she publicly apologized, a prosecutor was still investigating the complaint against her in November.

In October 2012, the Constitutional Tribunal declared that Bolivia's *desacato* provisions—under which insulting state officials is a criminal offense punishable by up to three years imprisonment—violated freedom of expression guarantees in the constitution. The court's president stated that the ruling was binding and that legislation to eliminate the provisions from the criminal code was therefore unnecessary. Several public figures were facing *desacato* charges at the time for insulting officials.

Key International Actors

Following a visit to Bolivia in September 2012, the UN special rapporteur on racism, Mutuma Ruteere, commended Bolivia's achievements in passing legislation and creating institutions for combating racism. However, he noted that the judiciary should determine whether the application of the anti-racism law conflicts with Bolivia's obligation to protect freedom of expression and opinion.

In September 2012, the United States government rejected a Bolivian request to extradite former President Gonzalo Sánchez de Lozada and two ministers of his administration to face trial on charges including genocide, homicide, and torture, for their alleged responsibility for the deaths and injuries during "Black October."

Brazil

Brazil is among the most influential democracies in regional and global affairs, yet it continues to confront very serious human rights challenges at home. Faced with high levels of violent crime, some Brazilian police units engage in abusive practices with impunity, instead of pursuing sound policing practices. Justice officials who seek to hold police officers accountable for unlawful practices face threats of violence.

Detention centers in various states are severely overcrowded, lengthy pre-trial detention is common, and torture continues to be a serious problem. Forced labor persists in some states despite federal efforts to eradicate it.

In 2012, Brazil took significant steps toward addressing grave human rights abuses that were committed during the country's military dictatorship (1964-1985). In May, a national truth commission began investigating abuse cases from that era, and in August, a federal judge ordered the first criminal trials of former state agents for their alleged roles in enforced disappearances committed in 1973 and 1974.

Public Security and Police Conduct

Widespread violence perpetrated by criminal gangs and abusive police plague many Brazilian cities. In Rio de Janeiro, for example, drug gangs routinely engage in violent crime and militias composed of police, jail guards, firefighters, and others have been implicated in far-reaching extortion schemes.

According to official data, police were responsible for 214 killings in the state of Rio de Janeiro and 251 killings in the state of São Paulo in the first 6 months of 2012. Police routinely claim these are "resistance" killings that occur in confrontations with criminals. While many police killings undoubtedly result from legitimate use of force by police officers, others do not, a fact documented by Human Rights Watch and other groups and recognized by Brazilian criminal justice officials.

In 2012, the state of Rio de Janeiro continued to award financial compensation for meeting crime reduction targets, including police homicides, as part of the System of Goals and Results Tracking, which was established in 2009. In April, more than US$20 million were distributed among 9,000 police officers. In addition, as of October, 28 Pacifying Police Units (UPP) had been installed in Rio since 2008 in order to establish a more effective police presence at the community level. However, the state has not yet taken adequate steps to ensure that police who commit abuses are held accountable.

Judges and magistrates who take on cases of violence by illegal militia and government corruption face threats of violence. On August 23, 2012, human rights defender Diego Luiz Berbare Bandeira was gunned down outside his home in the state of São Paulo, apparently in retaliation for exposing abuses and corrupt practices by police officers and prison authorities in Caraguatatuba.

President Dilma Rousseff signed a law in July 2012 to allow criminal cases involving organized crime to be adjudicated by panels of three judges. In September, the president signed a law increasing prison sentences for paramilitary and militia activities.

Detention Conditions, Torture, and Ill-Treatment of Detainees

Many Brazilian prisons and jails are violent and severely overcrowded. According to the Ministry of Justice's Integrated System of Penitentiary Information (InfoPen), Brazil's incarceration rate increased approximately 40 percent over the last five years and the prison population now exceeds half a million people—two-thirds more than the prisons were built for. Delays within the justice system contribute to the overcrowding: nearly 175,000 inmates are in pre-trial detention. For example, the Unidade de Internação do Plano Piloto juvenile detention center in Brasilia operated at more than double its capacity in 2012. Three children were killed there in August and September, reportedly by gang members.

Inhumane prison conditions facilitate the spread of disease, and prisoners' access to medical care remains inadequate. In April 2012, nearly 500 detainees at the Complexo Penitenciário Advogado Antônio Jacinto Filho in the state of

Sergipe rioted in protest against alleged beatings by prison guards and inadequate food.

Torture is a chronic problem throughout Brazil's detention centers and police stations. The United Nations Subcommittee on Prevention of Torture and other Cruel, Inhuman or Degrading Treatment visited penitentiary and police institutions in the states of São Paulo, Rio de Janeiro, Espírito Santo, and Goiás in September 2011 and reported receiving "repeated and consistent" accounts from inmates of beatings and other allegations of ill-treatment during police custody such as the obligation to sleep in unsanitary cells without proper access to water and food.

At this writing, the Chamber of Deputies had yet to vote on legislation proposed by President Rousseff in September 2011 to create a national mechanism—the National System to Prevent and Combat Torture—to monitor detention centers throughout the country and investigate allegations of torture and ill-treatment.

Reproductive Rights and Gender-Based Violence

Although Brazil has significantly lowered its maternal mortality rate over the last two decades, national statistics mask severe disparities based on race, economic status, region, and urban or rural settings.

In February 2012, the Supreme Court upheld the constitutionality of Federal Law 11340 on domestic violence (the Maria da Penha law) and ruled that prosecutors may bring domestic violence cases regardless of whether the victim presses charges or not.

Brazil's criminal code criminalizes abortion except in cases of rape or when necessary to save a woman's life. Women and girls who obtain an abortion outside of these two exceptions face sentences of up to three years in jail, while people who perform abortions face up to four years. In March 2012, federal police in the states of Mato Grosso and Goiás arrested a doctor and 10 pharmacy workers for allegedly providing illegal abortions or selling abortion-inducing drugs.

On April 12, the Supreme Court ruled that abortion is also constitutional in cases of anencephaly, in which the fetus has a fatal congenital brain disorder, given the woman's right to dignity, autonomy, privacy, and physical, psychological, and moral integrity.

Sexual Orientation and Gender Identity

In May 2012, the Senate Human Rights Committee approved a bill providing for civil unions between two persons, without specifying gender, and the conversion of civil unions to civil marriages. This follows the 2011 rulings by the Supreme Court and the Superior Justice Court that recognize equal rights for same-sex unions and that same-sex marriage is permitted under the civil code.

Forced Labor

The federal government has taken important steps to eradicate forced labor since 1995, and official data suggests that more than 41,000 workers have been freed from slave-like conditions since then. However, the Pastoral Land Commission reported that nearly 4,000 workers were subject to forced labor in 2011. Criminal accountability for offending employers remains relatively rare.

Congress approved a constitutional amendment in May 2012 that permits the government to confiscate properties where forced labor is used without providing compensation.

Rural Violence

Indigenous leaders and rural activists continue to face threats and violence. According to the Pastoral Land Commission, 29 people involved in land conflicts were killed and 38 were victims of attempted murder throughout the country in 2011, and the number of rural conflicts nationwide rose to 1,363 that year. More than 2,000 rural activists have received death threats over the past decade.

Confronting Past Abuses

In May 2012, a truth commission, charged with "examining and clarifying" human rights abuses committed between 1946 and 1988, began its work. The commission announced in September that it will only investigate grave human rights violations committed by or on behalf of state agents.

Prosecutors in São Paulo state filed criminal charges against a retired army colonel and a civil police precinct chief in April 2012 for grave abuses committed in the 1970s. This was the second case in Brazil in which criminal charges have been brought against a Brazilian official for human rights crimes committed during the country's military dictatorship. A 1979 amnesty law has thus far been interpreted to bar most prosecutions of state agents, an interpretation that the Supreme Court reaffirmed in April 2010.

Brazil has granted more than US$1 billion in financial compensation to more than 12,000 victims of abuses committed by state agents during the military dictatorship.

Freedom of Expression and Access to Information

At least seven journalists were killed in Brazil in 2012 and many more were threatened and assaulted. In May 2012, the Ministry of Human Rights proposed creating an observatory to monitor violence against journalists.

An access to information law went into effect in May 2012, expanding access to documents under the custody of local, state, and federal government officials. The law ensures that information regarding violations of fundamental rights shall not be subject to access restrictions.

In September, a state court in São Paulo ordered Youtube to remove the movie "Innocence of Muslims" from its website in a lawsuit brought by the National Union of Islamic Entities against Google Brasil Internet Ltda.

Key International Actors

The Inter-American system has played an important role in addressing key human rights issues in Brazil. In November 2010, the Inter-American Court of Human Rights (IACrtHR) ruled that the country's amnesty law cannot prevent the investigation and prosecution of serious human rights violations and crimes against humanity committed by state agents during the military regime. In

February and September 2011 resolutions, the court also instructed the state of Espírito Santo to take steps to address alleged abuses against juveniles detained at the Unidade de Internação Socioeducativa (UNIS) detention center.

In April 2011, the Inter-American Commission on Human Rights (IACHR) issued precautionary measures for Brazil due to an alleged failure to consult with indigenous groups prior to beginning the construction of the Belo Monte hydro-electric dam, slated to be the world's third largest. The Rousseff administration publicly rejected the commission's findings and characterized them as "premature and unjustified." It also recalled its ambassador to the Organization of American States (OAS) and withdrew its candidate for the Inter-American Commission. It has since supported efforts to weaken the Inter-American system of human rights—most recently at the OAS annual assembly in June 2012—including a proposed reform that would reduce the commission's power to issue precautionary measures.

In August 2012, a federal district court in Brasília halted construction of the Belo Monte dam on the grounds that Brazil's congress had failed to consult local indigenous communities before construction. However, when this judgment was appealed to the Supreme Court, the chief justice authorized the work at Belo Monte to proceed. In September 2012, federal prosecutors requested that the chief justice reconsider his decision.

Brazil has emerged as an important and influential voice in debates over international responses to human rights issues at the UN. At the UN Human Rights Council (HRC) from July 2010 to June 2011, Brazil consistently voted in support of resolutions addressing country situations, including on Sudan, North Korea, Iran, Belarus, and Syria. Brazil will again be a member of the council in 2013.

At the UN General Assembly, Brazil voted in favor of two resolutions condemning state-sponsored violence in Syria in February and August 2012. During a Universal Periodic Review (UPR) at the HRC in September 2012, Brazil accepted most of the country recommendations regarding torture, detention conditions, and public security.

The UN special rapporteur on adequate housing expressed concern in April 2011 regarding allegations of displacement and evictions potentially leading to human rights violations as Brazil prepares to host the 2014 World Cup and 2016 Olympic Games.

In February 2012, the UN Committee on the Elimination of All Forms of Discrimination Against Women (CEDAW) acknowledged the country's efforts to implement measures for reducing the maternal mortality rate, but also expressed concern that the sole focus on care services for pregnant women may not sufficiently address all causes of maternal mortality in Brazil.

Chile

During 2011 and 2012, Sebastián Piñera's government faced student unrest and other protests that often ended in the destruction of property and violent clashes between police and demonstrators. Police abuses, including inappropriate use of anti-riot weapons and ill-treatment of detainees, were reported. The Piñera administration has ended the trial of civilians by military courts and amended elements of counterterrorism legislation that were incompatible with international standards of due process. However, military courts that lack independence from the military hierarchy still try police accused of human rights abuses. Although the government has not pressed terrorism charges against indigenous protesters, some prosecutors have continued to bring charges against them under the counterterrorism law for actions that should be considered common crimes.

Most recorded cases of extrajudicial executions and enforced disappearances committed during military rule (1973-1990) have been heard in court or are now under judicial investigation. Judges continue to convict former military personnel for these crimes. However, final sentences are often unacceptably lenient given the seriousness of the crimes.

The passage of a law protecting sexual minorities and other vulnerable groups from discrimination was a notable advance in 2012. Abortion continues to be prohibited in all circumstances, even when the mother's life is at risk.

Police Abuses

In 2011 and 2012, student marches and occupations demanding educational reforms sometimes ended in violent clashes in which police were injured and public and private property destroyed. A policeman was shot dead in September 2012 during disturbances on the anniversary of the 1973 military coup. *Carabineros* (uniformed police) sometimes used excessive force against protestors, including the misuse of non-lethal anti-riot weaponry such as tear gas and rubber bullets, arbitrary arrests, and the ill-treatment of detainees.

During February and March protests over regional economic and social demands in Aysen, southern Chile, local human rights monitors reported that police special anti-riot forces fired water-cannons and tear gas into homes, and shot tear gas cartridges directly at people. A 49-year-old mechanic, Teófilo Haro, was blinded by a steel pellet in the eye fired by a *Carabinero*, according to press reports. At a meeting of the Congressional Human Rights Commission, the head of *Carabineros* admitted the use of excessive force, and that metal shotgun pellets had been used incorrectly. The government spokesperson said in August 2012 that abuses by the police were "completely and categorically rejected, and immediately investigated."

At this writing, a police sergeant faced charges before a military court for unlawful use of lethal force in connection with the fatal shooting of 16-year-old student Manuel Gutiérrez Reynoso while he was watching a demonstration in August 2011 from a Santiago footbridge during a national strike.

Reports of police abuses against Mapuches during evictions of occupied land and attempts to arrest suspects in Mapuche communities continue. In July 2012, *Carabineros* fired rubber bullets at a group of Mapuches outside a hospital in Collipulli, in the southern region of Araucanía, where doctors were checking the injuries of people detained during a land eviction. According to an eyewitness, the shots were fired at short range, without provocation or warning, wounding seven people, including a 13-year-old girl and two 17-year-old boys.

Military Jurisdiction

Police accused of human rights abuses continue to be tried by military courts that are not independent. Following the recommendations of the Inter-American Court of Human Rights (IACrtHR) in its 2005 ruling against Chile in the Palamara case, legislation introduced by Piñera's administration and approved by Congress in September 2010 finally ended the jurisdiction of military courts over civilians.

However, the reforms did not address jurisdiction over abuses against civilians by *Carabineros*, which is still exercised by military courts composed of military officers on active service. Apart from their lack of independence, these courts do not provide the due process guarantees that have existed in ordinary criminal proceedings since their reform in 2005.

Investigations are secret, criminal proceedings are conducted mainly in writing, and lawyers representing victims of police abuse have limited opportunities to cross-examine witnesses. Decisions by the *Corte Marcial* (the military appeals court) in cases involving the alleged unlawful use of lethal force by *Carabineros* have not inspired confidence in the court's impartiality. At this writing, the government was preparing a bill to restructure the military justice system.

Counterterrorism Laws

The inappropriate use of counterterrorism legislation to deal with common crimes against property, such as arson, committed by indigenous Mapuche activists remains an important due process issue. In September 2010, following concern expressed by the United Nations and regional human rights bodies, the government amended the counterterrorism law. Some due process guarantees were strengthened, such as allowing witnesses whose identity can be concealed to be cross-examined by defense attorneys, and children could no longer be tried under the law. However, the inclusion in the law of crimes against property was left unchanged and prosecutors continue to apply the law in such cases, even though the government has refrained from doing so.

Confronting Past Abuses

More than three-quarters of the 3,186 documented killings and "disappearances" during the Augusto Pinochet dictatorship (1973-1990) have been heard by courts or are now under court jurisdiction, according to Diego Portales University's Human Rights Observatory, a nongovernmental organization that monitors progress in human rights trials.

Between 2000 and September 2011, more than 800 former state security agents had been indicted or convicted, and as of August 2012, 64 agents were serving prison sentences. In many cases, the Supreme Court has used its discretionary powers to reduce sentences against human rights violators in recognition of the time elapsed since the criminal act. Others had their sentences commuted.

These practices raise concerns about Chile's fulfillment of its obligation to hold accountable perpetrators of crimes against humanity by imposing appropriate punishments or sanctions.

Prison Conditions

Overcrowding and poor conditions in many prisons continue to be a problem. As of May 2012, the official capacity of the prison system was 39,832, but there were 54,339 prisoners.

Following a fire in December 2010 in Santiago's San Miguel prison in which 81 prisoners died, the Ministry of Justice undertook important reforms both to improve conditions and reduce overcrowding. In June 2012 a law entered into force that allowed the release of low-risk inmates, including women with young children who were within six months of completing two-thirds of their sentence, and the voluntary return of non-Chilean inmates to their countries of origin. Another law, promulgated the same month, provides six alternatives to prison for low risk offenders, including community service and the use of electronic bracelets.

Sexual Orientation and Gender Identity

In July 2012, President Piñera promulgated a law to provide legal protection for Chile's vulnerable minorities, including lesbian, gay, bisexual, and transgender (LGBT) individuals. The law explicitly includes sexual orientation and gender identity as prohibited grounds of discrimination. It also creates a special judicial process aimed at providing rapid redress to victims of discriminatory acts, which allows judges to halt or reverse them and provide protection for victims and toughens penalties. However, the law does not provide victims of discrimination with a mechanism for compensation.

Reproductive Rights

Chile in is one of only three countries in Latin America (the other two being El Salvador and Nicaragua) with an absolute prohibition on abortion, even prohibiting medical necessity as a defense. In April 2012, the Senate rejected three bills to legalize abortion in cases in which the mother's life was at risk or the fetus was unviable. Such an absolute prohibition violates a woman's fundamental right to the highest attainable standard of health, life, nondiscrimination, physical integrity, and freedom from cruel, inhuman, or degrading treatment.

Key International Actors

In February 2012, the IACrtHR found that Chile had violated the rights of Karen Atala, a lesbian, and her three children to equal treatment and to non-discrimination. Atala lost custody of her children when Chilean courts ruled that, due to her sexual orientation, her children would be at risk if she were to raise them with her female partner.

As reparations for the violation of Atala's rights, the court ordered Chile, inter alia, to invite the victims and the organizations that represented them in the case to a public event in which the state would recognize its responsibility. The court also ordered Chile to implement training programs for judges and other public officials to ensure respect for the rights of the LGBT population.

Colombia

Colombia's internal armed conflict continued to result in serious abuses by irregular armed groups in 2012, including guerrillas and successor groups to paramilitaries. More than 4 million Colombians have been internally displaced, and more than 100,000 continue to be displaced each year. Human rights defenders, community leaders, trade unionists, journalists, indigenous and Afro-Colombian leaders, and displaced persons' leaders face death threats and other abuses. The administration of President Juan Manuel Santos has publicly condemned threats and attacks against rights defenders.

Chronic lack of accountability for human rights abuses continued to be a serious problem. While justice authorities have made notable progress in some areas, impunity remains the norm, and there have been very limited results in holding accountable those with high-level responsibility for atrocities. Furthermore, constitutional amendments backed by the Santos administration concerning transitional justice and the military justice system threaten to dramatically reverse recent progress and secure impunity for egregious abuses by guerrillas, paramilitaries, and the military.

In 2012, Colombia began to implement the Victims and Land Restitution Law, which aims to return millions of acres of abandoned and stolen land to internally displaced persons (IDPs) who fled their homes over the past two decades. Implementation has advanced slowly, and there have been threats and attacks against individuals seeking land restitution, in some cases by paramilitary successor groups or others interested in maintaining control over the stolen land.

The Colombian government and Revolutionary Armed Forces of Colombia (FARC) guerrillas formally initiated peace talks in October 2012.The negotiations represent Colombia's first opportunity in over a decade to reach a settlement to end the nearly 50-year conflict.

Guerrillas

The FARC and the National Liberation Army (ELN) continue to commit serious abuses against civilians. The FARC in particular is often involved in killings, threats, forced displacement, and recruiting and using child soldiers. On August 12, 2012, presumed FARC members shot and killed Lisandro Tenorio, a leader of the Nasa indigenous community in Caloto, Cauca department, southwest Colombia.

The FARC and ELN frequently use antipersonnel landmines and other indiscriminate weapons. The government reported that landmines and unexploded munitions killed 25 civilians and injured 94 between January and June 2012.

In June 2012, the Santos administration secured passage of the Legal Framework for Peace constitutional amendment, which would regulate administration of justice in the context of peace agreements with guerrilla groups. The amendment contains several provisions that facilitate impunity for egregious abuses by guerrillas, paramilitaries, and the military. First, it empowers Congress to limit the scope of prosecutions of atrocities to individuals found "most responsible," and provide statutory immunity to the other guerrillas, paramilitaries, and military members who participated in planning, executing, and covering up the same crimes—but who are not deemed "most responsible." Second, it gives Congress authority to exempt entire cases of serious abuses from criminal investigation. Third, the reform enables Congress to fully suspend prison sentences or apply non-judicial punishments for all guerrillas, paramilitaries, and military personnel convicted of atrocities, including those found "most responsible" for Colombia's worst crimes.

Paramilitaries and Their Successors

Since 2003 more than 30,000 individuals have participated in a paramilitary demobilization process. However, there is substantial evidence that many participants were not paramilitaries, and that part of demobilized paramilitary organizations' membership remained active and reorganized into new groups. Successor groups to paramilitaries, largely led by members of demobilized paramilitary organizations, maintain a strong presence throughout Colombia. While authorities have made notable progress in capturing their leaders, public security force members have tolerated and colluded with paramilitary successor groups, contributing to their continued power.

Like the paramilitary organizations that demobilized, the groups commit widespread abuses against civilians, including massacres, killings, disappearances, sexual violence, recruiting children, threats, and forced displacement. They continue to threaten and attack social leaders, rights defenders, and victims of paramilitary groups seeking justice and land restitution. The government's Human Rights ombudsman's office reported receiving 1,500 complaints of possible international humanitarian law violations by paramilitary successor groups in 2011, more than half the total reported violations attributed to identified armed actors that year.

On November 7, 2012, alleged members of the Rastrojos paramilitary successor group opened fire and tossed a grenade at workers on a farm in Antioquia department, killing 10.

Implementation of the Justice and Peace Law, which offers dramatically reduced sentences to demobilized paramilitaries who confess their atrocities, has been slow and uneven. As of July 2012, seven years after the law was approved, special prosecutors had only obtained eight convictions.

Paramilitary Accomplices

In 2012, Colombia's Supreme Court continued to make progress investigating Congress members accused of collaborating with paramilitaries. Since the "parapolitics" scandal erupted in 2006, more than 150 former and current members of Congress have come under investigation, and approximately 55 have been convicted. The sudden decision by the criminal chamber of the Supreme Court to remove auxiliary magistrate Iván Velásquez from his position as coordinator of the investigations—and his subsequent resignation in September 2012—raised questions as to whether the cases will continue to advance significantly.

While demobilized paramilitaries have also made statements about extensive collaboration with local officials, senior military officers, and businesspersons, the attorney general's office's investigations into such individuals, who fall under their jurisdiction, have produced limited results. One important exception is the August 23, 2012 conviction and 25-year sentence handed down to former army General Rito Alejo del Río for a murder committed in 1997 during a joint army-paramilitary operation in Chocó department.

In 2011 and 2012, several former paramilitaries alleged that former President Álvaro Uribe (2002-2010) maintained links to paramilitary groups. Uribe has denied the allegations. On August 20, 2012, Uribe's security chief while he was president, retired police General Mauricio Santoyo, pleaded guilty in United States federal court to collaborating with paramilitaries between 2001 and 2008.

Military Abuses and Impunity

Over the past decade, the Colombian Army committed an alarming number of extrajudicial killings of civilians. In many cases—commonly referred to as "false positives"—army personnel murdered civilians and reported them as combatants killed in action, apparently in response to pressure to boost body counts.

The government does not keep statistics for cases of "false positives" as a separate category of crimes. However, as of August 2012, the Human Rights Unit of the attorney general's office was investigating 1,727 cases of alleged extrajudicial executions committed by state agents throughout the country involving nearly 3,000 victims. Most cases are attributed to the army and occurred between 2004 and 2008. There has been a dramatic reduction in cases of alleged extrajudicial killings attributed to the security forces since 2009; nevertheless, some cases were reported in 2011 and 2012.

Investigations into alleged extrajudicial killings continue to advance, but the vast majority of cases have not been resolved. As of August 2012, the Human Rights Unit of the attorney general's office had obtained convictions for less than 10 percent of the 1,727 cases under investigation. The successful prosecutions led to the convictions of 539 army members, of whom 77 were officers, including two lieutenant colonels and two colonels. The office of the prosecutor of the International Criminal Court (ICC) reported in November 2012 that the existing judicial proceedings in false positive cases "have largely failed to focus on the persons who might bear the greatest responsibility for the commission of these crimes."

Accountability achieved to date is due to the fact that civilian prosecutors are investigating most cases. However, the Santos administration is promoting a constitutional amendment that would result in military atrocities—including extrajudicial killings, torture, and rape—being investigated and tried by the military justice system. The amendment would likely also lead to the transfer of past cases of "false positives" from civilian prosecutors to the military justice system, which would virtually guarantee impunity for such crimes.

Violence against Trade Unionists

The number of trade unionists killed annually in recent years is less than a decade ago, but remains high: 47 trade unionists were murdered in 2009, 51 in 2010, 30 in 2011, and 12 from January to September 15, 2012, according to the National Labor School (ENS), Colombia's leading NGO monitoring labor rights. Threats against trade unionists are widespread: the ENS reported 539 such cases in 2011, and 255 between January and September 15, 2012.

No one has been held accountable for the vast majority of the more than 2,900 trade unionist killings that the ENS has reported since 1986. As of May 2012, the attorney general's office's sub-unit of prosecutors dedicated to anti-union violence had opened investigations into 815 cases of trade unionists killings, and in combination with other prosecutors from the Human Rights Unit, reported having obtained convictions for 263 cases. This progress is largely due to confessions by paramilitaries participating in the Justice and Peace process, and there have been severely limited results in prosecuting crimes committed since 2007, which are not covered by the demobilization law.

Internal Displacement and Land Restitution

More than 100,000 Colombians continue to be forcibly displaced annually, making them one of the world's largest populations of IDPs. Colombia's government registered 3.9 million IDPs between 1997 and December 2011, compared to 5.4 million that CODHES, a respected Colombian nongovernmental organization, reported between 1985 and December 2011. The government registered more than 140,000 newly displaced people in 2011, while CODHES reports that nearly 260,000 Colombians were displaced that year. Threats, forced recruitment, and killings were the top causes of forced displacement in 2011, according to government figures, which also show that nearly 25 percent of those displaced that year identified themselves as Afro-Colombian—a disproportionately high percentage compared to the government's latest estimate of the overall Afro-Colombian population.

At this writing, the Colombian government had progressed slowly in implementing its land restitution program under the 2011 Victims and Land Restitution Law. The government estimated that there would be 2,100 judicial rulings in land restitution cases under the Victims Law in 2012, and 60,000 rulings by 2014; however, as of mid-September 2012, less than 200 claims had been brought before specialized land restitution judges, and no land had been returned under the law. Abuses against displaced land claimants and their leaders in recent years—including threats, forced displacements, and killings—have created a climate of fear for those seeking restitution in several areas of the country, such as Urabá, Montes de María, and Cesar.

Gender-Based Violence and Displacement

Gender-based violence (GBV) is widespread in Colombia, but studies show that it may be higher for displaced women and girls. The government has laws, policies, and programs to address such violence, and the particular risk to displaced women and girls. However, lack of training and poor implementation of protocols create obstacles for women and girls seeking post-violence care. These include the failure of health facilities to properly implement relevant laws and policies—with the result that women and girls may not be adequately screened for signs of GBV, may be mistreated, may face delays in accessing essential services or be arbitrarily denied medical care altogether.

Barriers to justice for GBV victims include mistreatment by authorities, evidentiary challenges, and fear of retribution. Women and girl victims of this kind of violence are at times not informed about their legal rights, including where and how to access services. Perpetrators of GBV crimes are rarely brought to justice.

Human Rights Defenders

Human rights defenders are routinely threatened and attacked by perpetrators who are virtually never brought to justice. On February 28, a pamphlet allegedly signed by the "Águilas Negras-Bloque Capital" paramilitary successor group threatened two United Nations agencies and numerous human rights organizations, including several women's rights groups. Human Rights Watch documented several cases of rape of women human rights defenders in late 2011 and 2012.

The Ministry of Interior runs a protection program that covers more than 10,000 members of vulnerable groups, including human rights defenders and trade unionists. The program is unparalleled in the region, but its beneficiaries continue to report deficiencies in protection measures.

Key International Actors

The United States remains the most influential foreign actor in Colombia. In 2012, it provided approximately US$482 million in aid, about 58 percent of which went to the military and police. A portion of US military aid is subject to human rights conditions, which the US Department of State has not enforced. In August 2012, the State Department certified that Colombia was meeting human rights conditions. However, it noted that "[t]hreats and attacks against human rights defenders, land activists, trade unionists, journalists and other vulnerable groups continued to be a concern…. Armed Forces and civilian authorities could do more to investigate allegations of collusion with illegal armed groups, which persist."

The European Union provides social and economic assistance to Colombia. Norway and Cuba were named "guarantors" of the peace negotiations between the FARC and Colombian government, with Venezuela and Chile listed as "accompaniers" of the process.

The Organization of American States' Mission to Support the Peace Process in Colombia, charged with verifying paramilitary demobilizations, noted in its 2012 report that paramilitary successor groups' presence and illegal activities in certain regions "put at risk the return of people displaced by violence [to their homes]."

The office of the prosecutor of the ICC continued to monitor local investigations into crimes that may fall within the ICC's jurisdiction. The Office of the High Commissioner for Human Rights (OHCHR) is active in Colombia, and in November 2010 its mandate in the country was extended for three years. The International Committee of the Red Cross (ICRC) is also active in Colombia, where its work includes providing assistance to IDPs.

Cuba

Cuba remains the only country in Latin America that represses virtually all forms of political dissent. In 2012, the government of Raúl Castro continued to enforce political conformity using short-term detentions, beatings, public acts of repudiation, travel restrictions, and forced exile.

Although in 2010 and 2011 the Cuban government released dozens of political prisoners on the condition that they accept exile in exchange for their freedom, the government continues to sentence dissidents to one to four-year prison terms in closed, summary trials, and holds others for extended periods without charge. It has also relied increasingly upon arbitrary arrests and short-term detentions to restrict the basic rights of its critics, including the right to assemble and move freely.

Political Prisoners

Cubans who dare to criticize the government are subject to criminal prosecution. They do not benefit from due process guarantees, such as the right to fair and public hearings by a competent and impartial tribunal. In practice, courts are "subordinated" to the executive and legislative branches, thus denying meaningful judicial independence. Political prisoners are routinely denied parole after completing the minimum required sentence as punishment for refusing to participate in ideological activities such as "reeducation" classes.

The death of political prisoner Orlando Zapata Tamayo in 2010 after his 85-day hunger strike, and the subsequent hunger strike by dissident Guillermo Fariñas, pressured the government to release the political prisoners from the "group of 75" (75 dissidents who were sentenced to long prison terms in a 2003 crackdown). Yet most were forced to choose between ongoing prison sentences and forced exile, and dozens of other dissidents have been forced abroad to avoid imprisonment.

Dozens of political prisoners remain in Cuban prisons, according to human rights groups on the island. These groups estimate there are more political prisoners whose cases they cannot document because the government does not allow independent national or international human rights groups to access its prisons.

Rogelio Tavío López—a member the Unión Patriótica de Cuba dissident group— was detained in March 2012 in Guantanamo province after organizing a protest to demand the release of political prisoners. He has since been held in detention without being brought before a judge or granted access to a lawyer.

Arbitrary Detentions and Short-Term Imprisonment

In addition to criminal prosecutions, the Cuban government has increasingly relied on arbitrary detention to harass and intimidate individuals who exercise their fundamental rights. The Cuban Commission for Human Rights and National Reconciliation—an independent human rights group that the government views as illegal—received reports of 2,074 arbitrary detentions by state agents in 2010, 4,123 in 2011, and 5,105 from January to September 2012.

The detentions are often used preemptively to prevent individuals from participating in events viewed as critical of the government, such as peaceful marches or meetings to discuss politics. Many dissidents are subjected to beatings and threats as they are detained, even though they do not try to resist.

Security officers virtually never present arrest orders to justify the detentions and threaten detainees with criminal sentences if they continue to participate in "counterrevolutionary" activities. Victims of such arrests are held incommunicado for several hours to several days, often at police stations. In some cases, they are given an official warning, which prosecutors may later use in criminal trials to show a pattern of delinquent behavior. Dissidents said these warnings are aimed at discouraging them from participating in future activities seen as critical of the government.

In July, at least 40 people were arbitrarily detained in Havana at the funeral of dissident Oswaldo Payá, who died in a car accident. Police officers broke up the non-violent procession and beat participants. The detainees were taken to a prison encampment where they were held incommunicado for 30 hours before being released without charge.

Freedom of Expression

The government controls all media outlets in Cuba and tightly restricts access to outside information, which severely limits the right to freedom of expression. Only a tiny fraction of Cubans have the chance to read independently published articles and blogs because of the high cost of and limited access to the internet.

A small number of independent journalists and bloggers manage to write articles for foreign websites or independent blogs, yet those who use these outlets to criticize the government are subjected to public smear campaigns, arbitrary arrests, and abuse by security agents. The authorities often confiscate their cameras, recorders, and other equipment. According to the independent journalists' group Hablemos Press, authorities arbitrarily detained 19 journalists in September 2012, including Calixto Ramón Martínez Arias, who remained in prison without charge at this writing.

The Cuban government uses selective allocations of press credentials and visas, which are required by foreign journalists to report from the island, to control coverage of the island and punish media outlets seen as overly critical of the regime. For example, in anticipation of the March 2012 visit of Pope Benedict XVI to Cuba, the government denied visas to journalists from *El Pais* and *El Nuevo Herald*, newspapers whose reporting it has criticized as biased.

Human Rights Defenders

The Cuban government refuses to recognize human rights monitoring as a legitimate activity and denies legal status to local human rights groups. Meanwhile, government authorities harass, assault, and imprison human rights defenders who attempt to document abuses. In the weeks leading up to and during Pope Benedict XVI's visit to Cuba, authorities detained, beat, and threatened scores of human rights defenders.

Travel Restrictions and Family Separation

The Cuban government forbids the country's citizens from leaving or returning to Cuba without first obtaining official permission, which is often denied to those who criticize the government. For example, acclaimed blogger Yoani Sánchez, who has been critical of the government, has been denied the right to leave the island at least 19 times since 2008, including in February 2012 after the Brazilian government granted her a visa to attend a documentary screening.

The Cuban government uses forced family separation to punish defectors and silence critics. It frequently bars citizens engaged in authorized travel from taking their children with them overseas, essentially holding children hostage to guarantee their parents' return.

The government restricts the movement of citizens within Cuba by enforcing a 1997 law known as Decree 217. Designed to limit migration to Havana, the decree requires Cubans to obtain government permission before moving to the country's capital. It is often used to prevent dissidents traveling to Havana to attend meetings and to harass dissidents from other parts of Cuba who live in the capital.

Prison Conditions

Prisons are overcrowded, unhygienic, and unhealthy, leading to extensive malnutrition and illness. More than 57,000 Cubans are in prisons or work camps, according to a May 2012 article in an official government newspaper. Prisoners who criticize the government, or engage in hunger strikes and other forms of protest are often subjected to extended solitary confinement, beatings, restrictions on family visits, and denial of medical care. Prisoners have no effective complaint mechanism to seek redress, giving prison authorities total impunity.

In January 2012, Wilman Villar Mendoza, 31, died after a 50-day hunger strike in prison, which he initiated to protest his unjust trial and inhumane prison conditions. He had been detained in November 2011 after participating in a peaceful demonstration, and was sentenced to four years in prison for "contempt" in a summary trial in which he had no lawyer. After beginning his hunger strike, he was stripped naked and placed in solitary confinement in a cold cell. He was transferred to a hospital only days before he died.

Key International Actors

The United States' economic embargo on Cuba, in place for more than half a century, continues to impose indiscriminate hardship on the Cuban people, and has done nothing to improve human rights in Cuba. At the United Nations General Assembly in November, 188 of the 192 member countries voted for a resolution condemning the US embargo.

In 2009, President Barack Obama enacted reforms to eliminate limits on travel and remittances by Cuban Americans to Cuba, which had been put in place during the administration of President George W. Bush. In 2011, Obama used his executive powers to ease "people-to-people" travel restrictions, allowing religious, educational, and cultural groups from the US to travel to Cuba. However, in May 2012 the Obama administration established additional requirements to obtain "people to people" licenses, which has reduced the frequency of such trips.

The European Union continues to retain its "Common Position" on Cuba, adopted in 1996, which conditions full economic cooperation with Cuba on the country's transition to a pluralist democracy and respect for human rights.

In June, the UN Committee Against Torture (CAT) issued a report on Cuba in which it expressed concern about reports of inhumane prison conditions and the use of ambiguous preventive detention measures such as "social dangerousness," among other issues for which it said the Cuban government failed to provide key information.

Ecuador

President Rafael Correa has undercut freedom of the press in Ecuador by subjecting journalists and media figures to public denunciation and retaliatory litigation. Judicial independence continued to suffer in 2012 due to transitional mechanisms for judicial reform that have given the government and its supporters in Congress a powerful say in appointing and dismissing judges.

Freedom of Expression

In February 2012, President Correa won a US$2 million judgment against the co-authors of a book, *The Big Brother*, which dealt with questionable contracts between the president's brother and state institutions. Correa subsequently desisted from the demand, and also pardoned Emilio Palacio, former head of the opinion section of the newspaper *El Universo* and three of its directors, who had been sentenced to three years each in prison in 2011 and ordered, together with the newspaper, to pay him damages totaling $40 million. In August, Palacio was granted asylum in the United States.

President Correa continues to denounce his critics during national broadcasts *(cadenas)* that private media are obliged to transmit and in his weekly address on state media. In June 2012, for example, after *El Universo* published an article critical of the president of the state investment bank, Correa showed a photo of the newspaper's editor on his weekly address and asked the Ecuadorian people to "look at him and not to forget him, because he is the clearest example of this country's bad press."

According to official statistics cited in the press, the state broadcasting authority closed 20 private radio and television outlets in the first six months of 2012. The Committee to Protect Journalists (CPJ) found that in some instances government regulators ordered closures before judicial appeals had been heard, and that more than half the stations closed had been critical of the government.

In January 2012, President Correa introduced changes to electoral legislation that prohibit the media from disseminating "messages" or "reporting" that could favor or detract from a "political thesis" or candidate or electoral preference. The law grants the National Electoral Council sweeping powers to censor media deemed to violate the prohibition. In July 2012, the measures entered into force after the Constitutional Court lifted their temporary suspension while it considered a challenge to their constitutionality. In October, the court supported the ban on media "directly or indirectly" "promoting" a candidate or party.

Misuse of Anti-Terrorism Laws

Since President Correa took office in 2007, prosecutors have repeatedly applied a "terrorism and sabotage" provision of the criminal code against participants engaged in public protests against environmental and other issues. Involvement in acts of violence or obstructing roads during such protests should be ordinary criminal offenses. Yet Ecuador's criminal code includes, under the category of sabotage and terrorism, "crimes against the common security of people or human groups of whatever kind or against their property," by individuals or associations "whether armed or not." Such crimes carry a possible prison sentence of four to eight years. Many of those charged with terrorism have benefited from amnesties. In other cases, terrorism charges have subsequently been dropped for lack of evidence, or trials have proceeded under lesser charges, such as obstruction or damage to property. However, people engaging in public protest continue to face the risk of prosecution for terrorism.

In July 2012, a prosecutor charged 10 people with "terrorist acts," and breaching state security after their arrest while holding a peaceful meeting to plan their participation in a public protest. According to their lawyers, the only evidence that prosecutors had produced against them consisted of personal objects like innocuous books, t-shirts, and music found during a police raid on their homes.

Accountability for Past Abuses

A truth commission created by the Correa administration published a report in June 2010 documenting 118 cases of human rights violations committed between 1984 and 2008 involving 456 victims (including 68 victims of extrajudicial execution and 17 of enforced disappearance).

As of November 2012, more than two years after the creation of a special prosecutorial unit charged with investigating the 118 cases of human rights violations, prosecutors had charged one perpetrator, a police captain, with the fatal shooting of Damián Peña, a student, during a 2002 demonstration.

Judicial Independence

Corruption, inefficiency, and political influence have plagued Ecuador's judiciary for years. Despite a judicial reform program that the Correa administration initiated in 2011, political influence in the appointment and conduct of judges remains a serious problem.

During 2012, the Judicial Council—a body composed of independent jurists responsible for selecting, promoting, and dismissing judges—was replaced by a transitional council with three members, one of whom was appointed by the president, one by the legislature (where Correa has majority support), and one by the Transparency and Social Control Function, the citizens' branch established in the 2008 constitution.

In November 2011, six expert observers from Argentina, Brazil, Chile, Guatemala, Mexico, and Spain, chaired by Spanish Judge Baltazar Garzón, convened to monitor and make recommendations on the process of judicial reform. The observers reported in May 2012 that replacements would have to be found for 2,903 judges and court officials, over 1,500 of whom were removed after disciplinary proceedings, poor evaluations, or forced retirements. Many were replaced by temporary appointees without appropriate training.

In July 2012, 210 permanent first instance judges appointed by the transitional council took their seats. The results of the qualifying exams were widely criticized for alleged anomalies. Those who failed to achieve a minimum mark in a final training course held by the council—in which an interview was a key component—were rejected without the right to appeal, even though they rated highly in their overall grade. Two judges who had ruled in Correa's favor in the *El Universo* case were appointed to permanent posts although their overall scores were lower than others who were rejected. Among its preliminary recommendations, the observers' group suggested that "the excessive weighting" given to the final interview be reconsidered.

A memorandum issued by the transitional council in July warned judges that they would face sanctions and possible dismissal if they accepted appeals for the protection of constitutional rights against the state. Such threats constitute unwarranted interference in judicial independence and discourage judges from contesting the selection process organized by the council.

In July 2012, a prosecutor, Antonio Gagliardo, dismissed charges of prevarication and forgery against Judge Juan Paredes—who had convicted Palacio and his colleagues from *El Universo* in July 2011—as well as Gutemberg Vera, Correa's lawyer, despite credible evidence that the latter had given Paredes a draft of the sentence in a pen drive beforehand. Paredes was selected for a permanent judicial post, and in October Gagliardo was appointed to the Constitutional Court.

Human Rights Defenders

Correa's government has sought to discredit human rights defenders by accusing them of receiving foreign funds to destabilize the government. In April 2012, President Correa accused Fundamedios—a nongovernmental organization that in October 2011 had testified at a meeting convened by the Organization of American States' (OAS) special rapporteur on freedom of expression—of being a US government "informant." In July 2012, a top government official accused Fundamedios of meddling in Ecuadoran politics and of receiving funds from USAID to destabilize the government. Correa has repeatedly singled out Fundamedios Director César Ricaurte for criticism, and shown photographs of him during his weekly address.

A presidential decree adopted in July 2011, regulating international NGOs with offices in Ecuador, allows the government to monitor all their activities and rescind their authorizations if they engage in activities different from those described in their application, resort to "political interference," or "attack public security and peace."

Disability Rights

In June 2012, Ecuador's Congress approved a law promoting the rights of people with disabilities, which includes improvements in pensions, social security provisions, and school curricula. It also created a National Council for Persons with Disabilities (CONADIS) to monitor and propose reforms on provisions and rights of people with disabilities.

Key International Actors

In December 2011, after the Inter-American Commission of Human Rights (IACHR) and its Office of the Special Rapporteur on Freedom of Expression raised concerns regarding press freedoms in Ecuador, President Correa called for the IACHR to be replaced by a new regional human rights body. He also pushed for the OAS to limit the special rapporteur's funding and effectiveness. At the OAS annual assembly in June 2012, Correa again vehemently criticized the commission and the special rapporteur and promoted measures that would seriously undermine their autonomy and effectiveness.

In May 2012, Ecuador's human rights record came under scrutiny in the UN's Human Rights Council's (HRC) Universal Periodic Review (UPR) for restrictions on freedom of expression, efforts to regulate NGOs, and delays in implementing judicial reform. Ecuador rejected a recommendation to end criminal sanctions for the expression of opinions.

Guatemala

President Otto Pérez Molina, a former military officer who was elected in 2011, has increasingly used the Guatemalan military in public security operations, despite the serious human rights violations it committed during the country's civil war.

While impunity remains the norm in Guatemala, the prosecutor's office made progress in several prominent human rights cases in 2012, including bringing charges against the former head of state, retired General Efraín Ríos Montt, for atrocities committed in the early 1980s, and against eight members of the army for allegedly killing protesters in October.

Public Security and the Criminal Justice System

Powerful criminal organizations contribute significantly to violence and intimidation, which they use to further political objectives and illicit economic interests. Mexican drug cartels, in particular the Zetas, have added to the violence, as have transnational gangs such as Mara Salvatrucha. These groups have carried out lethal attacks against rivals and those who defy their control, such as those who refuse to pay extortion money.

Guatemala's justice system has proved largely incapable of curbing violence and containing organized crime and gang activity. According to official figures, 98 percent of crimes in Guatemala do not result in prosecutions. Deficient and corrupt prosecutorial and judicial systems, as well as the absence of an effective witness protection system, all contribute to this alarmingly low prosecution rate.

Despite these obstacles, prosecutors made significant advances in 2012 in recent cases involving torture, extrajudicial killings, and corruption—due in large part to the work of Attorney General Claudia Paz y Paz and the United Nations International Commission against Impunity in Guatemala (CICIG). In March, former director of the National Police Marlene Raquel Blanco Lapola was charged with the extrajudicial execution of three people in 2009 for allegedly orchestrating a plan to kill individuals suspected of extorting transport workers.

Yet the progress made by the public prosecutor's office and CICIG in bringing charges against officials has been undercut by the dilatory practices of defendants' lawyers, leading to trial postponements of up to several months or even years. Efforts to reform the criminal code and other laws to limit such practices have not advanced.

Use of Military in Public Security Operations

The Pérez Molina administration has increasingly relied on the military to carry out law enforcement duties, in particular efforts to combat organized crime. States of emergency have been declared on several occasions, allowing for the suspension of basic rights, and the military has repeatedly been used to assist police responding to public protests.

In October, soldiers intervened when protesters blocked a highway in Totonicapán. Soldiers opened fire on the protesters, killing six people and wounding more than 30 others, according to charges that the public prosecutor's office later brought against seven members of the military, including an army colonel.

In the aftermath of the shooting, Pérez Molina said the military would no longer be used to respond to public protests, but would continue to assist the police in public security duties. He pledged to draft a legislative proposal clarifying the role of the military in public security operations. At this writing, no proposal had been submitted to Congress.

Accountability for Past Abuses

In January, Efraín Ríos Montt—a retired general who led the military regime from 1982 to 1983 that carried out hundreds of massacres of unarmed civilians—was charged with genocide and crimes against humanity, and placed under house arrest. He had been immune from prosecution during the previous 12 years while serving in Congress.

In May, Ríos Montt was charged in a separate case for his role in a 1982 massacre in the town of Dos Erres, in the Petén region, in which soldiers murdered more than 250 people, including children. In both cases, Guatemalan courts denied appeals by his lawyers for amnesty under the National Reconciliation Law. However, his lawyers continued to file numerous legal challenges that have prevented the judicial proceedings from advancing.

President Pérez Molina, commenting on Ríos Montt's prosecution, asserted that while state actors may have carried out serious abuses, the crimes committed during the civil war do not constitute genocide. Such statements represent undue interference with the judicial process.

In March, a former member of army special forces, Pedro Pimentel, was sentenced to 6,060 years in prison for his role in the Dos Erres massacre. His conviction followed the sentencing in 2011 of four other retired officers who participated in the massacre and received similar sentences. In August, a Guatemalan court sentenced the former chief of detectives of the National Police, Pedro García Arredondo, to 70 years in prison for his involvement in the disappearance of a university student in 1981.

In June, Secretary of Peace Antonio Arenales Forno announced that the government was closing the Office of the Peace Archives, which had been created in December 2008 to systematize and analyze official documents from the internal conflict, such as secret police records. While the government said that over two million documents had been digitalized and would remain accessible, the office's closure ended the staff's efforts to document evidence of past abuses, which had played a key role in the prosecution of former officials.

Labor Rights and Child Labor

A high level of anti-union violence, including attacks and threats against trade unionists, endangers freedom of association and the right to organize and bargain collectively. The International Trade Union Confederation (ITUC) reported that at least 10 trade unionists were killed in 2011.

In 2010, the United Nations Children's Fund (UNICEF) found that, despite the basic minimum age for work being 14, 21 percent of children aged 5 to 14 were involved in child labor, many of them forced. Upon concluding an August 2012 visit to Guatemala, UN High Commissioner for Human Rights Navi Pillay said children continued to be widely exploited in sexual tourism, child pornography, and organized crime—problems that the government has failed to address effectively.

Gender-Based Violence

Violence against women is a chronic problem in Guatemala and perpetrators rarely face trial. According to Guatemala's human rights prosecutor's office, rapes and sexual assaults of women increased by 34 percent from 2008 to 2011, while in 9 of every 10 of these cases, those responsible are not punished.

Palliative Care

Palliative care is very limited in Guatemala, even though more than 10,000 people die of cancer or HIV/AIDS each year, many in severe pain. In 2012, Guatemala took the positive step of authorizing the use of immediate-release oral morphine, although the drug is not widely available, and set up a national commission to develop public palliative care policies. Nevertheless, Guatemala has failed to ensure health care workers are adequately trained in modern pain treatment methods or reform its regulatory policies, which continue to discourage doctors from prescribing pain medication and limit patients from accessing pain treatment.

Human Rights Defenders

Attacks and threats against human rights defenders are common, significantly hampering human rights work throughout the country. Those responsible are rarely prosecuted.

Key International Actors

The CICIG, established in 2007, plays a key role in assisting the Guatemala's justice system in prosecuting violent crime. The commission's unique mandate allows it to work with the Attorney General's Office, the police, and other government agencies to investigate, prosecute, and dismantle criminal organizations operating in Guatemala. The CICIG can participate in criminal proceedings

235

as a complementary prosecutor, provide technical assistance, and promote legislative reforms. As of September 2012, it had initiated 289 investigations, which had resulted in 70 people being sentenced. President Pérez Molina has expressed support for extending CICIG's mandate, which is set to expire in 2013, by two additional years.

Three former Guatemalan officials allegedly involved in a plan to execute prisoners and escapees involved in a prison break are currently being investigated in foreign countries. Erwin Sperisen, the head of Guatemala's police from 2004 to 2007, was arrested in August in Switzerland, where he has dual citizenship, while former Interior Minister Carlos Vielman, and Sperisen's former deputy, Javier Figueroa, have been charged in Spain and Austria, respectively. All three investigations remain ongoing.

In September, Jorge Vinicio Orantes Sosa, the former Guatemalan soldier who allegedly participated in the Dos Erres massacre, was detained in Canada and extradited to the United States, where he has been charged with making false claims in his application to become a US citizen. If convicted, he could be sent to Guatemala after serving his sentence.

In January, Guatemala ratified the Rome Statute, making the country party to the International Criminal Court (ICC).

The Pérez Molina government has asked the US to lift suspensions established in 1990 on US military aid because of the Guatemalan military's history of committing serious abuses with impunity. In August, the US deployed 171 marines to Guatemala to collaborate with security forces as part of a joint counternarcotics mission.

Haiti

Political instability, the lasting effects of the January 2010 earthquake, and the persistence of a deadly cholera epidemic continue to hinder the Haitian government's efforts to meet the basic needs of its people and address long-standing human rights problems, such as violence against women and girls, inhumane prison conditions, and impunity for past abuses.

The February resignation of Prime Minister Garry Conille, and the government's failure to hold key elections in 2012, left critical political posts vacant. In May, the terms of one-third of Haiti's senators ended. However, at this writing elections had still been held to replace them, undermining the body's ability to legislate.

In February, after President Michel Martelly announced his decision not to re-establish the Haitian army, disbanded in 1995 after decades of committing grave human rights abuses, former army personnel occupied old military bases and other buildings. The Haitian National Police (HNP), with the support of United Nations forces, intervened to end the illegal occupations.

The UN estimates nearly 400,000 internally displaced persons (IDPs) were living in camps in June 2012. More than 65,000 people have been evicted from camps since July 2010, and an additional 80,000 camp residents faced the threat of eviction at this writing. A cholera epidemic is estimated to have killed more than 7,440 people and infected 600,000 since October 2010.

Justice System

Dismissals and resignations of high-ranking officials undercut efforts to increase the effectiveness of the justice system. Minister of Justice Josué Pierre-Louis resigned in late 2011 amid controversy over the arrest of a member of parliament.

Haiti's capital, Port-au-Prince, has had seven chief prosecutors since President Martelly took office in May 2011. In September 2012, Chief Prosecutor Jean Renel Sénatus alleged he was fired for denying a request by Minister of Justice

Jean Renel Sanon to issue 36 illegal arrest warrants for government opponents, including three esteemed human rights lawyers.

Martelly formally established the Superior Council of the Judiciary in July 2012. A 2007 law provided for this body to promote judicial independence in a justice system long troubled by politicization, corruption, and lack of transparency. Within the first month of operation, two council members resigned over allegations that the executive had wielded undue influence when appointing the Permanent Electoral Council (CEP). As of November 2012, the council struggled to fulfill its mandate as controversy continued to engulf the CEP appointments.

The HNP's weak capacity contributes to overall insecurity in Haiti. While the government and the UN Stabilization Mission in Haiti (MINUSTAH) have made reforming the police a priority, there have been difficulties training sufficient numbers of entry-level cadets. According to the UN Office of the High Commissioner for Human Rights (OHCHR), Haitian authorities have made little progress in investigating allegations of extrajudicial killings, arbitrary arrests, and ill-treatment of detainees by police that occurred in 2011.

Detention Conditions

Haiti's prison system remains severely overcrowded, in large part due to high numbers of arbitrary arrests and prolonged pre-trial detentions. For example, in the prison in St. Marc, western Haiti, 36 inmates occupy a cell designed to hold only 8, and must take turns sitting and sleeping because of limited space. The UN reported a dramatic increase in prisoner deaths in the first half of 2012—from 43 in all 2011 to 69 in the first half of 2012—due to a resurgence of cholera and tuberculosis in Haiti's prisons.

A review of potential cases of arbitrary detention by prison and judicial officers led to numerous individuals being released in 2012.

Women's Rights

While Haiti has long suffered from high rates of sexual violence, the precarious conditions after the earthquake have left some women and girls more vulnerable to such abuse. Even as displacement camps close, gender-based violence continues to be a problem. Victims face challenges in accessing post-rape medical services to prevent unwanted pregnancy or sexually transmitted diseases.

The justice sector fails to respond adequately to these crimes, yet 2012 saw progress in some cases: courts in Port-au-Prince convicted at least 13 individuals for rape in August 2012. Two of these convictions were obtained with the support of forensic evidence, an advance for Haiti's judicial system.

Children's Rights

Prior to the earthquake, only about half of primary school-age children in Haiti attended school. In 2011, President Martelly introduced a plan for free universal primary education. By the beginning of 2012, an estimated 772,000 children had received tuition assistance through the program.

Use of child domestic workers—known as *restavèks*—continues, despite efforts to end the practice. *Restavèks*, 80 percent of whom are girls, are sent from low-income households to live with wealthier families in the hope that they will be schooled and cared for in exchange for performing light chores. These children are often unpaid, denied education, and physically or sexually abused.

After numerous reports of improper adoption procedures immediately after the earthquake, some children's rights advocates raised concerns that the government lacked adequate adoption procedures. To ensure greater protection of children in the adoption process, parliament ratified the 1993 Hague Convention on Protection of Children and Co-operation in Respect of Intercountry Adoption in June 2012.

Accountability for Past Abuses

Former President Jean-Claude Duvalier returned to Haiti in January 2011 after nearly 25 years in exile. He was charged with financial and human rights crimes allegedly committed during his 15-year tenure as president. From 1971 to 1986, Duvalier commanded a network of security forces that committed serious human rights violations, including arbitrary detentions, torture, disappearances, summary executions, and forced exile.

In January 2012, the investigating judge in the case found, contrary to international standards, that the statute of limitations prevented prosecuting Duvalier for his human rights crimes. An appeal was pending at this writing.

Key International Actors

MINUSTAH has been in Haiti since 2004. In October 2010, allegations surfaced that a contingent of UN peacekeepers were the source of the cholera epidemic. A UN independent investigation found that the cholera epidemic was caused by a confluence of circumstances, while numerous scientific analyses claim evidence that MINUSTAH soldiers most likely introduced the strain.

In November 2011, the Institute for Justice and Democracy in Haiti and the Bureau des Avocats Internationaux filed a complaint with the UN on behalf of 5,000 cholera victims, alleging that MINUSTAH was the proximate cause of their illness. The complaint seeks the installation of a national water and sanitation system, financial compensation for individual victims, and a public apology from the UN. At this writing, no progress had been reported in the case.

Sexual abuse and exploitation by UN forces in Haiti remains a problem. According to UN figures, at least 60 allegations of sexual abuse have been made against peacekeepers in the last five years. In 2012, several Pakistani peacekeepers were accused of raping a 14-year-old boy. Pakistani authorities court-martialed two of them on a UN base, sentencing each of them to one year in prison in Pakistan. Local Haitian authorities were not notified until after the trial.

The UN Security Council extended MINUSTAH's mandate through October 15, 2013.

Haiti's parliament ratified the International Covenant on Economic, Social and Cultural Rights (ICESCR) in January 2012.

Honduras

Honduras made very limited progress in 2012 in addressing the serious human rights violations committed under the de facto government that took power after the 2009 military coup, despite efforts by the human rights unit in the attorney general's office to investigate abuses, and the 2011 Truth and Reconciliation Commission report documenting those that occurred.

Violence and threats by unidentified perpetrators against journalists, human rights defenders, prosecutors, peasant activists, and transgender people remain serious problems. Perpetrators are rarely brought to justice.

Lack of Accountability for Post-Coup Abuses

Following the June 2009 military coup, the de facto government suspended key civil liberties, including freedom of the press and assembly. In the ensuing days, the military occupied opposition media outlets, temporarily shutting their transmissions. Police and military personnel responded to generally peaceful demonstrations with excessive force. This pattern of the disproportionate use of force led to several deaths, scores of injuries, and thousands of arbitrary detentions.

In July 2011, a truth commission, established by President Porfirio Lobo's administration to investigate events before and after the coup, issued a report documenting 20 cases of excessive use of force and killings by state security forces. The commission also reported that police and army officials were responsible for "systematic obstruction" of investigations into these abuses.

As of October 2012, only one police officer had been held accountable for any of the serious abuses that occurred in the context of protests in support of the ousted president, Manuel Zelaya. In February 2012, a police officer was sentenced to eight years in prison for the illegal arrest and torture of a protester after a demonstration in San Pedro Sula in August 2009. Human rights prosecutors face obstacles conducting investigations, including limited collaboration by security forces, lack of sufficient resources, and an ineffective witness protection program.

Attacks on Journalists

Honduras has the region's highest rate journalists killed per population, according to the United Nations special rapporteur on the promotion and protection of the right to freedom of opinion and expression. At least 20 journalists have died at the hands of unidentified attackers since 2009. In May 2012, for example, Alfredo Villatoro, a radio journalist, was abducted after having received death threats. His body was found less than a week later in the outskirts of Tegucigalpa, the capital. Impunity continues to be the norm in these cases.

Rural Violence

More than 60 people have been killed in the Bajo Aguán Valley since November 2009, when peasants occupied land being cultivated by large agricultural enterprises. Many victims were members of peasant associations who were allegedly gunned down by security guards working for the enterprises. Other victims included private security guards and law enforcement officials. According to the attorney general's office, as of November 2012, four security guards were facing trial for the killing of five peasants in Trujillo, Colón department, in November 2010. Two police officers had been charged with attempted homicide and illegal arrest in connection with a public protest in Tocoa, Colón, in August 2010, when police opened fire on peasants to clear a road they were occupying. No one has yet been convicted for any of the Bajo Aguán crimes.

Violence against Transgender Persons

Bias-motivated attacks on transgender people are a serious problem in Honduras. According to local rights advocates, more than 70 members of the lesbian, gay, bisexual, and transgender (LGBT) population were killed between September 2008 and March 2012. The alleged involvement of members of the Honduran police in some of these violent abuses is of particular concern. Impunity for these cases has been the norm. In January 2011, the government established a special unit in the attorney general's office in Tegucigalpa to investigate killings of transgender women, among other vulnerable groups. In January 2012, a similar unit was established in San Pedro Sula. As of November 2012, no one had been convicted for these crimes. According to an official in the attorney general's office, suspects had been charged in 25 cases under investigation by the special prosecutorial teams.

Prison Conditions

Overcrowding and poor prison conditions, including inadequate nutrition and sanitation, are longstanding problems in Honduras. The country's 24 prisons, which have a capacity of 8,000, held 13,000 prisoners, according to local press accounts. In February 2012, more than 300 inmates were killed and dozens were injured during a fire in the Granja Prison in Comayagua. In May 2012, Congress passed legislation to reform the prison system. At this writing, President Lobo had not yet signed it into law.

Police Reform

In December 2011, Congress established an independent body, the Directorate for Investigation and Evaluation of the Police Career, to evaluate police performance and remove officers implicated in corruption and criminal activity, including human rights abuses. As of October 2012, the unit had referred only two police officers—including a former director of the police criminal investigation division—to the attorney general's office for prosecution for their alleged involvement in the escape of four officers accused of the 2011 killing of two university students.

In June 2012, President Lobo established an independent commission consisting of three Honduran and two foreign experts to propose wide-ranging reforms of the police, the attorney general's office, and the courts.

Judicial Independence

In May 2010, the Supreme Court arbitrarily fired four judges who had publicly opposed the coup on grounds that they had participated in politics, while taking no action against judges who had publicly supported the ouster of former President Zelaya. In 2011, Congress approved a constitutional reform creating the Council of the Judiciary and Judicial Career, an elected body responsible for appointing and removing judges. As of October 2012, however, legislators had yet to appoint the council's members.

Human Rights Defenders

Violence and threats against human rights defenders are serious problems in Honduras. For example, in September 2012, Antonio Trejo Cabrera, a lawyer who advocated for peasant land rights and publicly opposed the creation of special autonomous development zones, was shot several times and killed after attending a wedding south of Tegucigalpa. Trejo had received death threats on multiple occasions.

The ability of the Human Rights Unit of the attorney general's office to investigate these crimes is undermined by the alleged participation of members of the police, who have impeded and obstructed investigations. The unit's staff has also been subject to threats and violence. In September 2012, unidentified assailants shot and killed one of the unit's prosecutors, Manuel Eduardo Díaz Mazariegos.

Key International Actors

The Inter-American Commission on Human Rights (IACHR) has played an active role in Honduras since the coup, producing press releases and comprehensive reports documenting abuses, including killings, threats, and attacks on journalists.

Since August 2010, the Office of the UN High Commissioner for Human Rights (OHCHR) has maintained a representative in Honduras to advise the government on human rights policies and support the work of local human rights defenders. In September 2012, the high commissioner urged the government to address the vulnerability of human rights defenders and journalists.

United States legislation granting military and police aid to Honduras states that 20 percent of the funds will only be available if the Honduran government meets human rights requirements, including implementing policies to protect freedom of expression and ensuring that abuses by police and military personnel are investigated and prosecuted by civilian authorities.

In August 2012, the US State Department issued a report stating that Honduras had met the requirements but nonetheless decided to withhold funds to police forces under the command of a police chief who is alleged to have been involved in past abuses. The US Congress has also put a hold on tens of millions of dollars of aid to Honduras in light of existing human rights concerns.

Mexico

Mexican security forces have committed widespread human rights violations in efforts to combat powerful organized crime groups, including killings, disappearances, and torture. Almost none of these abuses are adequately investigated, exacerbating a climate of violence and impunity in many parts of the country.

In an historic decision in August 2012, the Supreme Court ruled that the use of military jurisdiction to prosecute a human rights violation was unconstitutional. Nonetheless, most abuses by military personnel continue to be prosecuted in military courts, which lack independence and impartiality.

Criminal groups and members of security forces continue to threaten or attack human rights defenders and journalists. The government has failed to provide these vulnerable groups with adequate protection or investigate the crimes committed against them. In April, Mexico passed legislation to create a protection mechanism for human rights defenders and journalists, but protocols to evaluate risk and assign protection are still being designed.

Military Abuses and Impunity

Mexico has relied heavily on the military to fight drug-related violence and organized crime. While engaging in law enforcement activities, the armed forces have committed grave human rights violations. From January 2007 to mid-November 2012, Mexico's National Human Rights Commission issued detailed reports of 109 cases in which it found that members of the army had committed serious human rights violations, and received complaints of 7,350 military abuses.

One of the main reasons military abuses persist is because the soldiers who commit them are virtually never brought to justice. This occurs largely because such cases continue to be investigated and prosecuted in the military justice system. The military prosecutor's Office opened nearly 5,000 investigations into human rights violations by soldiers against civilians from January 2007 to April

2012, during which time military judges sentenced only 38 military personnel for human rights violations.

In August 2012, the Supreme Court ruled that the killing of an unarmed man by soldiers at a military checkpoint should be prosecuted in civilian jurisdiction, and that the article of the Military Code of Justice used to claim jurisdiction over human rights cases was unconstitutional. Nevertheless, efforts to reform the Military Code of Justice in Mexico's Congress have met with stiff resistance. The military has stated that it will continue to claim jurisdiction over cases of alleged abuses until its justice code is reformed.

Torture

Torture remains a widespread practice in Mexico to obtain forced confessions and extract information about organized crime. Torture is most frequently applied in the period between when victims are arbitrarily detained and when they are handed to prosecutors, a time when they are often held incommunicado on military bases or other illegal detention sites. Common tactics include beatings, asphyxiation, waterboarding, electric shocks, sexual torture, and death threats.

One perpetuating factor is that some judges continue to accept confessions obtained through torture and ill-treatment, despite the fact the constitution prohibits the admission of such statements. Another is the failure to investigate and prosecute most torture cases. Only two federal officials have been sentenced for torture since 1994. In contrast, the National Human Rights Commission received more than 100 complaints of torture and over 4,700 complaints of ill-treatment from 2007 to 2011.

Mexico has committed to applying the Istanbul Protocol, an internationally recognized set of guiding principles to assess the condition of a potential victim of torture or ill-treatment. Yet justice officials rarely follow it, and medical examiners often omit evidence of abuse from their reports.

Criminal Justice System

The criminal justice system routinely fails to provide justice to victims of violent crimes and human rights violations. The various causes of this failure include corruption, inadequate training and resources, and the complicity of prosecutors and public defenders.

In June 2008, Mexico passed a constitutional reform that creates the basis for an adversarial criminal justice system with oral trials, and contains measures that are critical for promoting greater respect for fundamental rights. But implementation of the reform, which authorities have until 2016 to complete, has been sluggish, and most changes have yet to be translated into practice. Many states continue to operate under Mexico's traditional system and tolerate its most insidious practices. Meanwhile, the few states where the new system has been introduced have passed significant counter-reforms or inserted exceptions that undercut the key modifications of the oral system.

In addition to its positive aspects, the reform also introduced the provision of *arraigo*, which allows prosecutors, with judicial authorization, to detain individuals suspected of participating in organized crime for up to 80 days before they are charged with a crime. Detention without charge for up to 80 days violates Mexico's obligations regarding liberty and security and due process under international law. Many detainees are held well beyond the 80-day limit, and in some cases are subjected to torture in *arraigo* detention centers.

Prison Conditions

Prisons are overpopulated, unhygienic, and fail to provide basic security for most inmates. Prisoners who accuse guards or inmates of attacks or other abuses have no effective system to seek redress.

Approximately 60 percent of prisons are under the control of organized crime, and corruption and violence are rampant, according to the National Human Rights Commission. Criminal groups use their control to extort the families of prisoners, threatening to torture inmates if they do not pay. In February 2012, guards in Apodaca prison in Nuevo León state allowed prisoners from one criminal group to execute 44 prisoners who belonged to a rival group, and then allowed many of those responsible to escape.

Freedom of Expression

Journalists, particularly those who have reported on drug trafficking or have been critical of security forces and authorities, have faced serious harassment and attacks. From 2000 to July 2012, 82 journalists were killed and 16 more disappeared. Participants in social media networks and the offices of news outlets have increasingly been the targets of violence. While many attacks on the press in 2012 were attributed to organized crime, evidence points to the involvement of state officials in some instances.

Authorities have routinely failed to adequately investigate and prosecute crimes against members of the press or to protect journalists who face serious risk, fostering a climate of impunity and self-censorship. Mexico created a special prosecutor's office for crimes against freedom of expression in 2006, and endowed it with greater authority in 2010, but it has failed to effectively prosecute cases. More than 630 attacks on the press were reported from 2006 through mid-2012, yet the special prosecutor has obtained only one criminal sentence.

In June 2012, Mexico passed a constitutional amendment that makes attacks on the press a federal crime, giving federal prosecutors the power to take over such investigations from local prosecutors, who are more susceptible to corruption and threats. Implementing legislation of the reform is pending.

Gender-Based Violence

Mexican laws do not adequately protect women and girls against domestic violence and sexual violence. Some provisions, including those that make the severity of punishments for some sexual offenses contingent on the "chastity" of the victim, contradict international standards. Women who have suffered these types of human rights violations generally do not report them to authorities, while those who do report them are generally met with suspicion, apathy, and disrespect.

Reproductive Rights

In August 2008, the Supreme Court affirmed the constitutionality of a Mexico City law that legalized abortion in the first 12 weeks of pregnancy. Since that time 16 of Mexico's 32 states have adopted reforms that recognize the right to life from the moment of conception, limiting women's ability to exercise their right to health. In 2010, the Supreme Court ruled that all states must provide emergency contraception and access to abortion for rape victims. However, in practice many women and girls face serious barriers to accessing abortions after sexual violence, including inaccurate information, undue delays, and intimidation by officials.

Same-Sex Marriage

In August 2010, the Supreme Court recognized the right of same-sex couples in Mexico City to adopt children and to marry, and ruled that all Mexican states must recognize same-sex marriages that take place in Mexico City. Yet the ruling does not require that states recognize the right themselves, and many still deny same-sex couples the right to marry.

Access to Palliative Care

Although since 2009 Mexican law provides for a right to home-based palliative care for patients with terminal illnesses—one of very few countries to do so—implementing regulations have not been passed. Consequently, tens of thousands of patients continue to face major and often insurmountable obstacles in accessing end-of-life care, leading to unnecessary suffering.

Migrants

Hundreds of thousands of undocumented migrants pass through Mexico each year and many are subjected to grave abuses en route—such as disappearances and physical and sexual assault—at the hands of organized crime, migration authorities, and security forces. Approximately 22,000 migrants are kidnapped annually, according to the National Human Rights Commission, often with the aim of extorting payments from their relatives. Authorities have not taken adequate steps to protect migrants, or to investigate and prosecute those who abuse them. Migration officials rarely inform migrants of their rights, such as the right to seek asylum. Authorities and criminal groups have threatened and harassed the staff of migrant shelters for assisting migrants.

Labor Rights

Agreements negotiated between management and pro-management unions continue to obstruct legitimate labor-organizing activity. These agreements often restrict workers' ability to obtain effective representation, undermining their ability bargain collectively and earn benefits beyond the minimums mandated by Mexican law. Workers who seek to form independent unions risk losing their jobs, as loopholes in labor laws and poor enforcement generally fail to protect them from retaliatory dismissals. In November 2012, Congress passed a far-reaching reform of labor law that imposes onerous preconditions for striking and makes it easier for employers to replace regular employees with workers on short-term contracts supplied by third-party brokers, further undermining fundamental labor rights and protections for workers.

Human Rights Defenders

Human rights defenders continue to suffer harassment and attacks, sometimes directly at the hands of state officials. Meanwhile authorities consistently fail to provide adequate protection or to investigate crimes against defenders such as Margarita Martinez, who fled Chiapas state in June 2012 after repeated death threats and attacks tied to her work denouncing police abuses.

In April 2012, Mexico's Congress passed a law to protect human rights defenders and journalists, which mandates formal protocols to evaluate the risk faced by individuals from these groups and protection when necessary. At this writing, the implementation of these processes—with civil society participation— remained ongoing.

Key International Actors

The United States has allocated over US$2 billion in aid to Mexico through the Merida Initiative, a multi-year aid package agreed upon in 2007 to help Mexico combat organized crime. Fifteen percent of select portions of the assistance can be disbursed only after the US secretary of state reports to the US Congress that the Mexican government is meeting four human rights requirements, which include ensuring that military abuses are investigated in the civilian justice system, and prohibiting the use of testimony obtained through.

However, the impact of these requirements has been undermined by the fact that the US State Department has repeatedly reported to the US Congress that they are being met, despite overwhelming evidence to the contrary, leading Congress to release the funds. For example, the State Department's 2012 human rights report on Mexico found that "widespread impunity for human rights abuses by officials remained a problem in both civilian and military jurisdictions," which violates one of the requirements.

In November 2011, a Mexican lawyer submitted a petition asking the Office of the Prosecutor of the International Criminal Court (OTP) to open an investigation into the alleged responsibility of President Felipe Calderón and other officials for war crimes and crimes against humanity, which was signed by more than 23,000 Mexicans. A press release that the presidency released in response called the accusations in the petition slander, and said it was exploring legal options against those who had made them. The prosecutor's office was still reviewing this petition at this writing.

The Inter-American Court of Human Rights (IACtHR) has issued decisions in four cases since 2009 mandating that the military justice system should not be used to investigate and prosecute human rights abuses committed by the military. These rulings precipitated a Supreme Court decision in July 2011, which recognized that the jurisprudence of the Inter-American Court was binding and stated that Mexican judges should take its rulings into account in their judgments.

The United Nations Working Group on Enforced or Involuntary Disappearances (WGEID) conducted a fact-finding mission to Mexico in 2011, concluding that, "sufficient efforts are not being made to determine the fate or whereabouts of persons who have disappeared, to punish those responsible and to guarantee the right to the truth and reparation."

Mexico appeared before the UN Committee Against Torture (CAT) in October 2012. During the hearing, committee experts expressed concern regarding the ongoing use of torture to obtain confessions and the unlawful practice of *arraigo* detention, among other abusive patterns.

Peru

In recent years, public protests against large-scale mining projects, as well as other government policies and private sector initiatives, have led to numerous confrontations between police and protesters, and resulted in the shooting deaths of civilians by state security forces. As of September 2012, 18 civilians had been killed during protests since President Ollanta Humala took office in July 2011.

Efforts to prosecute those responsible for the many egregious abuses committed during Peru's internal armed conflict (1980-2000) have had mixed results. The conviction in 2009 and 2010 of former President Alberto Fujimori, his advisor Vladimiro Montesinos, several army generals, and members of a government death squad were notable advances in accountability. However, progress on cases involving abuses committed under earlier administrations has been very limited.

Violence during Crowd Control Operations

The use of lethal force against public protesters is an ongoing problem. In addition to the 18 civilians killed during protests since President Humala took office, 165 civilians were killed during the administration of his predecessor, Alan García (2006-2011).

In some cases, the Peruvian police and army appear to have used lethal force unlawfully. For example, in July, four civilians were fatally shot in Celendín, Cajamarca, when soldiers reportedly opened fire on unarmed protesters.

Police guidelines require police officers to observe international norms on the use of force, but a bill under debate in Congress in November 2012 would undercut these guidelines and authorize the use of lethal force in circumstances that international standards do not permit.

Military Justice

Military courts that lack independence and impartiality continue to conduct trials of police and military officials accused of human rights abuses. Legislative Decree 1095—which was issued in 2010 by then President Alan Garcíato to regulate the use of the armed forces in public security operations—provides that "illicit conduct committed by military personnel when applying the decree or during the course of their duties" is subject to military court jurisdiction. This violates earlier rulings of Peru's Supreme Court and Constitutional Tribunal, and of the Inter-American Court of Human Rights (IACtHR).

Confronting Past Abuses

Peru's Truth and Reconciliation Commission estimated that almost 70,000 people died or were subject to enforced disappearance during the country's armed conflict between 1980 and 2000. Many were victims of atrocities by the Shining Path and other insurgent groups; others were victims of human rights violations by state agents.

Former President Fujimori was sentenced in 2009 to 25 years in prison for killings and "disappearances" in 1991 and 1992. His intelligence advisor, Vladimiro Montesinos, three former army generals, and members of the Colina group, a government death squad, are also serving sentences ranging from 15 to 25 years for the assassination in 1991 of 15 people in the Lima district of Barrios Altos, and for 6 "disappearances."

In July 2012, the Permanent Criminal Chamber of the Supreme Court reduced the sentences in the Barrios Altos case on appeal. By denying that the crimes were crimes against humanity, the court undercut the jurisprudence established by the Supreme Court's Special Criminal Chamber in the Fujimori case. The Ministry of Justice and Human Rights filed an appeal for the sentence to be annulled on constitutional grounds. In September, the Permanent Criminal Chamber rescinded the sentence, after the IACtHR ruled that it was incompatible with the country's human rights obligations.

Progress to hold accountable those responsible for human rights violations under earlier governments has been very limited. Prosecutors have not yet presented charges or have closed hundreds of cases, partly due to the Ministry of Defense and the army failing to cooperate in providing information essential to identify perpetrators.

Torture

Torture continues to be a problem. The Human Rights ombudsman's office received 62 denunciations of torture and ill-treatment by the police in 2011, and 18 during the first 6 months of 2012. A third of the 144 victims whose cases were being monitored in 2012 by the nongovernmental organization, COMISEDH, died or suffered permanent physical disabilities as a result of torture. According to COMISEDH, many victims do not make formal complaints about their torture, and those who do have trouble obtaining judicial redress and adequate compensation.

Freedom of Media

Journalists continue to receive suspended prison sentences and face fines for defamation. In June 2012, a court gave two journalists from the newspaper *Diario 16*, Juan Carlos Tafur and Roberto More, two-year suspended prison sentences and ordered each to pay compensation of 60,000 nuevos soles (about US$23,000) to a former police general whom the newspaper had linked to a family whose members faced money-laundering charges.

A bill that would replace prison sentences of up to three years for defamation—as stipulated in the current law—with community service and fines, is still awaiting a vote in the legislature. Although Congress approved the bill in July 2011, former President García lodged objections that must still be debated and voted on before the bill can become law.

In August 2012, President Humala introduced a bill that would introduce prison sentences of up to eight years for anyone who "approves, justifies, denies or minimizes the crimes committed by members of terrorist organizations" for which courts have issued a final verdict. The bill contains broad language that could criminalize publishing legitimate criticism of judicial decisions, such as the guilt of an alleged offender or the penalty imposed, if a "social group" affected by terrorism felt belittled, offended, or insulted by it. By the end of October, Congress had still to debate the bill.

Journalists in Peru's provinces face threats and physical attack for criticizing local authorities. Some of these attacks have been attributed to individuals hired by elected officials. For example, a police investigation found that a mayor in Casma, Ancash, ordered the murder of Pedro Alonso Flores, the director of a local TV news program who was his staunch critic. Flores was shot to death in Ancash in September 2011 after reportedly receiving death threats. At this writing, the prosecutor had brought no charges.

Disability Rights

Under Peru's system of judicial interdiction, judges can determine that individuals with certain multisensory, intellectual, or mental disabilities are "incompetent" and assign them legal guardians, effectively suspending their basic civil rights, including the right to vote. International and regional human rights bodies have called on Peru to abolish judicial interdiction because it is incompatible with Peru's obligations under the Convention on the Rights of Persons with Disabilities (CRPD).

In June 2012, the General Law on People with Disabilities passed an initial vote in Congress. The proposed law would help bring existing national legislation into line with the convention, protecting the right of people with disabilities to act in their own interests, with appropriate support when necessary. As of November, a final vote on the bill was still pending.

Ill-Treatment of People with Drug Dependency

In January and May 2012, at least 41 people were killed and 5 critically injured in fires that swept through two privately run "drug rehabilitation" facilities, where patients were trapped behind locked doors and barred windows. Local authorities subsequently inspected and closed some unlicensed centers. In May, Congress passed a law permitting involuntary detention for treatment of drug dependence in broad circumstances, raising concerns that people who use drugs would continue to face involuntary detention and ill-treatment in circumstances that violate international standards.

Indigenous Rights

In September 2011, pursuant to Convention 169 of the International Labour Organization (ILO), the government promulgated a law giving Peru's indigenous communities the right to be consulted over legislative or administrative issues that directly affect them. The first consultation under the law, over an oil exploration project affecting indigenous communities in Loreto department in the Peruvian Amazon, is scheduled for early 2013.

Reproductive Rights

Women and girls in Peru have the right to seek abortions only in cases of medical necessity; however the country lacks clear protocols that enable health providers to determine in which specific circumstances an abortion may be lawful. Both the United Nations Committee on the Elimination of Discrimination against Women (CEDAW) and the UN Committee on Economic, Social and Cultural Rights (CESCR) have called on Peru to establish such protocols, as well as to legalize abortion in cases in which the pregnancy is the result of rape. At this writing, the government had failed to comply with these recommendations.

Human Rights Defenders

On at least two occasions in 2012, police arbitrarily detained or mistreated human rights workers when they tried to protect detainees' rights. In May 2012, police arrested two workers at the Vicariate of Solidarity of Sicuani, a church-based human rights group, as they waited in a jeep outside a mining camp in Espinar, Cusco, while lawyer colleagues checked on detainees reportedly held there. The police told a prosecutor they had found ammunition under the back seat. A judge found that the arrests were illegal.

Police in Cajamarca prevented Genoveva Gómez, a lawyer from the Human Rights ombudsman's office, and Amparo Abanto, a lawyer from the NGO GRU-FIDES, from intervening to help detainees they thought were being beaten in the

HUMAN
RIGHTS
WATCH

"I Want to be a Citizen
Just like Any Other"

Barriers to Political Participation for People with Disabilities in Peru

police station during protests in the city in June 2012. Gómez was wearing a jacket and a card that identified her as a member of the ombudsman's office. She reported that about 20 police forced her out of the building, insulted her, pulled her hair, hit, and kicked her. The Human Rights ombudsman's office filed a complaint with the attorney general's office, but at this writing, no action had been taken against the police involved in the incident.

Key International Actors

In September 2012, the Inter-American Court of Human Rights (IACtHR) ruled that the verdict of the Supreme Court's Permanent Criminal Chamber in the Barrios Altos case was incompatible with Peru's obligation to ensure that the events were fully investigated and those responsible held accountable.

In December 2011, the Inter-American Commission on Human Rights asked the IACtHR to open a case against Peru for the alleged extrajudicial execution of three former members of the Tupac Amaru Revolutionary Movement (MRTA) who were killed in April 1997 during a commando operation to free hostages held by the MRTA in the Lima residence of the Japanese ambassador. The commission had recommended that the case, which a military court had closed in 2004, reopen under civilian jurisdiction. In October 2012, a Lima court found that one of the MRTA members had been extrajudicially executed, but acquitted the three main suspects, including Vladimiro Montesinos.

Venezuela

President Hugo Chávez, who has governed Venezuela for 14 years, was elected to another six-year term in October 2012. During his presidency, the accumulation of power in the executive branch and the erosion of human rights guarantees have enabled his government to intimidate, censor, and prosecute Venezuelans who criticize the president or thwart his political agenda. President Chávez and his supporters have used their powers in a wide range of cases involving the judiciary, the media, and human rights defenders.

While many Venezuelans continue to criticize the government, the prospect of facing similar reprisals—in the form of arbitrary or abusive state action—has undercut the ability of judges to adjudicate politically sensitive cases, and forced journalists and rights defenders to weigh the consequences of publicizing information and opinions that are critical of the government.

Prison violence and police abuse remain serious problems.

Judicial Independence

In 2004, Chávez and his legislative allies conducted a political takeover of the Supreme Court, filling it with government supporters and creating new measures that make it possible to purge justices from the court. The court—re-packed with Chávez supporters in 2010—has largely abdicated its role as a check on executive power. Its members have openly rejected the principle of separation of powers and publicly pledged their commitment to advancing the political agenda of President Chávez. This political commitment has been reflected in the court's rulings, which have repeatedly validated the government's disregard for international human rights norms.

Individual judges may face reprisals if they rule against government interests. In December 2009, Judge María Lourdes Afiuni was detained on the day she authorized the conditional release of a government critic who had spent nearly three years in prison awaiting trial on corruption charges. Although Afiuni's ruling complied with a recommendation by United Nations human rights monitors—and was consistent with Venezuelan law—she was promptly arrested. A provisional judge who had publicly pledged his loyalty to President Chávez ordered her to stand trial. The day after her arrest, Chávez publicly branded Afiuni a "bandit" who should receive the maximum 30 years in prison. Afiuni spent more than a year in pretrial detention, in deplorable conditions, together with convicted prisoners—including many she herself had sentenced—who subjected her to repeated death threats. In the face of growing criticism from international human rights bodies, Afiuni was moved to house arrest in February 2011, where she remained at this writing while awaiting trial.

Freedom of Media

The Chávez government has expanded and abused its powers to regulate the media. While sharp criticism of the government is still common in the print media, on the private TV station Globovisión, and in some other outlets, fear of government reprisals has made self-censorship a serious problem.

Laws contributing to a climate of self-censorship include amendments to the criminal code in 2005 extending the scope of *desacato* laws that criminalize disrespect of high government officials, and a broadcasting statute allowing arbitrary suspension of channels for the vaguely defined offense of "incitement." In December 2010, the National Assembly broadened this statute to include the internet. Amendments to the telecommunications law grant the government power to suspend or revoke concessions to private outlets if it is "convenient for the interests of the nation."

The Chávez government has used its regulatory authority to expand the number of government-run and pro-Chávez media outlets, while reducing the availability of media outlets that engage in critical programming. Venezuela's oldest private television channel, RCTV, which was arbitrarily removed from the public airwaves in 2007, has since been driven off cable TV by the government, leaving Globovisión as the only major channel that remains critical of Chávez.

The government has pursued administrative sanctions against Globovisión, imposing a fine of US$2.1 million in one case for allegedly violating the broadcasting statute when it aired images of a prison riot in 2011. Another six cases remain pending against the station, which could lead to another heavy fine, or to its closure or suspension. In addition, the government has targeted media outlets for sanction and/or censorship for their critical reporting on the government's response to issues of public interest.

The government has also targeted other media outlets for arbitrary sanction and censorship. For example, after the weekly newspaper *6to Poder* published a satirical article in August 2011 depicting six high-level female officials as dancers in a cabaret entitled, "The Revolution" directed by "Mr. Chávez," the paper's director and president were arrested, and the newspaper received a court order barring it from publishing text or images that might constitute "an offense and/or insult to the reputation, or to the decorum, of any representative of public authorities."

Human Rights Defenders

The Chávez government has intensified its efforts to marginalize the country's human rights defenders by repeatedly accusing them of seeking to undermine Venezuelan democracy with the support of the United States government. While some human rights nongovernmental organizations have received funding from US sources—a common practice among independent groups throughout Latin America—there is no credible evidence that the independence and integrity of their work has been compromised as a result.

The weight of the government's unfounded allegations has been compounded by Chávez supporters, who have filed multiple criminal complaints against leading NGOs for receiving foreign funding. In addition, the Supreme Court ruled in 2010 that individuals or organizations that receive foreign funding could be prosecuted for "treason" under a provision of the criminal code that establishes a prison sentence of up to 15 years for anyone who "collaborates directly or indirectly with a foreign country or Republic ... or provides or receives money from them ... that could be used against the Bolivarian Republic of Venezuela, the integrity of its territory, its republican institutions, citizens, or destabilizes the social order." The National Assembly, moreover, has enacted legislation blocking organizations that "defend political rights" or "monitor the performance of public bodies" from receiving international assistance.

These efforts to harass and discredit human rights defenders have contributed to an environment in which they feel more vulnerable to acts of intimidation by government officials and violence or threats by its supporters.

The Chávez government has also enacted rules that dramatically reduce the public's right to obtain information held by the government. In combination, these measures have significantly increased the government's ability to prevent or deter human rights defenders from obtaining the funding, information, legal standing, and public visibility they need to be effective advocates.

Police Abuses

Violent crime is rampant in Venezuela, and extrajudicial killings by security agents remain a grave problem. The minister of the interior and justice has estimated that police commit one of every five crimes. According to the most recent official statistics, law enforcement agents allegedly killed 7,998 people between January 2000 and the first third of 2009.

Impunity for police abuses remains the norm. In 2011, prosecutors charged individuals allegedly responsible for abuses in less than 4 percent of cases investigated.

In April 2008, Chávez's administration issued a decree that established a new national police force and enacted measures to promote non-abusive policing proposed by a commission comprised of government and NGO representatives. At this writing, there had been no independent evaluation of the new police force's performance.

Prison Conditions

Venezuelan prisons are among the most violent in Latin America. Weak security, deteriorating infrastructure, overcrowding, insufficient and poorly trained guards, and corruption allow armed gangs to effectively control prisons. Hundreds of violent prison deaths occur every year. For example, in August 2012, a clash between rival prison gangs in Yare 1 prison, Miranda state, left 24 inmates and one visitor dead and 43 people injured.

Labor Rights

The National Electoral Council (CNE), a public authority, has the power to organize and certify all union elections, violating international standards that guarantee workers the right to elect their representatives in full freedom, according to conditions they determine. Established unions whose elections have not been CNE-certified may not participate in collective bargaining.

For several years, the government has promised to reform the relevant labor and electoral laws to restrict state interference in union elections. In April 2012, President Chávez adopted a new labor law by decree. Although the law states that unions are free to organize elections without interference, it lays down the voting system that unions must incorporate into their statutes, as well as the maximum length of tenure of union officers. These provisions limit the full freedom that unions should have under international norms to draw up their constitutions and rules and elect their representatives.

Key International Actors

Venezuela has increasingly rejected international monitoring of its human rights record, rejecting binding rulings of the Inter-American Court of Human Rights (IACtHR) and refusing to allow the Inter-American Commission on Human Rights (IACHR) to conduct in-country monitoring of human rights problems. In September 2012, Venezuela formally announced its withdrawal from the American Convention on Human Rights.

In March 2012, the UN Human Rights Council (HRC) adopted the Universal Periodic Review (UPR) report of Venezuela. The government has rejected several key recommendations aimed at protecting free speech, strengthening judicial independence, complying with the IACtHR's binding rulings, and supporting the independent work of NGOs. At this writing, the government had yet to authorize in-country visits by several UN human rights experts.

HUMAN
RIGHTS
WATCH

"Will I Get My Dues ... Before I Die?"

Harm to Women from Bangladesh's Discriminatory Laws
on Marriage, Separation, and Divorce

WORLD REPORT
2013

ASIA

Afghanistan

Afghans feel enormous anxiety as the 2014 deadline for withdrawing international combat forces from Afghanistan looms, and powerbrokers jockey for position.

The Afghan government's failure to respond effectively to violence against women undermines the already-perilous state of women's rights. President Hamid Karzai's endorsement in March of a statement by a national religious council calling women "secondary," prohibiting violence against women only for "un-Islamic" reasons, and calling for segregating women and girls in education, employment, and in public, raises questions about the government's commitment to protecting women. The minister of justice's description of battered women shelters as sites of "immorality and prostitution" deepens that skepticism.

Government efforts to stifle free speech through new legislation and targeting individual journalists were a worrying new development in 2012, while a crackdown on a political party that advocates prosecuting warlords provided a troubling indication of the government's approach to the rights to freedom of association and expression of political parties ahead of the 2014 presidential election.

Civilian casualties from the civil armed conflict remained alarmingly high, and re-vetting of the Afghan Local Police (ALP) was underway due to abuses by these forces. Rising numbers of "green on blue" attacks where members of the Afghan security forces target foreign soldiers prompted joint operations with foreign troops to be curtailed during the year.

Taliban laws-of-war violations against civilians continued, particularly indiscriminate attacks causing high civilian losses. Following the end of the United States military "surge," many areas of Afghanistan remained under Taliban control, where Taliban abuses, particularly against women and girls, were endemic.

HUMAN
RIGHTS
WATCH

"I HAD TO RUN AWAY"
The Imprisonment of Women and Girls for "Moral Crimes" in Afghanistan

Violence and Discrimination against Women and Girls

A series of high-profile attacks on women highlighted the heightened danger that the future holds for Afghan women. The Law on Elimination of Violence Against Women, adopted in 2009, remains largely unenforced. Women and girls who flee forced marriage or domestic violence are often treated as criminals rather than victims. As of spring 2012, 400 women and girls were in prison and juvenile detention for the "moral crimes" of running away from home or sex outside marriage.

The late December 2011 arrest and subsequent trial of the in-laws of Sahar Gul— a girl sold into marriage at 13, locked in a basement, and tortured by her in-laws after she refused their demands that she become a prostitute—underlined the threat posed to Afghan girls by unchecked violence against women.

The unsolved February murder in Bamiyan of an adolescent girl named Shakila led to street protests in Kabul and Bamiyan, and complaints from Bamiyan officials to President Karzai over what was seen as a cover-up by government officials of a murder. In July, a videotaped public execution of a woman in Parwan for the alleged "crime" of adultery followed by the assassination of the head of the government's Department of Women's Affairs in Laghman highlighted the erosion of legal protections for Afghan women.

In the spring and summer, a series of "poisonings" at girls' schools in several provinces, alleged by the Afghan government to have been perpetrated by opponents of girls' education, escalated fear for schoolgirls and their families. World Health Organization (WHO) investigations of some cases pointed to mass hysteria as the likely cause. The Afghan government made several arrests, prompting the United Nations to accuse the Afghan government of extracting forced confessions from the alleged perpetrators.

Armed Conflict

The security transition moved rapidly, with international forces handing over large areas of the country to Afghan security forces. NATO claimed no increases in insurgent attacks in most areas, while evidence emerged of the failure by Afghan security forces to maintain control in other areas including formerly peaceful Bamiyan province. Afghan security forces increasingly assumed a leadership role in military operations, according to NATO, including controversial "night raids."

The Afghan government continues to allow well-known warlords, human rights abusers, corrupt politicians, and businesspeople to operate with impunity, further eroding its public support. Worries about the potential for a civil war along geographic and ethnic lines following the withdrawal of international forces led to reports of re-arming and preparations for conflict by warlords.

Civilian casualties from fighting remained high with 3,099 civilian casualties (1,145 civilians killed and 1,954 injured) in the first 6 months of the year, down from 2011's high of 3,654 civilian casualties (1,510 killed and 2,144 injured) during the same period, according to the UN. Most civilian casualties were due to Taliban attacks that failed to distinguish between combatants and civilians, or sometimes intentionally targeted civilians.

Pro-government security forces were also responsible for abuses against civilians. In September, concerns about the US-backed ALP prompted a temporary suspension of training of new recruits while all 16,300 members of the program were re-vetted. While ALP abuses included reports of extortion, assault, rape, and murder of civilians, ALP "reform" by the US and NATO focused solely on measures to halt the rapidly escalating number of "green on blue" killings where members of Afghan security forces, including possible Taliban infiltrators, attack their international military mentors.

In May, a number of "uprisings" against the Taliban began in Ghazni as apparently spontaneous community reactions and spread to other provinces. The view that these local actions could help solidify government control of the country were tempered by the apparent involvement of Hezb-i-Islami, an insurgent Taliban-rival group. In September, the suggestion by International Security Assistance Force (ISAF) Commander John Allen that the US might support arming these groups raised the specter of yet another untrained, undisciplined militia operating with impunity.

Negotiations for a political settlement with the Taliban made little progress in 2012. Preliminary discussions between the Taliban and the US, ongoing since

2011, were widely reported to have broken down in March over failure to agree on a US transfer of key Taliban prisoners from the US military facility at Guantanamo Bay to Qatar.

Efforts by the Afghan government and some international experts to portray the Taliban as significantly reformed since 2001 were undermined by the Taliban's continued abuses. These included the Taliban's March attack on a Kabul restaurant, its announcement in May of a spring offensive specifically aimed at killing key civilians— including senior government officials, members of parliament, High Peace Council members, contractors, and "all those people who work against the Mujahideen"—and its order in April that schools in Ghazni be closed, which led to local uprisings against the group in some communities.

The Taliban also continued to attack schools and to recruit children, including as suicide bombers. The UN reported 34 attacks against schools in the first 6 months of 2012 (6 of which involved targeted assassinations of school staff or education officials),

Ethnic violence between Tajiks and Hazaras in Kabul in September renewed fears of rising sectarian strife, which has plagued neighboring Pakistan but has so far been largely avoided in Afghanistan.

Abuse of Prisoners and Detainees

A March agreement between the Afghan and US governments set a deadline of September for full transfer of the US-run Bagram detention facility to the Afghan government. The handover occurred, but amid recriminations as the US refused to hand over a number of prisoners, as well as disagreement over the continuing role of the US in holding and interrogating detainees.

Provisions of the Afghan-US agreement also obliged the Afghan government to establish an administrative detention system, which would permit the government to hold conflict-related detainees without charge. Agreed upon in secret, Afghan lawmakers criticized the deal as unconstitutional under Afghan law. However, both governments agreed on plans for the US to maintain custody of approximately 50 non-Afghan "third country national" prisoners being held indefinitely at Bagram without trial until the US makes arrangements for their transfer or release.

The January 2012 transfer of responsibility for the Afghan prison system back to the Ministry of Interior from the Ministry of Justice raised serious concerns about potential torture and other ill-treatment of prisoners. The government had shifted responsibility for prison operations from the former to the latter in 2003 as part of an effort to reform the justice system and reduce torture by the abusive Interior Ministry.

In March, additional concerns about the transfer were raised when a newly appointed Ministry of Interior warden ordered invasive vaginal searches of all female visitors at Pul-i-Charkhi, Kabul's main men's prison.

In September, Karzai's appointment of Asadullah Khalid to head the National Security Directorate, the country's intelligence service, sparked domestic and international dismay. Khalid, a former governor of Ghazni and Kandahar provinces, has been accused of abuses that include operating a private, unlawful prison where torture was routine during his tenure as governor of Kandahar from 2005-2008. The intelligence service has a long and well-documented history of torture of detainees.

Human Rights Defenders and Transitional Justice

The Afghanistan Independent Human Rights Commission (AIHRC) is an independent government agency that has been praised globally as an example of an effective human rights body. However, in December 2011, Karzai announced the dismissal of three of its nine commissioners. The three positions remained vacant at this writing. The move effectively disabled the commission. A fourth position has been vacant since January 2011 when the commissioner responsible for children's rights was killed with her husband and four children in a Kabul supermarket bombing.

Karzai may have sought to undermine the AIHRC by intervening to block the release of one of the commission's key projects—a 1,000-page report that maps war crimes and crimes against humanity in Afghanistan since the communist era. Completed in December 2011, it is needed to provide a foundation for future steps to prosecute those implicated in past abuses.

Freedom of Expression and Association

The rights to freedom of expression and association of the media and political parties, hailed as one of the few clear human rights success stories since 2001, came increasingly under threat in 2012. In March, the Afghan government supported calls for banning and prosecuting a political party that sponsored a protest calling for prosecution of suspected war criminals, some of whom are current government officials. The Afghan government repeatedly lashed out at journalists. In April, one reporter was detained without charge after his TV station broadcast a show critical of the Kabul mayor.

In May, the government accused a foreign journalist of being a spy after she alleged government corruption, but took no further action, and in November reacted harshly to an International Crisis Group (ICG) report, calling the group's activities "detrimental to Afghanistan's national interests" and said it was "assessing the ICG's operations in the country."

In June, the government presented a new draft media law that sought to dramatically tighten government control of media through measures including establishing a government-controlled media complaints body, creating a long list of media "violations," limiting broadcast of foreign programming, and establishing special courts and attorneys across the country to deal with media violations. The draft law was significantly revised following outcry from Afghan journalists, but the October creation of a new media standards committee raised concerns that the government was simply taking a new approach in its effort to crack down on the media. In September, the media commission instructed the attorney general's office to launch criminal investigations of two Afghan media organizations accused of broadcasting "immoral" programs.

Key International Actors

Growing international fatigue with Afghanistan negatively impacted human rights in 2012, particularly by reducing political pressure on the government to respect women's rights. In spite of efforts by many countries to sign partnership agreements with Afghanistan, and pledges of goodwill and support at the 2012 Tokyo Conference on Afghanistan, commitments to support human rights in Afghanistan remain glaringly short on details.

Diplomats admit behind closed doors that willingness to continue high-level support to Afghanistan is fading fast, and the planned military drawdown by 2014 is already prompting further disengagement when it comes to using political pressure and providing aid. Cuts in international aid are already leading to the closure of some schools and health clinics.

Afghanistan remained under preliminary analysis by the prosecutor of the International Criminal Court (ICC). Since 2007, the court has been looking into allegations of crimes, including torture, recruitment of child soldiers, attacks on humanitarian targets and the UN, and attacks on objects or locations protected under international law that are not military targets.

Bangladesh

Bangladesh's overall human rights situation worsened in 2012, as the government narrowed political and civil society space, continued to shield abusive security forces from accountability, and flatly ignored calls by Human Rights Watch to reform laws and procedures in flawed war crimes and mutiny trials. Civil society and human rights defenders reported increased governmental pressure and monitoring.

The security forces' practice of disguising extrajudicial killings as "crossfire" killings or legitimate confrontations between alleged criminals and security forces continued, as did disappearances of opposition members and political activists. A prominent labor activist was kidnapped and killed, and other labor activists threatened.

After June 2012 sectarian violence in Arakan state in neighboring Burma, the government responded to an influx of Rohingya refugees by pushing back boatloads of refugees and insisting that it had no obligation to provide them sanctuary. The government curtailed the activities of nongovernmental organizations operating in pre-existing Rohingya refugee camps in Cox's Bazaar in Chittagong.

Flawed trials against those accused of war crimes in the 1971 war for independence continued, as did mass and unfair trials of the Bangladesh Rifles (now Bangladesh Border Guards) accused of mutineering in 2009.

The government continued to demand that Indian border guards stop killing Bangladeshi nationals who cross into India for smuggling or other crimes.

Extrajudicial Killings, Torture, and Impunity

Although there was a decline in overall numbers of civilians killed by security forces in 2012, the Rapid Action Battalion (RAB)—a force comprised of military and police—continued to carry out extrajudicial killings. The ruling political party, the Awami League, pledged to bring the RAB under control when it assumed office, but abuses persisted.

The government continued to persecute 17-year-old boy, Limon Hossain, whom RAB officials shot and maimed in March 2011. Although the government initially said that Hossain was injured in a botched RAB operation, it quickly retracted the statement and filed criminal charges against him. In August 2012, an alleged RAB informant attacked and beat Hossain in a street in his hometown. Instead of protecting Hossain, the government filed further charges against him, and accused him and his relatives of murdering a bystander.

The authorities failed to investigate and prosecute the RAB or other security forces responsible for extrajudicial killings or torture. While the RAB set up an internal investigative unit with technical assistance from the United States, no RAB member has ever faced criminal prosecution for a human rights violation.

In April, Elias Ali, secretary of the Sylhet Division of the opposition Bangladesh Nationalist Party (BNP), disappeared without trace. Prime Minister Sheikh Hasina called on the police to investigate Ali's disappearance, but undermined the effort by claiming that Ali and his driver were "hiding" at his party's orders to allow the opposition to blame the government. Human rights groups reported more than 20 disappearances in 2012.

Labor Rights

Aminul Islam, a prominent labor rights activist, was found tortured and killed in April 2012. In response to an intense outcry, the Home Ministry set up a high-level commission to investigate his killing, but there had been no progress in the investigation at this writing. While there was no suggestion of political responsibility, Prime Minister Hasina made public statements downplaying the significance of the killing.

Workers in Bangladesh faced poor working conditions, low wages, and excessive hours. Government repression and collusion with factory owners prevented them from organizing effectively.

The government continued legal action against the Bangladesh Center for Worker Solidarity (BCWS), an NGO that works closely with trade unions. Over a dozen labor rights leaders, including BCWS leaders, faced criminal charges on a variety of spurious grounds, including under the Explosive Substances

Ordinance Act, which carries the death penalty as a sentence. Labor rights groups faced registration problems that affected their funding and operations.

Hazaribagh Tanneries

The Hazaribagh neighborhood of Dhaka, the capital, is considered to be one of the world's most polluted urban sites; some 150 leather tanneries discharge 21 thousand cubic meters of untreated effluent into the nearby Buriganga River each day. Local residents complain of fevers, skin diseases, and respiratory and stomach illnesses due to contamination, while tannery workers suffer from skin and respiratory diseases due to exposure to tanning chemicals, and limb amputations caused by accidents in dangerous tannery machinery. In some tanneries, children as young as 11 work directly with chemicals, operate heavy tannery machinery, or slice hides with razor blades.

In 2001, Bangladesh's High Court ordered the government to ensure that the tanneries installed adequate waste treatment facilities. The government ignored that ruling. Officials from the Department of Environment and the Department of Labour confirmed that the government does not enforce labor and environmental laws in Hazaribagh, which exports most of its leather to China, South Korea, Japan, Italy, Germany, Spain, and the United States.

Restrictions on Civil Society and Political Opposition

The government was increasingly hostile in 2012 to civil society groups. Following the July 2012 publication of a Human Rights Watch report on the 2009 Bangladesh Rifles mutiny, Bangladeshi officials threatened action against domestic rights groups who had helped conduct the research.

Of particular concern is a draft law aimed at regulating foreign donations to Bangladeshi NGOs. Many NGOs, such as BCWS or Odhikar, had already been facing years of delays in getting critical foreign funds released for their projects. The bill appeared aimed at severing funds for organizations engaged in publicly criticizing the government. In August 2012, the government announced plans to establish a new commission charged solely with regulating NGO activities, in

HUMAN
RIGHTS
WATCH

TOXIC TANNERIES

The Health Repercussions of Bangladesh's Hazaribagh Leather

addition to the NGO Affairs Bureau that already exists in the prime minister's office.

Refugees and Asylum Seekers

The government's response to the influx of Rohingya refugees fleeing sectarian violence in Arakan state, Burma, exposed its failure to respect the United Nations Refugee Convention. Bangladesh pushed Rohingyas back at the border, regardless of the risk they faced when they return to Burma, and blocked critical humanitarian assistance.

The government suspended any third-country resettlement of the Rohingya refugees, arguing it would encourage other Rohingya in Burma to seek refuge in Bangladesh. Government officials labeled Rohingya "intruders" and "criminals," and blamed them for destroying Buddhist temples in mass riots in October, without offering evidence to prove they were responsible.

International Crimes Tribunal and Bangladesh Rifles Mutiny

Trials against those accused of war crimes during the 1971 war of independence continued, despite calls by the US war crimes ambassador, Stephen Rapp, and several international groups to amend the International Crimes Tribunal Act (ICT Act) to ensure it complied with international fair trial standards.

The trial chamber allowed several prosecution witnesses statements as evidence, without any live testimony being heard. While the prosecution claimed the witnesses were unavailable, the defense produced safe house logbooks that showed they were available at the time when they were meant to appear in court. However, the tribunal rejected the defense's claims. In the first trial against the accused Delwar Hossain Sayedee, defense lawyers claimed that they could not produce their witnesses due to intimidation and threats against them by the prosecution. The prosecution denied the claims.

Mass military trials against the 6,000 soldiers of the Bangladesh Rifles (since renamed Bangladesh Border Guards) continued, with nearly every accused soldier being found guilty. A mass trial in a civilian court of over 800 soldiers con-

HUMAN
RIGHTS
WATCH

"The Fear Never Leaves Me"
Custodial Deaths, Torture, and Unfair Trials
after the 2009 Bangladesh Rifles Mutiny

Photo: Members of Bangladesh Rifles (BDR) accused of mutiny are
summoned for a hearing before a special court in Dhaka July 12, 2010.
© 2010 Reuters/Andrew Biraj

tinued in 2012. In addition to the allegations of torture, most of the accused did not have proper access to lawyers and were often unaware of the charges against them. The government rejected Human Rights Watch's concerns—published in a July 2012 report—concerning these mass trials, which involved as many as 800 accused being tried at one time, in one courtroom. Instead, the government mounted a public relations campaign that denounced Human Rights Watch and local groups that had helped to research the report.

Women's and Girls' Rights

While Bangladesh has a strong set of laws and judicial guidelines to tackle violence against women, implementation remains poor. Violence against women including rape, dowry-related assaults, and other forms of domestic violence, acid attacks, and illegal punishments in the name of fatwas or religious decrees and sexual harassment continue.

Bangladesh reported the highest prevalence of child marriages in the world. Archaic and discriminatory family laws for Muslims, Hindus, and Christians, continued to impoverish many women when they separate from, or divorce spouses, and trap them in abusive marriages for fear of destitution. The Law Commission of Bangladesh researched and recommended reforms to these laws in 2012.

International Community

The international community continued to press the government to respect civil and political rights in the face of increased restrictions on political opposition groups and civil society. The donor community was particularly vocal in calling for swift and meaningful investigations into the murder of Aminul Islam and the disappearance of Elias Ali, as well as calling on the government to give Rohingya refugees sanctuary. The government often responded by suggesting that critics were part of a conspiracy against it.

Under persistent pressure from Bangladesh, Indian authorities committed to end all unlawful killings at their shared border.

In June, the World Bank announced that it was withdrawing its US$1.2 billion credit assistance for building the Padma Multipurpose Bridge across the Padma River due to evidence of serious corruption by senior government officials. In September, the government agreed to put in place conditions that the World Bank had demanded when the deal was suspended, including placing all public officials suspected of involvement in the corruption scheme on leave from government employment, appointing a special inquiry and prosecution team, and granting an external international expert body access to investigate the corruption charges and advise the bank. When the government announced in September 2012 that the Padma Bridge deal was back on track, the World Bank issued a public rejoinder stating that the project would resume only once all its conditions had been fully and unconditionally fulfilled.

Burma

Burma's human rights situation remained poor in 2012 despite noteworthy actions by the government toward political reform. In April, opposition leader Aung San Suu Kyi and her National League for Democracy party won 43 of 44 seats it contested in a parliamentary by-election; the parliament consists of 224 seats in the upper house and 440 in the lower house, the majority of which remain under the control of military representatives or former military officers.

President Thein Sein welcomed back exiles during the year, and released nearly 400 political prisoners in five general prisoner amnesties, although several hundred are believed to remain in prison. Freed political prisoners face persecution, including restrictions on travel and education, and lack adequate psychosocial support. Activists who peacefully demonstrated in Rangoon in September have been charged with offenses. In August 2012, the government abolished pre-publication censorship of media and relaxed other media restrictions, but restrictive guidelines for journalists and many other laws historically used to imprison dissidents and repress rights such as freedom of expression remain in place.

Armed conflict between the Burmese government and the Kachin Independence Army (KIA) continued in Kachin State in the north, where tens of thousands of civilians remain displaced. The government has effectively denied humanitarian aid to the displaced Kachin civilians in KIA territory. In conflict areas in Kachin and Shan States, the Burmese military carried out extrajudicial killings, sexual violence, torture, forced labor, and deliberate attacks on civilian areas, all which continue with impunity. Ceasefire agreements in ethnic conflict areas of eastern Burma remain tenuous.

Deadly sectarian violence erupted in Arakan State in June 2012 between ethnic Arakanese Buddhists and ethnic Rohingya Muslims, a long-persecuted stateless minority of approximately one million people. State security forces failed to protect either community, resulting in some 100,000 displaced, and then increasingly targeted Rohingya in killings, beatings, and mass arrests while obstructing humanitarian access to Rohingya areas and to camps of displaced Rohingya around the Arakan State capital, Sittwe. Sectarian violence broke out again in 9

of the state's 17 townships in October, including in several townships that did not experience violence in June, resulting in an unknown number of deaths and injuries, the razing of entire Muslim villages, and the displacement of an additional 35,000 persons. Many of the displaced fled to areas surrounding Sittwe, where they also experienced abuses, such as beatings by state security forces.

Despite serious ongoing abuses, foreign governments—including the United States and the United Kingdom—expressed unprecedented optimism about political reforms and rapidly eased or lifted sanctions against Burma, while still condemning the abuses and violence.

Limited Political Change and Ongoing Abuses

Burma's national parliament and 14 regional and state assemblies completed a first full year in operation in 2012 since the formal end of military rule. Former military generals hold most senior ministerial portfolios and serving generals are constitutionally guaranteed the posts of ministers of defense, home affairs, and border affairs security. Many former military officers hold important positions in the ruling military-backed Union Solidarity and Development Party.

Two new laws passed in 2012 related to land use fail to adequately protect farmers' rights. A new law on peaceful assembly—signed in December 2011 and hailed as a reform by Western governments—fails to meet international standards, providing for imprisonment for permit violations, and requiring that protest slogans be pre-approved.

Thirteen activists in Rangoon faced charges for failing to get permission for a demonstration held peacefully in September to oppose the armed conflict in Kachin State. Other laws that have been used to imprison peaceful activists, lawyers, and journalists remain on the books, including, among others, the Unlawful Associations Act, the Electronics Act, the State Protection Act, and the Emergency Provisions Act.

Media freedoms improved in 2012 but remain highly restricted. In August, the government abolished pre-publication censorship that had been in place nearly 50 years but retained 16 guidelines restricting publication of articles critical of the government or related to corruption, illicit drugs, forced labor, and child soldiers. Editors continue to self-censor out of concern for arrest and hesitate to publish stories regarding government abuses.

The National Human Rights Commission, created in September 2011, continued to disappoint in 2012. The commission exists by executive order and lacks independence from the government, contrary to the Paris Principles—minimum standards endorsed by the UN on the functioning of national human rights commissions. Statements from Burma's commission on Kachin and Arakan States failed to mention any abuses by the state security forces, or government-imposed restrictions on delivering humanitarian aid to tens of thousands of internally displaced persons (IDPs).

After spending a total of 15 years under house arrest since 1989, and otherwise facing travel restrictions, Aung San Suu Kyi's right to travel domestically and internationally was restored, and she traveled to five European countries in June, including Oslo to accept her 1991 Nobel Peace Prize. In September she travelled to the US where she accepted the Congressional Gold Medal in recognition of her non-violent struggle for democracy and human rights, awarded in 2008 while she was under house arrest

However, other former political prisoners continue to face persecution, including restrictions on travel and education. The Ministry of Home Affairs refused to issue passports to many former political prisoners, including democracy and human rights activists, public interest lawyers, and journalists, preventing them from traveling abroad.

While parliament in 2012 appointed a commission to investigate land confiscation, the practice continues throughout the country. Farmers lose their land to private and state interests and in some cases are effectively forced to work as day laborers on their own land. Numerous disputes about land confiscations under the prior military juntas remain largely unresolved.

Forced labor continued in various parts of the country despite the government's commitment to end the practice by 2015 in an action plan agreed to with the International Labour Organization (ILO). The army continued to have child soldiers in its ranks, but in June, signed an action plan with the United Nations to halt further recruitment of children and demobilize and reintegrate those already in the army within 18 months. Several non-state armed groups continue to use and recruit child soldiers and the government continues to prevent UN agencies from accessing ethnic areas controlled by non-state armed groups to focus on demobilization and reintegration of child soldiers.

Ethnic Conflict and Displacement

Fighting slowed between government forces and most ethnic armed groups in eastern Burma as negotiations on tenuous ceasefires continued. In northern Burma, however, fighting continued between the Burmese armed forces and the KIA.

The Burmese military continues to engage in extrajudicial killings, attacks on civilians, forced labor, torture, pillage, and use of antipersonnel landmines. Sexual violence against women and girls remains a serious problem, and perpetrators are rarely brought to justice. The KIA and some other ethnic armed groups have also committed serious abuses, such as using child soldiers and antipersonnel landmines.

Internally displaced Kachin swelled to an estimated 90,000 in 2012, and the government continued to prevent international nongovernmental organizations and UN agencies access to IDP camps in KIA-held territory to provide humanitarian assistance. Kachin fleeing to China to escape violence and persecution were not welcome. Several thousand Kachin refugees temporarily in Yunnan province in southwest China lacked adequate aid and protection. In August, China forced back more than 4,000 Kachin to conflict zones in northern Burma.

More than 550,000 people remain internally displaced in Burma, including 400,000 due to decades of conflict in eastern Burma. There are an additional 140,000 refugees in camps in Thailand and several million Burmese migrant workers and unrecognized asylum seekers who suffer due to inadequate and ad hoc Thai policies causing refugees to be exploited and unnecessarily detained and deported.

Some 30,000 ethnic Rohingya refugees live in an official camp in Bangladesh and another 200,000 live in makeshift settlements or surrounding areas. Bangladeshi authorities ordered three international aid agencies to close humanitarian operations for Rohingya refugee camps and pushed back thousands of Rohingya asylum seekers to Burma in 2012.

Sectarian Violence and Ensuing Abuses

Burmese security forces committed killings, rape, and mass arrests against Rohingya Muslims after failing to protect both them and Arakanese Buddhists during deadly sectarian violence in western Burma in June 2012. Over 100,000 people were displaced by widespread abuses and arson. State security forces failed to intervene to stop the sectarian violence at key moments, including the massacre of 10 Muslim travelers in Toungop that was one of several events that precipitated the outbreak. State media published incendiary anti-Rohingya and anti-Muslim accounts of the events, fueling discrimination and hate speech in print media and online across the country.

Violence erupted again in late October in 9 of the state's 17 townships, with coordinated violence and arson attacks by Arakanese against Rohingya and Kaman Muslims—a government-recognized nationality group, unlike the Rohingya. In some cases violence was carried out with the support and direct involvement of state security forces and local officials, including killings, beatings, and burning of Muslim villages, displacing an additional 35,000 Rohingya and non-Rohingya Muslims.

Government restrictions on humanitarian access to the Rohingya community have left tens of thousands in dire need of food, adequate shelter, and medical care. The authorities indefinitely suspended nearly all pre-crisis humanitarian aid programs, affecting hundreds of thousands more Rohingya who were otherwise unaffected by the violence and abuse.

Local security forces detained hundreds of Rohingya men and boys—primarily in northern Arakan State—and held them incommunicado without basic due process rights. UN and international NGO staff were among the arrested and charged. Many remain detained at this writing.

The Rohingya number approximately one million in Burma and were effectively stripped of their citizenship in 1982 through the discriminatory Citizenship Law. There has been little political will to repeal the law due to widespread prejudice

HUMAN
RIGHTS
WATCH

"The Government
Could Have Stopped This"
Sectarian Violence and Ensuing Abuses in Burma's Arakan State

against Rohingya, including by prominent pro-democracy figures. The government has long restricted their rights to freedom of movement, education, and employment.

President Thein Sein suggested in July that the Rohingya be expelled from Burma to "third countries" or to camps overseen by the United Nations High Commissioner for Refugees (UNHCR). He later appointed a 27-member commission to investigate the violence in Arakan State and make recommendations, but failed to include a Rohingya representative on the panel.

Key International Actors

In 2012, foreign governments expressed unprecedented optimism about Burma's political changes, despite evidence of ongoing human rights abuses. In April, the European Union suspended all of its sanctions for one year, enabling investment by European companies and lifting travel and visa bans on nearly 500 people, but retained an arms embargo.

In July, the United States eased sanctions to allow American companies to invest in all sectors of Burma's economy, including the controversial and opaque oil and gas sector. The US maintained targeted sanctions against some Burmese military officers and companies they control, and appointed its first ambassador to Burma in 22 years.

Tomas Ojea Quintana, the UN special rapporteur on Burma, conducted his sixth visit in late July and early August, expressing concern over alleged abuses in Arakan State and calling for a credible investigation and a review of the 1982 Citizenship Law, which he said discriminates against Rohingya. He also voiced concern about ongoing abuses in Kachin State and the need to release remaining political prisoners.

Several high-profile visits to Burma in 2012 were ostensibly aimed to show support for ongoing changes, including visits in November by US President Barack Obama—the first by a sitting US president—in April by British Prime Minister David Cameron, and UN Secretary-General Ban Ki-moon. President Obama gave a historic speech at Rangoon University raising human rights concerns, including the military's role in parliament, ethnic conflicts, national reconciliation, and abuses against Rohingya Muslims. Other high-profile visits were explicitly more economically motivated, including visits in May by India's Prime Minister Manmohan Singh, and in September by China's top legislator, Wu Bangguo, chairman of the Standing Committee of China's National People's Congress.

Others expressed concerns for the plight of Burma's Rohingya Muslims, including visits by Turkey's foreign minister and a high-level delegation from the Organization for Islamic Cooperation (OIC), which in September reached an agreement with the Burmese government to open an office in the country to facilitate delivery of humanitarian aid in Arakan State. President Thein Sein terminated the agreement in October following several protests in Sittwe, Mandalay, and Rangoon led by anti-Rohingya Buddhist monks opposing the OIC's involvement in the issue.

Members of the Association of Southeast Asian Nations (ASEAN) continue to invest in and trade extensively with Burma, especially in the extractive and hydropower industries. Burma continued to earn billions of US dollars in natural gas sales to Thailand, little of which is directed into social services such as health care and education. Gas dollars will increase markedly when a gas pipeline from Arakan State to Yunnan in China is operational in 2013. Work continues on that project, which passes through northern Shan State where the Burmese army has moved in to secure territory and where armed conflict has led to abuses such as torture, forced labor, and forced displacement of Kachin and Shan.

Russia, China, and North Korea continued to sell arms to Burma in 2012, and there are concerns that North Korean sales breached UN Security Council punitive sanctions on North Korea passed in 2006 and 2009. In May, Thein Sein assured South Korean President Lee Myun-bak that his government would cease buying weapons from North Korea.

Cambodia

The human rights situation in Cambodia deteriorated markedly in 2012 with a surge in violent incidents, as the ruling Cambodian People's Party (CPP) prepared for national elections scheduled for July 28, 2013. On June 1, Prime Minister Hun Sen reached his 10,000th day (more than 27 years) in office, making him one of the 10 longest-serving leaders in the world. The prime minister, now 60, has said he wants to remain in office until he is 90.

Violence involving state security forces occurred amidst increasing land-taking by powerful business and security interests, and growing labor unrest due to dissatisfaction with an economic policy that relies heavily on state authorities' often-corrupt promotion of unbridled foreign investment, especially via granting economic and other land concessions, which continued despite the government's May 2012 announcement of a moratorium.

Opposition party leader Sam Rainsy remained in exile in France rather than face prison sentences totaling 12 years as a result of politically motivated and manifestly unfair trials. At least 35 other political and social activists and residents involved in defending human rights, opposing land grabs, and demanding better working conditions were killed, wounded, arbitrarily arrested, threatened with arrest, or kept in exile by CPP-led security forces and the CPP-controlled judiciary.

Cambodian judicial officers working at the Extraordinary Chambers of the Courts of Cambodia (ECCC) continued to implement Hun Sen's pronouncements by refusing to investigate additional Khmer Rouge suspects, including CPP-linked perpetrators from Pol Pot's 1975-1979 Khmer Rouge regime. At the same time, as chair of the Association of Southeast Asian Nations (ASEAN), Cambodia's government played a leading role in stymying efforts by regional civil society organizations to adopt a credible and effective human rights mechanism.

Attacks, Harassment, and Prosecutions against Activists and Protesters

On February 20, three young women factory workers were wounded by gunfire during a large peaceful protest demanding increased wages and allowances for foreign enterprise employees in Bavet municipality of Svay Rieng province, eastern Cambodia. While evidence suggests that the CPP mayor, Chhouk Bandit, intentionally fired directly into the crowd, a provincial court only placed him under investigation for unintentional injury without holding him for trial.

On April 26, noted environmental activist Chhut Wutthy was shot dead after military police and company security guards stopped him from documenting illegal logging activities in Koh Kong province, southwestern Cambodia. Although the exact circumstances of his death remain unclear, government and judicial investigations into his killing appeared designed to shield those most responsible and further conceal their unlawful economic activities. The killing had a chilling effect on efforts by others to uncover similar activities.

On May 16, security force gunfire killed Heng Chantha, a 14-year-old girl, during a government military operation against villagers in Kratie province, eastern Cambodia, who were protesting the allegedly illegal seizure of their land by a foreign concessionaire. Instead of launching a criminal investigation into police conduct, Hun Sen accused protesters of organizing a "secessionist movement" and then ordered the arrest of its leaders.

The government also used the incident to falsely accuse Mom Sonando—the 71-year-old owner of Cambodia's main independent radio station and an outspoken critic of the government—of being the ringleader of the supposed succession. Sonando was arrested on July 12 and later sentenced to 20 years' imprisonment during a trial in which no credible evidence against him was presented.

The government also targeted for prosecution leading investigators of ADHOC, a major Cambodian human rights organization, apparently to punish them for their human rights activities. A court in Phnom Penh, the capital, ordered Chan Sovet to appear on August 24 in connection with the land protests in Kratie noted above to answer allegations that he provided a small amount of humanitarian assistance to a community organizer who fled the government operation suppressing the protests, saying the aid constituted intentional assistance to a known perpetrator of a felony. A local court in Ratanakiri province, northeastern Cambodia, summoned Pen Bonnar on October 1 in connection with land disputes there.

On May 24, prominent Buddhist monk Luon Sovath, who had on many occasions expressed sympathy and support for victims of land-grabbing, was briefly detained while en route to observe the trial of 13 women activists (the "Boeng Kak 13") opposing evictions in Phnom Penh. On February 14, he had been secretly indicted on frivolous grounds for "incitement to commit a felony," leaving him vulnerable to arrest at any time. Sovath was named winner of the prestigious Martin Ennals human rights prize in October.

Also on May 24, the court sentenced the 13 women, including a 72-year-old, to two-and-a-half years in prison for involvement in a campaign protesting evictions and demanding proper resettlement for people displaced by a development project owned by a Hun Sen crony and a Chinese investor in Phnom Penh's Boeng Kak area. Under domestic and international pressure, an appeal court released the 13 on June 27, but upheld their convictions.

In August and September, a provincial court repeatedly summoned Rong Chhun, president of the Cambodian Confederation of Unions who is widely seen as the country's most determined labor leader, to answer allegations that he had incited a supposedly illegal garment worker strike in a factory near Phnom Penh, also putting him at risk of imprisonment.

In early September, two more leaders of protests against urban evictions, Yorm Bopha and Tim Sakmony, were arrested after apparently politically motivated allegations lodged with the Phnom Penh court. They were held pending trial and faced prison sentences if convicted.

Khmer Rouge Tribunal (ECCC)

CPP political interference effected via government-appointed judges, prosecutors, and other personnel at the ECCC precipitated the resignation—with effect from May 4—of Laurent Kasper-Ansermet, an investigating judge nominated by the United Nations secretary-general. Kasper-Ansermet claimed that government interference and lack of cooperation made it impossible for him to do his job. His court submissions detailed how that interference had blocked his efforts to investigate five suspects whom Prime Minister Hun Sen had not approved.

The CPP's longstanding strategy of attempting to control the court via delaying tactics and passive non-cooperation contributed to reducing the prosecution of Nuon Chea, Ieng Sary, and Khieu Samphan—three Hun Sen-authorized indictees among former Khmer Rouge leaders—to a "mini-trial" in which only a few of the crime against humanity counts against them would be adjudicated. It appeared unlikely that they would ever go on trial for the additional charges of genocide and war crimes laid against them in December 2009, even though the tribunal is the most expensive international or hybrid criminal tribunal ever, calculated in terms of cost per accused put on trial.

Impunity for Human Rights Violators

Hun Sen's protection of perpetrators of Khmer Rouge crimes and failure in 2012 to credibly investigate killings involving security forces bookended a consistent pattern of impunity for human rights abuses committed during his prolonged rule. These include torture and forced labor in the 1980s, political killings when the UN attempted to midwife a democratic transition in the early 1990s, and a string of extrajudicial executions, assassinations, and attempted assassinations in the years between then and 2011.

These crimes have targeted journalists, opposition party organizers, labor leaders, activists, and intellectuals—with the dead numbering in the hundreds. The crimes, and impunity for them, have characterized Hun Sen's rise and hold on power, and the surge of human rights violations in 2012 confirmed that he considers their perpetration as fundamental to his rule and to preventing popular and democratic challenges.

Drug Detention Centers

In December 2011, revisions to Cambodia's drug law enabled drug users to be detained for compulsory "treatment" for up to two years. Despite a March 2012

HUMAN
RIGHTS
WATCH

"Tell Them That I Want
to Kill Them"
Two Decades of Impunity in Hun Sen's Cambodia

call by 12 UN agencies to close drug detention centers, various government agencies—including security forces—continued to operate 10 centers across the country. Former detainees reported that they had been held without due process, subjected to exhausting military exercises, and ill-treated and even tortured by staff.

Migrant Workers

A 2011 government moratorium on temporary migration of Cambodians as domestic workers to Malaysia, announced after revelations of grave abuses during recruitment in Cambodia and work in Malaysia, remained in place. Officials made statements about lifting the ban, despite uncertain prospects for a Cambodian-Malaysian agreement to establish minimum protections for these migrants, and new media reports of ill-treatment of Cambodian domestic workers in Malaysia. Available statistics pointed to a general increase in the international trafficking of Cambodian workers, many of whom worked in conditions amounting to forced labor.

Key International Actors

The United States, China, and Vietnam provided security assistance to Cambodia in the form of training, equipment, or both. Although US law required that beneficiaries of its training be vetted to ensure none were human rights violators, the vetting process remained deeply flawed. There were no human rights safeguards in Chinese and Vietnamese security aid.

Japan continued to be a major provider of economic assistance without effective conditions. Large-scale state and private Chinese, Vietnamese, and South Korean aid and investment lacked any mechanisms for community participation in decisions related to land or the local environment. Conversely, the World Bank continued to withhold funding for new projects pending a satisfactory government resettlement solution for evictees from the Boeng Kak development project in Phnom Penh, while the Asian Development Bank agreed to review its performance in addressing deteriorations in living conditions suffered by people affected by a bank-financed railway project.

The US made a number of public and private demarches to the government on specific human rights concerns, including the Boeng Kak 13. However, a September donor conference in Phnom Penh was almost silent on the deteriorating human rights situation.

The government reacted with invective to reports by the UN special rapporteur on the situation of human rights in Cambodia that recommended reforming electoral and land concession systems.

China

China's new leadership, consisting of the Communist Party's seven permanent standing committee members, assumed power at the 18th Party Congress in November, ending the decade-long leadership of Hu Jintao and Wen Jiabao.

That era saw sustained economic growth, urbanization, and China's rise as a global power, but little progress on human rights. The government rolled back protections on the administration of justice, presided over a significant rise in social unrest, including the largest inter-ethnic incidents in decades in Tibet and Xinjiang, and expanded the power of the security apparatus.

Chinese people had no say in the selection of their new leaders, highlighting that despite the country's three decades of rapid modernization, the government remains an authoritarian one-party system that places arbitrary curbs on freedom of expression, association, religion, prohibits independent labor unions and human rights organizations, and maintains party control over all judicial institutions. The government also censors the press, internet, and publishing industry, and enforces highly repressive policies in ethnic minority areas in Tibet, Xinjiang, and Inner Mongolia.

At the same time, citizens are increasingly prepared to challenge authorities over volatile livelihood issues, such as land seizures, forced evictions, abuses of power by corrupt cadres, discrimination, and economic inequalities. Based on law enforcement reports, official and scholarly statistics estimate that there are 250-500 protests each day, with anywhere from ten to tens of thousands of participants. Despite facing risks, internet users and reform-oriented media are aggressively pushing censorship boundaries by advocating for the rule of law and transparency, exposing official wrongdoing, and calling for political reforms.

Despite their precarious legal status and surveillance by the authorities, civil society groups continue to try to expand their work. An informal but dedicated network of activists monitors and documents human rights cases under the banner of a country-wide *weiquan* (rights defense) movement. These activists face a host of repressive state measures.

The government announced in its 2012-2015 "National Human Rights Action Plan" that it would interpret its international legal obligations on human rights with a new vaguely defined "principle of practicality"—departing from the its previous rhetorical commitment to the principle of universality of human rights. The new principle appears to be another iteration of the government's oft-repeated justification that China's "national conditions" do not allow for participatory politics.

Human Rights Defenders

Human rights defenders in China regularly face police harassment, house arrest, short-term detention, "reeducation through labor," forcible commitment to psychiatric facilities, or imprisonment on criminal charges, often on state security or public order grounds.

Nobel Peace Prize laureate Liu Xiaobo is serving an 11-year sentence in Heilongjiang province for incitement to subvert state power. His wife, Liu Xia, has been missing since December 2010. She is believed to be under house arrest in the capital Beijing to prevent her from campaigning on her husband's behalf.

Li Tie, a writer and dissident from Wuhan in Hubei province, was sentenced on January 18 to 10 years in prison for subversion. Li's especially harsh sentence was the last of several given to several long-standing democracy activists in the wake of the Arab Spring.

After a year in detention, veteran activists Ni Yulan and Dong Jiqin were sentenced on April 10 to two years and eight months, and two years respectively for "creating a disturbance." An appeal court shortened Ni's sentence by two months in July.

In late April, the blind activist Chen Guangcheng escaped from his home in Shandong province where he had been unlawfully confined with his family since his release from an unjustified prison term for "intentionally damaging property and gathering crowds to disturb transport order." In September 2010, helped by a network of activists, Chen sought refuge at the United States Embassy in Beijing. Following tense negotiations between the US and China over several weeks, Chen was finally allowed to leave with his family on May 19 to study in the US, after central government envoys gave assurances there would be an investigation into his unlawful detention. Chen Kegui, Chen's nephew, faces homicide charges for injuring several guards who raided Chen's brother's home in the middle of the night after they realized Chen had escaped. Local judicial authorities barred Chen Kegui's lawyers from representing him, claiming they had already appointed a legal aid lawyer for him.

On July 25, Hunan activist Zhu Chengzhi was formally arrested on a charge of "inciting subversion of state power" for exposing the suspicious conditions surrounding the alleged suicide of veteran dissident Li Wangyang. Li, who spent most of his life imprisoned, was found hanged in a hospital room in Shaoyang city, Hunan province, on June 6, his feet touching the ground. His suspicious death prompted an internet outcry amongst Chinese rights activists and led to several large demonstrations in Hong Kong. Relatives and supporters of Li were placed under house arrest to stop them challenging the results of a second party-led investigation into the case, which Li's supporters see as a part of the official cover- up.

On August 13, police detained a dozen activists in Beijing and arrested another, Peng Lanlan, in Hunan province. These activists had pressed the State Council to disclose government-held information about implementing measures of the country's second National Human Rights Action plan, publicized earlier in June.

Legal Reforms

While legal reforms effectively stalled under the Hu-Wen leadership and the government rejects judicial independence, large parts of the legal community continue to be a force for change, spurred by increasing popular legal awareness and activism. The party maintains authority over all judicial institutions and mechanisms, and coordinates the work of the judiciary through its political and legal committees. The Public Security, or police, remains its most powerful actor. Forced confessions under torture remain prevalent and miscarriages of justice frequent due to weak courts and tight limits on the rights of the defense.

In March 2012, in an effort to reduce such cases and improve the administration of justice, the government adopted comprehensive revisions to the Criminal Procedure Law (CPL). However, the new revisions also legalize the power of the police to place "state security, terrorism, and major corruption" suspects in detention in a location of the police's choice, outside the formal detention system, for up to six months. These measures put suspects at risk of torture while giving the government a justification for "disappearance" of dissidents and activists.

Domestic critics of the administrative detention system of "reeducation through labor," frequently used against people petitioning the authorities for redress, received a boost following a national outcry over the police sentencing to 18 months a woman who had pressed officials over the rape of her 11-year-old daughter. She was released after approximately a week in detention.

China continued in 2012 to lead the world in executions. The exact number remains a state secret but experts estimate it to be 5,000 to 8,000 a year.

Freedom of Expression

Government restrictions on journalists, bloggers, and an estimated 538 million internet users continued to violate domestic and international legal guarantees of freedom of press and expression. Sina Weibo, the largest of China's social media microblog services, gives 300 million subscribers space to express opinions and discontent to an extent previously unavailable. But like all online content, Weibo is subject to strict scrutiny and manipulation by China's censors tasked with shaping online debate in line with government policy. Alternative social media operations including Twitter, YouTube, and Facebook are blocked.

In mid-June, internet censors blocked all searches for Yili milk powder, an infant formula, after the company recalled products contaminated with mercury. Government censors excised eight pages of *Southern Weekend* newspaper's coverage of the disastrous July 21-22 Beijing flood that caused widespread property damage and disrupted transportation infrastructure. On September 12, censors banned searches for the name "Jinping" amid frantic speculation as to why Chinese Vice President Xi Jinping had disappeared from public view and from mention in Chinese state media for almost two weeks. He later reappeared with no official explanation for his absence.

At least 27 Chinese journalists were serving prison terms in 2012 due to ambiguous laws on "revealing state secrets" and "inciting subversion." Journalists are also at risk of perceived violations of censorship restrictions. *Southern Metropolitan* editor Yu Chen was removed from his position after an anonymous posting to the paper's website criticized the Chinese Communist Party's control over the People's Liberation Army. *Xian Evening News* reporter Shi Junrong was suspended on July 2 for an unspecified time for writing a June 27 expose about local Communist Party member spending money on cigarettes. He remained suspended at this writing.

Journalists who report on sensitive topics remained vulnerable to physical violence in 2012. In one of the higher profile of such incidents, Lei Zhaohe, a reporter with Hong Kong's Asia Television, was punched and kicked by two men on August 10 while filming police detain protesters outside a courthouse in Hefei, Anhui province. Other journalists at the scene identified the two men as plainclothes police.

2012 marked the first expulsion of a foreign journalist since 1998. On May 7, the Chinese government expelled Al Jazeera correspondent Melissa Chan for alleged violations of unspecified rules and regulations. On August 21, the Foreign Correspondents' Clubs of Hong Kong, China, and Shanghai issued a joint statement expressing "extreme concern" over four incidents between July 28-August 12 in which seven foreign journalists were "threatened, harassed and even beaten." The statement said that several of those incidents "involved members of the official security forces and associated elements."

The Chinese government sought to extend its stringent controls on freedom of expression overseas on at least two occasions. In March, the Chinese government successfully pressured the organizers of the annual London Book fair to exclude any dissident or exiled Chinese writers from the list of official participants. In September, the Chinese consulate in San Francisco unsuccessfully sought to persuade the mayor of Corvallis, Oregon, to remove a mural on a private building that supported Tibetan and Taiwanese independence.

Freedom of Religion

Despite a constitutional guarantee of freedom of religion, the Chinese government restricts religious practices to officially approved mosques, churches, temples, and monasteries. The government also audits the activities, employee
details, and financial records of religious bodies. Religious personnel appointments, religious publications, and seminary applications are subject to government review.

Unregistered spiritual groups such as Protestant "house churches" are deemed
unlawful and the government subjects their members to fines and prosecution.
The government classifies Falun Gong—a meditation-focused spiritual group
banned since July 1999—as an "an evil cult" and arrests, harasses, and intimidates its members.

In February, municipal religious management officials in Wugang city, Hunan
province, required parents to sign a guarantee to not participate in "evil cult"
activities as a condition for registering their children in city schools. The registration was part of a wider municipal campaign against Falun Gong and
Protestant house churches during the Chinese Lunar New Year period.

On August 22, the Shanghai municipal government indefinitely suspended
classes at the city's Sheshan Catholic seminary as a reprisal related to the July 7
decision of Ma Daqin, the new auxiliary bishop of Shanghai, to resign from the
official Chinese Catholic Patriotic Association. Ma has been under house arrest
following his decision and remained so at this writing.

The government continues to heavily restrict religious activities in the name of
security in ethnic minority areas. See sections below on Tibet and Xinjiang.

Health and Disability Rights

The government remains hostile towards claims for compensation stemming
from the 1990s blood scandal in Henan province. On August 27, baton-wielding
police beat several members of a group of 300 people with HIV-AIDS protesting
outside headquarters of the Henan provincial government headquarters in
Zhengzhou. The crowd was protesting the government's refusal to pay compen-

sation to those infected with the virus via government-organized mass blood plasma sales in Henan province in the 1990s.

The government's National Human Rights Action Plan (2012-2015) issued on June 11 commits the government to greater protection from widespread heavy metal pollution, yet no redress or medical attention had materialized at this writing for children poisoned by lead in in Henan, Yunnan, Shaanxi, and Hunan in recent years.

Although it is a party to the Convention on the Rights of Persons with Disabilities (CRPD), China's protections of the rights of persons with disabilities remains inadequate. During China's first CRPD review on September 18-19 in Geneva, government officials generally denied the existence of abuses and their failure to provide people with disabilities access to information, justice, and basic services.

On October 26, the Chinese government adopted a mental health law, which had been in the works for more than 20 years. The law has numerous flaws, including inadequate safeguards to protect against involuntary detention in psychiatric institutions.

Women's Rights

Women's reproductive rights and access to reproductive health remain severely curtailed under China's family planning regulations. The government continues to impose administrative sanctions, fines, and coercive measures, including forced abortion. In recent years coercive birth control policies increasingly extend to ethnic minority areas such as Tibet and Xinjiang. These policies contribute to an increasing gender-imbalance (118.08 males for every 100 females according to the 2010 census), which in turn contribute to different rights violations, including forced marriage and trafficking.

The government's erratic and punitive crackdowns on sex work often lead to serious abuses, including physical and sexual violence, increased disease risk, and constrained access to justice for the country's estimated 4 to 10 million sex workers.

Although the government acknowledges that domestic violence, employment discrimination, and discriminatory social attitudes are acute and widespread, it limits the activities of independent women's rights groups and discourages public interest litigation.

Migrant and Labor Rights

Chinese workers are becoming more active and outspoken in their efforts to improve wages and conditions despite the absence of meaningful union representation. The official All-China Federation of Trade Unions (ACFTU) is the sole legal representative of China's workers due to a ban on independent labor unions.

Nongovernmental labor groups devoted to protecting migrant workers' rights in Guangdong province's assembly manufacturing areas came under sustained attack from government officials and security forces in 2012. In 2012, government authorities or landlords under pressure from local government officials targeted at least a dozen other migrant labor NGOs in Shenzhen with forced evictions. On August 30, two dozen plainclothes thugs who appeared to be operating at official behest attacked the Shenzhen office of Little Grass Center for Migrant Workers, smashing windows and breaking the front door in an apparent act of intimidation.

In June, joint research by the official All-China Women's Federation and the Guangdong provincial judiciary revealed that thousands of children left behind in rural villages by their migrant worker parents due to restrictions of the *hukou* (household registration) system are victims of sexual abuse. The *hukou* system, which the government has pledged to abolish, unfairly limits the access of China's 220 million migrant workers to education, medical services, and housing.

Sexual Orientation and Gender Identity

The Chinese government stopped classifying homosexuality as a mental illness in 2001 following decriminalization of homosexual behavior in 1997. In June, more than 80 lesbian, gay, bisexual, and transgender (LGBT) activists gathered in Beijing for China's first LGBT conference. However, activists describe deliberate official harassment through occasional police raids on popular gay venues. China also lacks anti-discrimination laws based on sexual orientation and the state does not recognize same sex relationships or adoption rights.

In September, parents of gay men and women protested the publication of an educational booklet produced for Zhejiang province's Hangzhou Education Bureau that described homosexuality as "sexual deviance" and advocated that parents seek to "prevent" it. The publishing company later announced those passages would be excised from the booklet's second edition in October.

In May, for the second year in a row, the Beijing LGBT Center was the target of a forced eviction after the center's landlord insisted that homosexuality was "too sensitive" a topic for his property and demanded the center relocate. The facility subsequently relocated.

Tibet

The situation in the Tibet Autonomous Region (TAR) and the neighboring Tibetan autonomous areas of Qinghai, Sichuan, Gansu, and Yunnan provinces remained tense following the massive crackdown on popular protests that swept the plateau in 2008, and the introduction of measures designed to place all Tibetan monasteries under the direct control of government officials who will be permanently stationed there.

The government has yet to indicate that it will accommodate the aspirations of Tibetan people for greater autonomy, even within the narrow confines of the country's autonomy law on ethnic minorities' areas. At this writing, 85 Tibetans had self-immolated since the first recorded case on February 27, 2009—72 of them in 2012 alone. At least 69 of those who self-immolated have died.

Chinese security forces maintain a heavy presence and the authorities continue to tightly restrict access and travel to Tibetan areas, particularly for journalists and foreign visitors. Tibetans suspected of being critical of political, religious, cultural, or economic state policies are systematically targeted on charges of "separatism." On June 18, a Sichuan province court sentenced senior Tibetan cleric, Yonten Gyatso, to seven years in prison for disseminating information about the situation in Tibet and contacting human rights organizations abroad.

Secret arrests and torture in custody remains widespread. In June, a 36-year-old Tibetan monk named Karwang died due to prolonged torture in police custody in Ganzi (Kardze in Tibetan). He had been arrested mid-May on suspicion of having put up posters calling for Tibetan independence.

As part of its drive to build "a New Socialist Countryside" on the Tibetan plateau, the government continues to implement large development programs mandating rehousing or relocating up to 80 percent of the rural population. The relocation policies have been carried out—contrary to Chinese government claims—with no effective choice and without genuine consultation of those affected, while compensation mechanisms are opaque and inadequate. Pastoralists deprived of their traditional livelihood face declining living standards and increased dependency on government subsidies.

Xinjiang

Under the guise of counterterrorism and "anti-separatism" efforts, the government maintains a pervasive system of ethnic discrimination against Uighurs and other ethnic minorities in the Xinjiang Uighur Autonomous Region, and sharply curbs religious and cultural expression. Politically motivated arrests are common.

A pervasive atmosphere of fear among the Uighur population contributes to growing ethnic polarization. Factors contributing to this bleak atmosphere include the omnipresence of the secret police, the recent history of disappearances, and an overtly politicized judiciary.

Also contributing to this polarization is the legacy of the Urumqi riots of July 2009, the most deadly episode of ethnic unrest in recent Chinese history. The government has not accounted for hundreds of persons detained after the riots, investigated serious allegations of torture and ill-treatment of detainees that have surfaced in testimonies of refugees and relatives living outside China, or released definitive numbers or names of victims—the majority of whom were ethnic Chinese—killed during the riots.

HUMAN
RIGHTS
WATCH

Isolated in Yunnan

Kachin Refugees from Burma in China's Yunnan Province

Several violent incidents took place in a year of increasing restrictions on religious and cultural expression. In one of the most severe, On February 28, a group of Uighurs, led by a man the government claimed was an underground radical cleric, attacked passers-by in a mainly Chinese-inhabited street of Yechen (Kargilik in Uighur), killing at least 12 people. The cleric, Abdudukeremu Mamut, was sentenced to death on March 26.

A policy to raze traditional Uighur neighborhoods and relocate or forcibly evict inhabitants, accompanied by a campaign to settle the majority of the nomadic and pastoralist population of Xinjiang, are the most visible aspects of a comprehensive development policy launched in 2010 that is supposed to reduce socio-economic disparities and lift the livelihood of ethnic groups and help "smash separatist sentiment."

Hong Kong

Civic groups and the public have challenged the Hong Kong government on rights issues. Hong Kong authorities appear unwilling to deviate much from pro-Beijing interests. They have not moved towards universal suffrage as mandated by the territory's mini-constitution, and have shown weakness in safeguarding the territory's autonomy, civil and political freedoms, and the rule of law.

In September, the government bowed to popular pressure and suspended introducing patriotic education teaching material aimed at inculcating loyalty to the Chinese Communist Party. Concerns continue to grow about the use of excessively restrictive methods by the police in controlling assembly and procession, and over the Immigration Department's arbitrary bans on individuals critical of Beijing. Concerns are also growing about the failure of the government to properly investigate the rising number of claims that mainland security personnel or individual working at their behest are operating in the territory, monitoring or intimidating critics of the Beijing government.

In July, two mainland petitioners were each sentenced to 14 months of "reeducation through labor" in their home province of Jiangxi for having participated to the annual July 1st pro-democracy demonstration in Hong Kong, the first known such instance.

Key International Actors

Despite claims to "making unremitting efforts" at peace in Syria, the Chinese government, along with Russia, vetoed three resolutions aimed at pressuring the Syrian government. China also demonstrated its disdain for international law by pushing back from Yunnan province at least 7,000 ethnic Kachin refugees into a conflict zone in northern Burma, insisting that they were not refugees.

Although the United States won praise for helping Chen Guangcheng and his family, neither it nor other governments moved to alter or improve their largely ineffective bilateral human rights dialogues with the Chinese government. Few of these dialogues involve meaningful participation by civil society groups.

In early April, Japanese Diet members adopted a highly unusual resolution on Tibet calling for the Chinese government to resume talks with the Dalai Lama. Beijing also found itself forced to respond to critical South Korean press reports that China had forcibly repatriated North Koreans; in response, Beijing allowed a handful of North Koreans sheltered in the South Korean consulates in China to depart for Seoul.

India

India, the world's most populous democracy, continues to have significant human rights problems despite making commitments to tackle some of the most prevalent abuses. The country has a thriving civil society, free media, and an independent judiciary. But longstanding abusive practices, corruption, and lack of accountability for perpetrators foster human rights violations.

Government initiatives, including police reform and improved access to health care and education, languish due to poor implementation. Many women, children, Dalits (so-called untouchables), tribal communities, religious minorities, people with disabilities, and sexual and gender minorities remain marginalized and continue to suffer discrimination because of government failure to train public officials in stopping discriminatory behavior.

Impunity remains a serious problem, particularly for abuses committed by security forces in Jammu and Kashmir, the northeast, and areas in central and eastern India facing a Maoist insurgency. Resource extraction and infrastructure projects often have deleterious environmental and economic impacts, and may infringe upon the rights of affected communities.

The central government tightened restrictions on internet content, insisting the measures are to contain threats to public order. It used a colonial-era sedition law to stifle peaceful dissent in 2012 on issues ranging from the government's handling of the Maoist insurgency and corruption, to protests against a nuclear power plant in the southern state of Tamil Nadu. The protection of religious minorities received a boost from the prosecutions of several suspects in the 2002 Gujarat riots, resulting in over 75 convictions in 2012. These included the August conviction of Maya Kodnani, a former minister and a leader of Bajrang Dal, a militant Hindu organization.

Impunity

Members of security forces implicated in serious rights abuses continued to enjoy impunity, in large measure due to India's laws and policies.

The Indian defense establishment resisted attempts in 2012 to revoke or revise the Armed Forces Special Powers Act (AFSPA), which permits soldiers to commit serious human rights violations with effective immunity.

Maoist Insurgency

Maoists operations extend to nine states in central and eastern India, finding support in regions with weak governance, infrastructure and basic public services, such as health care and education.

Maoist insurgents known as Naxalites continued to target government schools and hospitals. Paramilitary forces continued to occupy and use schools as bases, despite a Supreme Court order to vacate all schools by May 2011. In September, government officials in Chhattisgarh, central India, stated they would remove forces from 36 schools and hostels because of their impact on children's education.

At this writing, Maoist-related violence in 2012 had resulted in 257 deaths, including 98 civilians. In June, security forces killed 19 villagers in Chhattisgarh state in a night operation, prompting widespread condemnation.

Civil society activists in Maoist areas remain increasingly at risk from both Maoists and state security forces. Many activists have been arbitrarily arrested, tortured, and charged with politically motivated offenses that include murder, conspiracy, and sedition. The Maoists have threatened or attacked activists they believe are linked to the government.

Jammu and Kashmir

While violence in the northern state of Jammu and Kashmir has been on a decline, security forces responsible for serious rights abuses remain effectively immune from prosecution under the AFSPA.

In September, the state government rejected calls for DNA testing of 2,730 corpses that a police investigative team found in unmarked graves at 38 sites in north Kashmir in July 2011. Some of the gravesites are believed to hold victims

of enforced disappearance and extrajudicial execution by government security forces dating back to the 1990s.

A number of elected village council leaders resigned in September following threats and attacks from armed separatist militants who oppose any election in Jammu and Kashmir.

Violence in Assam

In July, violence between indigenous Bodo tribes and Muslim migrant settlers started in Kokrajhar and spread to several districts in Assam, resulting in the deaths of at least 97 people and displacing over 450,000. Authorities in Assam failed to prevent the violence, despite information about increasing tensions between the communities, which have clashed in the past over access to land and resources.

Freedom of Expression

In 2012, the central government used the Information Technology (Intermediary Guidelines) Rules to tighten internet censorship, raising concerns about restrictions on the right to free speech. Under the rules, intermediaries such as internet service providers and search engines are required to remove content within 36 hours that is deemed offensive. However, criteria for prohibited content are ambiguous and frequently used to stifle criticism of the government.

The government used the colonial-era sedition law without regard for a Supreme Court ruling that sedition requires evidence of incitement. In September, police in Mumbai arrested political cartoonist Aseem Trivedi, acting on a complaint that his cartoons mocked the Indian constitution and the national emblem. He was released after widespread protests. In May, in the southern state of Tamil Nadu, police filed sedition complaints against thousands of people who peacefully protested the construction of a nuclear power plant. In Orissa and Chhattisgarh states, sedition cases have been filed against activists and lawyers suspected of supporting armed Maoist groups.

The government continued to use the Foreign Contributions Regulation Act (FCRA) to restrict access to foreign assistance by domestic nongovernmental organizations.

Protection of Children's Rights

Children remained at risk of abuse, with a large number forced into dangerous forms of labor, and without proper access to health care and education.

India has one of the largest populations of malnourished children in the world. According to government estimates, at least 40 percent of children are vulnerable to sex trafficking, homelessness, forced labor, drug abuse, and crime—and need protection.

The government took some significant steps in 2012 to improve children's rights. In April, the Supreme Court upheld the government decision to provide universal access to primary education, requiring that private schools reserve 25 percent of seats for underprivileged children. In May, parliament passed a new law to protect children from sexual abuse. In August, the government issued a blanket ban on employing children under 14, reversing a former law that only prohibited employment in hazardous jobs.

Women's Rights

Violence against women and girls continued in 2012, with increased reports of sexual assault, including against those with disabilities. The government had yet to properly investigate and prosecute sexual abuse in police custody.

In June 2012, Pinki Pramanik, a renowned woman athlete, was arrested on allegations of rape. Male police officers mistreated her while taking her into custody and authorities conducted "gender determination" tests in violation of her rights to consent, privacy, and dignity. A video of her undergoing some part of the abusive examination was made public.

India has yet to enact amendments to reform its penal laws to recognize a wide range of sexual offenses. While the central government modified its protocols for handling rape investigations, removing questions on the degrading "two-finger test," the changes still fall short of World Health Organization (WHO) guidelines on sexual assault, especially regarding medical treatment for victims.

India has a strong law to curb child marriages but the government also pursues discriminatory policies. In central India's Madhya Pradesh state, for example, adult candidates are barred from taking state civil service exams if they were forced to marry as children. The government continued to limit its nutrition programs for pregnant mothers in many states to women ages 19 and older, and up to two live births only, excluding many young mothers from benefits.

Abuses in Extractive Industry

A breakdown in government oversight over India's mining sector has led to rampant corruption and, in some cases, to serious harm to health, environments, and livelihoods of mining-affected communities.

In September, the government of the western state of Goa canceled all mining licenses to examine whether proper procedures were followed to mitigate the negative impact on health and environment. The same month, after a year-long suspension, mining activity was allowed to partially resume in the southern Karnataka state, on condition that no environmental restrictions are violated. However, the government failed to enforce protection mechanisms in other parts of the country.

Access to Palliative Care

The Indian government took several important steps in 2012 to address the suffering of hundreds of thousands of persons with incurable diseases from pain and other symptoms. It has begun to actively encourage regional cancer centers, many of which do not currently offer palliative care, to ensure such services become available. The government is also preparing amendments to the Narcotic Drugs and Psychotropic Substances Act, which, if adopted, would improve the medical availability of morphine. More than seven million people in India require palliative care every year.

HUMAN
RIGHTS
WATCH

Out of Control
Mining, Regulatory Failure and Human Rights in India

Death Penalty

In November, India hanged Ajmal Kasab, the only surviving Pakistani gunman from the November 2008 Mumbai attacks in which 10 members of the Lashkar-e-Taiba Pakistan-based terrorist group killed more than 160 people. It was the first execution in India since 2004, ending an eight-year unofficial moratorium.

India maintains that it imposes capital punishment in only the "rarest of rare" cases. In July, 14 retired judges asked the president to commute the death sentences of 13 inmates erroneously upheld by the Supreme Court over the past nine years. This followed the court's admission that these death sentences were rendered *per incuriam* (out of error or ignorance). In November, the Supreme Court also conceded that the "rarest of rare" standard has not been applied uniformly over the years and that the principles for judging what constitutes "rarest of rare" crimes need "a fresh look."

International Role

India's foreign policy in the region continues to be influenced by strategic and economic concerns about China's growing influence in Burma, Nepal, Pakistan, and Sri Lanka.

India took some positive steps toward promoting human rights and accountability globally. In March, India voted for a United States-led resolution at the United Nations Human Rights Council (HRC) calling for post-war reconciliation and accountability in Sri Lanka. This marked a significant change of position by India, which has traditionally refrained from publicly criticizing the Sri Lankan government on well-documented war crimes and related abuses.

In February, India voted in favor of a UN Security Council resolution on Syria backing an Arab League plan concerning the escalating violence there. In July, India again voted with Western governments at the Security Council in favor of a resolution on Syria, which if adopted, would have extended the mandate of the United Nations Supervision Mission in Syria (UNSMIS) and threatened sanctions if demands that Syrian authorities end abuses were not met.

Key International Actors

India has traditionally followed a foreign policy based on the principle of non-interference and deems any criticism on human rights issues as interference in its domestic affairs. As a result, most countries, including the US and the European Union (EU), prefer to discuss these issues with India in private rather than publicly press it to improve its rights record.

However, in May, several UN member states made significant recommendations during the UN Universal Periodic Review (UPR) of India's human rights record. Recommendations included calls for India to ratify international treaties against torture and enforced disappearance, repeal the death penalty as well as the much-abused AFSPA, and protect the rights of Dalits, religious minorities, women, children, and tribal groups. The Indian government has responded by committing to address some of the recommendations, but ignored those that required substantive action against impunity.

India invited the UN special rapporteur on extrajudicial, summary, or arbitrary executions, and the UN special rapporteur on the sale of children, child pornography, and child prostitution-to visit the country. After his visit in March, Christof Heyns, the special rapporteur on extrajudicial, summary, or arbitrary executions, expressed concerns over "high levels of impunity" enjoyed by police and armed forces, recommended that the AFSPA be repealed, and called for establishing a commission of inquiry to investigate extrajudicial killings.

Indonesia

Competitive, credible, and fair local elections in Jakarta and the province of West Kalimantan in 2012 underscored the ongoing transition from decades of authoritarian rule in Indonesia. The government's willingness to accept numerous recommendations from United Nations member states during the UN's Universal Periodic Review (UPR) of Indonesia's human rights record was another hopeful sign of a growing commitment to respecting human rights.

However, Indonesia remains beset by serious human rights problems. Violence and discrimination against religious minorities, particularly Ahmadiyah, Bahai, Christians, and Shia deepened. Lack of accountability for abuses by police and military forces continues to affect the lives of residents in Papua and West Papua provinces.

Freedom of Expression

Indonesia's vibrant media routinely reports on crucial social and political issues including corruption, environmental destruction, and violence against religious minorities. But a rising climate of religious intolerance and an infrastructure of discriminatory national and local laws deny freedom of expression to Indonesia's religious minorities.

In May, the Indonesian government dismissed recommendations during its UPR to release more than 100 political prisoners, the majority in the Moluccas Islands and Papua. These activists are serving sentences of up to 20 years for acts of peaceful protest including staging protest dances or raising separatist flags. In January, the government refused to accept the UN Working Group on Arbitrary Detention's determination, issued in September 2011, that Papuan independence activist Filep Karma is a political prisoner. The working group called on Indonesia to immediately and unconditionally release Karma.

Indonesian police and government authorities failed to adequately protect artists, writers, and media companies targeted with threats and protests by militant Islamist groups. In May, neither police nor government officials intervened to prevent Islamist groups from disrupting the book tour of Canadian-Muslim writer Irshad Manji in the capital, Jakarta, and Yogyakarta. In June, Jakarta police bowed to pressure from the militant Islamic Defenders Front organization protesting the planned concert of US pop star Lady Gaga and revoked the permit to the concert organizers, prompting its cancellation.

Military Reform and Impunity

Impunity for members of Indonesia's security forces remained a serious concern, with the military courts having a poor prosecution record and no civilian jurisdiction over soldiers who commit serious rights abuses. On June 6, over 300 soldiers from the 756th Battalion rampaged in the Papuan village of Wamena as a reprisal for an incident in which in which villagers beat to death two soldiers involved in a fatal traffic accident. Soldiers randomly fired their weapons into shopping areas, burned down 87 houses, stabbed 13 villagers, and killed a native Papuan civil servant.

Although military officials on June 12 apologized for the incident and promised compensation, victims said military investigators failed to question them about the incident. They said rather than paying any compensation, the military has limited its response to the violence to a traditional Papuan "stone-burning" ceremony and declared the case closed.

Freedom of Religion

In 2012, incidents of violence against religious minorities were frequent and occasionally deadly. Islamist militants mobilized mobs to attack religious minorities with impunity. Light prison terms imposed on those prosecuted sent a message of official tolerance for such mob violence. Dozens of regulations, including ministerial decrees on building houses of worship, continue to foster discrimination and intolerance.

Throughout 2012, dozens of minority Christian congregations, including GKI Yasmin church in Bogor and HKBP Filadelfia church in the Jakarta suburb of Bekasi, reported that local government officials arbitrarily refused to issue them permits required under a 2006 decree on building houses of worship. Both churches had already won Supreme Court decisions to build such structures.

Senior government officials, including Religious Affairs Minister Suryadharma Ali and Home Affairs Minister Gamawan Fauzi, continued to justify restrictions on religious freedom in the name of public order. They both offered affected minorities "relocation" rather than legal protection of their rights.

Suryadharma Ali has himself inflamed tensions by making highly discriminatory remarks about the Ahmadiyah and Shia, suggesting that both are heretical. In September 2012, he stated that the "solution" to religious intolerance of Shia and Ahmadiyah was their conversion to the Sunni Islam that most Indonesians follow. That same month, President Susilo Bambang Yudhoyono called for the development of an international instrument to prosecute "religious blasphemy," which could be used to restrict free expression and the religious freedom of minorities.

According to Indonesia's Setara Institute, which monitors religious freedom, religious attacks increased from 216 in 2010 to 244 in 2011. In the first nine months of 2012 there were 214 cases.

On December 29, 2011, Sunni militants attacked a Shia village in Sampang regency, Madura Island, burning houses and the madrasa, causing around 500 Shia residents to flee. Police arrested and charged only one of the militants for the arson attack. On August 26, at the end of the holiday following the end of Ramadan, hundreds of Sunni militants again attacked the same Shia village and burned down around 50 Shia houses, killing one man and seriously injuring another. Several police officers at the scene failed to intervene to stop the attack.

In March, a court in Central Java sentenced Andreas Guntur, the leader of the spiritual group Amanat Keagungan Ilahi, to four years' imprisonment on charges of blasphemy on the basis of allegedly improper teachings of certain verses of the Quran.

In June, a West Sumatra court sentenced Alexander An, an administrator of the "Minang Atheist" Facebook group, to 30 months in prison and a fine of 100 million rupiah (US$11,000) for "inciting public unrest" via Facebook postings espousing atheism.

In July, an East Java district court sentenced Shia cleric Tajul Muluk to two years' imprisonment for blasphemy against Islam. The East Java high court later increased his sentence to four years and two months for causing "riots" in August.

In November, Acehnese villagers attacked a Muslim sect in Bireuen, Aceh, targeting the house of Muslim teacher Tengku Aiyub Syakuban. Mainstream Muslim clerics accused Syakuban of disseminating "heretical teachings." Hundreds of villagers burned and killed Syakuban and his student Muntasir. One attacker, Mansyur, also died in the melee.

Papua/West Papua

In March, a Jayapura court convicted five men—Selpius Bobii, a social media activist; August Sananay Kraar, a civil servant; Dominikus Sorabut, a filmmaker; Edison Waromi, a former political prisoner; and Forkorus Yaboisembut, a Papuan tribal leader—and sentenced them to three years in prison for statements made at a Papuan People's Congress in October 2011. The security forces had brutally attacked the congress, leaving at least three people dead.

In May, more than a dozen UN member countries raised questions and made recommendations during Indonesia's UPR in Geneva about human rights problems in Papua including impunity for abuses by security forces, restrictions on the rights to freedom of expression, and excessive restrictions and surveillance of foreign journalists and human rights researchers. In September, Indonesia rejected all the Papua-related UPR recommendations. The government instead denied that Indonesia has political prisoners and asserted that there is no impunity in Papua and that "national journalists" could travel freely in the region.

From May to August there was a marked upsurge in violence as Indonesian security forces apparently sought to crackdown on Papuan activists. Forty-seven reported violent incidents in this period left 18 dead, including one Indonesian security officer, and dozens of wounded, including a German tourist.

On June 14, police shot and killed KNPB deputy chairman Mako Tabuni, triggering riots in the Jayapura neighborhood of Wamena, over perceptions that Tabuni was the victim of an extrajudicial execution. Papua police suspected Tabuni of involvement in numerous shootings.

Aceh

In June, former Aceh guerilla leaders Zaini Abdullah and Muzakir Manaf took the offices of Aceh's governor and deputy governor respectively after winning an April 9 election.

In May, the Singkil regency closed down 19 churches and one house of worship belonging to followers of Pambi, a native faith among the Pakpak Dairi ethnic group, after protests from the militant Islamic Defenders Front who asserted the structures were "illegal." Governor Zaini refused to intervene in the dispute, blaming religious tension on unnamed "outsiders."

Aceh's provincial government continued to implement a repressive Sharia-inspired dress code and law on "seclusion," banning association between unmarried men and women in "isolated" places. The provisions are enforced primarily through a Sharia police force that harasses, intimidates, and arbitrarily arrests and detains women and men.

In September, a 16-year-old teenage girl arrested by the Sharia police in Langsa regency committed suicide after two daily newspapers reported that she was a "prostitute." In her suicide note, she denied the allegation and said she could not bear the shame.

Migrant Workers

More than four million Indonesian women work abroad in Malaysia, Singapore, and the Middle East as live-in domestic workers. These women often encounter a range of abuses, including labor exploitation, psychological, physical, and sexual abuse, and situations of forced labor and slavery-like conditions. The Indonesian government has become an increasingly vocal advocate for its workers abroad, successfully negotiating the pardon of 22 Indonesian women on Saudi Arabia's death row, calling for improved labor protections, and ratifying the Migrant Workers Convention.

However, Indonesia has consistently failed to rein in abusive recruitment agencies that send workers abroad. Many agencies charge workers high fees that leave them heavily indebted and give them deceptive or incomplete information about their work conditions. Revisions to its migration law remain pending.

Within Indonesia, an important draft law extending key protections to domestic workers has languished in parliament. The country's labor law excludes all domestic workers from the basic labor rights afforded to formal workers, such as a minimum wage, overtime pay, limits to hours of work, a weekly rest day, and vacation. Hundreds of thousands of girls, some as young as 11, are employed as domestic workers. Many work 14 to 18-hour days, seven days a week, with no day off. Many employers forbid child domestic workers from leaving the house where they work and pay little or none of their salaries. In the worst cases, girls are physically, psychologically, and sexually abused by their employers or their employers' family members.

Refugees and Asylum Seekers

Indonesia detains and mistreats thousands of asylum seekers, including children, from Sri Lanka, Afghanistan, Burma, and elsewhere. Asylum seekers face detention, abuses in custody, limited access to education, and have little or no basic assistance. In February 2012, an Afghan asylum seeker died from injuries allegedly inflicted by guards at the Pontianak Immigration Detention Center. There are at least 1,000 unaccompanied migrant children in Indonesia, approximately 200 of whom remain in detention with unrelated adults. Indonesia is not party to the 1951 Refugee Convention, and does not provide most migrants opportunities to obtain legal status, such as to seek asylum. Many migrants consider traveling on to Australia on boats arranged by smugglers a viable option, despite the risks of drowning in the dangerous sea crossing.

Key International Actors

In April 2012, British Prime Minister David Cameron visited Jakarta. Cameron applauded Indonesia's political progress, but challenged the government to stand up against "despicable violence and persecution" of religious minorities.

Much of US policy towards Indonesia has focused on cementing military ties, including with Indonesian special forces, which have long been implicated in serious abuses. In September, the US announced the sale of eight Apache attack helicopters to Indonesia.

In November, United Nations High Commissioner for Human Rights Navi Pillay visited Jakarta and asked the Indonesian government to address "increasing levels of violence and hatred towards religious minorities and narrow and extremist-interpretations of Islam."

Malaysia

In a nationally televised speech on Malaysia Day in September 2011, Prime Minister Seri Najib Tun Razak called for a Malaysia "which practices functional and inclusive democracy, where peace and public order are safeguarded in line with the supremacy of the Constitution, the rule of law and respect for basic human rights and individual rights." However he added that there had to be "checks and balances ... between national security and personal freedom," and ensuing reforms have favored security over internationally recognized human rights.

Parliamentary elections must be held no later than April 2013, and political tensions were already high in November with both the opposition and the government alleging engagement by their political opponents in election-related intimidation and violence.

Preventive Detention

In his September 2011 speech, Prime Minister Najib pledged to replace the notorious Internal Security Act (ISA), which permitted long-term detention without trial, and other rights-restricting legislation. The Banishment Act 1959 and the Restricted Residence Act 1933 were the first to be rescinded, followed by three emergency declarations and the emergency-related laws they made possible. One of the rescinded laws, the Emergency (Public Order and Crime Prevention) Ordinance 1969, had been regularly used to hold criminal suspects indefinitely without charge or trial.

The Security Offences (Special Measures) 2012 Act (SOSMA) replaced the ISA on July 31, 2012. On a positive note, SOSMA reduced initial detention without charge from 60 to no more than 28 days, and required that a suspect be charged in court or released thereafter. However, other provisions reduce human rights protections, including an overly broad definition of a security offense, allowing police rather than courts to authorize interception of communications during investigations, and permitting prosecutors to conceal the source of evidence and to keep the identities of witnesses secret, thereby preventing cross-examination. Even if a suspect is acquitted under SOSMA, the law permits a series of appeals, with bail disallowed, that could result in a suspect's indefinite detention. Malaysian authorities, using transitional authority at the time SOSMA replaced the ISA, still hold 27 ISA detainees.

Freedom of Assembly and Association

In 2012, the government continued to violate rights to free association and peaceful public assembly. While Prime Minister Najib agreed in September 2011 to review section 27 of the Police Act, which mandated police permits for public assemblies, the government hastily drafted and passed a replacement Peaceful Assembly Act on December 20, 2011.

The new law rescinded the requirement for a permit but also introduced major new restrictions, including a broad ban on "moving assemblies" of any kind. Static protests are also prohibited closer than 50 meters from many prohibited sites, making it virtually impossible to hold an assembly in an urban setting. Other restrictions include empowering the police to set assembly conditions such as time, place, and date after taking into consideration other groups' objections or "any inherent environmental factor." Police were also given the power to use all "reasonable force" to break up a protest.

City and federal officials sought to prevent an April 28 sit-in sponsored by Bersih 3.0, the Coalition for Clean and Fair Elections. They barred Bersih from using Dataram Merdeka (Independence Square) in central Kuala Lumpur and barricaded the area. Nevertheless, marchers numbering in the tens of thousands walked peacefully toward the barricaded square and when the announcement came that the rally was over began a peaceful dispersal. However, a small group breached the barricades. The police reacted with excessive force in what became a four-hour onslaught of tear gas, water cannon, and indiscriminate beatings and arrests.

On July 1, 2011, Home Affairs Minister Hishammuddin Hussein declared Bersih an illegal organization under the Societies Act. On July 24, 2012, the Kuala Lumpur High Court overturned that decision, ruling that the original decision was "tainted with irrationality."

Freedom of Expression

Most major newspapers and television and radio stations remain controlled by media companies close to political parties in the government coalition. A recent amendment to the Evidence Act has raised fears that intermediary liability on the internet will further decrease freedom of expression. The provision creates a legal presumption that an owner, administrator, host, editor, or subscriber to a network service who has in their custody or control any computer from which any publication originates is presumed to have published or republished the content of the publication unless the contrary is proven.

The Printing Presses and Publications Act (PPPA) retains its potency despite some reforms, such as ending the need to renew licenses annually and adding judicial oversight to what was the home minister's unchecked power to approve or reject license applications. New publications still require initial approval and licenses still may be arbitrarily revoked. Other means of control include calls from the ministry offering "advice" to editors and prison terms and fines for "maliciously" printing so-called false news. The home minister maintains absolute discretion over licensing of printing presses.

In 2012, Malaysian courts partially advanced the right of free expression. *Malaysiakini*, the largest online newspaper in Malaysia, had repeatedly and unsuccessfully applied to publish a daily print version. On October 1, the Kuala Lumpur High Court ruled the home minister's refusal was "improper and irrational" and the application should be resubmitted. In a significant statement contradicting the prevailing government view, the judge said that a license to publish was "a right, not a privilege." The attorney general's chambers and the Home Ministry appealed the court's decision.

Sisters in Islam, a local nongovernmental organization, also won a significant victory in July when the Court of Appeal dismissed a government appeal to overturn a 2010 High Court decision lifting the ban on *Muslim Women and the Challenge of Islamic Extremism*, a book of essays originally banned in 2008.

A civil court's decision that the arrest of political cartoonist Zunar under the Sedition Act and the PPPA in September 2012 was lawful had a more negative impact, reinforcing the unwillingness of printing presses, publishers, and book-stores to be associated with controversial books.

Police Abuses and Impunity

Human Rights Watch and local civil society groups have documented police abuses, including excessive use of force during arrests, suspicious deaths in custody, failure to adequately investigate such incidents and to hold account-able those responsible; and inadequate post-mortem inquiries and investiga-tions. Victims of police violence reported few effective avenues for redress and decried an apparent culture of police impunity for mistreatment.

Trial of Anwar Ibrahim

On January 9, 2012, a Kuala Lumpur court acquitted Anwar Ibrahim, parliamen-tary leader of Malaysia's political opposition, of sodomy on the grounds that it could not "be 100 percent certain that the [DNA] evidence can be accepted, as there could have been tampering." An appeal by the attorney general's cham-bers, could add months, if not years, to resolution of the case.

Human Rights Defenders

On July 3, 2012, government agencies initiated a multi-pronged investigation into Suaram, one of Malaysia's leading human rights NGOs. Government offi-cials and civil servant investigators accused Suaram of financial irregularities, accepting foreign donations to undermine the Malaysian government, and hid-ing an illegal association behind the group's registration as a company. Regulatory agencies, including the Companies Commission of Malaysia and the Registrar of Societies, demanded information and documents going back years, and interrogated Suaram staff and board members. No one had been charged at this writing.

Many observers believe the investigation was prompted by Suaram's decision in 2010 to become involved in a French judicial investigation examining alleged corruption in Malaysia's purchase of submarines from a French defense compa-ny.

Throughout September and October, pro-government media alleged that Suaram and a number of other NGOs critical of the government were receiving foreign funding in an attempt to destabilize the government.

Refugees, Asylum Seekers, and Trafficking Victims

Malaysian immigration law does not recognize refugees and asylum seekers. The government is not a party to the 1951 Refugee Convention and lacks domestic refugee law and asylum procedures. Malaysia refuses to permit refugees to work or to allow for education of refugee children.

In February, Malaysia denied the United Nations High Commissioner for Refugees (UNHCR) access to asylum seeker Hamza Kashgari, who appeared to be an asylum seeker from Saudi Arabia. He had fled after it was learned he had tweeted messages that some deemed insulting to the Prophet Muhammad. Kashgari was deported amid execution calls in his homeland. At this writing, he was still imprisoned.

The Anti-Trafficking in Persons and Anti-Smuggling of Migrants Act conflates trafficking and people smuggling, and fails to provide meaningful protection to victims of either crime. The government confines trafficking victims in sub-standard government shelters without access to services and assistance until legal cases they are involved with are adjudicated.

Detention and Drugs Policy

The Dangerous Drugs (Special Preventive Measures) Act continues to authorize preventive detention. During 2012, an estimated 700 people were held under the act.

The National Anti-Drugs Agency maintains over 20 *puspens* (drug detention centers) where users are held for a minimum of two years. Rates of relapse in Malaysia have been estimated at 70 to 90 percent and those re-arrested as users face long prison terms combined with caning. Drug traffickers face mandatory death sentences, but the number of people executed is not publicly available.

Sexual Orientation and Gender Identity

In 2012, discrimination against lesbian, gay, bisexual, and transgender (LGBT) persons reached new levels of intensity. On June 25, Prime Minister Najib publicly stated that LGBT activities do not "have a place in the country." On July 19, speaking before 11,000 imams and mosque committee members, he stated that "it is compulsory for us to fight" LGBT behavior.

In March, the High Court dismissed the application of the LGBT group Seksualiti Merdeka for a review of the police ban on their November 2011 festival, leaving the future of the annual festival in doubt.

Two October court rulings concerning transsexuals also caused alarm: in one, a transsexual was refused the right to change the gender recorded on her national identity card; and in the other it was ruled that Muslims born as males may not dress as females.

The government refuses to consider repeal of article 377B of the penal code which criminalizes adult consensual "carnal intercourse against the order of nature," or to replace article 377C on non-consensual sexual acts with a modern, gender-neutral law on rape.

Key International Actors

The United States has not strongly pressed Malaysia over its failure to honor international human rights standards. Other than its demands for a fair trial for Anwar Ibrahim, the US has allowed concern for security cooperation to trump speaking out about human rights. During Trans-Pacific Pact free trade negotiations, the US has failed to hold Malaysia accountable for its human rights violations.

Malaysia is a member of the UN Human Rights Council (HRC), but has not signed or ratified most core human rights treaties. The government has also opposed including protections on the basis of sexual orientation or gender identity in the Association of Southeast Asian Nations (ASEAN) Human Rights Declaration and has blocked consideration of a comprehensive agreement to protect the rights of all migrant workers in ASEAN.

Nepal

Nepal's six-year peace process between government forces and Communist party of Nepal (Maoist) combatants remained in limbo in 2012, and human rights commitments undertaken in the 2006 Comprehensive Peace Accord (CPA) remained unfulfilled.

Impunity for wartime abuses continued, with the government continuing to advocate for establishing a Commission of Inquiry on Disappeared Persons, Truth, and Reconciliation that would be empowered to recommend amnesty for suspects implicated in crimes committed during the decade-long conflict from 1996-2006. The government has also promoted government officials and security force members suspected of involvement in human rights abuses. The closure in March of the United Nations Office of the High Commissioner for Human Rights (OHCHR) symbolizes the government's retreat from promises for accountability.

In May, the Constituent Assembly, tasked to draft a new constitution, was dissolved amid political deadlock over extending its term. The collapse of the assembly, which also served as the country's parliament, left the country without a legislature. In September, the government announced elections for a new Constituent Assembly, without clarifying the date or terms of the vote.

The political stalemate, along with weak governance, corruption and impunity, contributed to ongoing political instability, and problems with law and order.

Accountability for Past Abuses

The government failed to provide redress in 2012 for wartime crimes, including enforced disappearances, torture, rape, and extrajudicial executions. The government pushed for a politically appointed Commission of Inquiry on Disappeared Persons, Truth, and Reconciliation, with discretionary powers to grant amnesties for crimes under international law.

In the absence of a legislature, the cabinet controversially forwarded the bill to the president for executive approval, a power that no president has exercised to date. The framework for a Truth and Reconciliation Commission was part of the November 2006 Comprehensive Peace Agreement. However, granting amnesty for crimes against humanity clearly violates international law and Nepal's Supreme Court decisions, and would undermine reconciliation.

The army continued to shield alleged perpetrators of human rights abuses. In July, the army recommended the promotion of Col. Raju Basnet, implicated in dozens of cases of enforced disappearance and torture, to the rank of brigadier general. The cabinet approved the promotion in October.

In September, the government promoted Kuber Singh Rana from additional inspector general of police to inspector general. Rana is a suspect in ongoing criminal investigations that the Supreme Court ordered in February 2009 related to the October 2003 enforced disappearance and extrajudicial killings of five students from Dhanusha district in Nepal's southern plains.

Integration of Maoist Combatants

In October, the government completed the integration of a total of 1,450 former Maoist fighters into the Nepalese army. The integration marked the conclusion of a November 2011 agreement that all political parties signed allowing for a maximum of 6,500 former combatants to be integrated into a specially created general directorate under the army in non-combat roles.

Forced Evictions of Squatters

In May, the municipal government of the capital, Kathmandu, and the city's armed police force started to forcibly evict residents of settlements along the Bagmati River to make way for a planned urban development project. Those forced evictions, which did not comply with UN-developed specific standards and due process, left over 800 people homeless, nearly half of them children. Authorities plan to evict some 12,000 people in Kathmandu for the planned project, without ensuring adequate and sustainable alternative housing.

Women's Rights

Trafficking of young girls, rape and sexual assault, domestic violence, and dowry-related violence remain serious concerns.

Migrants' Rights

Hundreds of thousands of Nepalis migrate every year to the Gulf and Malaysia for employment, primarily in construction and domestic work. The money they send home makes up approximately 20 percent of Nepal's gross domestic product. In August, the government banned young women under 30 years old from traveling to Gulf countries for work. The ban was a response to numerous cases of abuse of Nepali domestic workers, including unpaid wages, excessive work hours, and physical or sexual abuse.

International and national rights groups said the ban could push women to migrate through irregular channels and increase risk of exploitation. They called for the ban to be revoked and for better protections during training and recruitment. Nepali construction workers also face deception during recruitment, and exorbitant fees that leave them deeply in debt. This may put them at greater risk of getting trapped in abusive situations while working abroad. Corruption hampers effective monitoring of the recruitment industry. In October, Labor Minister Kumar Belbase resigned after he was caught seeking bribes from recruitment agencies.

Disability Rights

Despite policy advancements, children with disabilities face many barriers to education due to lack of implementation and monitoring. Nepal has ratified the Convention on the Rights of Persons with Disabilities (CRPD), and the government publicly promotes an inclusive education system in which children with and without disabilities attend school together in their communities. However in practice, many schools remain inaccessible and the current curriculum is inadequate for students with different learning needs. In addition, Nepal continues to have a system of separate schools for children who are deaf, blind, or have physical and intellectual disabilities, as well as segregated classes for children with disabilities in mainstream schools.

Sexual Orientation and Gender Identity

Nepal's government has made significant strides towards ensuring equality for lesbian, gay, bisexual, and transgender (LGBT) people in recent years. The government's 2011 census allowed citizens to self-identify as male, female, or "third gender," though independent observers reported problems with tallying census figures.

In May, the Ministry of Home Affairs issued a directive to allow citizens to identify as male, female, or "other" on citizenship documents based on self-identification, in line with a 2007 Supreme Court decision. However, the directive had yet to be implemented at this writing. In August, the UN Office of the High Commissioner for Human Rights (OHCHR) welcomed the government's announcement that citizens would be allowed to identify their own gender, including those who do not identify as male or female.

Statelessness

Flaws in the citizenship law continued to make it difficult for women to secure legal proof of citizenship, especially when male family members refuse to assist them or are unavailable to do so. Without proof of citizenship, Nepali women cannot assert their rights to marital property, inheritance, or land. Moreover, the current law continues to deny citizenship to children born to non-Nepali fathers, effectively leaving them stateless. The 2012 draft articles on citizenship, which did not rectify these flaws, stalled after the Constituent Assembly dissolved.

Tibetan Refugees

Under increasing pressure from China, the government continued to deny Tibetans safe passage to India. In 2012, authorities also obstructed peaceful gatherings by Tibetans and Nepalis of Tibetan origin, including detaining demonstrators in violation of orders from Nepal's Supreme Court.

The government continues to deny Tibetans the right to openly celebrate their holidays, including the Tibetan New Year. In March, 100 Tibetans were arrested during protests in Kathmandu to mark the 53rd anniversary of the Tibetan uprising against Chinese rule. In September, the police arrested seven Tibetans in Kathmandu. Six were released the same day, but the police charged one under the Public Offenses Act and were investigating his activities at this writing.

In September, following a meeting between Tibetan refugees in Kathmandu and Robert O. Blake, the United States assistant secretary of state for South and Central Asia, the government queried the US embassy as to why Nepali authorities had not been notified of the meeting before it took place.

Key International Actors

Geographically located between Asia's two powers, India and China, Nepal has a delicate balancing act to perform. India continues to exert a dominant external influence on Nepal's politics, sometimes resulting in negative Nepali public opinion of India. India also continues to compete with China to invest in large infrastructure projects in Nepal, especially hydropower.

In recent years, Nepal has accepted increasing amounts of financial aid from China to finance infrastructure development and support the Nepali military. In return, the Nepalese government explicitly supports Beijing's "one-China policy" that China has sovereignty over Tibet and Taiwan. Nepal also prohibits "anti-Chinese activities" within Nepal, even though there are no specific laws to support such prohibition.

In March, the Nepali government refused to extend the tenure of the OHCHR office in Kathmandu. The government has also failed to respond to OHCHR's request to place a human rights officer in the city's United Nations Development Programme (UNDP) office.

In September, the US removed the ruling Maoist party from its list of terrorist organizations, allowing US entities to legally interact with the party and its members after a nine-year ban.

North Korea

Kim Jong-Un's succession as North Korea's supreme leader after the death of his father, Kim Jong-Il, in December 2011 had little impact on the country's dire human rights record.

The Democratic People's Republic of Korea (North Korea) systematically violates the rights of its population. The government has ratified four key international human rights treaties and includes rights protections in its constitution, but does not allow organized political opposition, free media, functioning civil society, or religious freedom. Arbitrary arrest, detention, lack of due process, and torture and ill-treatment of detainees remain serious and pervasive problems. North Korea also practices collective punishment for various anti-state offenses, for which it enslaves hundreds of thousands of citizens in prison camps, including children. The government periodically publicly executes citizens for stealing state property, hoarding food, and other "anti-socialist" crimes, and maintains policies that have continually subjected North Koreans to food shortages and famine.

In April, the International Coalition to Stop Crimes against Humanity in North Korea (ICNK), which includes Human Rights Watch, filed a comprehensive submission on political prison camps to 11 United Nations special procedures operating under the mandate of the UN Human Rights Council (HRC), and called for the creation of a UN commission of inquiry to investigate crimes against humanity in North Korea.

On November 2, the UN special rapporteur on the situation of human rights in the DPRK recommended that the UN General Assembly and the international community should consider setting up a "more detailed mechanism of inquiry" into the egregious human rights abuses in the country.

Food Shortages and Famine

North Korea continues to face serious food insecurity in 2012, following a major famine in 2011. In November 2012, the World Food Program (WFP) and Food and Agriculture Organization (FAO) estimated that 2.8 million vulnerable people, equal to slightly more than 10 percent of all North Koreans, face under-nutrition and a lack of vital protein and fat in their daily diet. The troubling food situation is the result of several factors, including a dry spell that heavily impacted soybean production in the first half of 2012; economic mismanagement; and the government's blatantly discriminatory food policies that favor the military and government officials.

Torture and Inhumane Treatment

Testimony from North Korean refugees that Human Rights Watch gathered in 2012 indicates that individuals arrested on criminal or political charges often face torture by officials aiming to elicit confessions, extract bribes and information, and enforce obedience. Common forms of torture include sleep deprivation, beatings with iron rods or sticks, kicking and slapping, and enforced sitting or standing for hours. Detainees are subject to so-called "pigeon torture," in which they are forced to cross their arms behind their back, are handcuffed, hung in the air tied to a pole, and beaten with a club. Guards also rape female detainees.

Executions

North Korea's criminal code stipulates that the death penalty can be applied only for a small set of crimes, but these include vaguely defined offenses such as "crimes against the state" and "crimes against the people" that can be, and are, applied broadly. A December 2007 amendment to the penal code extended the death penalty to many more crimes, including non-violent offenses such as fraud and smuggling. Testimony that Human Rights Watch collected in 2012 revealed that authorities executed persons for "crimes" that included stealing metal wire from a factory, taking plate glass from a hanging photo of Kim Jong-Il, and guiding people to the North Korea-China border with intent to flee the country.

Political Prisoner Camps

Information provided by escapees who have fled North Korea in the past two years has again shown that persons accused of political offenses are usually sent to brutal forced labor camps, known as *gwalliso*, operated by the National Security Agency.

The government practices collective punishment, sending to forced labor camps not only the offender but also their parents, spouse, children, and even grand-children. These camps are notorious for horrific living conditions and abuse, including severe food shortages, little or no medical care, lack of proper hous-ing and clothes, continuous mistreatment and torture by guards, and execu-tions. Forced labor at the *gwalliso* often involves difficult physical labor such as mining, logging, and agricultural work, all done with rudimentary tools in dan-gerous and harsh conditions. Death rates in these camps are reportedly extremely high.

North Korea has never acknowledged that these camps exist, but United States and South Korean officials estimate some 200,000 people may be imprisoned in them, including in camp No. 14 in Kaechun, No. 15 in Yodok, No. 16 in Hwasung, No. 22 in Hoeryung, and No. 25 in Chungjin.

Refugees and Asylum Seekers

North Korea criminalizes leaving the country without state permission. Following the death of leader Kim Jong-Il, the new government decreed a shoot-on-sight order to border guards to stop illegal crossing at the northern border into China. Increased border security in both North Korea and China significantly reduced the numbers of North Koreas reaching Thailand, and ultimately, South Korea.

Those who leave face harsh punishment upon repatriation. Interrogation, tor-ture, and punishments depend on North Korean authorities' assessments of what the returnee did while in China. Those suspected of simple commerce or other money-making schemes are usually sent to work in forced labor brigades (known as *ro-dong-dan-ryeon-dae*, literally labor training centers) or *jip-kyul-so* (collection centers), low-level criminal penitentiaries where forced labor is required.

Others suspected of religious or political activities, especially including contact with South Koreans, are given lengthier terms in horrendous detention facilities known as *kyo-hwa-so* (correctional, reeducation centers) where forced labor is combined with chronic food and medicine shortages, harsh working conditions, and mistreatment by guards.

Beijing categorically labels North Koreans in China "illegal" economic migrants and routinely repatriates them, despite its obligation to offer protection to refugees under customary international law and the Refugee Convention of 1951 and its 1967 protocol, to which China is a state party. Former North Korean security officials who have defected told Human Rights Watch that North Koreans handed back by China face interrogation, torture, and referral to political prisoner or forced labor camps. In a high profile case, China forced back at least 30 North Koreans in February and March 2012, defying a formal request from South Korean President Lee Myung-Bak to desist from doing so, and despite protests in front of the Chinese Embassy in Seoul.

North Korean women fleeing their country are frequently trafficked in forced de facto marriages with Chinese men. Even if they have lived there for years, these women are not entitled to legal residence and face possible arrest and repatriation. Many children of such unrecognized marriages lack legal identity or access to elementary education because their parents fear that by attempting to register such the child, the Chinese authorities will identify the mother as an undocumented North Korean migrant, and arrest and forcibly repatriate her.

Government-Controlled Judiciary

North Korea's judiciary is neither transparent nor independent. The government appoints and tightly controls judges, prosecutors, lawyers, court clerks, and even jury members. In some cases designated as political crimes, suspects are not even sent through a nominal judicial process; after interrogation they are either executed or sent to a forced labor camp, often with their entire families.

Labor Rights

North Korea is one of the few nations in the world that is not a member of the International Labour Organization (ILO). The ruling Korean Workers' Party firmly controls the only authorized trade union organization, the General Federation of

Trade Unions of Korea. South Korean companies employ over 50,000 North Korean workers in the Kaesong Industrial Complex (KIC), close to the border between North and South Korea, where the law governing working conditions falls far short of international standards on freedom of association, the right to collective bargaining, and protection from gender discrimination and sexual harassment.

Freedom of Association, Information, and Movement

The government uses fear—generated mainly by threats of forced labor and public executions—to prevent dissent, and imposes harsh restrictions on freedom of information, association, assembly, and travel.

North Korea operates a vast network of informants who monitor and report to the authorities fellow citizens they suspect of criminal or subversive behavior. All media and publications are state controlled, and unauthorized access to non-state radio or TV broadcasts is severely punished. North Koreans found with unauthorized TV programs, such as South Korean drama and entertainment shows, are punished. The government periodically investigates the "political background" of its citizens to assess their loyalty to the ruling party, and forces Pyongyang residents who fail such assessments to leave the capital.

Key International Actors

The North Korean government continues to refuse to recognize the mandate of the UN special rapporteur on the situation of human rights in the DPRK, or cooperate with him.

In March, the HRC adopted a resolution against North Korea for the fifth year in a row condemning Pyongyang for its abysmal, systematic human rights violations. For the first time the resolution passed by consensus, marking a breakthrough in international recognition of the gravity of North Korea's human rights abuses. This followed condemnation by the UN General Assembly for the seventh straight year in a December 19, 2011 resolution that demanded North Korea halt its "systematic, widespread and grave violations of human rights" and reiterated UN member states' concerns about the country's "all-pervasive and severe restrictions on the freedoms of thought, conscience, religion, opinion and expression, peaceful assembly and association."

Both resolutions condemned North Korea's failure to state whether it accepted any of the 167 recommendations that it took under advisement from a HRC's Universal Periodic Review (UPR) session of its record in December 2009.

The six-party talks on denuclearizing the Korean peninsula—involving North and South Korea, China, Japan, Russia, and the US—remained moribund during the year. A potential breakthrough deal between the US and North Korea in February to provide substantial US food assistance in exchange for an end to uranium enrichment and missile testing by North Korea, and a return of International Atomic Energy Agency (IAEA) inspectors, fell apart when North Korea insisted on attempting to launch a rocket carrying a satellite to commemorate the 100th anniversary of the birth of North Korean founder Kim Il-Sung.

Japan continued to demand the return of 17 Japanese citizens that North Korea abducted in the 1970s and 1980s for, among other things, training North Korean spies. It returned five to Japan, but claimed eight had died and that the other four had never entered North Korea. Some Japanese civil society groups insist the number of abductees is much higher. South Korea's government continued to increase its attention and efforts to demand return of hundreds of its citizens it claimed were abducted by North Korean government agents.

Pakistan

Pakistan had a turbulent year in 2012, with the judicial ouster of Prime Minister Yusuf Raza Gilani, attacks on civilians by militant groups, growing electricity shortages, rising food and fuel prices, and continuing political dominance of the military, which operates with almost complete impunity. Religious minorities continued to face insecurity and persecution as the government failed to provide protection to those threatened or to hold extremists accountable. Islamist militant groups continued to target and kill Shia Muslims—particularly from the Hazara community—with impunity. In September, the southwestern province of Balochistan experienced massive flooding for the third year running, displacing some 700,000 people.

Ongoing rights concerns included the breakdown of law enforcement in the face of terror attacks, continuing abuses across Balochistan, ongoing torture and ill-treatment of criminal suspects, and unresolved enforced disappearances of terrorism suspects and opponents of the military. Abuses by Pakistani police, including extrajudicial killings, also continued to be reported throughout the country in 2012.

Relations between Pakistan and the United States —Pakistan's most significant ally and its largest donor of development and military aid—remained tense for much of the year due to the "Salala Attack" in November 2011, in which US forces killed 24 Pakistani soldiers during a military operation near the Afghan border.

Sectarian Attacks

In 2012, at least 325 members of the Shia Muslim population were killed in targeted attacks that took place across Pakistan. In Balochistan province, over 100 were killed, most of them from the Hazara community. On August 16, gunmen ambushed four buses passing through the Babusar Top area of Mansehra district in Khyber Pakhtunkhwa province. The attackers forced all the passengers to disembark, checked their national identity cards, and summarily executed 22 travelers whom they identified as belonging to the Shia community. A spokesman for the Tehrik-e-Taliban Pakistan, the Pakistani Taliban, claimed responsibility. On August 30, gunmen shot dead Zulfiqar Naqvi, a Shia judge, in Quetta, Balochistan's capital. In two separate attacks on September 1, 2012, gunmen attacked and killed eight Hazara Shia in Quetta.

Sunni militant groups, including those with known links to the Pakistani military, its intelligence agencies, and affiliated paramilitaries—such as the ostensibly banned Lashkar-e Jhangvi—operated with widespread impunity across Pakistan, as law enforcement officials effectively turned a blind eye to attacks.

Students and teachers were regularly attacked by militant groups. On October 9, 2012, gunmen shot Malala Yousafzai, a 15-year-old student and outspoken advocate for children's right to education, in the head and neck leaving her in critical condition. The Tehreek-e-Taliban Pakistan claimed responsibility for the attack in the Swat Valley. The attack on Yousafzai garnered condemnation from across the political spectrum in Pakistan. Militant Islamist groups also attacked more than 100 schools, and rebuilding is slow.

Religious Minorities and Women

Abuses under the country's abusive blasphemy law continued as dozens were charged in 2012 and at least 16 people remained on death row for blasphemy, while another 20 served life sentences. Aasia Bibi, a Christian from Punjab province, who in 2010 became the first woman in the country's history to be sentenced to death for blasphemy, continued to languish in prison. In July 2012, police arrested a man who appeared to suffer from a mental disability for allegedly burning the Quran. A mob organized by local clerics demanded that the man be handed to them, attacked the police station, pulled the victim out, and burned him alive.

On August 17, Islamabad police took into custody Rimsha Masih, a 14-year-old Christian girl from a poor Islamabad suburb with a "significantly lower mental age," who was accused of burning pages filled with Quranic passages. Police had to beat back a mob demanding that it be handed the girl so that it could kill her. Threats against the local Christian community forced some 400 families to flee their homes. But Islamist groups who support the blasphemy law took a significantly different position, demanding a full investigation. The accuser, local cleric Khalid Chishti, was himself arrested for fabricating evidence in order to rid the neighbourhood of Christians. On September 23, police officials stated they had found no evidence against Rimsha Masih, who was released and given state protection at an undisclosed location.

Members of the Ahmadi religious community continued to be a major target for blasphemy prosecutions and subjected to specific anti-Ahmadi laws across Pakistan. They faced increasing social discrimination as militant groups used provisions of the law to prevent Ahmadis from "posing as Muslims," forced the demolition of Ahmadi mosques in Lahore, barred Ahmadis from using their mosques in Rawalpindi, and vandalized Ahmadi graves across Punjab province. In most instances, Punjab provincial officials supported militants' demands instead of protecting Ahmadis and their mosques and graveyards.

Violence against women and girls—including rape, "honor" killings, acid attacks, domestic violence, and forced marriage—remained a serious problem. Intimidation and threats against women and girls out in public increased in major cities in 2012.

Freedom of Expression

At least eight journalists were killed in Pakistan during the year, including four in May alone. On May 9 and 10 respectively, Tariq Kamal and Aurangzeb Tunio were killed. On May 18, the bullet-riddled body of *Express News* correspondent Razzaq Gul was found dumped in a deserted area near Turbat in Balochistan province. Security agencies are suspected of involvement in his killing. On May 28, Abdul Qadir Hajizai was shot dead in Balochistan by armed men on a motorbike. The Baloch Liberation Front reportedly claimed responsibility for his killing. No one was held accountable in any of these cases.

A climate of fear impeded media coverage of the state security forces and militant groups. Journalists rarely reported on human rights abuses by the military in counterterrorism operations, and the Taliban and other armed groups regularly threatened media outlets over their coverage.

In June, gunmen shot at the building of Aaj TV, a private Urdu-language news channel, wounding two guards. The Pakistani Taliban claimed responsibility and threatened such attacks would continue if media outlets did not reflect the Taliban's priorities and positions in coverage. However, as has been the case since the return to civilian rule in 2008, journalists vocally critical of the government experienced less interference from elected officials than in previous years.

Judicial Activism and Independence

Pakistan's judiciary continued to assert its independence from the government in 2012. In December 2011, the judiciary began controversial hearings into the so-called "Memogate" scandal investigating Husain Haqqani, Pakistan's former ambassador to the US on charges that he attempted to conspire against Pakistan's military in collusion with the US. The court notably failed to investigate allegations from the same source that the head of the country's dreaded Inter-Services Intelligence (ISI) had conspired to oust the elected government.

In June, the Supreme Court controversially fired Prime Minister Yusuf Raza Gilani for refusing to sign a letter to Switzerland asking for an investigation into corruption allegations against President Asif Zardari.

Despite the adoption of a National Judicial Policy in 2009, access to justice remained abysmal and courts remained rife with corruption and incompetence. Case backlogs remain huge at all levels. The judiciary's use of *suo motu* proceedings—acting on its own motions—was considered so excessive that the International Commission of Jurists raised concerns about it.

While the Supreme Court was active in raising the issue of government abuses in Balochistan, no high-level military officials were held accountable for them. As has been the case since Pakistan's independent judiciary was restored to office in 2009, Chief Justice Iftikhar Chaudhry and the provincial high courts muzzled media criticism of the judiciary in 2012 through threats of contempt of court proceedings. In October, both the Lahore and Islamabad high courts effectively barred media from criticizing the judiciary or giving airtime to critics in the aftermath of a multi-million dollar corruption scandal involving Arsalan Iftikhar, the son of the Supreme Court chief justice.

Balochistan

The human rights crisis continued to worsen in the mineral-rich province of Balochistan. Human Rights Watch recorded continued enforced disappearances and killings of suspected Baloch militants and opposition activists by the military, intelligence agencies, and the paramilitary Frontier Corps. Baloch nationalists and other militant groups also stepped up attacks on non-Baloch civilians. Pakistan's military continued to publicly resist government reconciliation efforts and attempts to locate ethnic Baloch who had been subject to "disappearances." Pakistan's government appeared powerless to rein in the military's abuses. As a result, large numbers of Hazara community members sought asylum abroad.

Militant Attacks and Counterterrorism

Suicide bombings, armed attacks, and killings by the Taliban, al Qaeda, and their affiliates continued in 2012, targeting politicians, journalists, religious minorities, and government security personnel. Many of these attacks were claimed by groups such as the Haqqani network, the Lashkar-e-Jhangvi, and other al Qaeda affiliates.

Security forces routinely violated basic rights in the course of counterterrorism operations. Suspects were frequently detained without charge or were convicted without a fair trial. Thousands of suspected members of al Qaeda, the Taliban, and other armed groups—who were rounded up in a nationwide crackdown that began in 2009 in Swat and the Federally Administered Tribal Areas—remained in illegal military detention; few were prosecuted or produced before the courts. The army continued to deny lawyers, relatives, independent monitors, and humanitarian agency staff access to persons detained during military operations. Terrorism suspects, particularly in the Swat Valley, reportedly died inexplicably of "natural causes." However, lack of access to the detainees made independent verification of the cause of death impossible.

Aerial drone strikes by the US on suspected members of al Qaeda and the Taliban in northern Pakistan continued in 2012, with some 44 strikes taking place through early November. As in previous years, these strikes were often accompanied by claims from Pakistanis of large numbers of civilian casualties, although lack of access to the conflict areas largely prevented independent verification.

Human Rights Defenders

Community-based human rights activists faced increased threats. In June, Asma Jahangir, the country's most prominent human rights defender, alleged that she had discovered that an assassination attempt was being planned against her from "the highest levels of the security establishment." In the preceding months, Jahangir had been at odds with the Pakistani military in a series of high-profile standoffs, including over the military's policies in Balochistan and elsewhere.

Key International Actors

The US remained the largest donor of development and military aid to Pakistan, but relations remained abysmal through much of 2012. The US rejected apologizing for the "Salala Attack," prompting Pakistan to ban the movement of NATO supplies to Afghanistan through Pakistan. The routes were only reopened in July after the US offered a formulation of regret that Pakistan found acceptable. Major areas of bilateral tension remained, particularly Pakistan's alleged persistent support for the Haqqani network, a militant group that US officials accused of targeting US troops in Afghanistan. In September, the US declared the Haqqani network a terrorist body.

Pakistan and China continued to deepen extensive economic and political ties. Historically tense relations between Pakistan and nuclear rival India showed marked improvement in 2012. In September, the two countries signed landmark trade and travel agreements.

The United Nations Working Group on Enforced or Involuntary Disappearances (WGEID) visited Pakistan in September and reported in preliminary findings that there is "acknowledgment that enforced disappearances have occurred and still occur in the country."

Papua New Guinea

Papua New Guinea's (PNG) significant oil, gas, and gold reserves are powering strong economic growth. In the last four years, the country's gross domestic product has doubled. Yet poor governance and corruption prevent ordinary citizens from benefitting from this wealth. Large-scale extractive projects have generated environmental and human rights concerns that the government has failed to address, and disputes over compensating landowners impacted by these projects trigger protests and occasional violence.

One year after the United Nations special rapporteur on torture released a report on PNG, the government has failed to adequately respond to his recommendations. Police and security forces continue to commit abuses with impunity. Violence against women is rampant.

In 2012, political turmoil paralyzed the government. Parliament re-elected Peter O'Neill as prime minister after July's general election—despite a December 2011 Supreme Court ruling that the change of government in August 2011, in which parliamentarians first elected him prime minister, was unconstitutional. Former Prime Minister Sir Michael Somare, the country's dominant political figure for more than 40 years, joined O'Neill's coalition. While the new leadership has made positive strides in instituting a more transparent political culture, much work remains in reversing the legacy of corruption and unaccountable governance.

Extractive Industries

Extractive industries are PNG's key economic driver. The US$15 billion ExxonMobil Liquefied Natural Gas (LNG) project, currently under construction, is expected to begin output by 2014. LNG contractors had disputes in 2012 with local landowners over land use compensation, as well as with workers protesting benefits.

The Porgera gold mine, 95 percent owned by the Canadian firm Barrick Gold, accounts for approximately 11 percent of the country's GDP. A 2011 Human Rights Watch report implicated the mine's operators in serious abuses. The report documented gang rapes and other violent abuses at the mine site by private security personnel. In January 2011, Barrick fired six employees for involvement in, or failure to report, alleged sexual violence. In October 2012, Barrick began implementing a remediation framework to provide compensation and assistance to women who suffered sexual violence at the hands of its personnel. The company said that the program would include financial reparations, legal aid, and access to medical and psychological support services.

Torture and Other Police Abuse

Human Rights Watch has previously documented widespread abuse by PNG's police, including use of excessive force against demonstrators, torture, and sexual violence, including against children.

In September, a police officer was suspended from duty and charged with assault after attacking a school administrator for sending his son home from school. In October, an officer received a 15-year prison sentence for sexually assaulting a woman in police custody. That same month, another officer was found guilty of sexually assaulting his daughter. Yet despite these signs of progress, police impunity remains the norm.

Violence against Women and Girls

Women and girls are victims of rampant sexual violence in PNG. In March, the UN special rapporteur on violence against women, Rashida Manjoo, visited the country on a fact-finding mission and observed that violence against women "is a pervasive phenomenon ... in the home, the community and institutional settings." Manjoo also documented the government's failure to hold perpetrators to account. In June 2011, the draft Family Planning Law, which would criminalize domestic violence, was sent to the attorney general's office. More than a year later, the bill had yet to be sent to parliament for a vote.

Corruption

Corruption remains a serious problem in PNG. In October, Task Force Sweep, the government-appointed team tasked with investigating institutional graft, estimated that close to 3.8 billion PNG Kina (US$1.7 billion) from the country's budget was lost due to corruption between 2009 and 2011.

Earlier in May, the task force submitted its report on its seven-month investigation into corruption across government agencies including the departments of Health and National Planning and Monitoring. The report documented 20 politicians who had been referred to the ombudsman commission for further investigation and 24 public servants who had been suspended for "facilitating or benefiting from corruption." Systemic graft continues to negatively impact the country's ability to provide basic social and economic services, such as infrastructure improvements and access to health care and education.

Key International Actors

Australia is the country's most important international partner and provided over $500 million dollars in development assistance in 2012.

In September, after the Australian parliament approved legislation that authorizes the transfer from Australian territory of "irregular maritime arrival"— Australia and PNG agreed to reopen a processing center on Manus Island for asylum seekers who arrive in Australia by boat. However, that agreement does not release PNG from its obligations as a party to the 1951 Refugee Convention for ensuring a fair refugee status determination process and respect for the principle of non-refoulement ("non-return" to persecution), as well as being responsible for humane treatment of migrants and durable solutions for refugees.

In October, UN High Commissioner for Refugees Antonio Guterres sent a letter raising concerns about PNG's capacity to act as a regional processing country for asylum claims, including the absence of any national legal or regulatory framework for asylum processing, and its failure to sign international treaties against torture and in favor of protecting stateless people. At this writing, PNG authorities expected the processing center on Manus Island to begin operating in late 2012.

Philippines

The Philippines is a multi-party democracy with an elected president and legis-lature, an active civil society sector, and a vibrant media. Two years into power, President Benigno S. Aquino III continues to enjoy significant political capital and goodwill, in part because the economy has performed better in the past two years than during the administration of Gloria Macapagal-Arroyo. Aquino has expressed his commitment to improve the human rights situation and to undo the harm done to basic rights by his predecessor.

In 2012, the government pushed for legislation improving reproductive health and domestic workers rights, and actively engaged international bodies in seek-ing ways to improve the criminal justice system. In October, Congress passed legislation criminalizing enforced disappearances, the first of its kind in Asia.

The Aquino administration has promised to expedite human rights investiga-tions and to improve the capacity of investigators, prosecutors, and the courts. It has taken some action against high-profile officials implicated in abuses, including ordering that charges be filed against a high-ranking military officer, and a former governor implicated in the killing of a journalist. More importantly, extrajudicial killings and enforced disappearances have decreased since Aquino took office in 2010. However, harassment and violence against political activists and journalists continue. No one was convicted in any extrajudicial killing case since Aquino became president.

Military and police personnel frequently commit serious human rights viola-tions. Armed opposition forces, including the communist New People's Army (NPA), the separatist Moro Islamic Liberation Front, and the Islamist extremist group Abu Sayyaf, have often committed serious abuses against civilians. The Philippine government and the Moro Islamic Liberation Front signed a "frame-work agreement" in October, which promised an end to the four-decades-old conflict in the southern region of Mindanao.

Free expression suffered a serious setback when Congress passed a law in October that allows for stiff criminal sentences for online defamation.

Criminal Defamation and Media Freedom

While the Philippines has long had one of the world's freest cyberspaces, in 2012 Congress passed the Cybercrime Prevention Act, which Aquino signed into law on September 12. The law's criminal penalties for online libel and other restrictions are a serious threat to free expression in the Philippines. The new law drastically increases the penalty for computer-related libel, with the minimum punishment raised from six months to six years. In October, lawyers, journalists, and bloggers filed several petitions before the Supreme Court against the law. On October 9, the court issued a temporary restraining order suspending its implementation for 120 days.

Media and human rights organizations have long urged the government to decriminalize libel, which the United Nation Human Rights Committee (UNHRC) views as a violation of the International Covenant on Civil and Political Rights (ICCPR), but bills for this proposal have languished in Congress over the years. In October, Aquino said he "subscribes to the idea of decriminalizing libel." The bills were still in Congress at this writing.

Killings and harassment of journalists continued in 2012. According to media groups, three journalists were murdered in 2012 because of their work, bringing the total number to 10 since Aquino took office. Journalists also complained about being physically assaulted by men allegedly working for local politicians and of being threatened through text messages.

Extrajudicial Killings and Enforced Disappearances

The Aquino administration has failed to keep its commitment to hold those responsible for extrajudicial killings to account. Since 2001, hundreds of leftist activists, journalists, environmentalists, and clergy have been killed by alleged members of the security forces. Local human rights organizations reported approximately 114 cases of extrajudicial killings since Aquino came to office, and 13 at this writing.

Despite strong evidence that military personnel have been involved, investigations have stalled. No one was convicted for political killings in 2012. The government has attempted to hold some high-profile suspects accountable. Retired

Maj. Gen. Jovito Palparan, who is facing kidnapping and illegal detention charges for the 2006 abduction of activists Sherlyn Cadapan and Karen Empeño, went into hiding after the government announced plans in December 2011 to arrest him. Joel Reyes, a former governor of Palawan province and the alleged mastermind in the January 2011 killing of journalist and environmentalist Gerry Ortega, managed to leave the country.

Abuses by Paramilitary Forces

While the government claims that it has managed to reduce the number of "private armies" controlled by politicians, it has resisted calls for dismantling government-backed paramilitary forces.

Several extrajudicial killings have recently been attributed to members of the Citizen Armed Force Geographical Units (CAFGU), which the military controls and supervises, as well as the Special CAFGU Active Auxiliary, which the army trains but companies hire to protect their operations. In October 2011, Aquino authorized paramilitary forces to protect mining investments.

Aquino had at this writing still not fulfilled his promise during the 2010 election campaign to revoke Executive Order 546, which local officials cite to justify the provision of arms to their personal forces. Among those who benefited from this order is the Ampatuan political clan in Maguindanao, whose senior members are accused of the November 23, 2009 massacre of 58 supporters of a political opponent and media workers in Maguindanao province. The trial continued in 2012. Although authorities have identified 197 suspects in the massacre, only 99 have been arrested (one of them died in jail and the court dropped charges against another). Of the accused, only 78 have been indicted. Four of the 98 suspects still at large are soldiers; the rest are members of the Ampatuan militia. Some witnesses have been killed, while families of the victims reported being harassed and threatened in 2012.

Attacks on Environmentalists

Activists vocal in opposing mining and energy operations that they say threaten the environment and will displace tribal communities from their land continued to face attack in 2012. Many mining investments in the Philippines are in areas with large indigenous populations or controlled by tribal groups. In one case, Margarito J. Cabal, 47, organizer of a group opposing a hydroelectric dam in Bukidnon province, was gunned down on May 9. At this writing, no one had been arrested for the killing in October 2011 of Italian priest Father Fausto Tentorio in North Cotabato province, reportedly carried out by the Bagani ("tribal warriors") paramilitary group under military control. Tentorio was a longtime advocate of tribal rights and opposed mining in the area.

Death Squad Killings

So-called death squad killings in Davao City, in the southern Philippines, and other cities continued in 2012. In August, the Commission on Human Rights released a "resolution" on its investigation of the so-called Davao Death Squad. It affirmed reports of the targeted and systematic killings by the so-called Davao Death Squad in Davao City, mostly of suspected criminals, many of them young men and teenagers. The commission said it verified 206 out of an alleged 375 killings between 2005 and 2009 that it had previously listed. The commission called for the investigation of local officials and police, which had not started at this writing.

New People's Army Abuses

The military and the communist New People's Army continue to clash across the Philippines, particularly in southern Mindanao. Peace talks that began in 1986 between the government and the National Democratic Front, the political arm of the Communist Party of the Philippines, made no progress in 2012.

The NPA committed frequent abuses against civilians. On September 1, NPA rebels lobbed a grenade at a military outpost in Paquibato, Davao City, but instead hit and wounded civilians who were attending a nearby community fair. The NPA continued to kill individuals it deemed to have committed "crimes against the people" or the communist movement, among them tribal leader Abantas Ansabo, who was shot dead in July in North Cotabato province. The NPA claimed Ansabo was a paramilitary leader who committed abuses against local residents. In March, the NPA killed Patrick Wineger, a North Cotabato businessman of Swiss-Filipino descent, saying the victim had been engaged in "anti-communist activities."

Children and Armed Conflict

The NPA, the Moro Islamic Liberation Front and Abu Sayyaf allegedly continued to recruit and use children within their forces. The Philippine army at times used schools for military purposes, such as camping on school grounds and using school facilities during civil-military operations, despite a Philippine law prohibiting such activities. The latest reported incident of this violation occurred in Davao City in October.

Domestic Workers

The Philippines' ratification of the Domestic Workers Convention in September will bring the groundbreaking international treaty into legal force, promising better working conditions and key labor protections for millions of domestic workers worldwide. At this writing, Aquino had not signed into law a bill promising better wages and benefits, and more protection for the country's estimated 2 million domestic workers.

Key International Actors

In July, the European Union and the Philippines strengthened their relationship by signing a new Partnership and Cooperation Agreement that promises, among other things, better cooperation on such issues as human rights, security, migration, and energy.

The United States remained the Philippines's most influential ally and, together with Australia and Japan, the country's largest bilateral donors.

The US military has access to Philippine territory and seas under a Visiting Forces Agreement, and the two militaries held in October one of their annual joint exercises. In August, the US delivered military hardware as part of the Philippines' efforts to modernize its military. The US has made some effort to address the problem of extrajudicial killings in the Philippines by providing assistance to the Philippine Commission on Human Rights, training investigators and prosecutors, and supporting judicial reform. Despite Philippine government efforts to end restrictions, the US Congress continued in 2012 to withhold $3 million in annual assistance to the Philippines military because of human rights concerns.

In June, the European Parliament adopted a resolution calling on the Philippine government to end impunity for extrajudicial killings, torture, and enforced disappearances.

The Philippines is a member of the UN Human Rights Council (HRC), but during 2012, as in previous years, it failed to take a strong or principled stand on key votes. For example, it repeatedly abstained from voting on measures to improve the human rights situation in Syria. In March, the Philippines voted against the HRC resolution calling on the Sri Lankan government to take action to ensure justice and promote national reconciliation following the country's internal armed conflict.

Singapore

The Singapore government in 2012 continued to sharply restrict basic rights to free expression, peaceful assembly, and association. However, there were small signs of progress in other areas, including changes in mandatory death penalty laws, and limited improvements in protecting the rights of migrant workers and combating human trafficking.

Freedom of Expression, Peaceful Assembly, and Association

Singapore's constitution guarantees the rights to freedom of expression, peaceful assembly, and association, with exceptions for broadly worded restrictions in the name of security, public order, morality, and racial and religious harmony. A network of restrictive government regulations still applies to broadcast and electronic media, films, video, music, and sound recordings. In October, Singapore banned a satirical film "Sex, Violence, Family Values," on the grounds it offended the country's Indian population.

The Newspaper and Printing Presses Act requires that all newspapers renew their registration annually, and allows the government to limit the circulation of foreign newspapers it believes "engage in the domestic politics of Singapore."

The two corporations that dominate media regularly tow a pro-government line: MediaCorp, which is owned by a government investment company and dominates broadcasting, and Singapore Press Holdings Limited (SPH), a private company that dominates print media. The government must approve and can remove SPH shareholders, who in turn have the authority to hire and fire all directors and staff.

Outdoor gatherings of five or more persons still require police permits. The city-state's Speakers Corner—where people may demonstrate, perform, and hold exhibitions—remains the only outdoor space where uncensored speech is allowed in the country.

The Registrar of Societies must approve associations of 10 or more members, and can deny approval if it deems a body "prejudicial to public peace, welfare or good order."

The Singaporean government and senior government officials have frequently brought charges of "scandalizing the court," criminal and civil defamation, and sedition to silence and even bankrupt its critics.

In July 2012, the attorney general's chambers wrote to Alex Au, a prominent blogger and gay rights activist, demanding that he take down and apologize for a June post in his Yawning Bread blog that criticized the judiciary for showing deference to the executive. Au removed the post. In February, after being threatened, prominent domestic blog site TR Emeritus, apologized to Prime Minister Lee Hsien Loong for suggesting nepotism was a factor in Lee's wife obtaining a position to head a state-linked firm.

Criminal Justice System

Singapore's Internal Security Act (ISA) and Criminal Law (Temporary Provisions) Act permit the authorities to arrest and detain suspects for virtually unlimited periods of time without charge or judicial review. In September 2011, Singapore's Home Affairs Ministry said threats of subversion, espionage, terrorism, and racial and religious extremism keep the long-criticized ISA "relevant."

The Misuse of Drugs Act permits the authorities to confine suspected drug users in "rehabilitation" centers for up to three years without trial. Second-time offenders face prison terms and may be caned.

On November 14, 2012, Singapore's parliament passed new laws authorizing incremental changes in mandatory death penalty provisions that affect some 20 drug-related and intentional murder offenses. In drug cases, judges may drop the mandatory death sentence requirement and opt instead for life in prison with caning if two conditions are met: the accused must have functioned only as a courier, and either meaningfully cooperated with the Central Narcotics Bureau or have a "mental disability that impairs appreciation of his own actions."

However, a new section of the Misuse of Drugs Act limits judicial discretion by stating that the public prosecutor has "sole discretion" to determine whether a person has substantively assisted the Central Narcotics Bureau in disrupting drug trafficking activities. Deputy Prime Minister and Minister for Home Affairs Teo Chee Han has defended mandatory death sentences in drug-related cases, citing what he said is their known deterrent effect.

Parliament also passed less controversial amendments to the criminal law, which remove mandatory death sentences for murderers who had "no outright intention to kill." Courts may instead choose to impose life imprisonment.

All future death penalty cases will be automatically reviewed, and the new laws provide that all eligible existing death penalty cases will be reviewed for re-sentencing. There are some 35 inmates currently on death row, but all executions have been on hold since July 2011.

Judicial caning is a mandatory punishment for medically fit males between the ages of 16 and 50 who have been sentenced to prison for a range of violent and non-violent crimes, including drug trafficking, rape, and immigration offenses. A sentencing official may also order caning in cases involving some 30 other crimes. The United States State Department reported that in 2011 "2,318 convicted persons were sentenced to judicial caning, and 98.9 percent of caning sentences were carried out." During its United Nations Human Rights Council (HRC) Universal Periodic Review (UPR) in 2011, Singapore rejected all recommendations designed to eliminate caning.

Sexual Orientation and Gender Identity

Although the government has said it will not enforce the law, penal code section 377A still criminalizes sexual acts between consenting adult men. On August 21, 2012, the Court of Appeals found that legitimate grounds existed for a constitutional challenge to section 377A, and referred the case to the High Court. Sexual acts between women are not criminalized.

There was an unprecedented turnout on June 30 for Singapore's Pink Dot fourth annual festival, held at the Speakers Corner, supporting "freedom to love." However, lesbian, gay, bisexual, and transgender (LGBT) groups continue to report that LGBT people face a range of harassment and abuses, including physical assault.

Rights of Migrant Workers and Human Trafficking

Despite partial reforms introduced in recent years, including capping recruitment fees at two months' salary, Singapore's 208,000 foreign domestic workers are still excluded from the Employment Act and key labor protections, such as limits on daily work hours.

A March 2012 reform guaranteeing domestic workers who arrive on new contracts after January 1, 2013, a weekly rest day rather than the current monthly day off, contains a provision permitting employers to give domestic workers monetary compensation in lieu of rest so long as the worker agrees. Given the power imbalance, there is significant risk that an employer will coerce a worker to sign away their rest days.

In 2012, at least 11 foreign domestic workers fell to their deaths, many while washing windows or hanging laundry from apartments in high-rise buildings. In June, the government responded by strengthening safety requirements so that domestic workers only clean windows in the presence of their employers and if window bars have been installed and locked. In at least one case, an employer was fined S$5000 (US$4093) for negligence.

Foreign workers in Singapore, both men and women, are subject to forced labor through debts owed to recruitment agents, non-payment of wages, restrictions on movements, confiscated passports, and physical and sexual abuse. Although the government is still not in compliance with minimum standards for trafficking elimination, it has demonstrated some improvement in prevention and protection, but prosecutorial efforts have been weak.

A government-mandated standard contract for migrant workers does not address issues such as long work hours, poor living conditions, and enforced confinement. Instead of guaranteeing one day off per month and a set number of rest hours per day, it makes such breaks a matter of negotiation between employer and employee. It also fails to provide protections against denial of annual or medical leave.

Singapore is one of only nine countries that did not vote for passage of International Labour Organization (ILO) Convention No. 189 on Decent Work for Domestic Workers. It has not ratified the Protocol to Prevent, Suppress and Punish Trafficking in Persons.

Human Rights Defenders

Human rights defenders in Singapore risk being fined, imprisoned, bankrupted, and banned from traveling outside the country without government approval.

In September, opposition leader and human rights activist Chee Soon Juan announced that former Prime Ministers Lee Kuan Yew and Goh Chok Tong had accepted his SG$30,000 ($24,550) offer to settle his debts with them and annul his bankruptcy resulting from politically motivated defamation proceedings. The annulment will allow Chee to travel overseas and to stand in the 2016 parliamentary elections. However, in October, the High Court dismissed an application by Chee and three other defendants seeking a hearing to appeal their conviction for illegal assembly in 2008.

Members of Singaporeans for Democracy (SFD), a human rights organization, voted in June to disband due to the onerous government regulations imposed on its political advocacy and activities.

At its 2011 UPR, Singapore rejected the recommendation from other countries that it accept a visit by the UN special rapporteur on the situation of human rights defenders.

Key International Actors

The US and Singapore maintain strong military ties, including bilateral access agreements that allow the US to use a Singapore naval base, and to operate re-supply vessels, dock its aircraft carriers, and maintain a regional logistical command unit. Discussion of Singapore's poor human rights record was not part of the bilateral agenda.

Singapore continued to play a leading role in the Association of Southeast Asian Nations (ASEAN), but did little to ensure the regional body engaged meaningfully with civil society organizations, particularly during development of the ASEAN Human Rights Declaration, adopted in November.

Sri Lanka

The Sri Lankan government in 2012 continued its assault on democratic space and failed to take any meaningful steps towards providing accountability for war crimes committed by either side during the internal armed conflict that ended in 2009.

The government targeted civil society through threats, surveillance, and clamp-downs on activities and free speech. Statements by government officials and government-controlled media named and threatened human rights defenders who called for accountability for wartime abuses or criticized other government policies. Local activists expressed deep concern about the security of their staff and the people they assist.

Overly broad detention powers remained in place under various laws and regulations. Several thousand people continued to be detained without charge or trial. State security forces committed arbitrary arrests and torture against ethnic minority Tamils, including repatriated Sri Lankan nationals allegedly linked to the defeated Liberation Tigers of Tamil Eelam (LTTE). The Tamil population in the north benefitted from humanitarian groups having greater access to the area, but the government did not take adequate steps to normalize their living conditions.

President Mahinda Rajapaksa and his brothers continued to accumulate power at the expense of democratic institutions. Calls to restore the independence of the National Human Rights Commission (NHRC) and other government commissions that Rajapaksa marginalized via the Eighteenth Amendment to the constitution, which passed in 2010, went unheeded.

Accountability

Sri Lanka made no progress in 2012 toward ensuring justice for the victims of numerous violations of human rights and the laws of war committed by both sides during the 26-year-long conflict between the government and the LTTE. These violations include the government's indiscriminate shelling of civilians and the LTTE's use of civilians as "human shields" in the final months of the conflict, which ended in May 2009.

The government continued to ignore the 2011 report of the panel of experts appointed by United Nations Secretary-General Ban Ki-moon, which recommended establishing an independent international mechanism to monitor the government's implementation of the panel recommendations, conduct an independent investigation, and collect and safeguard evidence.

In March 2012, the UN Human Rights Council (HRC) adopted a resolution finding that the government's Lessons Learnt and Reconciliation Commission (LLRC) did not adequately address serious allegations of violations of international law, and called on Sri Lanka to take all necessary steps to ensure justice and accountability. It requested that the government expeditiously present a comprehensive plan detailing the steps it had taken to implement the LLRC's recommendations and to address accountability.

The Sri Lankan government responded by publicly threatening human rights defenders who had advocated for the resolution. In July, the government announced that it had adopted an action plan to implement LLRC recommendations. The plan vaguely calls for the government to look into civilian deaths and prosecute any wrongdoers. It sets out a 12-month timeframe to conclude disciplinary inquiries and 24 months for prosecutions. □□But the government proposal merely leaves responsibility for investigations with the military and police, the entities responsible for the abuses, using processes lacking in transparency.

There has been no information regarding actions of the special army courts of inquiry, supposedly established in 2012 to look into allegations of war crimes. Despite strong evidence that government forces were involved in the execution-style slayings of 17 aid workers and 5 students in separate incidents in 2006, no one was arrested for the crimes. Other recommendations, such as the need to restore the independence of the police and remove them from the purview of the Ministry of Defence, were tasked to parliamentary select committees that had yet to be established at this writing.

During its Universal Periodic Review (UPR) before the HRC in November 2012, the Sri Lankan government rejected 100 recommendations from member states, including some that have a direct impact on accountability.

Arbitrary Detention, Torture, and Enforced Disappearances

The police and security forces continue to enjoy overly broad detention powers. The president issued monthly decrees granting the armed forces search and detention powers, effectively granting police powers to the army.

Despite the end of the formal state of emergency in 2011, the government continued to hold without trial several thousand people initially detained under the emergency regulations. In spite of public commitments, the government also failed to publish comprehensive lists of the names of the detained, as well as places of detentions.

The government released most of the more than 11,000 suspected LTTE members detained at the end of the war and announced plans to prosecute 180 of those still detained.

Local rights groups reported arbitrary arrests, new enforced disappearances, abductions, and killings in the north and the east in 2012. The government lifted its restrictions on travel to the north, although it maintained a high security presence. Tamils with alleged links to the LTTE were increasingly at risk of arbitrary arrests and torture. In April, nearly 220 Tamil men and women in the Trincomalee area were arrested and held for several days without charge in military detention camps.

Tamils who returned to Sri Lanka, including deported asylum seekers, reported being detained and accused of having links to the LTTE or taking part in anti-government activities abroad. A number reported being tortured by the Central Intelligence Department and other security forces. On the basis of these reports, courts in the United Kingdom granted injunctions to stop the deportation of more than 30 Tamil asylum seekers.

The Prevention of Terrorism Act remained in place, giving police broad powers over suspects in custody.

Attacks on Civil Society

Free expression remained under assault in 2012. Government officials and state-owned media publicly threatened civil society and human rights activists who spoke in favor of March's HRC resolution. Their names and faces were publicized and they were branded as traitors. The government took no action against a cabinet minister, Mervyn de Silva, who threatened activists.

Media reported increased surveillance and clampdowns on free speech. In June 2012, the Criminal Investigation Department raided the offices of the *Sri Lanka Mirror*, a news website, and the *Sri Lanka X News* website of the opposition United National Party. The authorities confiscated computers and documents and arrested nine people on the grounds that the websites were "propagating false and unethical news on Sri Lanka." They were charged under article 120 of the penal code, which imposes up to two years in prison for those who "excite or attempt to excite feelings of disaffection to the president or to the government." The nine were released on bail the day after their arrest.

The government shut down at least five news websites critical of the government in 2012 and put in place onerous registration requirements and fees for all web-based media services. Many news websites moved their host proxies abroad to avoid the censorship. Frederica Jansz, then-editor of the anti-government *Sunday Leader* newspaper, reported that Gotabhaya Rajapaksa threatened her in July, when she criticized his decision to reroute a government plane in order to pick up a puppy from Switzerland. The paper retracted the story in November. There were reports of other independent or outspoken members of the media being pushed out of their positions due to political pressure. Unknown assailants gunned down the previous *Sunday Leader* editor, Lasantha Wickrematunge, in broad daylight near a police station in 2009. No investigation has been conducted into his death.

There were no further developments in the case of Prageeth Ekneligoda, a contributor to *Lanka E-news*, who disappeared on January 24, 2010. Attorney General Mohan Peiris, summoned to testify in Colombo, retracted a previous statement where he had claimed that Ekneligoda had not disappeared but had willingly moved abroad.

In September, elections for local provincial councils in the east were marred by allegations of violence and vote-rigging.

Internally Displaced Persons and Militarization

The last of the nearly 300,000 civilians illegally confined in military-controlled detention centers after the war—including Menik Farm near Vavuniya, which was closed in September 2012—moved back into communities, although not necessarily to their home areas. Tens of thousands of persons still live with host families or in temporary accommodation, and several thousand are not able to return home because their home areas have not been de-mined.

Although the government claimed to have considerably decreased its military presence in the north and east, credible accounts indicate that military personnel still frequently intervene in civilian life. A Defence Ministry video on the north and east showed the military involved in numerous civilian activities, including organizing school cricket competitions and celebrations in temples. Soldiers commit abuses against soldiers with impunity. Fishermen and farmers complained about the armed forces continuing to encroach into their coastal areas and onto their land, impacting their livelihoods.

Key International Actors

Sri Lanka's government faced mounting pressure from key international actors after it failed to take meaningful action on accountability issues. At the March HRC session, the government tried to block the council from adopting a resolution focusing on accountability. The resolution, which passed with 24 votes in favor, 15 against, and 8 abstentions, effectively overturned a May 2009 council resolution that ignored serious human rights concerns during the Sri Lankan war. Member countries voting for the resolution included Nigeria, Uruguay, and India, which faces pressure from Tamil Nadu state and civil society activists demanding accountability. The resolution calls on the UN Office of the High Commissioner for Human Rights (OHCHR) to report back in March 2013.

India continued to press the Sri Lankan government to address allegations of human rights violations, implement the LLRC recommendations, and initiate a reconciliation process with the Tamil minority.

China has emerged in recent years as an important ally of Sri Lanka's government. In addition to investing heavily in developing Sri Lankan infrastructure, China had several high-level diplomatic and military missions to the country during the year and vocally opposed the HRC resolution on Sri Lanka.

Thailand

The government of Prime Minister Yingluck Shinawatra, which won a landslide victory in July 2011 elections, has not yet addressed Thailand's many serious human rights problems, including lack of accountability for the 2010 political violence, abuses in southern border provinces, free speech restrictions, and violations of refugee and migrant rights.

Accountability for Political Violence

At least 90 people died and more than 2,000 were injured during violent political confrontations from March to May 2010 as a result of unnecessary or excessive use of lethal force by Thai security forces, as well as attacks by armed elements operating in tandem with the United Front for Democracy against Dictatorship (UDD), known as the "Red Shirts."

On September 17, 2012, the independent Truth for Reconciliation Commission of Thailand (TRCT) presented its final report, which blamed both sides for the 2010 violence but indicated that the security forces were responsible for the majority of deaths and injuries. The commission urged the Yingluck government to "address legal violations by all parties through the justice system, which must be fair and impartial."

The results of the first post-mortem inquest delivered by the Bangkok Criminal Court on September 17, 2012, found that UDD supporter Phan Khamkong was shot dead by soldiers during a military operation near Bangkok's Ratchaprarop Airport Link station on the night of May 14, 2010. However, in what appeared to be a response to pressure from Army Commander-in-Chief Gen. Prayuth Chanocha, the government adopted a policy that soldiers should be treated as witnesses in the investigations and protected from criminal prosecution.

At the same time, the status of investigations into alleged crimes by UDD-linked "Black Shirt" militants remains unclear. A number of those accused of violence against soldiers, police officers, and anti-UDD groups were released on bail with the expectation they would not be prosecuted. The UDD leadership and their supporters, including those holding positions in the government and the parlia-

374

ment, dismissed the TRCT findings and asserted that there were no armed elements within the UDD during the events of 2010.

The Yingluck government provided reparations to all those harmed by the 2010 violence. However, many victims and their families said they feared that financial compensation has been offered as a substitute to full investigations and commitment to bring perpetrators of violence to justice. Early drafts of a National Reconciliation Bill submitted to parliament in May 2012 by the ruling Pheu Thai Party and its coalition partners contained a proposal for a broad amnesty for leaders and supporters of all political movements, politicians, government officials, and members of the security forces involved in the 2010 violence.

On November 24, 2012, police deployed teargas, shields, and batons to push back anti-government Pitak Siam protesters, who charged at police lines and drove trucks through barricades. At least 52 protesters and 29 police officers were injured in the clashes.

Freedom of Expression and the Media

According to a study by the National Human Rights Commission of Thailand, the number of arrests and convictions for *lese majeste* (insulting the monarchy) offenses declined significantly since Prime Minister Yingluck came to office in 2011. On October 31, 2012, the Bangkok Criminal Court acquitted Red Shirt supporter Surapak Phuchaisaeng of *lese majeste* charges, ruling that the prosecutor had failed to prove Surapak's computer was used for posting on Facebook messages deemed insulting to the royal family. Arrested in September 2011, Surapak had been the first *lese majeste* case brought by the Yingluck government.

However, Thai authorities continue to use the *lese majeste* statute in article 112 of the penal code, and the Computer Crimes Act, to suppress and prosecute perceived critics of the monarchy.

On October 10, 2012, the Constitutional Court ruled that the restriction of freedom of expression and the penalty for *lese majeste* offenses were constitutional.

Since December 2011, Thai authorities have blocked more than 5,000 alleged *lese majeste* webpages.

Other persons charged with *lese majeste* offenses were denied bail and remained in prison for many months, awaiting trial. In most cases, their trials resulted in harsh sentences. Amphon Tangnoppakul, who was sentenced in November 2011 to 20 years in prison for sending four *lese majeste* SMS messages in 2010, died of cancer in prison on May 8, 2012.

Lese majeste prosecutions also target intermediaries, leading to widespread self-censorship in discussion about the monarchy. On May 30, 2012, the Bangkok Criminal Court sentenced Chiranuch Premchaiporn, website manager of the well-known online news portal Prachatai, to a suspended one-year prison term for *lese majeste* statements posted by others on the Prachatai webboard. Labor activist and magazine editor Somyos Pruksakasemsuk was arrested in April 2011 and charged with *lese majeste* in connection with articles written by someone else in his *Voice of Taksin* magazine. He was denied bail eight times during the course of his pre-trial detention, shackled, and compelled to appear in hearings in four different provinces, despite the fact that witnesses were resident in Bangkok. At this writing, the verdict was scheduled for December 19.

Deputy Prime Minister Chalerm Yubamrung and military commanders have publicly and repeatedly warned human rights activists, academics, and political movements from about calling for the reform of *lese majeste* laws.

Violence and Human Rights Abuses in Southern Border Provinces

Separatist insurgents in the network of National Revolution Front-Coordinate (BRN-Coordinate) continued in 2012 to target civilians in bomb attacks, roadside ambushes, drive-by shootings, and assassinations.

Civilians make up more than 90 percent of the more than 5,000 deaths in the southern border provinces since January 2004. Insurgent groups have used violence to intimidate and ultimately drive out ethnic Thai Buddhists in Pattani,

Yala, and Narathiwat, as well as to discredit Thai authorities for being unable to protect citizens and to keep ethnic Malay Muslims under control.

The Yingluck government initiated a government-funded compensation scheme for Malay Muslim victims of abuses committed by the security forces. However, Thai security forces faced few or no consequences for extrajudicial killings, torture, enforced disappearances, and other abuses.

Local human rights groups reported the "disappearance" of Nasulan Pi in Narathiwat's Joh Airong district on January 17, 2012, after two armed security personnel forced him into their pickup truck and drove away.

After former Prime Minister Thaksin Shinawatra and Malaysia's Prime Minister Najib Razak pressured exiled separatist leaders to enter negotiations with Thai officials, insurgents retaliated by attacking the commercial districts of Yala and Songkhla with car bombs on March 31, 2012. At least 16 civilians were killed and more than 400 wounded.

Insurgents continued to burn down government-run schools and attack teachers whom they accused of representing the ideology of the Thai Buddhist state. On November 22, 2012, insurgents shot dead Nanthana Kaewjan, a teacher from Pattani's Ban Thakamsam school. Since January 2004, insurgents have killed 154 teachers from government-run schools. Insurgents also recruited children from private Islamic schools to participate in armed hostilities and perform secondary tasks such as distributing separatist leaflets. They also used some private Islamic schools to assemble bombs.

Reacting to domestic and international concerns, the Fourth Region Army Commander Lt. Gen. Udomchai Thammasarorat ordered security units to stop using government schools as barracks.

In 2012, insurgents admitted that they planted antipersonnel landmines in and near rubber plantations owned by Thai Buddhists to force them to relinquish land ownership.

Anti-Narcotics Policy

While vowing to respect human rights and due process when implementing anti-narcotics policy, the Yingluck government still denied any official involvement in the more than 2,800 extrajudicial killings that accompanied then-Prime Minister Thaksin Shinawatra's 2003 "War on Drugs."

On March 14, 2012, the parliamentary Police Affairs Committee found that police officers from the Sakon Nakhon provincial anti-drug squad used excessive force in the 2011 fatal shooting of Pairote Saengrit, and had planted a bag of methamphetamine on his body after his death.

After a seven-year trial, the Bangkok Criminal Court found five police officers from Kalasin province guilty on July 30, 2012, for the murder of Kiettisak Thitboonkrong. Kiettisak's case was the first prosecution of more than 20 extrajudicial killings in Kalasin province allegedly committed by this group of police officers from 2003 to 2005. However, the judge released the convicted officers on bail pending the outcome of their appeal, raising serious concerns about the safety of witnesses.

As of November 2012, the Yingluck government had sent more than 500,000 drug users to so-called rehabilitation centers, mostly run by the military and the Interior Ministry, where the ostensible treatment is based on military-style physical exercise. Routinely detained in prison prior to compulsory rehabilitation, detainees get little or no medical assistance for drug withdrawal symptoms.

Human Rights Defenders

Since 2001, more than 20 environmentalists and human rights defenders have been killed in Thailand. Investigations into the killings have frequently suffered from shoddy police work, the failure of the Justice Ministry to provide adequate protection for witnesses, and political interference in law enforcement efforts.

In the southern border provinces, Malay Muslim human rights defenders, paralegals, and student activists have often been profiled by security agencies as "insurgent sympathizers" and subjected to surveillance, arbitrary arrest, and detention.

Refugees, Asylum Seekers, and Migrant Workers

Thailand is not a party to the 1951 Refugee Convention, and has no law that recognizes refugee status. Asylum seekers and refugees who are arrested often face long periods of detention until they are accepted for resettlement or agree to be repatriated at their own expense.

Burma's President Thein Sein called for Burmese exiles to return as his government signed preliminary ceasefire agreements with nearly all armed ethnic groups. But enormous obstacles remain, including a lack of firm political settlements, landmines, and still-blocked access of the office of the United Nations High Commissioner for Refugees (UNHCR) to the Burma side of the border. Prime Minister Yingluck publicly assured that, regardless of what appeared to be positive developments in Burma, the 140,000 refugees living in camps on the Thai-Burmese border would not be forced to return home.

Thai authorities continued to implement a policy of intercepting and pushing back boats carrying ethnic Rohingya Muslims from Burma and Bangladesh despite allegations that such practices led to hundreds of deaths in 2008 and 2009.

Thai labor laws afforded migrant workers little protection in 2012. A migrant worker registry and "nationality verification" scheme provides legal documentation for workers, but does little to counter the impunity with which employers violate such workers' rights. Migrant workers remain extremely vulnerable to labor exploitation, physical and sexual violence, and trafficking. Male migrants in particular face being trafficked onto fishing boats.

In October 2012, factory owners and local officials prevented thousands of Burmese workers living in the border town of Mae Sot from leaving the area to search for work elsewhere in Thailand, despite possessing legal work permits that allowed them to do so.

After receiving strong criticisms at home and abroad, Labor Minister Padermchai Sasomsap in July 2012 scrapped his plan to send home migrant workers who are three to four months pregnant.

HUMAN
RIGHTS
WATCH

Ad Hoc and Inadequate
Thailand's Treatment of Refugees and Asylum Seekers

Key International Actors

The United Nations, United States, Australia, European Union, Switzerland, and Norway expressed strong support for political reconciliation and greater human rights protections in Thailand in 2012, calling on the government and all other conflicting political factions to engage in dialogue and refrain from using violence. On September 18, 2012, the UN High Commissioner for Human Rights Navi Pillay urged the Yingluck government to act on the TRCT's recommendations by holding those responsible for the 2010 violence to account and addressing reforms identified by the omission.

Vietnam

The Vietnam government systematically suppresses freedom of expression, association, and peaceful assembly, and persecutes those who question government policies, expose official corruption, or call for democratic alternatives to one-party rule. Police harass and intimidate activists and their family members. Authorities arbitrarily arrest activists, hold them incommunicado for long periods without access to legal counsel or family visits, subject them to torture, and prosecute them in politically pliant courts that mete out long prison sentences for violating vaguely worded national security laws.

In 2012, police used excessive force in response to public protests over evictions, confiscation of land, and police brutality.

Land confiscation continues to be a flashpoint issue, with local farmers and villagers facing unjust confiscation of their lands by government officials and private sector projects. Those who resist face abuses from local authorities.

Following a series of arrests of well-connected tycoons and managers of state-owned companies, the Party Central Committee held its sixth plenum in October. During the session, factions led by Prime Minister Nguyen Tan Dung and by Communist Party Secretary General Nguyen Phu Trong and President Truong Tan Sang vied for control of the state's political and economic machinery in a still ongoing power struggle. However, neither faction has voiced or otherwise demonstrated a commitment to protect human rights.

Vietnam has stated that it will seek a seat on the United Nations Human Rights Council (HRC) for the 2014-2016 term.

Freedom of Expression, Assembly, and Information

On the surface, private expression, public journalism, and even political speech in Vietnam show signs of enhanced freedom. This trend was especially evident in a surge of criticism of Prime Minister Nguyen Tan Dung during the course of the 6th Plenum of the Party Central Committee in October, and a high-profile call for his resignation issued from the floor of the National Assembly in November.

However, there continues to be a subcurrent of state-sponsored repression and persecution of individuals whose speech crosses boundaries and addresses sensitive issues such as criticizing the state's foreign policies in regards to China or questioning the monopoly power of the communist party.

The government does not allow independent or privately owned media outlets to operate, and exerts strict control over radio and TV stations, and publications. Criminal penalties apply to those who disseminate materials deemed to oppose the government, threaten national security, reveal state secrets, or promote "reactionary" ideas. The government blocks access to politically sensitive websites and requires internet cafe owners to monitor and store information about users' online activities.

In April, the government revealed a draft Decree on Management, Provision, and Use of Internet Services and Information on the Network. As drafted, the decree will outlaw posting internet content that opposes the Vietnam government, national security, public order, customs and traditions, national unity, offends the reputation of an individual or group, or transgresses a number of other ill-defined areas of concern. The decree would also require domestic and foreign companies to filter whatever content the government finds objectionable. The National Assembly had not yet begun considering the draft at this writing.

In September, Prime Minister Nguyen Tan Dung ordered the Ministry of Public Security to target blogs and websites not approved by the authorities, and to punish those who create them.

On August 5, authorities forcibly dispersed peaceful marchers in Hanoi protesting Chinese foreign policies on sovereignty over the Paracels and Spratly islands. Authorities temporarily detained more than 20 protesters for disrupting public order. Yet on the same day, authorities did not interfere with over 100 people on bicycles participating in Vietnam's first public demonstration for lesbian, gay, bisexual, and transgender (LGBT) rights.

Repression of Rights Activists

During 2012, the Vietnam government used vaguely defined articles in the penal code that criminalize exercise of civil and political rights to send at least 33 activists to prison and arrest at least another 34 political and religious advocates. At least 12 other rights campaigners detained in 2011 were still being held, awaiting trial at this writing.

Rights activists continue to suffer from intrusive police surveillance, interrogation, monetary fines, and restrictions on domestic and international travel. Police use temporary house arrest to prevent them from participating in protests or attending trials of other bloggers and activists. In a number of instances in 2012, unidentified thugs have assaulted dissidents and police have done little or nothing to investigate.

In a prominent, internationally monitored trial that lasted only several hours on September 24, a court convicted the country's three most prominent dissident bloggers—Nguyen Van Hai (also known as Dieu Cay), Ta Phong Tan, and Phan Thanh Hai (also known as Anhbasg)—for violating article 88 of the penal code (conducting propaganda against the state). The court sentenced them to 12, 10, and 4 years in prison respectively. All are founding members of the Club for Free Journalists. United States President Barack Obama, US Secretary of State Hillary Clinton, and European Union High Representative Catherine Ashton have all raised concerns about their cases on different occasions during the year.

Authorities also widely used article 88 to silence other bloggers and rights activists. In October, musicians Tran Vu Anh Binh and Vo Minh Tri (also known as Viet Khang) were sentenced to a total of 10 years in prison for writing songs critical of the regime. In August, bloggers Dinh Dang Dinh and Le Thanh Tung were sentenced to six and five years in prison respectively. In June and July, labor rights activist Phan Ngoc Tuan in Ninh Thuan province and land rights activists Nguyen Kim Nhan, Dinh Van Nhuong, and Do Van Hoa in Bac Giang province were sentenced to a total of eighteen-and-a-half years in prison for conducting propaganda against the state for storing and distributing pro-democracy documents and leaflets. In March and May, five Catholic activists—Vo Thi Thu Thuy, Nguyen Van Thanh, Dau Van Duong, Tran Huu Duc, and Chu Manh Son—were jailed for a total of 17 years and 9 months for distributing pro-democracy leaflets, reduced to the total of 16 years and 3 months on appeal.

In March, the People's Court of Go Dau district in Tay Ninh province sentenced rights activists Ho Thi Hue and Nguyen Bich Thuy to three years each in prison for participating in protests against land confiscation in Tay Ninh province. Their sentences were reduced to two years each on appeal in August. In April and June, land right activists Nguyen Van Tu in Can Tho and Nguyen Van Tuan in Ba Ria-Vung Tau were sentenced to two and a half years and four years respectively in prison for "abusing rights to democracy and freedom to infringe upon the interests of the State." Both were accused of helping local people file petitions against land confiscation. Nguyen Van Tuan's sentence was reduced to two years on appeal in August.

Freedom of Religion

The government restricts religious freedom through legislation, registration requirements, and harassing and intimidating unsanctioned religious groups, including independent Protestant home churches, and individuals and congregations of Hoa Hao Buddhists, Cao Dai, the Unified Buddhist Church of Vietnam, and Falun Gong.

Religious groups must register with the government and conduct their operations under the direction of government-controlled management boards. The authorities do generally allow government-affiliated churches and pagodas to hold worship services. However, local authorities routinely harass and intimidate religious communities, especially unregistered ones, when they take up politically disfavored issues including land rights and freedom of expression; when they are were popular among groups that the government considers to be potentially disaffected, such as ethnic minorities with a history of resistance against central rule and assimilation policies; or when they simply refuse to conform to state-sanctioned religious organization.

In February and March, Phu Yen province police arrested at least 18 members of a Buddhism-based religious group that refers to itself as the Council for Public Law and Affairs of Bia Mountain. They face charges under penal code article 79 for "activities aiming to overthrow the people's administration." At this writing, the 18 members of the group were in police detention in Phu Yen province, awaiting trial.

In Gia Lai province in March, Pastor Nguyen Cong Chinh was sentenced to 11 years in prison for "undermining national unity" in violation of article 87 of the penal code. The same month, eight ethnic Hmong Protestant activists from Muong Nhe district in Dien Bien were each given sentences of between two to two-and-a-half years in jail for "disrupting security" after they participated in a mass protest in Muong Nhe in May 2011.

In April and June, three other Protestant activists, Kpuil Mel, Kpuil Lɖ, and Nay Y Nga, were sentenced to a total of 22 years in prison for transgressing article 87. All three were accused of practicing Dega Protestantism, which is outlawed by the state.

In May, three ethnic Montagnard activists, Runh, Jonh, and Byuk, were arrested in Gia Lai for being affiliated with the unregistered Ha Mon Catholic group and charged with "undermining national unity" according to article 87.

Police in An Giang prevented members of the unregistered Pure Hoa Hao Buddhist Association from gathering to commemorate key events, including the anniversary of the disappearance of the group's founder Huynh Phu So. Hoa Hao activist Bui Van Tham was sentenced to 30 months in prison for "resisting officials in the performance of official duties."

In June and July, local authorities sought to prevent Catholic priests from performing masses at the private homes of Catholic followers in Con Cuong and Quy Chau districts in Nghe An province. In both areas, local Catholics have filed multiple requests to authorities to form and register new parishes without success.

Criminal Justice System

Police brutality, including torture in detention and fatal beatings, continued to be reported in all regions of the country in 2012. At least 15 people died in police custody in the first 9 months of the year, according to state-controlled media.

Vietnamese courts lack independence since they are firmly controlled by the government and the Vietnam Communist party, and trials of political and religious dissidents fail to meet international fair trial standards. Police intimidate, and in some cases detain, family members and friends who try to attend trials or publicly display dissenting views during court proceedings.

Vietnamese law continues to authorize arbitrary "administrative detention" without trial. Under Ordinance 44 (2002) and Decree 76 (2003) persons deemed threats to national security or public order can be placed under house arrest, involuntarily committed to mental health institutions, or detained at "re-education" centers.

In June, the National Assembly passed the Law on Handling of Administrative Violations that will finally halt the practice of sending sex workers to administrative detention in the so-called "05 centers" where they often suffer abuse. Human rights observers welcome this rare example of a concrete and positive institutional reform.

The policy of detention of drug users, however, remained unchanged. The mainstay of Vietnam's approach to drug treatment remains detention in government centers where detainees are subjected to so-called "labor therapy." Some 123 centers across the country hold around 40,000 people, including children as young as 12 years old. Their detention is not subject to any form of due process or judicial oversight and routinely lasts as long as four years. Infringement of center rules—including the work requirement—is punished by beatings with truncheons, shocks with electrical batons, and imprisonment in disciplinary rooms where detainees are deprived of food and water. Former detainees report that authorities forced them to work in cashew processing and other forms of agricultural production, including potato or coffee farming, construction work, and garment manufacturing and other forms of manufacturing.

Key International Actors

Vietnam's complicated relationship with China plays a key role in domestic and foreign affairs. Hanoi pledges friendship with China, but domestically must respond to criticism that it fails to counter China's aggressive behavior in the disputed Spratly and Paracel Islands. Internationally, the government has increased cooperation with the US, the EU, Russia, India, Japan, and neighboring Association of Southeast Asian Nations (ASEAN) to counter-weight to China's growing influence.

The EU and Vietnam launched negotiations on a comprehensive free trade agreement in June. Two rounds of the EU-Vietnam human rights dialogue took place in January and October.

The relationship between Vietnam and the US continues to grow. The US is Vietnam's largest export market, and the June visit of US Defense Secretary Leon Panetta symbolized the growing ties between the two countries' militaries. The US and Vietnam are also negotiating a Trans-Pacific Partnership free trade agreement. However, during a July visit to Vietnam, Secretary of State Hillary Clinton publicly raised serious concerns about Vietnam's poor human rights record, and US policy makers indicated that failure to improve human rights could impose limits on the closeness of the relationship between the two governments.

Starting in 2013, Le Luong Minh, Vietnam's deputy foreign minister, will start his five- year term as secretary-general of ASEAN, greatly increasing Vietnam's influence in this regional bloc.

HUMAN
RIGHTS
WATCH

Boat Ride to Detention

Adult and Child Migrants in Malta

WORLD REPORT
2013

EUROPE
AND CENTRAL ASIA

Armenia

Armenia's ruling coalition retained a parliamentary majority following the May 2012 elections amid allegations of abuse of administrative resources, and intimidation of voters, observers, and journalists. Ill-treatment in police custody persists. The government has yet to offer conscientious objectors a genuine civilian alternative to military service and has failed to effectively investigate a troubling number of non-combat deaths in the military.

Politically motivated defamation lawsuits no longer appear to be a problem, but media pluralism is lacking, and some journalists covering the May 6 parliamentary elections suffered violent attacks by onlookers, some of them members of Armenia's ruling political party. Violence and discrimination based on sexual orientation are serious problems. Bureaucratic restrictions prevent people with terminal illnesses from accessing strong pain medications.

Parliamentary Elections

The Organization for Security and Co-operation in Europe's (OSCE) monitoring report assessed the May 6 parliamentary elections as competitive and largely peaceful, yet marred by "an unequal playing field" due to misuse of administrative resources, and party representatives and local authorities pressuring voters, interfering in voting, and hindering the work of journalists.

Several violent incidents occurred during the campaign period in Yerevan, including assaults on opposition party Armenian National Congress (ANC) candidate Babken Garoyan and three other ANC members on April 15, and on ANC candidate Karen Tovmasyan on April 17. In both cases, the ANC members were distributing campaign information. Police opened investigations into each case.

Helsinki Association campaign monitor Arman Veziryan filed complaints alleging that Yerevan resident Tigran Manukyan punched him and hindered his work as an observer while Veziryan observed an opposition activist distributing election pamphlets on April 30. Instead of investigating, prosecutors pressured Veziryan to withdraw the complaint and in June charged him with beating Manukyan, although Manukyan never claimed to be a victim. Veziryan was awaiting trial at this writing.

Torture and Ill-Treatment in Custody

According to local human rights defenders, torture and ill-treatment in police custody persist. Authorities often refuse to investigate ill-treatment allegations or coerce citizens into retracting complaints. The October report of the European Committee for the Prevention of Torture (CPT) on a follow-up visit in December 2011 noted overcrowding, unhygienic conditions, and inadequate medical care in two prison facilities. CPT also noted that it received no new cases of ill-treatment from these facilities in 2012.

The government has not effectively investigated a complaint from seven ANC activists that police beat them in detention in August 2011. The activists' lawyers also filed a complaint alleging police denied them access to their clients, refused their request for a medical examination for the activists, and detained the lawyers for seven hours, during which a lawyer witnessed police beating one of the activists, Artak Karapetyan. The activists testified about the abuse during trial, but a Yerevan court did not request an investigation.

In July, the court sentenced four of the activists—Karapetyan, Tigran Arakelyan, Sargis Gevorgyan, and David Kiramijyan—to two to six years' imprisonment for hooliganism and resisting authority. In November, the appeals court upheld their sentences. In August, police dropped charges against the other three for lack of evidence.

In October, the European Court of Human Rights (ECtHR) ruled that Armenia had violated the prohibition against inhuman or degrading treatment in the case of opposition party member Grisha Virabyan when police repeatedly hit him in the testicles with metal objects after detaining him following demonstrations in 2004. The court denounced the authorities' failure to effectively investigate.

Army Abuses

Local human rights groups reported 44 non-combat army deaths through September. On February 29, conscript Tigran Varyan was killed by a gunshot wound. The government-mandated autopsy revealed that Varyan was subject to violence, but investigators classified his death as suicide. A report by local human rights groups noted the Defense Ministry's failure to initiate investigations promptly, to account for signs of violence in cases of alleged suicides, and to disclose the circumstances of many deaths.

A January ECtHR ruling found Armenia had violated the right to religious freedom of two Jehovah's Witnesses by imprisoning them for refusing to perform mandatory military service in 2003.

According to Forum 18, an international religious freedom nongovernmental organization, 32 conscientious objectors were in prison as of September 20 for refusing military and alternative service, believing the alternative service was not independent of the military. In 2012, courts sentenced to prison terms 16 additional Jehovah's Witnesses for refusal to serve. The sentences were not enforced.

In 2011, authorities proposed amendments to the alternative service law. However, the OSCE and the Council of Europe (CoE) criticized the amendments for not making alternative service truly independent of the military and for making it 12-18 months longer than military service. In its July review of Armenia, the United Nations Human Rights Committee (HRC) urged the government to ensure a real alternative to military service, and release those imprisoned for refusing to perform military service or the existing alternative to it.

Freedom of Expression

Politically motivated defamation lawsuits no longer appear to be a serious problem. However, a June 2012 Parliamentary Assembly of the Council of Europe (PACE) report on media freedom in Europe found Armenian journalists' capacity to report was "hampered by pressures of self-censorship" and expressed concern about television stations' use of material from political advertisements in news coverage.

At least two journalists suffered attacks while covering the May elections. In Yerevan, a man punched Elina Chilingaryan as she filmed a bus arriving at a polling station, knocking her camera to the ground. Police brought charges against the assailant for interfering with the professional duties of a journalist. They later dropped the charges, claiming that Chilingaryan was not performing her professional duties at the time of the attack since she was not wearing her press badge. The authorities did not bring separate assault charges.

In Gyumri, four unidentified men approached journalist Karen Alekyan at a polling station, ripped off his press badge, and broke his camera. Alekyan filed a complaint. The investigation was ongoing at this writing.

Palliative Care

Armenia's complicated and time-consuming prescription and procurement procedures for opioid medications obstruct the delivery of adequate palliative care. UN statistics from 2009-2010 suggest that approximately 7,000 people die annually in Armenia from cancer and HIV/AIDS. However, analysis of strong pain medicine consumption suggests only about 600 patients with moderate to severe pain gained access in 2012 to adequate pain relief during the last stages of their illness.

Sexual Orientation and Gender Identity

In July, the NGO Public Information and Need of Knowledge (PINK) Armenia reported that lesbian, gay, bisexual, and transgender (LGBT) people experience employment discrimination, obstacles accessing healthcare, and physical and psychological abuse in the army, in families, and in public.

On May 8, unidentified people threw a homemade bomb at DIY, a Yerevan bar frequented by LGBT and women's rights activists. Graffiti identified LGBT people as targets. Deputy Speaker of Parliament Eduard Sharmazanov called the attack "right and justified." Police arrested two suspects who were released pending trial. Unidentified attackers destroyed bar property and made death threats against its owners in three subsequent May incidents. Police were called during each attack but intervened only once.

On May 21 in Yerevan, a group of people threatened violence and shouted homophobic slogans at participants in a march organized by PINK Armenia and the Women's Resource Center Armenia to celebrate diversity.

Human Rights Defenders

In April, about 200 people gathered outside the human rights nongovernmental Helsinki Citizens' Assembly's (HCA) Vanadzor office, throwing eggs and stones, breaking windows, and threatening staff with further violence if films made by Azerbaijani filmmakers were screened as planned. The group dispersed after HCA leaders agreed to cancel the films. As the crowed assembled HCA staff called the police, who failed to intervene.

In April, a court rejected a lawsuit by Lernapat Mayor Vano Yeghiazaryan against Artur Sakunts, head of HCA Vanadzor. In a 2011 newspaper interview Sakunts accused Yeghiazaryan of embezzlement and abuse of power. The court concluded that Yeghiazaryan, as a public official, "must be more tolerant towards opinions and publications relating to him."

Key International Actors

In its May European Neighborhood Policy Progress Report, the European Commission urged Armenia to address corruption, media freedom, low public trust in the judiciary, and inadequate investigation of ill-treatment. It commended the government for strengthening laws on gender equality and health care.

European Union foreign ministers' conclusions on the South Caucasus adopted in February at the Foreign Affairs council in Brussels highlighted the importance of free and fair elections and further judiciary reforms, political pluralism, freedom of and equal access to media, and protection of human rights defenders.

In his July visit to Yerevan, EU President Herman Van Rompuy welcomed Armenian authorities' efforts to deliver more competitive and transparent parliamentary elections, but cautioned that February 2013 presidential elections should be more democratic.

Following its July review of Armenia's compliance with the International Covenant on Civil and Political Rights (ICCPR), the HRC highlighted a host of concerns, including lack of comprehensive antidiscrimination legislation, violence against racial and religious minorities and LGBT people, discrimination and violence against women, lack of accountability for torture, and threats and attacks against rights defenders.

In May, the UN Office in Armenia condemned violence and intolerance based on sexual orientation and gender identity. The EU Delegation to Armenia and the CoE's European Commission against Racism and Intolerance expressed concern over Armenia's inadequate response to anti-LGBT hate speech and violence.

In a new strategy for Armenia adopted in May, the European Bank for Reconstruction and Development stressed the need for "further steps" such as police and judiciary reform and facilitating media pluralism.

Azerbaijan

Azerbaijan hosted the 2012 Eurovision Song Contest, casting an international spotlight on the government's deteriorating human rights record. The atmosphere for political activists and independent and pro-opposition journalists grew acutely hostile. Authorities used imprisonment as a tool for political retribution and forcibly dispersed a number of peaceful demonstrations, indiscriminately arresting activists and passersby. Restrictions on freedom of religion and the prosecution of unregistered religious groups continued. The government intensified its urban renewal campaign in the capital Baku, forcibly evicting thousands of families and illegally demolishing homes.

Foreign actors failed to fully realize the potential of their relationships with the government to press it to honor its human rights obligations.

Freedom of Media

In June, the Supreme Court released Bakhtiyar Hajiyev, a social media activist who had been serving a two-year prison sentence for allegedly avoiding mandatory military service. But Azerbaijani journalists continue to face prosecution on bogus charges, harassment, intimidation, and physical attacks. Defamation remained criminalized.

In November 2011, a court sentenced Aydin Janiyev, a *Khural* newspaper correspondent, to three years in prison on hooliganism charges, apparently in retaliation for his articles criticizing the authorities. Avaz Zeynalli, *Khural's* editor, in custody since his October 2011 arrest, was at this writing on trial on dubious extortion charges brought by a member of parliament from the ruling party. *Khrural,* which regularly published allegations of government corruption, closed in October 2011, when a court ordered that bailiffs seize its property to pay fines imposed in three defamation cases.

In March 2012, police arrested the executive director and editor-in-chief of Khayal TV, a local station, who remained in custody at this writing pending trial on charges of organizing social unrest and abuse of authority. The charges are linked to a video posted on YouTube showing the governor of the northern city of Guba insulting local residents in a speech, which many believe was the catalyst for the March 1 mass protests in the city.

In June, a court convicted Anar Bayramli, a journalist for the Iranian satellite television station Sahar TV, on trumped-up charges of illegal drug possession. In July, the Appeals Court halved his two-year prison sentence.

Hilal Mammadov, the editor-in-chief of *Tolishi Sado* newspaper who was arrested in June on bogus drug possession charges, remained in custody pending trial. In June, police also detained Mehman Huseynov, a blogger and photographer at the Institute for Reporters' Freedoms and Safety, a local media monitoring organization, and released him pending investigation on trumped-up charges of hooliganism.

In August, a court sentenced Faramaz Novruzoglu, a freelance journalist, to four-and-a-half years in jail on bogus charges of illegal border crossing and inciting mass disorder, stemming from spring 2011 Facebook postings, written using a pseudonym, calling for riots. Novruzoglu has denied the allegations and claims they are retribution for his investigations into business ties of high-level officials.

In April, police and private security personnel beat unconscious Idrak Abbasov, a journalist who was filming forced evictions and house demolitions. A police investigation was pending at this writing.

In March, unknown persons attempted to blackmail Khadija Ismailova, a Radio Liberty journalist, in retaliation for her investigation into the business holdings of the president's family and close associates.

In November 2011, Rafig Tagi, a journalist with *Sanet* weekly, was stabbed on the street near his apartment, and died of the wounds. No one had been charged for the attack at this writing.

In September 2012, the opposition daily *Azadlig* faced eviction threats from its premises at the state publishing house for failing to pay its outstanding debts, while at the same time a court fined the paper 30,000 AZN (about US$40,000) in a defamation suit brought by the head of Baku metro system.

Freedom of Assembly

The government limited freedom of assembly by breaking up peaceful protests, in some cases violently, and arresting protesters. In March, at the first sanctioned opposition protest since 2006, police detained two popular musicians as they played at the peaceful gathering. Police beat and denied them access to their lawyer. They were released after five and ten days of detention.

In April, police detained 20 activists distributing flyers encouraging people to attend an opposition rally. Courts sentenced 7 of the activists to 10 to 15 days of detention, and fined or released others.

In the days before and during May's Eurovision Song Contest, police broke up several protests in Baku's center. Police rounded up dozens of peaceful demonstrators, forcing them onto buses, and beating some as they did so. The demonstrators were released several hours later.

In October, police rounded up dozens of protesters in an unsanctioned rally in central Baku, roughed them up and forced them into buses. Courts imprisoned 13 on misdemeanor charges for up to 10 days, and fined several others.

In November, the parliament increased sanctions for participating and organizing unauthorized protests, establishing fines of up to 1,000 AZN ($ 1,274) for participation, and 3,000 ($ 3,822) for organization.

Political Prisoners

Imprisonment on politically motivated charges is a continuing problem. A June 2012 report by a committee of the Parliamentary Assembly of the Council of Europe (PACE) described the cases of 89 political prisoners in Azerbaijan. Just before the report's publication, nine were released under a presidential pardon. The PACE report documents the cases of journalists, human rights defenders, and activists who remain in detention in Azerbaijan on a range of trumped-up charges in retaliation for their work.

Ill-Treatment and Deaths in Custody

Torture and ill-treatment continue with impunity, and two men died in police custody in 2012. In the first eight months of 2012, the Azerbaijan Committee Against Torture, an independent prison monitoring group, received 136 complaints alleging ill-treatment in custody.

Forced Evictions and Illegal Demolitions

Since 2008, the authorities in Azerbaijan have been implementing a program of urban renewal in Baku, involving illegal expropriation of hundreds of properties—primarily apartments and homes in middle class neighborhoods—to make way for parks, roads, and luxury residential buildings. Most evictees have not received fair compensation based on market values of their properties. In 2012, hundreds of homeowners were affected as the authorities accelerated construction for the Eurovision Song Contest.

Freedom of Religion

The government continued to tighten restrictions on freedom of religion. In December 2011, the president signed legislative amendments criminalizing the illegal production, distribution, and import of religious literature not approved by the state; they were previously administrative offenses. A new criminal code article punishes the creation of a group that undermines social order under the guise of carrying out religious work.

According to Forum 18, an independent international religious freedom monitoring group, police raided several private homes on religion-related grounds.

Human Rights Defenders

Police arrested two human rights defenders associated with Kur Civil Union in retaliation for protecting flood victims in southern Azerbaijan. In April 2012, police arrested Ogtay Gulaliyev, the organization's coordinator, and charged him with hooliganism. In June, police released him, pending investigation and arrested Ilham Amiraslanov, another Kur activist. In September, a court sen-

tenced Amiraslanov to two years imprisonment on trumped-up weapons possession charges. No investigation was made into Gulaliyev's claim of ill-treatment
in custody, and after a preliminary inquiry the prosecutor's office refused to
investigate an ill-treatment complaint by Amiraslanov.

In April, a court sentenced Taleh Khasmammadov, a blogger and human rights
defender from Goychay, to a four-year prison term on charges of hooliganism
and physically assaulting a public official. Khasmammadov investigated allegations of abuse and corruption by law enforcement officials. Another human
rights defender from Goychay region, Vidadi Isganderov, remained in jail after
being convicted in August 2011 on false charges of interfering with parliamentary elections.

Azerbaijan Human Rights House, a member of the International Human Rights
House Network, remained closed following the Ministry of Justice suspending its
registration in March 2011.

Key International Actors

While expressing concern about Azerbaijan's worsening human rights record,
the European Union, United States, and other international and regional institutions did not impose policy consequences or make their engagement with
Azerbaijan conditional on concrete improvements.

A great number of foreign governments and international organizations condemned President Ilham Aliyev's decision to pardon Ramil Safarov, a military
officer, whom Hungary extradited to Azerbaijan so that he could serve out his
life imprisonment term there. In 2004, a Hungarian court convicted Safarov for
murdering an Armenian colleague at a NATO-sponsored training in Budapest.
Safarov confessed to the crime, which he justified by citing his victim's ethnicity.

The EU, Organization for Security and Co-Operation in Europe (OSCE), and the
US Embassy in Baku all condemned the assault on journalist Idrak Abbasov, and
called on the government to launch a prompt and thorough investigation, to no
avail.

In its May European Neighborhood Policy progress report, the EU highlighted Azerbaijan's failure to meet its commitments regarding electoral processes, human rights protections, and judicial independence. It also, for the first time, addressed concrete recommendations to the authorities.

The European Broadcasting Union, which oversaw the Eurovision Song Contest, made a public commitment to promote freedom of expression in Azerbaijan, but declined to take a strong public stand on the Azerbaijani government's record. It also refused to urge the government to properly compensate homeowners whose apartments were demolished in connection with the construction of Eurovision-related infrastructure.

While in Baku in June, US Secretary of State Hillary Clinton met with Bakhtiyar Hajiyev, and urged the authorities to release others imprisoned on politically motivated charges.

In a landmark vote on June 26, the Legal Affairs and Human Rights Committee of the Council of Europe's Parliamentary Assembly adopted a report on political prisoners in Azerbaijan. The government had refused to cooperate with the committee's rapporteur and denied him access to Azerbaijan.

In its March 2012 concluding observations, the UN Committee on the Rights of the Child (CRC) criticized Azerbaijan, for, inter alia, the lack of improvement in the juvenile justice system, and the lack of alternatives to institutionalization for children without families.

Belarus

The Belarusian government continues to severely curtail freedoms of association, assembly, and expression, and the right to fair trial. New restrictive legislative amendments paved the way in 2012 for even more intense governmental scrutiny of civil society organizations and activists. Governmental harassment of human rights defenders, independent media, and defense lawyers continues, including through arbitrary bans on foreign travel. At this writing, at least 12 political prisoners remain jailed. Allegations of torture and mistreatment in custody persist.

Parliamentary Elections

Parliamentary elections took place in September against a backdrop of stifled civil and political freedoms, and were marked by a lack of competitiveness and a low level of public confidence.

The continuing political crackdown impeded a competitive campaign. The elections resulted in 110 members elected for a four-year term to the lower chamber of the parliament. The opposition did not win any seats.

The elections complied with recent amendments to the electoral code, which the Organization for Security and Co-operation in Europe (OSCE) and the Venice Commission assessed as a positive but insufficient step towards a legal framework allowing for genuinely democratic elections. The OSCE's Office for Democratic Institutions and Human Rights and the OSCE Parliamentary Assembly found elections had fallen short of international standards, noting, in particular, irregularities during the vote count, a flawed process for considering complaints, and biased campaign coverage by state-controlled media.

Domestic monitors noted flaws in the rules on forming district and precinct election commissions, resulting in a low level of representation in the commissions by opposition parties. Monitors also documented incidents of intimidation by officials of opposition activists.

Days before the voting, the two registered opposition parties decided to boycott the elections, citing procedural violations, political repression, and the fact that opposition activists were imprisoned on politically motivated charges and could not run as candidates or vote.

Political Prisoners, Threats to Human Rights Defenders, and Civil Society Groups

In April, apparently responding to international criticism, the authorities released former opposition presidential candidate Andrei Sannikau and his aide, convicted in connection with the peaceful protests in 2010. In August and September 2012, the government pardoned three prisoners sentenced on criminal charges of "rioting" in connection with the December 2010 mass protests. All released prisoners had to sign a request for pardon that acknowledged their guilt.

Throughout the year, the authorities intensified the crackdown on dissent. Legislative amendments adopted in October 2011 established criminal liability for receiving foreign grants in violation of the law, and broadened the definition of treason to include "any form of assistance to a foreign state" that is detrimental to Belarus's national security. The amendments put civil society groups at risk of arbitrary prosecution if they receive foreign funding or engage in international advocacy.

In November 2011, a court sentenced leading human rights defender, Ales Bialiatski, to four-and-a-half years in prison on politically motivated charges of tax evasion. Prison officials have regularly subjected Bialiatski to arbitrary reprimands and other kinds of pressure. The authorities frequently sentence opposition activists and human rights defenders to arbitrary detention for "hooliganism" and other misdemeanor charges.

In February, opposition activist Siarhei Kavalenka was sentenced to 25 months' imprisonment for evading his supervised release, after being sentenced in 2010 for flying a banned pre-Lukashenka era national flag on a Christmas tree. He was freed in September 2012, after authorities forced him, including by making veiled threats regarding his son, to sign a request for pardon that acknowledged his guilt.

In May, a court handed human rights defender Aleh Vouchak a nine-day jail sentence on misdemeanor charges of "minor hooliganism," allegedly for swearing at police. Vouchak's arrest was apparently in retaliation for his human rights work and for meeting with a Human Rights Watch researcher a day earlier.

In June, the prosecutor's office issued a warning to human rights defender Andrei Bandarenka, for "discrediting" Belarus by participating in an ultimately unsuccessful campaign to convince the International Ice Hockey Federation not to hold the 2014 Men's World Ice Hockey Championship in Belarus because of its human rights record. At least 15 activists and journalists were banned during the year from leaving Belarus under arbitrary pretexts.

In July, President Aliaxander Lukashenka—in power since1994—signed a decree expanding the grounds on which the State Security Service (KGB) can impose travel bans on individuals.

Death Penalty

Belarus remains the only country in Europe to still use the death penalty. In March, Belarusian authorities executed Dzmitry Kanavalau and Uladzislau Kavalyou, convicted of carrying out a terrorist attack in the Minsk metro in April 2011 after a trial that raised serious due process concerns, including allegations of torture to extract confessions. The execution was carried out while a complaint regarding the men's treatment was pending with the United Nations Human Rights Committee. The committee had asked the authorities not to carry out the sentence until the review was complete.

Freedom of Assembly

Legislative amendments adopted in October 2011 further restricted freedom of peaceful assembly by broadening the definition of mass events and establishing criminal liability for organizing them in violation of the law. The amendments also required event organizers to report financing sources for mass events and expanded the powers of law enforcement during public gatherings to, among other things, limit access to the event site and conduct personal searches of participants.

Authorities regularly prohibit peaceful gatherings and use "hooliganism" or similar misdemeanor charges to intimidate activists and prevent them from carrying out their work. Dozens have been sentenced, some repeatedly, to short-term detention.

In April, riot police broke up the screening of "Europe's Last Dictator," a documentary about President Lukashenka, arrested all 19 viewers and staff, and took them to a police station for interrogation and fingerprinting. They were later released.

In February, a court sentenced activist Pavel Vinahradau to 10 days of detention for holding an "unsanctioned protest" for placing stuffed toys with anti-government slogans in front of government headquarters in Minsk. In August, two independent journalists, who were taking photos with teddy bears on a street in Minsk, were sentenced to fines for protesting.

Freedom of Expression

The government severely restricts freedom of expression. Most media is state-controlled, and television, radio, and internet censorship is widespread. The authorities continue to harass independent journalists for their work, including through arbitrary arrests, warnings, and criminal convictions. Journalists face great difficulties obtaining accreditation.

In June 2012, Belarusian authorities charged a journalist, Andrzej Poczobut, for libel against the president, a criminal offense punishable by up to five years' imprisonment. He was later released under his own recognizance. In a separate case brought in 2011, Poczobut had received a suspended sentence for allegedly defaming President Lukashenka.

In July, blogger Anton Suryapin was arrested and charged with complicity in an unlawful border crossing after posting in his blog photographs of a political stunt that month organized by Swedish activists who dropped teddy bears carrying freedom of speech messages from a plane into Belarusian territory. Suryapin denied involvement, and in August was released under his own recognizance. The trial was ongoing at this writing and Suryapin faces up to seven years in prison if convicted

In August, four Swedish journalists were refused entry into Belarus upon arriving in Minsk airport. Two of them had been accredited by the government to report on the September parliamentary elections.

In September, customs officials held an Australian journalist in Minsk airport and confiscated his laptop, phone, video camera, and memory cards. The journalist was released but his equipment was not returned.

Key International Actors

2012 marked a new low for the Belarusian government's pariah status in the international arena. The European Union and the United States government further tightened existing sanctions imposed against Belarusian officials, private individuals, and companies implicated in repression and human rights abuse. Responding to the continuing crackdown on civil society, the UN Human Rights Council (HRC) in July denounced abuses committed in Belarus, called for the release of all political prisoners, and appointed a special rapporteur to document and report back on violations in the country. The Belarusian Foreign Ministry swiftly announced that the government did not recognize the special rapporteur's mandate and refused to cooperate with it.

A diplomatic scandal unfolded in February when Lukashenka's government expelled the Polish and EU delegation ambassadors, and recalled Belarusian ambassadors in Warsaw and Brussels in response to the expansion of EU sanctions. All EU member states recalled their ambassadors from Belarus in solidarity. Belarus allowed all ambassadors to be reinstated after they later returned to Minsk.

In March, the European Parliament adopted a resolution urging additional sanctions that targeted several more officials and companies linked to the government and prohibited the export to Belarus of arms and materials that could be used for repression.

In a September 2012 report presented to the council, the UN high commissioner for human rights singled out Belarus among 16 countries where government intimidation of civil society activists is commonplace, and authorities mostly fail to hold accountable those responsible.

After the July teddy bear stunt, the government expelled the Swedish ambassador and closed the Swedish embassy in Minsk.

In September, the authorities refused visas to a Lithuanian politician and a German parliamentarian who planned to visit the country during parliamentary elections, stating that their presence in Belarus was "undesirable."

Bosnia and Herzegovina

There was little improvement in human rights in 2012 in Bosnia and Herzegovina (BiH) despite the formation of a national government in February after a delay of 14 months.

The government missed several deadlines to make changes to the constitution that were needed to end discriminatory restrictions on Jews and Roma holding political office. Roma remain subject to widespread discrimination. Some refugees and internally displaced persons (IDPs) wishing to return to their pre-war homes faced an obstacle in the courts, and there was no progress on implementing a return strategy. Journalists remained vulnerable to threats and attack.

Ethnic and Religious Discrimination

The new Bosnian government failed to implement a 2009 European Court of Human Rights (ECtHR) ruling ordering the country to amend its constitution to eliminate ethnic discrimination in the national tri-partite presidency and House of Peoples, both currently restricted to the three main ethnic groups (Bosniaks, Serbs, and Croats).

This was despite the government agreeing in June to present reform proposals by August 31, and a binding September 3 deadline set by the ECtHR itself. A joint working group established to propose changes has not met since March, and there are sharp disagreements among the main parties on the way forward. Local elections scheduled for October 2012 were held under the existing constitution.

A questionnaire for BiH's first national census since 1991, made public in April 2012 and scheduled for 2013, drew criticism from the International Monitoring Operation (IMO) and the Conference of European Statisticians. The IMO was established by the European Union and Council of Europe (CoE) to monitor the census. Criticism was based on questions requiring respondents to identify their ethnicity, religion, and mother tongue in the form of a closed question and limiting them to a single response. Amendments to the questionnaire largely failed to address the IMO's criticisms, and continued to require respondents to

411

identify their mother tongue, which may have a discriminatory effect on national minority groups and those who want to declare themselves as multilingual and multi-ethnic.

Roma remain the most vulnerable minority group, subject to widespread discrimination. Many Roma are still not on the national public registry that records births, deaths, and marriage, impeding their access to public services. Roma continue to face problems accessing health care due to registration restrictions, lower educational enrollment than other groups, and employment discrimination. Many Roma, particularly refugees and IDPs, including from Kosovo, remain in informal settlements. The practice of placing Roma in special schools in Mostar, a city in the Federation, instead of mainstream schools, continued during the year.

Most of the 100 Roma evicted from their homes in Mostar in October 2011 to make room for a housing project for other Roma families simply relocated to other informal settlements in the city and remain vulnerable to further evictions.

Refugees and Internally Displaced Persons

There was virtually no progress on implementing the 2010 strategy to support the return of refugees and IDPs to their pre-war homes, even after the new government was formed in February 2012. In the first 6 months of 2012, 185 refugees and 198 IDPs returned, according to the United Nations High Commissioner for Refugees (UNHCR), a slight increase relative to same period in 2011. According to the latest updates in June 2012, there were still 112,802 IDPs registered, down from 113,188 at the end of June of the previous year.

District court rulings awarding excessive compensation to temporary occupants of property were an obstacle to displaced people wanting to return to pre-war homes, prompting repeated criticism during the year by the Office of the International High Representative (OHR). Faik Zulcic, a returnee to Bjeljina in Republika Srpska, was evicted from his home in April after he was unable to pay 40,000KM (around US$26,000) to the former occupant as ordered in March 2012 by the Bjeljina District Court.

HUMAN
RIGHTS
WATCH

SECOND CLASS CITIZENS
Discrimination Against Roma, Jews, and Other National Minorities
in Bosnia and Herzegovina

National Security and Human Rights

BiH continued to subject foreign nationals to indefinite detention without trial on national security grounds. In February, the ECtHR halted the deportation of Imad Al Husin to Syria because of the risk of torture on return and ordered Bosnian authorities to charge him with a crime, find a third country to which he could safely travel, or release him. He remained in Bosnian detention without trial at this writing.

Also at this writing, Zeyad Khalad Al Gertani, another foreign national security suspect remained in detention without trial. Four others left BiH in 2012: Noureddine Gacci (deported to Algeria in January), Omar Frendi (deported to Algeria in March), Fadhil Al Hamadini (escaped house arrest to an unknown location in May), and Ammar Al Hanchi (deported to Tunisia in September after the ECtHR in June rejected his claim that he risked torture on return).

War Crimes Accountability

On May 16, the trial against Bosnian Serb wartime General Radtko Mladic commenced at the International Criminal Tribunal for the former Yugoslavia (ICTY). The trial was periodically delayed by Mladic's ill-health. Mladic is charged with genocide, including the murder of 8,000 men and boys from Srebrenica in 1995, war crimes, and crimes against humanity.

The trial of Radovan Karadzic, the Bosnian Serb wartime president who is charged with many of the same crimes as Mladic, continued at the ICTY with the prosecution concluding its case on May 25 and the defense seeking Karadzic's acquittal on all counts. The court upheld all charges except one genocide charge not involving Srebrenica, which it dismissed due to insufficient evidence. On September 24, the office of the prosecutor at the ICTY appealed this decision; the appeal procedure was ongoing at this writing.

On January 21, Bosnia police captured convicted war criminal Radovan Stankovic in the city of Foca. Stankovic had been at large since escaping from Foca prison in BiH in 2007, where he was serving a 20-year sentence for crimes against humanity committed in 1992 when he was serving as a soldier in the army of the Serb Republic of BiH.

The War Crimes Chamber of the State Court of BiH reached verdicts on 13 cases between September 2011 and 2012.

Inadequate capacity and funding for war crimes prosecutions continued to hamper implementation of the national war crimes strategy in cantonal and district courts. In May, the OHR and ICTY chief prosecutor discussed ways to strengthen local prosecutor and courts on war crimes cases. The mandate of the international judges and prosecutors is scheduled to expire by the end of 2012, having been extended once in 2009.

Human Rights Defenders

The national journalists' association and the Helsinki Committee in BiH expressed concern about the high frequency of verbal abuse of journalists leveled mostly by politicians but also by religious leaders and media regulators, with 42 violations of free expression and personal freedoms recorded between September 2011 and 2012, including 19 verbal assaults, 3 physical assaults, and one death threat.

On July 18, Stefica Galic, chief editor of the web portal tacno.net, was attacked in the city of Ljubuski after a documentary screening that honored her late husband's efforts to protect Bosniaks during the 1992 to 1995 Bosnian War. Nedjeljko Galic was a Croat living in the federation and helped hundreds of Bosniaks to leave Ljubuski during the war. Despite appeals by the EU, United States, and the Organization for Security and Co-operation in Europe's (OSCE) representative on freedom of the media to investigate the case thoroughly, the police failed to address the issue adequately, labeling it a minor offence against peace and order that was exaggerated by media.

In June, the local lesbian, gay, bisexual, and transsexual (LGBT) rights organization Sarajevo Open Centre reported a telephone threat to police relating to their work. The organization did not organize a Sarajevo Gay Pride parade for 2012 because it regarded other issues affecting LGBT people as more pressing.

Key International Actors

A March report on post-war justice in the Western Balkans from outgoing CoE Human Rights Commissioner Thomas Hammarberg recommended that Bosnian authorities strengthen local courts' capacity to try war crimes and protect witnesses, and expressed support for a regional truth and reconciliation commission.

In May, ambassadors to BiH from the US, Brazil, Germany, Norway, the Netherlands, Sweden, Switzerland, and the United Kingdom, together with the CoE office, issued a joint statement calling on the government of BiH to ensure equal rights for LGBT people.

In a September 2012 joint statement, EU Enlargement Commissioner Stefan Fule and CoE Secretary General Thorbjorn Jagland expressed their "great disappointment" that the BiH government had failed to meet the August deadline on constitutional reform. They affirmed that doing so remains a precondition for formal EU candidate status.

Also in September 2012, EU Special Representative Peter Sorensen, together with OSCE Representative on Freedom of the Media Dunja Mijatovic, and the head of the OSCE mission to Bosnia and Herzegovina, issued a statement calling for legal reforms to ensure media freedom in the country.

Following a country visit in late September, Rita Izsak, UN expert on minority issues, criticized continuing ethnic segregation in the education system and discrimination against Roma.

The European Commission's annual progress report on Bosnia and Herzegovina in October identified the failure to reform the constitution, discrimination against Roma, intimidation and violence against human rights advocates, and segregated education amongst its main concerns.

The UN Human Rights Committee in its concluding observations on BiH, adopted in

October, highlighted poor conditions in prisons and detention centers and urged the authorities to address overcrowding and combat prison violence.

Following a country visit in November, Rashida Manjoo, UN special rapporteur on violence against women, voiced concern about the prevalence of domestic violence in BiH.

In a report published in November, the OSCE Mission to BiH emphasized the need to combat hate crimes, including those committed against returning refugees and IDPs, Roma, Jews, and sexual minorities.

Croatia

As Croatia moved closer to European Union integration, expected in July 2013, human rights protection dipped. Croatian authorities took a significant step towards improving domestic war crimes trials. Abuses against persons with disabilities continue. A housing program aimed at Serbs stripped of property rights during the war helped only two out of more than a thousand households that were eligible, while the asylum system remains unable to cope with growing arrivals, mainly from Afghanistan and Somalia.

Accountability for War Crimes

In November, the International Criminal Tribunal for the Former Yugoslavia (ICTY) appeals chamber overturned the 2011 convictions of two Croatian generals, Ante Gotovina and Ivan Cermak, for war crimes and crimes against humanity committed against Serbs in the Krajina region in 1995.

The trial at the ICTY of Croatian Serb wartime leader Goran Hadzic charged with the killing and deportation of Croats and other non-Serbs began on October 17. Hadzic is the last of 161 indictees to be brought before the tribunal as it winds down its operations.

Fifteen domestic war crimes prosecutions were transferred in late 2011 and early 2012 from local county courts to four courts designated for war crimes cases, with only two remaining in local courts as of August, the most recent data available at this writing. Following the transfer, the designated courts suspended several cases, particularly those affecting Serbs, because the trials had been conducted in absentia, a long-standing concern about war crimes cases heard in local courts.

In March, five former Croatian armed forces soldiers were arrested on suspicion of 1993 war crimes against Serbs during the Medak Pocket operation in the village of Medak, eastern Croatia. Three were released the next day after questioning, while the court released a fourth, Josip Krmpotic, in October pending a prosecution review of the indictment against him for allegedly ordering executions of four prisoners of war. To date, General Mirko Norac remains the only high-ranking official convicted of war crimes during the operation.

The presiding judge in the trial of Zeljko Gojak, convicted in February 2012 of war crimes near Karlovac in 1991, ruled that Gojak's military service would not be used to reduce his nine-year sentence, a change to the judicial practice of considering participation in the Croatian armed forces as a mitigating factor in sentencing for war crimes.

The trial continued of Tomislav Mercep, the former police commander accused of having command responsibility for—and in some cases ordering—the illegal detention, torture, and killing of 53 Yugoslav Army soldiers in 1991. According to Croatian nongovernmental organizations, the Croatian government is paying for Mercep's defense, totaling almost 400,000 Kuna (US$69,000) as of August, the most recent data available. Mercep was released from detention on medical grounds in July 2012.

Rights of Persons with Disabilities

In September, Ministry of Social Policy officials closed down a privately run state-funded social care home for people with mental disabilities following findings of severe abuse, including lack of food, use of solitary confinement, and inadequate sleeping facilities. The ministry moved all 129 residents to other institutions in Croatia.

There was virtually no progress implementing the government's March 2011 master plan for deinstitutionalization. The number of people with intellectual or mental disabilities living in institutions remained steady at around 9,000, with a small increase in the number of places in community-based housing and support services (up to 425 from about 300 in 2010) for all people with disabilities. According to disability rights NGOs in Croatia, the government has directed greater resources to foster families for adults with disabilities, placements that may still amount to institutionalization.

Efforts by Croatia's parliament to amend the country's guardianship laws continued. But the proposed changes were limited to children, despite the need for reforms for almost 19,000 adults deprived of legal capacity at the end of 2011, including more than 16,000 deprived of all ability to make major life decisions.

Return and Reintegration of Serbs

Only 128 Serbs returned to Croatia during the last 6 months of 2011 and the first 6 months of 2012, down significantly from the 479 returns during the same period a year previously. According to the United Nations High Commissioner for Refugees (UNHCR), there were 2,059 internally displaced persons (IDPs) in Croatia as of the end of 2011, but most IDPs are now settled in their new homes or are in the process of being settled.

More than two years after the start of a program permitting Serbs stripped of tenancy rights during the 1991-1995 war to buy apartments at discounts of up to 70 percent, only 2 out of a total 1,317 eligible households had completed a purchase as of September. The UNHCR attributed the low up-take to onerous application and administrative procedures. Work on a regulation to better implement the program, begun in July, was ongoing at this writing.

The government made some progress in providing public housing for returnees. Of 8,930 approved requests for such housing, 8,047 units had been allocated at the end of June 2012. There were 237 new applications approved from November 2011 to June 2012, the vast majority of which were from Serb families.

There was some progress in processing Serb pension eligibility claims for recognition of wartime work in formerly rebel-held areas. According to the UNHCR, 27,090 requests had been processed (up from 23,568 a year earlier) at the end of June, although only 55 percent were resolved positively (down from 57 percent). Despite a ruling from the Croatian Constitutional Court broadening the standard for admissible evidence to prove years of working service, the High Administrative Court, which adjudicates final appeals in such cases, continued to require registration in a pension fund as evidence of employment.

Asylum and Migration

The number of people seeking asylum in Croatia increased as the country moved closer to EU membership. There were 704 asylum applications in the first 9 months of 2012, compared to 807 applications in 2011. Croatia had granted 11 people asylum in 2012 and 6 subsidiary protection during that period, bringing the total granted international protection since 2004 to 64.

Croatia continued to lack sufficient reception accommodation for asylum seekers. The state does not provide free legal aid in first instance proceedings. But the main issues facing asylum-seekers and new refugees in Croatia continues to be the lack of services available for their employment, education, and integration, according to the UNHCR.

Systems to provide special assistance to the growing number of unaccompanied migrant children (173 in the first nine months of 2012) remained inadequate. Guardians appointed to all unaccompanied migrant children upon arrival in Croatia lack capacity and guidance on how to secure the best interests of their wards, with no provision for interpreters or legal assistance (other than for asylum appeals).

Freedom of Media

On September 14, the Dubrovnik County Court approved the extradition of Vicdan Özerdem, a Turkish journalist wanted on terrorism charges in Turkey, following her arrest in Dubrovnik. The Croatian human rights ombudsman wrote to the Ministry of Justice in September calling on it to halt the extradition, citing violations of the UN Convention Against Torture because of the risk Özerdem would be tortured if returned to Turkey. An appeal against the extradition order was pending at this writing.

In May, the Organization for Security and Co-operation in Europe (OSCE) representative on freedom of media and the European Federation of Journalists expressed concerns about public television and radio station HRT conducting disciplinary proceedings and possibly dismissing Elizabeta Gojan, a journalist and Croatian Journalists' Association board member. HRT's actions followed an interview Gojan gave on German broadcaster Deutsche Welle criticizing the state of media freedom in Croatia.

Human Rights Defenders

In July 2012, the Human Rights Center and the People's Ombudsman's Office merged, after a law passed in 2011 to merge Croatia's five national human rights institutions. The three other national human rights institutions (the ombudspersons' offices for gender equality, children, and persons with disabilities) will remain separate until at least 2014 following a decision by the new government.

The Lesbian, Gay, Bisexual, and Transgender (LGBT) Pride March in Split went ahead in June without incident, after the 2011 march was marred by violence by anti-gay protesters.

Key International Actors

In January, the OSCE ended its Croatia presence after more than 15 years, following several years of winding down operations in the country, leaving a significant monitoring gap related to domestic war crimes accountability.

Croatia continued to proceed in negotiations to join the EU, slated for July 2013. The October 2012 EU monitoring report noted that Croatia needed to intensify efforts to tackle impunity for war crimes, protect Serb and Roma minorities, and ensure LGBT rights.

The Council of Europe's (CoE) European Commission against Racism and Intolerance (ECRI) released its fourth report on Croatia in September, noting positive developments in the impartiality of war crimes trials and investments related to property and pensions to promote the return and reintegration of Serbs. It noted that many Roma still lack citizenship or registration papers in Croatia, few attend secondary schools, and migrants and refugees face many barriers to integration.

European Union

In the face of a political and economic crisis affecting the European Union and many of its member states, protection of human rights was rarely a priority in 2012, especially when those negatively affected were marginalized or unpopular groups, such as Roma, migrants, and asylum seekers.

Despite deteriorating rights in Hungary and elsewhere, EU institutions largely failed to live up to the promise of the EU Charter of Fundamental Rights, with the European Council particularly reluctant to hold member states to account for abuse.

EU Migration and Asylum Policy

Despite efforts towards establishing the Common European Asylum System (CEAS) by the end of 2012, migrants and asylum seekers continue to experience gaps in accessing asylum and poor reception and detention conditions, including for unaccompanied children. At this writing, the EU had not adopted a coordinated response to the Syrian refugee crisis, and Syrians had access to varying levels of access to protection in different member states.

In May, the EU adopted the Action on Migratory Pressures strategy detailing a broad range of steps, including strengthening the capacity of countries outside the EU to control their borders and the capacity for those countries to provide refugee or humanitarian protection to individuals who might otherwise seek to travel on to EU countries.

Boat migration across the Mediterranean decreased, although over 300 people died at sea between January and November. In April, the Parliamentary Assembly of the Council of Europe (PACE) adopted a report documenting a "catalogue of failures" by EU member states, Libya, and NATO resulting in the deaths of 63 boat migrants in April 2011. Negotiations continued to create the European Border Surveillance System (EUROSUR) amid concerns that it lacked clear guidelines and mechanisms for ensuring rescue of migrants and asylum seekers at sea.

In September, the European Union Court of Justice (CJEU) annulled rules governing sea surveillance by the EU border agency Frontex, including where rescued boat migrants are to be disembarked, because the European Parliament had not approved them. The rules remain in effect until new ones are adopted. An inquiry that the European ombudsman launched in March into Frontex compliance with fundamental rights continued at this writing. Frontex appointed its new fundamental rights officer in September.

Efforts to revise common EU asylum rules progressed, with changes to the EU Qualification Directive agreed in December 2011 providing clearer recognition of gender-specific forms of persecution and gender identity as ground for protection. The European Parliament and the European Council were expected to give changes to the Reception Directive and Dublin II Regulation their final approval by the end of 2012. Changes on minimum reception conditions would improve access to employment and oblige states to identify vulnerable groups, but still allow detention of asylum seekers, including unaccompanied children.

Changes to Dublin II would block transfers to countries where an asylum seeker risks inhuman or degrading treatment, following a December 2011 ruling by the CJEU on Greece, and improve safeguards but leave intact the general rule that the first EU country of entry is responsible for claims. In September, the CJEU ruled that member states must provide minimum reception standards to all asylum seekers awaiting transfer under Dublin II.

In September, the European Commission released its mid-point assessment of the Action Plan for Unaccompanied Minors, noting improvements in coordination, dedicated European funding, and the European Asylum Support Office's positive role, but also problems with data collection. Discrepancies in age assessment procedures continued, with insufficient procedures in Greece, Italy, and Malta affecting access to appropriate services. Unaccompanied children faced detention in the EU, including Greece and Malta. In July, Malta initiated a review of immigration detention, including policies affecting children whose age is disputed.

In September, Denmark joined efforts by Norway, the UK, and Sweden—through the EU-funded European Return Platform for Unaccompanied Minors (ERPUM)—

to initiate the return of unaccompanied Afghan children to Afghanistan, despite serious risks of violence, military recruitment, and destitution. At this writing none had been returned.

In March, the EU adopted a framework for facilitating refugee resettlement, including increased funds. Five EU countries formally announced national resettlement programs in 2012, but resettling refugees displaced by conflict in Libya the previous year progressed slowly. In September, Germany resettled 195 refugees who had taken shelter in Tunisia.

In June, EU interior ministers endorsed a proposal allowing member states to reinstate border controls within the Schengen area—a free movement zone comprising 25 EU and other countries—if a country fails to control external EU borders. There were enduring concerns that countries, including France, Germany, the Netherlands, and Italy, use ethnic profiling to conduct spot-checks at internal borders. In response to a 73 percent increase over last year in asylum applications from Balkan countries—primarily from Roma and ethnic Albanians from Serbia and Macedonia, the vast majority rejected—some member states including Germany and France pressed for renewed visa restrictions on Balkan citizens, and in October, the European Commission called on Balkan states to do more to arrest the trend.

Discrimination and Intolerance

A Fundamental Rights Agency survey published in May showed destitution and social exclusion among Roma in 11 EU countries, with high levels of unemployment (over 66 percent) and low levels of secondary school graduation (around 15 percent). In May, a European Commission assessment on progress by member states in integrating Roma found gaps in health care and housing. In August, the commission announced it was monitoring evictions and removals of Eastern European Roma from France, and in September wrote to Italy asking for information about discrimination against Roma.

The European Commission against Racism and Intolerance (ECRI) warned in May that economic downturn and austerity were feeding intolerance and anti-immigrant violence. Council of Europe (CoE) Commissioner for Human Rights Nils

Muižnieks called in July for a "European Spring" to counter anti-Muslim prejudice, citing bans on full-face veils and ethnic profiling by police as examples.

In October, the EU adopted a directive on minimum standards for victims, obliging states to ensure access to justice without discrimination, including for undocumented migrants.

At this writing, 14 EU member states had signed (but not ratified) the CoE Convention on preventing and combating violence against women and domestic violence, including the United Kingdom in June, and Belgium and Italy in September.

Counterterrorism

European parliamentarians and victims continued to demand accountability for complicity in counterterrorism abuses. The European Court of Human Rights (ECtHR) heard arguments in May in its first case on European complicity in rendition to torture by the United States concerning German citizen Khaled al-Masri who was detained in Macedonia in 2003 before the US rendered him to torture in Afghanistan. At this writing, similar cases against Poland, Romania, and Lithuania remained pending before the court.

A European Parliament report and accompanying September resolution condemned the lack of transparency and use of state secrecy impeding public accountability for collusion in abuses. The report urged full inquiries in Romania, Lithuania, and Poland, and called on other EU countries to disclose information about secret CIA flights on their territory.

Human Rights Concerns in Select EU Member States

France

A summer campaign to evict Roma camps and remove migrant Roma from France echoed a similar push in 2010, raising questions about pledges by Socialist President François Hollande, elected in June, to tackle discrimination.

By mid-September, an estimated 4,000 people had been forcibly evicted, and hundreds returned to Eastern Europe.

The UN special rapporteurs on housing, migrants' rights, minority rights, and racism issued a joint statement in August expressing concern over authorities' failure to provide alternative housing, the risk of collective expulsions, and stigmatization of Roma. The French government moved in September to ease restrictions on access to employment for Eastern Europeans, including Roma, and signed a new agreement with Romania on deportations providing for reintegration projects.

In September, the government backtracked on a proposal to introduce stop forms for identity checks—a way to improve police accountability and address persistent concerns about ethnic profiling—in the face of strong opposition from police unions. The rights ombudsman recommended reforms in October and legal rules on pat-downs during such checks. In June, France's highest criminal court ruled that police powers to ask individuals to prove their right to be in France, regardless of behavior, violated EU free movement norms.

The government moved to limit detention of children with their families pending deportation, after an ECtHR ruling in January against France for detaining two young children with their parents for two weeks in 2007. A July government circular clarified that detention of families with children remained possible if families do not respect the conditions of compulsory residence in a particular place or if one or more family members abscond.

In February, the ECtHR ruled in a case brought by a Sudanese asylum seeker that the fast-track asylum procedure, including lack of suspensive appeal, did not provide effective protection against refoulement.

The European Committee for the Prevention of Torture (CPT) expressed concern in April about conditions and treatment in police and immigration detention, prisons, and psychiatric facilities, recommending further reforms to ensure that all suspects can access a lawyer from when they first enter police custody.

Parliament adopted a new sexual harassment law in late July, after the Constitutional Court struck down previous legislation for vagueness. The new law protects a broader range of situations beyond employment and introduces protections based on gender identity. In November the government tabled a bill to legalize same-sex marriage.

In October, one man was killed and eleven arrested in multi-city raids following a mid-September grenade attack on a Jewish supermarket outside Paris. At this writing, parliament was examining draft legislation to criminalize acts of terrorism abroad by French citizens. The measure, first proposed by the previous administration after a man claiming to be inspired by al-Qaeda shot seven people in March—including three Jewish children and a rabbi—would allow prosecution for participating in terrorism training abroad.

Germany

The Federal Constitutional Court ruled in July that asylum seekers and refugees should receive the same welfare benefits as German citizens, ordering retroactive payments starting from 2011 to approximately 130,000 people. The suicide of an asylum seeker in Würzburg in March launched a series of nationwide protests about conditions in reception centers, restrictions on freedom of movement, and obstacles to employment for asylum seekers.

German states, including Lower Saxony and Nordrhein-Westfalen, continued to deport Roma to Kosovo despite concerns about inadequate reception conditions, including problems accessing and integrating into the educational system.

Three senior intelligence officials resigned in July after repeated failures to correctly identify and investigate a neo-Nazi cell responsible for murdering nine immigrants and a policewoman. In October, a Frankfurt court upheld a 2002 ruling that awarded compensation to a man later convicted of murdering a child because a police officer had threatened violence during his interrogation.

At this writing, the lower house of parliament was examining two different bills to make racist motivation an aggravating circumstance during sentencing for criminal offenses, as well as a bill to introduce hate crimes as a specific category. In October, the Koblenz administrative appeals court ruled that it was unlawful and a violation of anti-discrimination law for German police to use racial profiling to conduct checks for irregular migrants, annulling an earlier February decision that had permitted the police tactic.

In September, the federal justice minister drafted legislation to clarify the legality of religiously motivated circumcisions, following a June Cologne court ruling that circumcising young boys amounted to criminal bodily harm. The ruling provoked considerable debate about freedom of religion and rights of the child. The same month, Chancellor Angela Merkel called for greater tolerance towards Muslims.

Greece

There was widespread hardship and protest in 2012 amid economic crisis. The far-right anti-immigrant Golden Dawn party entered parliament for the first time with 7 percent of the vote in the June general election.

Legislation passed in April permits police to detain migrants and asylum seekers on overly broad public health grounds, including susceptibility to infectious disease based on national origin and living in conditions that do not meet minimum hygiene standards, prompting condemnation by the UN Committee Against Torture (CAT).

The new government continued its predecessor's heavy-handed immigration control approach. Construction of a 12.5-kilometer fence along the border with Turkey, begun in February, neared completion at this writing. A vast sweep operation launched in August had by mid-November led to more than 50,000 presumed undocumented migrants being detained for questioning based on appearance alone, and more than 3,700 arrests. By the end of October, over 1,900 of these had been deported and 1,690 had returned home under the International Organization for Migration's (IOM) voluntary program. The operation continued at this writing.

Critical problems with the asylum system persisted. New government bodies inaugurated in March to oversee asylum reception and application processing were not fully operational due to staffing delays by November. Severe obstacles to submitting asylum applications remained, and latest available figures show

HUMAN
RIGHTS
WATCH

Hate on the Streets
Xenophobic Violence in Greece

Greece remained in 2011 the country with the lowest overall protection rate at first instance in Europe (2 percent).

In July, September, and November, the ECtHR ruled in five separate cases that Greece had subjected undocumented migrants and asylum seekers in detention to inhuman and degrading treatment. In October, the government extended permissible detention of asylum seekers to 3 to 15 months (and from 6 to 18 months for those who applied for asylum only once detained), a decision likely to increase overcrowding in detention.

Greece established five new detention camps for undocumented migrants between April and October, with more facilities planned on islands in response to increased arrivals in 2012, including of Syrians. The European Commission, the CPT, and CAT noted problematic conditions in detention centers, while non-governmental reports documented substandard detention conditions on islands including overcrowding, poor hygiene, and limited access to health care, water, and food.

Xenophobic violence reached alarming proportions with regular attacks on migrants and asylum seekers, and growing evidence of the involvement of Golden Dawn members. In October, the public order minister presented a draft presidential decree to create specialized police units to tackle racist violence, following a commitment in September by the justice minister to initiate legislative reforms to toughen hate crime sentencing.

The Council of State, the highest administrative court, ruled in November that criteria for acquiring citizenship under a 2010 law were too lenient; the government announced it would present stricter requirements shortly.

The Joint United Nations Programme on HIV/AIDS, voiced its concern in May after the government published photos and personal information, including HIV status, of accused sex workers after police arrested them for allegedly having unprotected sex with customers while HIV positive.

In May, the UN Committee on the Rights of the Child (CRC) expressed deep concern about inhumane conditions experienced by children with disabilities at the

Lechaina Children's Care Center and urged Greece to ensure that children with disabilities are never placed in such conditions.

Hungary

A new constitution and cardinal laws entered into force on January 1, 2012, weakening human rights protection, stripping the constitutional court of some powers, and undermining judicial independence, including a forced retirement affecting 300 judges. In November, the CJEU ruled that lowering the retirement age for judges constituted unjustified age discrimination.

In January, 348 religious groups lost their status as "churches" under the new constitution. The constitution also defines the right to life as starting from conception, raising concerns about reproductive rights; limits the right to vote for persons with mental disabilities; and defines family in a way that excludes lesbian, gay, bisexual, and transgender (LGBT) people.

In November, the Hungarian Constitutional Court ruled unconstitutional a law adopted in April criminalizing homelessness with repeat offenders subject to fines or imprisonment. No one was prosecuted while the law was in force.

Despite criticism by the CoE, the European Commission, and the Organization for Security and Co-operation in Europe (OSCE) representative on media freedom, the Hungarian government failed to sufficiently amend problematic media laws. The main media regulator, the Media Council, lacks political independence, potential fines for journalists are excessive, and requirements for content regulation are unclear. Journalists and media outlets reported self-censorship and editorial interference. At this writing, the Media Council had yet to renew the long-term broadcast license of leading independent news station Klubradio, despite three court rulings in the station's favor.

Roma continue to face discrimination and harassment. In July and August, right-wing paramilitary groups marched through Romani settlements threatening residents and attacking homes. In August, paramilitaries threw stones and bottles at Romani houses and shouted threats in Devecser during a march against "gypsy crime." Police were present at the time but made no arrests. A police investigation was ongoing at this writing.

There were several anti-Semitic attacks against Jewish leaders and memorials. In October, two assailants beat and insulted a Jewish leader in Budapest. He suffered minor injuries. Police later arrested the attackers, who were in custody at this writing.

Hungary continued to return asylum seekers and migrants to neighboring countries, including Serbia and Ukraine, despite lack of access to asylum, risk of return to persecution in third countries, and in the case of Ukraine, risk of ill-treatment in detention. In October, the ECtHR ruled in two separate cases that Hungary had unlawfully detained asylum seekers in 2010 without effective judicial review of their detention.

Italy

An estimated 18,000 asylum seekers who arrived in 2011 remained in reception centers, including emergency facilities, many awaiting final decisions on their applications. To date, 30 percent of those who arrived from North Africa since early 2011 had received some form of protection, including refugee status, subsidiary protection, or humanitarian leave to remain in the country.

In October, the Italian government issued rules for the reexamination of denied claims that could allow authorities to grant temporary protection. At this writing, it remained unclear what would happen to those housed in facilities at year's end, when the "North Africa Emergency," which the government declared in February 2011, is set to expire.

Concern over living conditions and integration for asylum seekers and refugees, including the risk of homelessness and destitution, led German courts, as well as the ECtHR, to block transfers to Italy under Dublin II.

In February, the ECtHR ruled that Italy's summary "push-backs" of migrant boats to Libya in 2009 amounted to collective expulsions and exposed people to torture and cruel, inhuman, or degrading treatment in Libya or their countries of origin. The government indicated it would respect the ruling, but commitments reached with the new Libyan authorities in April raised questions over continued efforts to externalize border control in ways that violate human rights.

Summary returns to Greece continued, including of unaccompanied children and asylum seekers who stow away on ferries to Italy. In September and October respectively, Commissioner Muižnieks and UN Special Rapporteur on Migrants' Rights François Crépeau urged Italy to suspend all returns to Greece due to grave deficiencies in the country's asylum system.

Muižnieks urged the government to ensure implementation of the first national strategy on Roma inclusion, which it adopted in February, by establishing precise targets and allocating adequate resources. Roma continued in 2012 to face evictions from informal camps and segregation

In March, the ECtHR ruled Italy's expulsion of a Tunisian terrorism suspect in 2010 violated the prohibition of torture and ill-treatment and the court's order to stay removal.

In March, the UN Committee on the Elimination of Racial Discrimination (CERD) expressed serious concerns about racist violence in Italy, and urged measures to improve prevention, investigation, and prosecution. In June, the UN special rapporteur on violence against women recommended that Italy adopt a specific law on violence against women and ensure access to justice for victims, including Roma, Sinti, and undocumented migrant women.

In July, Italy's highest criminal court upheld the convictions of senior police officers for falsifying evidence in relation to police violence during the 2001 G8 summit in Genoa; it also upheld controversial long prison sentences of up to 15 years for some protesters over property destruction, ordering others to be reviewed.

In September, the same court upheld the 2011 in absentia convictions of 23 US citizens for the 2003 abduction and rendition to Egypt of an Egyptian imam known as Abu Omar, and ordered the retrial of five Italian intelligence officers, including two senior officials, whom lower courts had acquitted citing state secrecy.

The Netherlands

The People's Party for Freedom and Democracy and Dutch Labor Party formally took power in a coalition government in November after winning the September elections. The anti-immigrant Freedom Party lost nine seats.

In September and October, parliament suspended deportations of children who have been living in the Netherlands for at least five years, and to postpone implementation of tighter family reunification requirements. Both measures will be considered now that a government has been formed.

The Council of State, the highest administrative court, ruled in July that Somalia was not a safe country of return, and ordered that dozens of Somali failed asylum seekers be released from immigration detention. The previous government halted deportations of gay Iraqis in June, and in July announced a policy to grant protection to Iraqis seeking asylum based on sexual orientation or gender identity.

In August, the Dutch national ombudsman and the CPT criticized conditions in immigration detention. The CPT expressed concern over families with children being detained for longer than the 28-day maximum permitted by law. They urged the government to only detain children in exceptional circumstances and without locking them in cells.

During the Netherlands' Universal Periodic Review (UPR) at the Human Rights Council (HRC) in May, numerous countries recommended measures to combat discrimination and racism.

At this writing, parliament was due to examine draft legislation tabled in August to eliminate the sex reassignment surgery requirement for transgender people who want to get a new identification document.

Poland

In March, news emerged that Poland's former intelligence chief had been charged over complicity in CIA secret detention on Polish territory. The ECtHR agreed in July to examine a case brought by a Saudi national, currently held in

Guantánamo Bay, who alleges he was held incommunicado and tortured in a secret CIA facility in Poland in 2002-2003.

In September, parliament passed a law authorizing appointed provincial governors, rather than the courts, to decide on appeals against denials of permission to hold a public demonstration. In September, the OSCE called for Poland to repeal its defamation laws after a court convicted Robert Frycz, editor of the *Antykomor.pl* website, for insulting the president, and sentenced him to 15-months of community service.

In September, parliament voted against a bill to liberalize access to abortion and contraception, and institute comprehensive sex education. In October, the ECtHR ruled that Poland violated the rights of a 14-year-old rape victim who was denied a legal abortion.

Romania

A political crisis between the president and prime minister led the government to take steps that undermined separation of powers and the rule of law.

Following a May constitutional court ruling that the president, rather than the prime minister, should represent Romania in EU meetings, the government in July stripped the court of its powers to overrule parliamentary decisions, replaced the ombudsman with a party loyalist, and took control of the official gazette that publishes court decisions and laws, in order to delay Constitutional Court rulings coming into effect.

In July, the European Parliament, European Commission, and CoE criticized these actions as contrary to the rule of law, with Commission President José Manuel Barroso referring to possible infringement proceedings. A July European Commission report raised serious concerns about Romania's commitment to the rule of law. It called on the country to reverse measures impacting judicial independence and appoint an ombudsman with cross-party support.

Romanian authorities continued in 2012 to deny allegations that they housed a secret CIA prison to detain and interrogate terrorism suspects, despite a joint investigation by the Associated Press and German public television ARD

Panorama, and German newspaper *Süddeutsche Zeitung*, which in December 2011 identified the former location of the prison in Bucharest.

Discrimination and marginalization of Roma remained a concern. Approximately 150 Roma were forcibly evicted in June from informal settlements in Baia Mare, northwestern Romania, and relocated to a former chemical plant without adequate accommodation or sanitation. Several hundred more faced imminent eviction from other informal settlements in Baia Mare.

Spain

Demonstrations continued throughout 2012 as the government imposed austerity measures amid a deepening economic crisis, and protester and police violence that included use of rubber bullets. The UN Committee on Economic, Social and Cultural Rights (CESCR) expressed concern in June that austerity measures disproportionately affect vulnerable groups, highlighting forced evictions without due safeguards, curtailed access to health services for undocumented migrants, and deep cuts in education budgets.

In July, the ECtHR found that Spain had violated anti-torture and non-discrimination obligations by failing to investigate allegations that in 2005, police conducted a racially abusive identity check on an African woman who was a legal resident. In a separate ruling the same month, the court found that retroactive lengthening of prison sentences, limiting eligibility for parole for people convicted of terrorism offenses, violated fair trial standards. The ECtHR agreed in November to hear the Spanish government's appeal against the ruling.

In April, Frontex attributed continued low levels of boat migration to Spain to sea patrols and the country's migration cooperation with African countries. Spain forcibly removed to Morocco around 70 sub-Saharan Africans from a nearby Spanish island in September, despite media and NGO reports of migrant ill-treatment in Morocco and dumping at the Algerian border. Two women and eight children were transported to Spanish mainland. In February, CAT published its decision against Spain for failing to investigate the responsibility of a Spanish coast guard unit in the 2007 drowning of a Senegalese man off Ceuta, the Spanish enclave in Morocco.

In February, the Spanish Supreme Court acquitted Judge Baltasar Garzón of abusing his judicial powers by investigating enforced disappearances during the Franco era between 1939 and 1975, despite Spain's amnesty law. Earlier that month, the same court convicted Garzón of ordering unlawful wiretaps in a corruption case and suspended him from the bench for 11 years.

In September, parliament rejected an opposition bill initiated under the previous government to improve Spain's anti-discrimination legislation. In November, the Constitutional Court upheld Spain's law on marriage equality. The justice minister announced his intention in July to limit access to abortion laws, but at this writing no draft legislation had been tabled.

United Kingdom

In May, the government reduced pre-charge detention in terrorism cases from 28 to 14 days, but left open the possibility for parliament to reinstate 28 days in an emergency. Replacements to control orders on terrorism suspects no longer permit forced relocation and are subject to stricter time limits. But the new measures can still be based in part on secret evidence, and parliament can quickly approve harsher powers in an emergency.

A draft law in parliament at this writing would widen use of secret hearings in civil courts on national security grounds and prevent material that shows UK involvement in wrongdoing by other countries being disclosed. In September, the UN special rapporteur on torture expressed concern that the draft law could inhibit accountability for torture.

In January, the government halted a widely criticized inquiry into UK involvement in rendition and torture. It cited new criminal investigations into UK complicity in rendition and torture in Libya by former dictator Muammar Gaddafi's security forces. Although the government promised a second inquiry, it was unclear at this writing when it would begin, and whether it would have the necessary independence and powers.

In January, the ECtHR blocked deportation of Jordanian terrorism suspect Abu Qatada due to the risk of evidence obtained through torture being used against him at trial upon return, but also held that diplomatic assurances were sufficient to protect him from torture or ill-treatment. In November, a UK court ordered Qatada's release from custody saying it was not satisfied that he would received a fair trial in Jordan; he was placed under house arrest.

In October, the UK extradited five terrorism suspects to the US after the ECtHR in September definitively rejected their appeals that they would face ill-treatment.

In June, the government signed the CoE Convention on preventing and combating violence against women and domestic violence, but continued to reject calls to sign the International Labour Organization (ILO) Convention on Decent Work for Domestic Workers. Instead, in April it changed immigration rules that will make it harder for foreign domestic workers to leave abusive situations without losing their immigration status.

The UK continued to deport failed Sri Lankan Tamil asylum seekers, including 25 on a chartered flight in September, despite evidence of torture upon return for some Tamils with perceived links to Sri Lanka's separatist Tamil Tigers.

Official statistics published in August revealed that the number of children being detained with their parents pending deportation was rising, although such detention is limited to one week. In April, the UK Border Authority suspended a pilot program to use dental x-rays to determine age, amid medical ethics concerns.

In September, the UK's chief prosecutor announced he would develop guidelines related to prosecuting offensive speech on the internet and social media after a series of controversial convictions raised free expression concerns.

Georgia

The October 2012 parliamentary elections marked Georgia's first peaceful transition of power since independence. The opposition Georgian Dream coalition, led by billionaire Bidzina Ivanishvili, defeated President Mikheil Saakashvili's ruling United National Movement (UNM), gained a majority in parliament, and formed a new government. Harassment and intimidation of opposition party activists and other violations marred the pre-election environment. Authorities used administrative (misdemeanor) charges to detain activists for minor public order breaches without full due process.

Graphic video material showing torture and ill-treatment of inmates illustrated a long-standing problem. Lack of judicial independence is a serious problem.

Parliamentary Elections

International observers, led by the Organization for Security and Co-operation in Europe (OSCE), concluded that the October 1 parliamentary elections were in line with Georgia's commitments. However, the pre-election environment was polarized and tense, with some instances of violence. Georgian Dream activists were targeted in several violent incidents in June and July.

On June 26, during Ivanishvili's campaign visit to Mereti village, ruling party supporters, including civil servants, allegedly provoked a fistfight. Several people sustained injuries. Police detained four, including two opposition supporters, and the courts sentenced them to ten days of administrative imprisonment. No officials were held accountable.

A similar incident took place on July 10, when government supporters in Karaleti village threw stones and swore at opposition supporters campaigning in the village. Thirteen people, including ten journalists, sustained injuries and were hospitalized. Police arrested six, including four opposition members, and sentenced them to fifteen days of administrative imprisonment.

Domestic observers reported misuse of administrative resources by the incumbent party. UNM candidates at times had preferential access to public venues and transport, and some of them had their campaign offices in local administration buildings.

The State Audit Office, which monitors parties' compliance with campaign financing rules, overwhelmingly targeted the opposition. In March, it summoned and questioned over 100 opposition supporters as witnesses in cases of possible breaches of campaign finance regulations. OSCE said the authorities selectively targeted the opposition, "raising questions about the impartiality of enforcement." According to Georgia's ombudsman, in some cases the authorities investigated these individuals without respecting due process and in an intimidating manner that may have deterred other potential donors. Courts imposed staggering fines—sometimes as high as five times the amount of the donation— on donors they found to have violated regulations, often leading to seizure of their property.

Administrative (Misdemeanor) Detentions

The government continued to resist reforming its system of administrative detention. Georgia's Code of Administrative Offences sets out misdemeanor sentences of up to 90 days. Although the sentence is equivalent to a criminal penalty, detainees do not have access to full due process rights. Although defense counsel is permitted, some detainees had difficulties accessing a lawyer in part because they are not allowed to inform their families of their detention. Lawyers who act for those facing administrative charges have sometimes as little as 10 to 15 minutes to prepare a defense. Defendants also often cannot present evidence or call witnesses in court.

For example, in September, police detained at least seven individuals under similar circumstances in four separate incidents in Tbilisi. The Ministry of Interior stated that all seven defendants disobeyed police orders and insulted them. Courts sentenced the detainees to administrative imprisonment ranging from 10 to 40 days. Two of those detained alleged ill-treatment in police custody and bore visible bruises at a trial, but the court failed to refer this for investigation.

Administrative detainees are held in Ministry of Interior holding cells. Although some of them were renovated, many are unsuitable for long-term detention, with inadequate access to exercise and hygienic and medical care.

Torture and Ill-treatment

In September, local media broadcast a series of video recordings showing graphic images of beating and sexual abuse of prisoners in several penitentiary facilities. Hours before the videos were released, the Ministry of Interior said that it arrested three officials of Tbilisi's Gldani prison for ill-treatment of inmates. The ministry released footage depicting two prison guards beating an inmate, and a television station broadcast further video materials showing Gldani prison officials beating and humiliating newly arrived inmates. Shortly afterward, another television station aired further footage graphically depicting prison staff raping inmates.

The authorities acknowledged both the systemic nature of prison abuse and their failure to react effectively to years of warnings about such abuse. The ministers for prisons and interior resigned, and police arrested 16 penitentiary staff, pending investigations.

Judicial Independence

In March, the Georgian Young Lawyers' Association published a report showing that in all 520 cases it monitored at the Tbilisi City Court during a six-month period between 2011 and 2012, the judges granted all motions filed by the prosecution regarding the admissibility of evidence, while denying all defense motions that prosecution did not support.

The court satisfied all requests for pre-trial custody and of the 113 judgments it handed down during the six months there was not a single acquittal. Since the Tbilisi City Court accounts for about 40 percent of all cases handled by Georgia's courts, the report raised serious questions on the independence of the judiciary.

Prison Conditions

The policy of zero tolerance towards crime and high conviction rates led to a rise in the prison population. According to the ombudsman's 2012 report, prison overcrowding is a persistent problem, leading to poor prison conditions. The report noted that in four prisons, inmates did not have "their own personal beds."

Freedom of Media

Georgia's print media presents diverse political views, but nationwide television broadcasting was limited to the state-funded public broadcaster and two pro-government stations, which were often biased in favor of the government. One partial improvement was an amendment to the election code requiring cable networks and satellite content providers to broadcast all television stations that carry news for 60 days ahead of elections. This allowed the three pro-opposition private channels, Maestro, Kavkasia, and TV 9, to increase their penetration into the urban areas being reached by cable networks. Most networks continued to broadcast all stations following the elections.

In July, the cable network provider Global Contact Consulting (GCC) and Maestro TV unsuccessfully attempted to increase their penetration by distributing satellite receivers. The authorities seized their satellite dishes on grounds that they were intended for "vote-buying" and released them only after the polls. In June, the authorities detained and questioned Alexander Ronzhes, a United States citizen and GCC shareholder. During questioning, authorities claimed Ronzhes had been involved in suspicious financial transactions but they released him the same day without charges.

In July, the OSCE media freedom representative, Dunja Mijatovic, expressed concern over violence against journalists, highlighting the Mereti and Karaleti incidents when journalists were physically and verbally assaulted.

In September, Giorgi Abdaladze—one of four photographers arrested in 2011, charged with espionage and released after plea bargaining—said in a media interview that prison staff and investigators coerced him into rejecting his legal counsel and making a false confession under threats of ill-treatment.

Lack of Accountability for Excessive Use of Force

The authorities still failed to ensure full accountability for excessive use of force on May 26, 2011, when police used water cannons, tear gas, rubber bullets, and other violence to disperse anti-government protests in Tbilisi.

Authorities' failure to fully address excessive use of force by police was further tainted by the continued lack of effective investigations into past instances of abuse, including the events of November 7, 2007, when police used excessive force against largely peaceful protestors in Tbilisi, injuring at least 500, and the June 15, 2009 police attack against 50 opposition supporters outside police headquarters in which at least 17 demonstrators were injured.

In October, the European Court of Human Rights (ECtHR) ruled that Georgia had violated the prohibition against inhuman or degrading treatment in the case of Giorgi Mikiashvili. Police used excessive force when they arrested Mikiashvili in 2005, causing multiple bruises on his face and head. The court denounced the authorities' failure to effectively investigate the incident.

Key International Actors

The United States, the European Union, the Council of Europe (CoE), OSCE, and other institutions and bilateral partners of Georgia welcomed the October parliamentary elections and subsequent peaceful political transition as a significant step forward in the country's democratic development.

A large number of foreign governments and international organizations condemned the abuses depicted in the prison video footage and urged the authorities to ensure prompt, thorough, and transparent investigation and accountability for those responsible.

In its May European Neighborhood Policy progress report, the EU expressed concerns about a dominant executive branch, weak parliamentary oversight, and lack of judicial independence. It also, for the first time, made concrete recommendations to the authorities to address these and other concerns.

While visiting Georgia in June, US Secretary of State Hillary Clinton highlighted the importance of the 2012 and 2013 parliamentary and presidential elections in meeting the country's "Euro-Atlantic aspirations". She also stressed the importance of labor rights, judicial independence, and media independence.

In its June report, the UN special rapporteur on the rights to freedom of assembly and association expressed concern about a "climate of fear and intimidation" against members of opposition political parties and civil society.

Kazakhstan

Kazakhstan's human rights record seriously deteriorated in 2012, following violent clashes In December 2011 between police and demonstrators, including striking oil workers, in western Kazakhstan. Authorities blamed outspoken oil workers and political opposition activists for the unrest. Freedom of assembly is restricted and dozens were fined or sentenced to administrative arrest in early 2012 for participating in peaceful protests. A restrictive law on religious freedoms remained in force. Media remains under tight control and there were attacks on independent journalists. Legislation regulating workers' rights is vague and burdensome, and a ban on strikes in certain sectors of the economy improperly restricts workers' rights.

Parliamentary Elections

Despite the state of emergency in effect in the western Kazakh oil town of Zhanaozen, Kazakhstan held early parliamentary elections on January 15, 2012. The Observation Mission of the Organization for Security and Co-operation in Europe's (OSCE) Office for Democratic Institutions and Human Rights (ODIHR) concluded that the vote did "not meet fundamental principles of democratic elections," and the authorities did not provide "the necessary conditions for the conduct of genuinely pluralistic elections."

Conduct of Police and Security Forces

On December 16, 2011, clashes broke out between police and demonstrators, including striking oil workers, who had gathered in Zhanaozen's central square. In response to the clashes and subsequent mayhem, police and government troops opened fire, killing 12 and wounding dozens, according to government figures. Three further people died in the clashes and several police officers were injured. On December 17, police shot dead a protester in Shetpe. The security forces' use of force and firearms did not appear to be justified or proportionate. In May 2012, five officers were convicted for "abuse of power," but no officers were held accountable for the sixteen killings. In trials that did not adhere to international human rights standards, courts convicted a total of 45 oil workers and demonstrators for participating or organizing mass riots, putting 17 behind bars.

Detention of Activists

During 2012, the authorities amnestied a number of imprisoned activists, including, Kazakhstan's most prominent human rights defender Yevgeniy Zhovtis, union lawyer Natalia Sokolova, and political activist Aidos Sadykov. Vadim Kuramshin, a civil society activist arrested in January on various charges, including extortion, was released in August on a one-year suspended sentence. However, after he spoke at an OSCE meeting in September in Warsaw, an appeals court sent his case for retrial. Kuramshin was rearrested, raising fears his detention was retribution for his public criticism of the government. His case was ongoing at this writing.

Starting in January, authorities misused criminal charges to arrest over a dozen others, including Vladimir Kozlov, the leader of the unregistered opposition party *Alga!*, civil society activist Serik Sapargali, and oil worker Akzhanat Aminov. On October 8, in a politically motivated trial marred by due process violations and vague and overbroad criminal charges, a court sentenced Kozlov to seven-and-a-half years in prison. Sapargali and Aminov will serve suspended sentences. Following Kozlov's conviction, the United States expressed serious concern about "the government's apparent use of the legal system to silence political opposition." In November, Kozlov's sentence was upheld on appeal.

Torture

Detainees made credible and serious allegations of torture in 2012, particularly in the aftermath of the Zhanaozen violence. The authorities failed to take any meaningful steps to thoroughly investigate these allegations or hold the perpetrators accountable, reinforcing a culture of impunity.

Between December 16 and 19, 2011, police detained hundreds of people in Zhanaozen, several of whom stated that police kicked and beat detainees with

HUMAN
RIGHTS
WATCH

Striking Oil, Striking Workers
Violations of Labor Rights in Kazakhstan's Oil Sector

truncheons, stripped them naked, walked on them, and subjected them to freezing temperatures. In March, defendants at one of the trials following the Zhanaozen events testified that guards and investigators subjected them to physical and psychological abuse, including beatings, suffocation, and threats of rape or harm to family members. The prosecutor's office declined to open a criminal investigation.

On December 22, Bazarbai Kenzhebaev, 50, died from wounds he sustained in police custody. Kenzhebaev had described to his family how police severely beat him, forced him to undress, lie face down on the floor and walked on him, stepping on his head. In May, the former director of the Zhanaozen temporary detention facility was sentenced to five years in prison, but those directly responsible for the beatings that led to Kenzhebaev's death have not been held accountable.

Human rights groups expressed concern about Vladislav Chelakh, a 19-year-old border guard accused of murdering 15 colleagues at a Kazakhstan-China border post. The groups said the authorities held him incommunicado for weeks and coerced his confession. His case, ongoing at this writing, had been marred by irregularities.

Freedom of Expression

In December 2011, Kazakh authorities declared a state of emergency in Zhanaozen, temporarily blocking several key websites, including Twitter, across Kazakhstan. Other popular websites, including the blogging platform Livejournal, remained blocked at this writing. Independent journalists continued to be targeted for their work. One journalist, Lukpan Akhmedyarov, was hospitalized in March 2012 following a vicious attack by unknown assailants. Libel remains a criminal offense and journalists are forced to pay prohibitive fines in defamation lawsuits.

In January, President Nazarbaev signed a new controversial broadcast law even though the previous month the OSCE Representative on Freedom of the Media Dunja Mijatović had urged the president to veto the bill.

In January and February, authorities arrested civil society activists for "inciting social discord," a vague and overbroad charge that can be used to criminalize legitimate exercise of the rights to freedom of expression and association as protected under international human rights law. They arrested *Vzglyad* editor-in-chief Igor Vinyavskii in January on charges of "calling for the forcible overthrow of the constitutional order." He was released two months later after his case received sustained international attention, including from the OSCE representative on freedom of the media, who in January called for his "immediate release."

Freedom of Assembly

Kazakh authorities maintain restrictive rules on freedom of assembly. In response to a series of public protests in the first half of 2012, the authorities detained and fined opposition and civil society activists and others for organizing and participating in unsanctioned protests, sentencing some to up to 15 days in prison and fining others up to US$550.

Freedom of Religion

Following the 2011 adoption of a restrictive law on religion—which outlaws any practice of religion in association with others without state permission—respect for religious freedoms continued to decline, according to Forum 18, an independent, international religious freedom group. In 2012, hundreds of small religious communities have been forced to close, unable to meet the 50 person membership requirements for re-registration, compulsory under the new law.

Makset Djabbarbergenov, a protestant pastor from Uzbekistan who sought asylum in Kazakhstan in 2007, was arrested by Kazakh authorities on September 5, 2012, and currently faces extradition to Uzbekistan where he faces criminal charges of illegally teaching religion and distributing religious literature.

Child Labor in Agriculture and Labor Rights

The Kazakhstan government and several companies violated fundamental labor and other rights of thousands of workers employed in the country's petroleum sector in 2011. Burdensome collective bargaining requirements and a broad prohibition on the right to strike violate workers' rights. Proposed amendments to Kazakhstan's law on unions, and administrative and criminal codes, would further restrict workers' rights and did not appear to meet international standards concerning freedom of association.

Risk of debt bondage and cases of hazardous child labor persist on some farms, despite steps by Philip Morris Kazakhstan, a subsidiary of Philip Morris International, to increase protections for migrant tobacco workers, including insisting on written contracts and improved training. Following her September visit, UN Special Rapporteur on Contemporary Forms of Slavery Gulnara Shahinian indicated that complex legal requirements for employing migrants and obstacles to migrant children attending schools may undermine the government's progress in preventing forced labor and hazardous child labor.

Key International Actors

Kazakhstan's key international partners have failed to respond to serious human rights abuses in Kazakhstan in 2012 with any discernible policy consequences. Instead, in February 2012, the US upgraded relations by agreeing to commence "Strategic Partnership" dialogues in place of the annual bilateral consultations. No known human rights benchmarks were set in advance of upgrading US-Kazakhstan relations.

In 2012, the European Union and Kazakhstan held several rounds of negotiations on an enhanced Partnership and Cooperation Agreement (PCA), which promises preferential political and economic ties to Kazakhstan. However, the EU has not set any clear human rights benchmarks for enhanced engagement, despite a March 2012 statement by the EU High Representative for Foreign Affairs and Security Policy Catherine Ashton that the "successful conclusion of the negotiations will be influenced by the advancement of democratic reforms," and a March 2012 European Parliament resolution that states "progress in the negotiation[s] ... must depend on the progress of political reform."

In July, United Nations High Commissioner for Human Rights Navi Pillay visited Kazakhstan where she issued a highly critical statement on the country's deteriorating rights record and calling for "an independent international investigation into the [December] event" in Zhanaozen. Previously, in December 2011 and February 2012, Ashton had called for an "objective and transparent investigation of the events." The US also called for a "complete impartial investigation" into the Zhanaozen violence.

Kyrgyzstan

Kyrgyzstan has failed to adequately address abuses in the south, in particular against ethnic Uzbeks, undermining long-term efforts to promote stability and reconciliation following inter-ethnic clashes in June 2010 that killed more than 400 people. Despite an uneasy calm in southern Kyrgyzstan, ethnic Uzbeks are still subjected to arbitrary detention, torture, and extortion, without redress.

Human rights defender Azimjon Askarov remains wrongfully imprisoned. Authorities blocked access to an independent news portal and banned a film about gay men. Violence and discrimination against women and lesbian, gay, bisexual, and transgender (LGBT) persons remain serious concerns.

Following a visit by the United Nations special rapporteur on torture in December 2011, authorities adopted new legislation and made reforms to the criminal code to address incompatibilities with international standards on the prevention of torture. However, ill-treatment and torture remain pervasive in places of detention, and perpetrators go unpunished.

Access to Justice

Local human rights nongovernmental organizations reported that the overall number of reported incidents of arbitrary detention and ill-treatment in police custody continued to decrease in 2012 in the south, although they still document new cases. Groups also reported the growing problem of law enforcement extorting money, in particular from ethnic Uzbeks, threatening criminal prosecution related to the June 2010 events. Victims of extortion rarely report incidents for fear of reprisals.

Investigations into the June 2010 violence have stalled. Trials of mostly ethnic Uzbeks connected to the violence continued to take place in violation of international fair trial standards, including the trials of Mahamad Bizurukov and Shamshidin Niyazaliev, each of whom was sentenced to life in prison in October 2012. According to Kylym Shamy, a Bishkek-based human rights group, some victims of the violence have not received financial compensation promised by the government.

Lawyers in southern Kyrgyzstan continued to be harassed in 2012 for defending ethnic Uzbek clients who were charged with involvement in the June 2010 violence, perpetuating a hostile and violent environment that undermined defendants' fair trial rights. On January 20, a group of persons in Jalalabad verbally and physically attacked a lawyer defending the ethnic Uzbek owner of an Uzbeklanguage television station. No one has been held accountable for such violence against lawyers.

Torture

UN Special Rapporteur on Torture Juan Mendez concluded after his December 2011 mission to Kyrgyzstan that "the use of torture and ill-treatment to extract confessions remains widespread" and that "general conditions in most places of detention visited amount to inhuman and degrading treatment." In October 2012, the European Court of Human Rights (ECtHR) cited the "widespread use of torture against members of the Uzbek minority in the southern part of Kyrgyzstan" in a ruling in the case of *Ergashev v. Russia*, concerning an ethnic Uzbek man threatened with extradition from Russia. In November, as many as 37 detainees alleged they were beaten by police in a pretrial detention facility in Jalalabad, and some said they were stripped naked and humiliated. In statements to the media, the Ministry of Internal Affairs said they found no evidence of a crime during a preliminary review.

In July, the government adopted a law on the National Center for the Prevention of Torture, fulfilling Kyrgyzstan's obligation under the Optional Protocol to the United Nations Convention against Torture (CAT) to establish a national torture prevention mechanism. Concurrently, criminal code amendments went into effect, bringing the definition of torture in line with international standards.

In June, government agencies, international organizations, and domestic NGOs concluded a Memorandum of Understanding (MoU) on Human Rights and Fundamental Freedoms, which allows the signatories to make unannounced visits to places of detention. However in practice some NGOs still encountered restrictions despite the MoU.

In hearings related to the June 2010 violence, judges continue to dismiss, ignore, or fail to order investigations into torture allegations. In a rare exception, four police officers were charged with torture after the August 2011 death of Usmonzhon Kholmirzaev, an ethnic Uzbek, who succumbed to internal injuries after he was beaten by police in custody. Repeated delays in proceedings have meant that over a year later, the trial has yet to conclude. In June, after Abdugafur Abdurakhmanov, an ethnic Uzbek serving a life sentence in relation to the June 2010 violence, died in prison, authorities did not open an investigation, alleging he committed suicide.

Farrukh Gapirov, an ethnic Uzbek, was awarded damages in March for unlawful imprisonment and torture in custody. He was arrested in 2010 on charges related to the inter-ethnic violence and later acquitted.

Freedom of Expression

In February, state-controlled KyrgyzTelecom began to block access to Ferghana.ru, an independent Central Asia news website, enforcing a June 2011 parliament resolution adopted after *Ferghana.ru*'s critical reporting on the June 2010 violence. NGOs and Kyrgyzstan's international partners strongly criticized the blocking of the site. The Organization for Security and Co-operation in Europe (OSCE) Representative on Freedom of the Media Dunja Mijatović called for it to be "lifted immediately." KyrgyzTelecom continues to block access to Ferghana.ru, although the site can be accessed through other providers.

Mijatović also expressed concern about the case of Vladimir Farafonov, a journalist who, on July 3, was fined US$1,000 for inciting inter-ethnic hatred in articles posted online, stating the verdict "might negatively influence the journalistic community in Kyrgyzstan." Farfonov had written articles about growing Kyrgyz nationalism and ethnic Russians in Kyrgyzstan.

In 2012, some journalists were physically or verbally attacked while doing their work. Several times in October, Ata-Jurt political party supporters attacked journalists during protests. Journalists reported that police did not intervene. "Insult" and "insult of a public official" remain criminal offenses.

In September, the authorities banned a documentary about gay Muslims which was to be screened during the One World human rights film festival in Bishkek, finding it "extremist." Officials and others pressured human rights defender Tolekan Ismailova not to show the film.

Sexual Orientation and Gender-Based Violence

Authorities have not effectively addressed long-standing problems of gender-based violence, including widespread domestic violence and bride kidnapping, which continue, largely with impunity. On September 20, a court sentenced Shaimbek Aimanakunov, 35, to 6 years in prison on a conviction for incitement to suicide, rape, and forced marriage. Two days after Aimanakunov had kidnapped, raped, and forcibly married a nineteen-year-old university student, she hung herself.

Gay and bisexual men are at serious risk of entrapment, extortion, beating and sexual violence. Such abuses largely go unpunished. In May, the prosecutor general's office refused to investigate approximately 10 cases of entrapment and extortion on the grounds that the victims declined to be identified. Lesbian and bisexual women continue to be subjected to forced marriages and "curative rapes," according to Labrys, a local NGO focusing on LGBT rights.

Human Rights Defenders

Azimjon Askarov, a human rights defender who has worked on documenting police treatment of detainees, is serving a life sentence, despite a prosecution marred by serious violations of fair trial standards. Askarov was found guilty of "organizing mass disorders," "inciting ethnic hatred," and taking part in killing a police officer on June 13, 2010. On December 20, 2011, Kyrgyzstan's Supreme Court upheld the verdict. Prosecutorial authorities refused to open a criminal investigation into Askarov's credible allegations of torture in custody. In May, the prosecutor general's office denied a request filed by Citizens Against Corruption, a local human rights NGO, to reopen the case on grounds of new evidence. In November, Askarov and his lawyers submitted a complaint on his case to the Human Rights Committee.

In January, parliamentarians introduced a draft law on foreign assistance that, if adopted, would "make foreign financing of NCOs [non-commercial organizations] more difficult and may lead to restriction of activities of NCOs in Kyrgyzstan," according to the International Center for Not-for-Profit Law (ICNL). At this writing, work on this law remained suspended.

In March, human rights activist Ravshan Gapirov won compensation from the state for being unlawfully held in pretrial detention in 2008, after it was determined that articles he had written did not incite hatred.

Key International Actors

In June, UN High Commissioner for Human Rights Navi Pillay presented her second report to the Human Rights Council (HRC) on Kyrgyzstan following the 2010 violence, in which she noted that "serious institutional deficiencies have hampered the delivery of justice and undermined the rule of law" and "lack of progress in addressing these matters impacts on reconciliation and peacebuilding efforts." The report includes recommendations to address discrimination, ill-treatment and torture, and minority rights, among others.

During her July visit to Kyrgyzstan, Pillay called attention to human rights issues including torture, discrimination on ethnic, religious and gender grounds, and violations of fair trial standards. She "urged the president...[to make] clear public statements stressing there will be zero tolerance for torture."

In February, the European Union held an EU-Kyrgyzstan Civil Society Seminar on Human Rights, and in September held its fourth annual human rights dialogue with Kyrgyzstan. The EU's voice on rights violations in Kyrgyzstan was overall muted.

United States Ambassador to the OSCE Ian Kelly publicly criticized the imprisonment of Askarov, discrimination against ethnic minorities, and restrictions on media freedoms. In late October, the US-Kyrgyzstan Annual Bilateral Consultations took place in Bishkek .

During a September mission, the UN Subcommittee on the Prevention of Torture (SPT), under the CAT's Optional Protocol (OPCAT), visited temporary detention facilities, prisons, and psychiatric institutions. The SPT presented confidential conclusions and recommendations to help the government "establish effective safeguards against the risk of torture and ill-treatment in places of deprivation of liberty."

Russia

Mass protests following Russia's December 2011 parliamentary elections prompted promises of political reforms. However, after his return to the presidency, Vladimir Putin oversaw the swift reversal of former President Dmitry Medvedev's few, timid advances on political freedoms and unleashed an unprecedented crackdown against civic activism. New laws in 2012 restrict nongovernmental organizations and freedoms of assembly and expression. New local laws discriminate against lesbian, gay, bisexual, and transgender (LGBT) people. Abuses continue in the counterinsurgency campaign in the North Caucasus.

Undermined Reforms

Russia's international partners initially praised reforms to Russia's electoral system that took place early in 2012, when parliament adopted legislative amendments that restored popular election of regional governors (since 2004, governors had been appointed by the Kremlin). However, under these reforms, gubernatorial candidates are required to secure support from local legislatures, which the ruling party dominates.

Amendments also lowered the minimum number of members for political party registration from 50,000 to 500 and lowered the threshold of votes a party needs for parliamentary representation from 7 to 5 percent. However, the ban on electoral blocs and the requirement that parties field candidates or risk losing registration attenuated the reforms' potential to strengthen political pluralism. The reforms were adopted too late to apply to the December 4, 2011 parliamentary vote, which saw the ruling party win 49.3 percent of the vote.

Freedom of Assembly

The September 2011 announcement by Medvedev and Putin that they would essentially switch posts became a tipping point for people dissatisfied with a decade of "soft" authoritarianism, bringing tens of thousands to the streets of

Russia's capital for unprecedented protests a day after the December parliamentary vote.

Thousands protested alleged electoral fraud, and riot police attacked some protesters and randomly detained about 300, some of who were sentenced to 15 days' detention. Protests and detentions continued in following days in Moscow and large Russian cities, but police subsequently ceased interfering with mass rallies.

However, on May 6, the day before Putin's inauguration, there were clashes in Moscow between police and demonstrators. By May 8, police detained over 1,000 people, many for simply wearing the protest movement's symbolic white ribbons, and even raided several cafes favored by protesters, detaining patrons. At this writing, 17 people awaited trial for alleged participation in mass disorders and attacking police, punishable by up to 10 years in prison. Witnesses and video recordings indicate that some people were detained when they arrived at the demonstration before they could engage in any action, violent or otherwise.

One month later, the Duma rushed through amendments that increase by 30-fold fines for violating rules on holding public events, essentially making them equivalent to fines for criminal offenses. The amendments also imposed new restrictions, for example, allowing authorities to compile lists of permanent public event-free locations.

Freedom of Association

Legislative amendments adopted in July require advocacy groups that accept foreign funding to register and identify themselves publicly as "foreign agents," demonizing them in the public eye as foreign spies. The authorities may suspend organizations that fail to register for up to six months, without a court order. The law imposes additional reporting requirements and stiff civil and criminal penalties.

Golos, the election monitoring organization, faced severe pressure, including a fine for allegedly violating the election law, a smear campaign in pro-government media, and hacker attacks. During the parliamentary vote, the authorities harassed Golos election monitors and at times denied them access to polling stations.

In October, parliament adopted a broad, expanded legal definition of the crime of treason that could lead to criminal action against those who conduct international advocacy on human rights issues. Despite his promise to "look into the law" and possibly narrow down the overly broad and vague definition of treason, President Putin signed it in November.

Some civil society groups lost an important source of funding in October 2012 when the Russian government expelled the United States government assistance organization, USAID, and banned its programming in Russia. The Russian government increased funding to local NGOs, but groups working on sensitive issues, such as human rights abuses related to counterinsurgency, right to free and fair elections, and police torture, are unlikely to benefit from it.

Freedom of Expression

In February, the Federal Drug Control Service (FSKN) blocked the Andrey Rylkov Foundation's website for including information about methadone, which is classified as an essential medicine by the World Health Organization for opiate dependence treatment, but illegal in Russia. The website included international research findings showing that methadone treatment reduces HIV risk among heroin and other opiate users and helps them stay on AIDS and TB treatments.

In July, the Duma adopted amendments recriminalizing certain kinds of libel seven months after it had been decriminalized. The new law provides for harsh financial penalties instead of prison terms. A special provision "on libel against judges, jurors, prosecutors, and law enforcement officials" could restrict legitimate criticism of public officials.

A July law requires internet providers to block web content that a court deems to be "extremist" or that competent federal agencies deem harmful to children. In practice, this forces internet-hosting services to block offending websites upon authorities' instructions.

In August, three young women from the feminist punk band Pussy Riot were sentenced to two years' imprisonment for a forty40-second political stunt in a Moscow cathedral that criticized Putin and the Russian Orthodox Church's close relationship with the Kremlin. The court supported the prosecutor's view that the women were motivated by hatred for Christian Orthodox believers. The authorities could have brought misdemeanor charges, punishable by a fine, against the women for their disruptive behavior under the code of administrative offenses but instead pursued criminal charges. In October, one of the women was given a suspended sentence on appeal and was released from prison.

Sexual Orientation and Gender Identity

By the end of 2012, legislation banning "homosexual propaganda" was in force in nine Russian provinces. The "propaganda" bans could be applied for such things as displaying a rainbow flag or a gay-friendly logo. In May, prominent Russian LGBT rights activist Nikolai Alekseev became the first person to be fined under the new St. Petersburg law after he picketed city hall with a poster declaring, "Homosexuality is not a perversion."

In 2010, the European Court of Human Rights (ECtHR) had firmly rejected the Russian government's argument that there is no general consensus on issues relating to the treatment of "sexual minorities." In spite of the court's ruling, Moscow city authorities in both 2011 and 2012 banned the Gay Pride event.

Harassment of Kremlin Critics and Human Rights Defenders

In the lead-up to Putin's inauguration, authorities in some cities repeatedly tried to intimidate political and civic activists, and interfered with news outlets critical of the government through arbitrary lawsuits and detentions, threats by state officials, beatings, and other forms of harassment. State-controlled media ran articles seeking to discredit the protest movement and government critics. Police also threatened several activists' families.

In June 2012, according to the independent print outlet *Novaya Gazeta,* the head of Russia's Investigation Committee, Alexander Bastrykin, abducted Sergei

Sokolov, deputy chief editor of the newspaper, took him to a forest in the out-skirts of Moscow and threatened his life. Bastrykin was not dismissed.

In April, two men attacked Elena Milashina, a *Novaya Gazeta journalist*, inflict-ing multiple bruises and kicking out a tooth. Investigators termed the attack a common mugging and arrested and charged two people who Milashina said did not resemble the attackers.

In October, Leonid Razvozzhaev, a political activist under investigation on suspi-cion of organizing riots during the May 6 demonstration in Moscow, was allegedly kidnapped in Kiev, Ukraine. He had stepped out of the office of the local partner organization of the United Nations High Commissioner on Refugees (UNHCR) during a break in his asylum interview, when he disappeared. Several days later he reappeared in custody in Russia. According to Razvozzhaev, after the kidnapping he was forced to sign a confession under duress while in incommunicado detention. The UNHCR expressed concern over the situation and called for an investigation. At this writing, Ravozzhaev was in custody awaiting trial in Moscow.

Human rights defenders working in the North Caucasus remained especially at risk, and impunity for past attacks continues.

The investigation into the 2009 murder of leading Chechen rights activist Natalia Estemirova remains inadequate with no progress made in 2012 in bring-ing the perpetrators to justice. At this writing, investigators had also yet to hold accountable the perpetrators of the December 2011 murder of Gadzhimurad Kamalov. Kamalov was the founder and publisher of *Chernovik,* Dagestan's independent weekly known for its reporting on corruption and human rights abuses.

In January 2012, Umar Saidmagomedov, a local lawyer who frequently defended individuals arrested on insurgency-related charges and worked closely with local human rights activists, died from gunshot wounds in the Dagestani capi-tal, Makhachkala, together with local resident Rasul Kurbanov. According to offi-cial reports, Kurbanov opened fire on police officials, who responded, killing both men. Saidmagomedov's colleagues, however, argued that the circumstances of the killing were different and that law enforcement officials killed the lawyer in retaliation for his work. Police did not examine this allegation.

The Joint Mobile Group of Russian Human Rights Organizations in Chechnya, which investigates human rights violations by law enforcement officials in the region, faced severe harassment. On January 21, police in Nizhny Novgorod detained one of the group's leading members, Anton Ryzhov, interrogated him about the organization's work, and confiscated his work laptop and memory sticks for eight months.

In June, Chechen leader Ramzan Kadyrov threatened three Mobile Group lawyers at a televised meeting they were forced to attend, sending a clear warning to victims to avoid the organization. In July, federal investigators interrogated Mobile Group head Igor Kalyapin as part of a criminal inquiry regarding alleged disclosure of secret information regarding a torture case. This inquiry, which was still ongoing at this writing, represented the authorities' third attempt in two years to open criminal proceedings against Kalyapin.

In the course of 2012, three Chechen activists reported to Human Rights Watch that they received death threats. One of them chose to leave Chechnya, fearing for the well-being of family members.

In October, a local group well known for publishing periodic online bulletins on the situation in Chechnya stopped working. According to the group's leadership, their decision resulted from pressure by the authorities.

In May, a police official in Kabardino-Balkaria explicitly threatened Rustam Matsev, a lawyer with the Memorial Human Rights Center, insinuated that Matsev supported Islamic insurgents, and warned he could be "eliminated." According to Matsev, his complaints against the official to competent authorities yielded no result.

North Caucasus

The Islamist insurgency remained active, especially in Dagestan. According to official data, in the first six months of 2012, insurgents perpetrated 116 "terrorist crimes" in Dagestan, killing 67 people, including seven civilians. In April, in an unprecedented move, the state-supported Sufi community and adherents of Salafism—a strand of Sunni Islam that promotes a literalist interpretation of the Koran—signed a resolution for cooperation. The authorities tend to view adherents of Salafism as supporting the Islamist insurgency. In August, a suicide bomber killed the region's leading Sufi sheikh who had actively promoted negotiations for the April resolution.

Adherents of Salafism are especially vulnerable to persecution and counterinsurgency-related abuses, such as enforced disappearances, torture, and extrajudicial executions. According to Memorial, six local residents were "disappeared" following abduction-style detentions between January and August 2012. Most were adherents of Salafism.

In Ingushetia, four local residents were abducted, two of whom "disappeared" between January and August, according to Memorial.

In Chechnya, law enforcement and security agencies under Ramzan Kadyrov's de facto control continued collective punishment against relatives and suspected supporters of alleged insurgents. Victims increasingly refuse to speak about violations due to fear of official retribution, meaning that abuses remain largely under-reported

Kadyrov's "virtue" campaign for women in Chechnya continued in 2012, with pressure on women to wear headscarves in all public places. Women must wear headscarves in most public buildings. According to local women's activists, "honor" killings have become more frequent in Chechnya.

Cooperation with the European Court of Human Rights

At this writing, the European Court of Human Rights (ECtHR) had issued more than 210 judgments holding Russia responsible for grave human rights violations in Chechnya. While Russia continues to pay the required monetary compensation to victims, it fails to meaningfully implement the core of the judgments by not conducting effective investigations, failing to hold perpetrators accountable, and using statutes of limitation and amnesties acts to avoid holding perpetrators to account.

Palliative Care

Restrictive government policies and limited availability of pain treatment continued in 2012 to be a major obstacle to the delivery of palliative care. Each year, tens of thousands of dying cancer patients (up to 80 percent) are denied their right to adequate relief. Such inexpensive drugs as oral immediate-release morphine are largely unavailable through the public healthcare system.

In 2012, the Russian Ministry of Health and Social Development acknowledged the need to significantly increase the number of hospices. But drug regulations have not been revised, and training of healthcare workers on pain management still does not meet World Health Organization (WHO) standards.

Disability Rights

In May, Russia ratified the UN Convention on the Rights of Persons with Disabilities (CRPD). However, the 13 million people with disabilities in Russia continue to face a range of barriers that limit their participation in society, including inaccessible public buildings and transportation for people with physical disabilities and confinement of people with mental disabilities to institutions for long periods of time against their will and without appropriate legal safeguards for their rights.

Abuses Linked to Preparations for the 2014 Olympic Games

Authorities expropriated property from hundreds of Sochi families for building venues for the 2014 Winter Olympics. Most homeowners received compensation, but in many cases amounts were unfair and the process was opaque. In September, authorities forcibly evicted a family of six without any compensation.

Some migrant workers building sports venues and other infrastructure for the Olympics reported that employers were failing to provide contracts or promised wages and demanded excessively long working hours.

Some journalists reporting on Olympics-related concerns faced censorship and threats of dismissal. Activists faced harassment and arrest. For example, police in early fall detained three activists who peacefully voiced concerns about a proposed thermal power plant. Administrative charges against two of them were later dropped.

Key International Actors

Many actors were forthright in their criticism of the restrictive legislation described above. Concerns centered on the shrinking space for vibrant civil society. For example, the re-criminalization of libel was flagged as a "step backwards" by the Organization for Security and Co-operation in Europe (OSCE) and the Council of Europe's Parliamentary Assembly (PACE). The UN commissioner for human rights expressed "concern" that the law would "stifle all criticism of government authorities."

Similarly, the "foreign agents" law was adopted despite public criticism by key international actors, including the UN, the US, and the European Union; the Council of Europe's (CoE) secretary general said the law did "not belong to a democratic society."

Most of these governments and institutions publicly voiced concern about the Pussy Riot trial, legislative amendments restricting public assemblies, the new treason law, and homophobic legislation.

A PACE resolution adopted in October welcomed electoral reforms while cautioning that other developments "must call the authorities' real intentions into question."

The International Olympic Committee (IOC) intervened with the Russian authorities on cases involving human rights abuses occurring in the run-up the 2014 Winter Olympics. However, the IOC has not insisted on comprehensive reforms to prevent and remedy violations.

In October, the European Parliament called for a visa ban and asset freeze against Russian officials allegedly responsible for the death in custody of whistleblower tax lawyer Sergei Magnitsky and recommended that the European Council draw up a list of implicated Russian officials. At this writing, a vote was pending on similar legislation in the US Congress, named for Magnitsky, which would apply to government officials around the world involved in the torture or killing of whistleblowers. In response, Russia banned entry for US officials allegedly involved in abuses in counterterrorism operations in Afghanistan.

In November, the UN Committee Against Torture (CAT) reviewed Russia's periodic report and noted persistent problems with torture and inhuman and degrading treatment by law enforcement officials.

Serbia

Despite being granted status as a candidate for European Union membership in March, Serbia did little to improve its human rights record in 2012. The situation of ethnic minorities remains precarious, especially for Roma. Journalists still face a hostile environment, despite some progress in bringing perpetrators of attacks to justice. The asylum system remains weak and overburdened. Relations with Kosovo remain tense, exemplified by Kosovo and Serbian police carrying out tit for tat arrests of Serbian election officials and Kosovo Albanian activists in the run-up to the May 6 Serbian elections.

Accountability for War Crimes

There was ongoing progress in domestic war crimes prosecutions. In September, the Belgrade War Crimes Chamber convicted 11 members of the Kosovo Liberation Army's (KLA) "Gnjilane group" to a combined total of 116 years in prison for crimes against civilians, mainly Roma and Ashkali, during the 1999 Kosovo war. In June, the chamber sentenced 14 former members of the Yugoslav People's Army (JNA) to a combined total of 126 years in prison for war crimes against Croat civilians in the Croatian village of Lovas in 1991. The Serbian war crimes prosecutor indicted three people for crimes against civilians during 2012. Sixteen cases were pending at this writing.

However, Chief Prosecutor Serge Brammertz at the International Criminal Tribunal for the former Yugoslavia (ICTY) in a June report criticized Serbia's lack of efforts to uncover the networks that helped war crimes fugitives wanted by the ICTY to evade justice. The Serbian war crimes prosecutor's office subsequently began investigating 13 suspects, including a former high-ranking security official. In his report Brammertz also criticized Serbia's failure to sign a proposed protocol on war crimes cooperation between the Serbian prosecutor and his Bosnian counterpart.

Freedom of Media

Journalists continue to face a hostile environment, although the authorities brought some perpetrators of attacks on journalists to justice.

In February, a cameraman from Studio B television was punched and kicked in the capital Belgrade. The sole assailant was arrested by police and charged in June for the assault. In February, a Belgrade appeals court increased the prison sentences of two men for the 2008 attack on journalist Bosko Brankovic while he reported on a demonstration in support of Radovan Karadizic, the Bosnian Serb wartime president, on trial at the ICTY for genocide and crimes against humanity. The court upheld sentences for two others.

Despite having 24-hour police protection since October 2005, threats continued against Vladimir Mitric, a journalist specializing in uncovering corruption. In September, Mitric was threatened twice by the same person and told not to report on particular individuals. On the second occasion the person making the threats was accompanied by a police officer who had been responsible for Mitric's protection. The person making the threats was charged with minor offences in September, but at this writing the police officer had not been disciplined.

In October, the homes of three journalists were attacked, although it is unclear whether the attacks were linked to their reporting. Unknown assailants lobbed Molotov cocktails at the Belgrade homes of Biljana Vujovic, a presenter at TV Kopernikus, and Damir Dragic, director of Belgrade-based tabloid Informer. No one was injured but Dragic's car was destroyed by the fire. It is unclear whether the incidents were connected to their reporting. An explosive device, which did not detonate, was placed near the home of Tanja Jankovic, an investigative journalist at TV B92 in Vranje, southern Serbia. At this writing, all three incidents were under police investigation.

In July, a Belgrade appeals court sentenced freelance journalist Laszlo Szasz to 120 days in prison for a 2007 commentary criticizing the leader of the Hungarian nationalist 64 Counties Youth Movement. Szasz was released after receiving a presidential pardon on August 3.

In September, Information Minister Bratislav Petkovic announced that the government was preparing legislation guaranteeing freedom and independence of the media. The same month, the government announced it would establish an international commission to investigate unsolved murders of three prominent journalists more than a decade ago.

Treatment of Minorities

Roma continued to experience harassment, threats, discrimination when accessing education, and problematic forced evictions.

In April, around 1,000 Roma were forcibly evicted from the Belvil informal settlement in Belgrade. Those internally displaced Romani families from Kosovo and those with permanent residency in Belgrade were rehoused in metal containers on the outskirts of Belgrade. Families with residency registered in other parts of Serbia were returned there, including four families returned to Nis, southern Serbia, where they were housed in an abandoned warehouse without access to water or electricity.

On May 1, 15 to 20 masked persons armed with baseball bats approached the Jabucki Rit container settlement occupied by Roma. They shouted racist slogans and drew a swastika on one metal container. At this writing, police had made only one arrest and the case remained under investigation.

There was progress in addressing problems of undocumented persons, many of whom are Roma. A new law adopted in September removes administrative barriers and simplifies registration procedures for birth certificates.

Tension rose in the Vojvodina region, northeast Serbia, between members of the Serb majority and Hungarian minority. In September, approximately 20 Serbs armed with iron rods attacked eight Hungarian children and young adults in the town of Subotica, allegedly because the victims spoke Hungarian. Police were investigating at this writing.

Sexual Orientation and Gender Identity

Serbia made some progress in protecting the rights of lesbian, gay, bisexual, and transgender (LGBT) people. In February, Simo Vladicic was sentenced to a three-month jail term for making threats against LGBT people via a Facebook group called "500,000 Serbs against Gay Pride." In March, a Belgrade court sentenced Mladen Obradovic, leader of the right-wing extremist movement Obraz, to 10 months in prison for threatening gays and inciting hatred in the run-up to the 2009 Gay Pride Parade, which was then cancelled on security grounds. In a separate case, Obradovic was sentenced to two years in prison in April 2011 for inciting violence during the 2010 Gay Pride Parade, a sentence that was under appeal at this writing. The Serbian Ministry of Interior banned the October 6 parade and other public gatherings citing security reasons, but took no measures to try to facilitate the parade in face of the threats of violence. Serbian authorities also banned the Belgrade Pride Parade in 2011 due to violent incidents during and after the 2010 event that injured policemen and participants.

Asylum Seekers and Displaced Persons

The Office of the United Nations High Commissioner for Refugees (UNHCR) said in September that the defects in Serbia's asylum system mean that it cannot be considered a safe country of asylum or safe third country and that countries should refrain from sending asylum seekers from other countries back to Serbia. Hungary, Greece, and Turkey are among the countries sending asylum seekers back to Serbia. In the first eight months of 2012, 1,454 asylum seekers were registered in Serbia, down from 2,134 during the same period in 2011.

There were concerns about inadequate capacity in Serbia's two asylum centers, which can only accommodate a total of 280 people. The Asylum Office, which makes initial decisions on asylum claims, has not granted refugee status or temporary protection to any applicant since it assumed responsibility for the asylum procedure in 2008.

There was little progress towards finding a lasting solution for refugees and internally displaced persons (IDPs) from the Balkan wars. According to the UNHCR, in July there were 66,563 refugees in Serbia, most from Croatia, and

228,215 IDPs of whom 210,146 hail from Kosovo. A successful international donors conference in Sarajevo in April raised financial support for the housing needs of 74,000 of the most vulnerable IDPs in Serbia, Bosnia and Herzegovina, Croatia, and Montenegro.

In October, the EU renewed calls on Serbian authorities to stop the influx of asylum seekers, mainly Roma, to EU countries, adding that failure to do so risked losing the right for Serbian citizens to travel to the EU without visas. There were credible reports by international human rights NGOs throughout 2012 that Serbian border guards prevent persons of perceived Romani origin from crossing the border from Serbia into Hungary.

Key International Actors

On March 1, EU heads of state granted candidate status to Serbia following a February 28 recommendation by the General Affairs Council, which made clear the decision was linked to Serbia's progress on cooperation with Kosovo, including on management of their border, and made no reference to human rights. The European Commission's annual progress report on Serbia stressed the need to strengthen the rule of law, ensure judicial reforms and protect vulnerable groups, particularly Roma. The commission said that Serbia needed to increase efforts to fight corruption and protect freedom of expression in the media.

A joint US and EU Balkans tour led by US Secretary of State Hillary Clinton and EU High Representative Catherine Ashton in late October and early November failed to emphasize the importance of improving human rights protection in Serbia and instead focused on political dialogue between authorities in Belgrade and Pristina.

In June, the European Committee for the Prevention of Torture (CPT) published a report on its 2011 visit to Serbia expressing concerns about allegations of ill-treatment of detainees by law enforcement officials and overcrowding in all prisons it visited.

The UN special rapporteur on human rights defenders expressed concern about allegations of harassment of LGBT human rights defenders in Serbia in her February global report.

In April 2012, Serbia signed the Council of Europe (CoE) Convention on preventing and combating violence against women and domestic violence.

Kosovo

There was no significant improvement in human rights protection in Kosovo in 2012. Tensions in the divided north sometimes flared into violence. Roma, Ashkali, and Egyptian (an Albanian speaking group that claims roots in Egypt) continue to be marginalized and vulnerable to discrimination. The justice system remains poor with large case backlogs. Mechanisms for human rights protection remain weak.

On September 10, the countries comprising the International Steering Group, which oversaw Kosovo after it unilaterally declared independence from Serbia in 2008, proclaimed an end to its supervision of Kosovo's self-governance. The decision signals a downgrading of international engagement.

Protection of Minorities

Roma, Ashkali, and Egyptians (RAE) remained among the most vulnerable groups in Kosovo. They continued to face discrimination in areas such as housing, education, and access to public services. A June 2012 United Nations Development Programme (UNDP) report found that around three-quarters of RAE lack formal employment, compared to around 45 percent of the general population. Many are displaced and unable to rebuild or return to their original homes.

Tensions between the Serb minority and the Albanian majority remained high in 2012, particularly in the divided city of Mitrovica in northern Kosovo. In April, an explosion in the majority Serb "Three Towers" neighborhood in the city killed an ethnic Albanian man and wounded two of his children. Police were investigating at this writing. In July, a Serb community activist, Milovan Jevtic, and his wife were shot dead in their home south of Pristina, the capital. Jevtic worked for the return of Kosovo Serb families and peaceful coexistence with Kosovo Albanians, raising concerns that the deaths may have been intended to discourage such returns. European Union Rule of Law Mission (EULEX) and local authorities were conducting a joint investigation at this writing.

Following confrontations in June between members of the Kosovo Police Service (KPS) and ethnic Serbs at four border crossings, unknown perpetrators in

Pristina pelted two buses carrying Serb children aged between 8 and 16 with Molotov cocktails and stones. Sixteen children sustained light injuries. Police were still investigating at this writing.

Despite these events, the KPS recorded only 16 inter-ethnic incidents during the first eight months of the year, a reported decline from 2011, when 60 inter-ethnic incidents were recorded. They comprised two attacks resulting in serious injuries and five in light injuries, seven other unspecified physical attacks, and two cases of property damage. There were concerns among international observers that many inter-ethnic incidents are unreported, unregistered, and misclassified.

Return of Refugees and Internally Displaced Persons

During the first 10 months of the year, the Office of the United Nations High Commissioner for Refugees (UNHCR) registered 785 voluntary returns, including those outside Kosovo and internally displaced persons (IDPs), compared to 989 returns during the same period in 2011.

Deportations to Kosovo from Western Europe continued, with limited assistance provided upon return. Between January and September, the UNHCR registered 1,717 forced returns to Kosovo, including 546 deportations of minorities, mostly from Sweden (235) and Germany (196): 327 Roma, 105 Ashkali, 2 Egyptians, 21 Serbs, 8 Albanians, 32 Bosniaks, 44 Gorani, 7 Turks, and 8 Albanians to Serb majority areas.

Roma, Ashkali, and Egyptian forced returnees continued to face particular hardships upon return, including difficulties accessing public services. A United Nations Children Fund (UNICEF) report in March stated that three out of four children deported from Germany drop out of school due to language barriers.

There was little progress in implementing two national strategies designed to facilitate the integration of returnees (the Strategy for Reintegration of Repatriated Persons) and for Roma generally (the Roma, Ashkali, Egyptian Integration Strategy), with central and local authorities failing to allocate needed resources, and local authorities often unaware of their responsibilities.

At this writing, the lead-contaminated Osterode camp outside Mitrovica was still open, with five remaining Romani families waiting to be resettled. Work had begun to construct apartments in the north to house the families.

Impunity, Accountability, and Access to Justice

On November 29, the International Criminal Tribunal for the former Yugoslavia (ICTY) acquitted Ramush Haradinaj, the former prime minister of Kosovo, and his two co-defendants, Lahi Brahimaj and Idriz Balaj, former Kosovo Liberation Army (KLA) commanders, after their retrial for crimes against humanity against Serb Roma and Albanian civilians in the Jablanica detention camp in 1998.

The EULEX special investigation team continued its investigation into allegations that some KLA members, including senior officials in Kosovo, had participated in post-war abductions, enforced disappearances, killing of Serbs, and organ trafficking.

In the first nine months of 2012, EULEX judges handed down three war crimes judgments, including in May sentencing Zoran Kolic to 14 years' imprisonment for war crimes against prisoners in Lipjan prison in May 1999, and confirmed one new war crimes indictment in October. During January and September, local judges handed down 20 other verdicts. As of October 78 war crimes cases were under investigation and in November, EULEX police arrested three former KLA members suspected of war crimes against civilians during 1998-1999. At this writing the case was being investigated by the Special Prosecutorial Office, which did not render details about the charges.

In November, the Supreme Court of Kosovo ordered the retrial of Fatmir Limaj and three other former KLA members on charges of war crimes against Serb and Albanian civilians and prisoners of war held in a detention center in the village of Klecka in 1999. The four were acquitted in May by a Pristina district court, including a EULEX judge. In March, the same court acquitted six other defendants in the case.

Freedom of Media

The Kosovo National Assembly adopted a new criminal code in April containing provisions that criminalized defamation and force journalists to reveal sources, raising media freedom concerns. In light of those concerns, Kosovo President Atifeta Jahjaga in May sent the code back to the National Assembly for reconsideration. But in June, the assembly adopted the criminal code without revising the controversial provisions. In September, it finally approved government amendments abrogating the controversial provisions, which will be removed from the criminal code once it enters into force on January 1, 2013.

Threats against journalists continued to be a serious problem. In March, journalists at the *Express* newspaper received threatening phone calls following an article on corruption in the fuel industry. Halil Matoshi, an outspoken journalist reporting on corruption, was assaulted in Pristina in July by three unidentified men, one of them armed with a knife. Matoshi escaped with minor injuries and the police were investigating at this writing.

In May, a EULEX judge at the Pristina municipal court confirmed indictments against Rexhep Hoti and four other staff at Kosovo daily *Infopress* and Skenderaj Mayor Sami Lushtaku for threats made against Balkan Investigate Reporting Network (a regional news group) Kosovo Director Jeta Xharra in 2009. In October, the Kosovo Special Prosecution Office launched a separate investigation against Lushtaku for threats made in March, May, August, and September against Adem Meti, a correspondent for the leading daily newspaper *Koha Ditore*, due to his reporting on corruption.

Key International Actors

The end of supervised independence of Kosovo on September 10 resulted in the closure of the International Civilian Office. EULEX's mandate was extended until 2014.

UN Secretary-General Ban Ki-moon in July expressed concern over escalating ethnic tensions in northern Kosovo and stressed that the basic needs and rights of affected communities in the north must be democratically represented.

An October report from the European Commission recommended opening negotiations with Kosovo on a Stabilization and Association Agreement (SAA), a
framework for closer relations seen as a prelude to candidate status for EU
membership, subject to progress on rule of law, including cooperation with the
EULEX task force, and respect for minority rights. The commission's assessment
made clear that signing the agreement would require tackling impunity and
access to justice, improving media freedom, implementing programs to secure
the rights of Roma, and taking steps to facilitate the return of displaced Serbs.

Following a July meeting with Kosovo President Atifete Jahjaga, European
Council President Herman Van Rompuy stressed the need for progress on the
rule of law, public administration reform, electoral reform, and outreach to
minority communities.

In October, German Defense Minister Thomas de Maiziere said that the EULEX
was "on the wrong track" and that its failure—together with that of the KPS—to
deal with ethnic violence was placing an unreasonable burden on NATO forces.
An OSCE report in October said authorities need to take concrete action to
implement laws on anti-discrimination and protection against domestic violence, among others.

In October, Council of Europe (CoE) Secretary General Thorbjorn Jagland emphasized the importance of an effective investigation into allegations contained in
the 2010 CoE report by Swiss Senator Dick Marty alleging that some KLA members, including senior officials in post-war Kosovo, had participated in the post-
war abductions, enforced disappearances, and killing of Serbs, as well as
alleged organ trafficking and organized crime, including weapons and drug
smuggling.

Tajikistan

The human rights situation in Tajikistan remains poor. The government persisted in 2012 with enforcing a repressive law on religion, and introduced new legislation further restricting religious expression and education. Authorities restricted media freedoms and targeted journalists for their work. Domestic violence against women and children and torture remain widespread human rights concerns.

Tajik authorities took positive steps during the year, including accepting a visit by the United Nations special rapporteur on torture. They also removed slander and insult from the criminal code, making them misdemeanors subject to fines. However, the government also restricted space for free expression, further tightening restrictions on religious practice, and denying the National Movement of Tajikistan, a new political party that had called for reducing presidential powers and reducing the presidential term from seven to five years, the right to register.

In July, dozens of deaths and numerous injuries were reported in Khorog, the provincial capital of Gorno-Badakhshan, after the Tajik government sent troops to the southeastern region to arrest those responsible for the fatal stabbing of the local state security chief. By late July, official sources reported that 17 government soldiers, 30 gunmen, and 20 civilians had died in the violence, but independent sources reported greater numbers of casualties among the general population. Human Rights Watch has not been able to verify the casualty reports.

Criminal Justice and Torture

Torture remains an enduring problem, and is used to extract confessions from detainees, who are often denied access to family and lawyers in pre-trial custody. Despite periodic discussions with the International Committee of the Red Cross (ICRC), authorities have not granted ICRC access to places of detention.

While torture is practiced with near impunity, authorities took a few significant steps in 2012 to hold perpetrators accountable. In early 2012, Tajikistan's criminal code was revised to include a definition of torture in line with international law. In March, authorities announced they would implement some of the recommendations on torture from the UN Human Rights Council's (HRC) Universal Periodic Review (UPR), including ensuring access for detainees to legal and medical assistance when in custody; and amending the criminal procedural code to ensure that the identity of law enforcement officers involved in arrests is recorded.

In September, authorities instituted the first-ever criminal prosecution under the newly amended article on torture. A court in Khatlon province sentenced police officer Mashraf Aliyev to seven years' imprisonment on charges of "torture" and "abuse of powers." Prosecutors charged Aliyev after Khoushvakht Mahmadsaid, a minor who was a suspect in a theft investigation, was found hanged at home in the village of Kulobod following torture and beatings that his family and lawyers allege Aliyev used to extract a forced confession.

Nongovernmental organizations and local media also reported on the death in September of Hamza Ikromozoda, 27, at the central detention center in Dushanbe. Relatives report that his body, which was returned to them on September 21, bore traces of torture, including burns from a heated iron. The center's officials refused to explain the cause of Ikromzoda's death to reporters, while a representative of the Penitentiary Control Board said "nobody tortures anyone in Tajik jails."

In October, a court in northern Tajikistan granted a Ministry of Justice petition to shut down one of Tajikistan's leading human rights organizations on charges that appeared politically motivated. The group, the Association of Young Lawyers (Amparo), investigates torture and serves as an advocate for the rights of army conscripts and other vulnerable groups. The rights group was shut down on what appear to be minor charges, including allegations that the group was conducting activities outside the province where they were originally registered and illegally operating a website.

For several years the group has been an active member of the Coalition against Torture, which brings together several leading Tajik civil society organizations that collect and report on torture allegations from across the country, and jointly encourage the government to meet its international commitments to end the practice.

Beyond investigating cases of torture, Amparo also conducted summer camps for youth to raise awareness about constitutional protections and international human rights norms. The Ministry of Justice filed a motion to liquidate Amparo on June 29, the day after ministry officials visited the group's Khujand office to conduct an unannounced, wide-ranging audit. The visit came just weeks after a representative of Amparo spoke publicly about the need to monitor reports of torture and severe forms of hazing in Tajikistan's army at a civil society seminar organized by the European Union in Dushanbe.

Freedom of Media

In 2012, Tajikistan witnessed further restrictions on media freedoms. Authorities frequently blocked access to critical websites, and continued to intimidate journalists. While July's decriminalization of libel was a step towards freedom of speech, the new legislation retained criminal sanctions for insulting the president.

Beginning in March, authorities ordered internet providers on several occasions to block access to independent local and international news and social networking sites. Following the publication of a critical article, the government blocked the Russian analysis site *zvezda.ru*. Three news sites that subsequently published the article were also blocked, as was Facebook, following user discussions deemed overly critical of the government.

In July and August, armed clashes in Gorno-Badakhshan prompted authorities to restrict, and at some points completely shut down, internet and telephone communications. News sites including the independent news site Asia Plus, as well as the BBC, RIA-Novosti, *Lenta.ru*, and *Centrasia.ru* that reported on the violence were blocked. Access to YouTube was also blocked after videos of demonstrations were posted.

Despite the absence of a clear definition of libel under Tajik law, state telecommunications chief Beg Zukhurov announced in July the formation of a "citizens' organization" to monitor online publications and websites for insulting or libelous content.

Journalists continue to suffer threats and violent attacks. On May 8, two unknown assailants beat unconscious Daler Sharifov, a state television reporter and host of the anti-corruption NGO, Step by Step. Also in May, two other journalists, Ravshan Yormakhmadov and Salim Shamsiddinov, were beaten in attacks that appeared to be connected to their work.

Freedom of Religion

Tajik authorities further tightened restrictions on religious freedoms, and due to newly adopted legislation, the government now extends far reaching controls over religious education and worship. According to a statement that the international religious freedom watchdog Forum 18 issued in August, authorities continue to try to suppress unregistered Muslim education throughout the country, brought administrative charges against Muslim teachers, and closed unregistered mosques.

In May, authorities closed the Muhammadiya mosque, one of Tajikistan's most popular, which is run by the family of Haji Akbar Turajonzoda, a theologian and charismatic leader during the country's civil war in the mid-1990s.

Authorities added further punishments, through changes to the administrative code that were enacted in July, for violating Tajikistan's restrictive religion law and increased the powers of the State Committee for Religious Affairs to administer punishments without investigation by police or prosecutors. The new provisions impose significant fines on those violating the religion law's tight restrictions on sending citizens abroad for religious education, teaching religious doctrines, and establishing ties with religious groups overseas.

The steady tightening of state controls led rights groups, religious groups, and international bodies in 2012 to continue to criticize the highly controversial Parental Responsibility law, which President Emomali Rahmon signed in August 2011. The law stipulates that parents must prevent their children from participating in religious activity, except for state-sanctioned religious education, until they are 18 years old.

Under the pretext of combating extremist threats, Tajikistan continues to ban several peaceful minority Muslim groups. Some Christian minority denominations, such as Jehovah's Witnesses, are similarly banned. Local media continued to report on prosecutions of alleged members of Hizb ut-Tahrir and the Islamic Movement of Uzbekistan.

Women's and Children's Rights

Women and girls in Tajikistan continue to face gender-based discrimination and violence at home. Despite a draft law that has been under discussion for many years, the government has yet to adopt a law prohibiting domestic violence.

In July, the country's Organization for Security and Co-operation in Europe (OSCE) mission hosted a meeting where civil society representatives spoke about the growing number of domestic violence cases, and the difficulties of holding perpetrators accountable and ensuring that victims can access courts. One major obstacle, for example, is the legal requirement that victims, rather than police or prosecutors, collect evidence of the domestic violence they have suffered before authorities will initiate charges.

Key International Actors

UN Special Rapporteur on Torture Juan Méndez visited Tajikistan in May 2012. In a statement issued at the end of his mission, Mendez reported that "pressure on detainees, mostly as a means to extract confessions is practiced ... in various forms, including threats, beatings (with fists and kicking but also with hard objects) and sometimes by applying electric shock." The statement added that Mendez was "persuaded that [torture] happens often enough and in a wide variety of settings that it will take a very concerted effort to abolish it or to reduce it sharply."

In June, the EU organized a civil society seminar in Dushanbe focused on torture, and submitted the resulting recommendations to the government.

In March, in response to the worsening climate for religious freedom, the United States Commission on International Religious Freedom (USCIRF) downgraded

Tajikistan from its "watch list" of violators of religious freedom, naming it a "country of particular concern." The commission censured Tajik authorities for "systematic, ongoing, and egregious violations of freedom of religion or belief," stating that Dushanbe "suppresses and punishes all religious activity independent of state control, and imprisons individuals on unproven criminal allegations linked to religious activity or affiliation."

Turkey

Turkey's Justice and Development Party (AKP) government maintained economic growth in 2012 despite a slowdown, and a strong focus on developing a leading regional role, but failed to take convincing steps to address the country's worsening domestic human rights record and democratic deficit. Prosecutors and courts continued to use terrorism laws to prosecute and prolong incarceration of thousands of Kurdish political activists, human rights defenders, students, journalists, and trade unionists. Free speech and media remained restricted, and there were ongoing serious violations of fair trial rights.

Cross-party parliamentary work on a new constitution to uphold the rule of law and fundamental rights continued, although it was unclear at this writing whether the government and opposition would reach a consensus on key issues such as minority rights, fundamental freedoms, and definition of citizenship.

In March, parliament passed legislation to establish a National Human Rights Institution, and in June, an ombudsman institution to examine complaints against public officials at every level. Human rights groups criticized government control of appointments to the national institution's board and its failure to meet the test of independence from the government that United Nations guidelines recommend.

With the AKP condoning the mass incarceration of Kurdish activists, and the outlawed Kurdistan Workers' Party (PKK) escalating attacks, 2012 saw a spiraling descent into violence with armed clashes resulting in hundreds of deaths of soldiers and PKK members, significantly higher than recent years. Throughout 2012, the PKK kidnapped security personnel and civilians, including local politicians, one parliamentarian, and teachers, releasing them periodically. A suspected PKK attack in Gaziantep in August left nine civilians dead, including four children. The non-resolution of the Kurdish issue remained the single greatest obstacle to progress on human rights in Turkey.

Turkey was amongst neighbouring countries most affected by the armed conflict in Syria. By mid-October 2012, the number of Syrian refugees hosted by Turkey had risen to around 100,000. Turkey responded to an October cross-border mortar attack from Syria that killed five Turkish citizens in Akçakale with military fire, and the Turkish parliament authorized the use of military force against Syria.

Freedom of Expression, Association, and Assembly

While there is open debate in Turkey, government policies, laws and the administration of justice continue to lag behind international standards. Prosecutors frequently prosecute individuals for non-violent speech and writing, and politicians sue their critics for criminal defamation. Courts convict with insufficient consideration for the obligation to protect freedom of expression. The government has yet to carry out a comprehensive review of all existing laws that restrict freedom of expression, although a draft reform package was expected in late 2012 at this writing.

The so-called third judicial reform package came into force in July 2012. It ends short-term bans of newspapers and journals, which the European Court of Human Rights (ECtHR) has criticized as censorship. The law suspends investigations, prosecutions, and convictions of speech-related offenses carrying a maximum sentence of five years that were committed before December 31, 2011, provided the offense is not repeated within three years. Critics fear the threat of reinstatement will continue to muzzle debate.

Thousands charged with alleged terrorism offenses remained in prison throughout their trials, although some well-known figures like academic Büşra Ersanlı, publisher Ragip Zarakolu, and journalists Ahmet Şık and Nedim Şener were released, though still face terrorism charges for activities amounting to exercising their rights to non-violent expression and association. Most of those in prison are Kurdish activists and officials of the Peace and Democracy Party (BDP) standing trial for alleged links to the Union of Kurdistan Communities (KCK/TM), a body connected with the PKK, and in general the ongoing clampdown on the BDP and Kurdish political activism intensified in 2012 with repeated waves of mass arrests and prolonged imprisonment. The trial of 44 Journalists and media workers (31 in detention) began in Istanbul in September. They are among the many journalists, students, lawyers, trade unionists, and human rights defenders imprisoned and prosecuted for association with the KCK.

There was little progress in the main Diyarbakır KCK trial of 175 defendants. The 108 defendants who have been in custody for up to three-and-a half-years include Human Rights Association Diyarbakir branch head Muharrem Erbey, six serving local BDP mayors, several local BDP council members, and five elected BDP parliamentarians.

Two parliamentarians from the Republican People's Party and one from the Nationalist Action Party, defendants in the Ergenekon and Sledgehammer trials, discussed below, are also in prison and unable to take up their parliamentary seats. Holding elected politicians, who have not been convicted of an offence, in prolonged pre-trial detention and failure to ensure they receive a prompt trial in line with international standards undermines the right to political representation and participation.

The July reform package also introduced and encouraged alternatives to remand imprisonment pending trial. But there were no indications that courts apply this to those already held in prolonged prison detention under terrorism charges. Statistics from the Ministry of Justice from May, the most recent data available, indicated that 8,995 of the 125,000-strong prison population were charged with terrorism offenses, and that half of the 8,995 were awaiting an initial verdict.

Violence against Women

In March, parliament passed the new Law on the Protection of the Family and Prevention of Violence against Women, aiming to offer protection from violence and practical support to family members and all women regardless of marital status, and to establish local centers to implement and monitor the law's application. Violence in the home remained endemic, with police and courts regularly failing to protect women who have applied for protection orders.

Torture, Ill-Treatment, and Use of Lethal Force by Security Forces

Police violence against demonstrators and in public places remained a serious problem. Authorities often mask the problem by investigating individuals who report police abuse for resisting police dispersal or police orders rather than their complaints.

In June, a cell phone video captured a group of uniformed police officers in Istanbul attacking and beating Ahmet Koca, a 22-year-old man. The incident reportedly began with an altercation between the police and Koca over right of way. The General Security Directorate's inspectorate imposed disciplinary sanctions on seven of the eleven police officers involved, including docking wages and reassigning them to other provinces, but did not dismiss any. The prosecutor's criminal investigation against them was pending at this writing. In contrast, following police complaints, a separate prosecutor indicted Koca for resisting police during the same incident. He faces up to five years' imprisonment in a trial that was expected to begin in December.

The government's July decision to promote police officer Sedat Selim Ay to a senior position in the Istanbul Security Directorate's Anti-Terror Branch provoked media and opposition-party criticism and seriously conflicts with efforts to eradicate torture and impunity. Selim Ay avoided final conviction for torture, despite the findings by two domestic courts that he had committed torture in the 1990s when working as an officer in the anti-terror branch, only because one case exceeded the statute of limitations in force and another sentence was suspended. He or his unit were the subject of European Court of Human Rights (ECtHR) rulings in 2006, 2009, and 2010 that Turkey failed to prevent, conduct effective investigations into, or provide a remedy for torture.

Combating Impunity

Great obstacles remain in securing justice for victims of abuses by police, military, and state officials. There was no progress in uncovering the full plot behind the January 2007 murder of journalist Hrant Dink or probing state collusion, though in January 2012 an Istanbul court convicted Yasin Hayal of "directing" Ogun Samast (already convicted of the murder in a juvenile court) and others as accessories to murder. The Dink family immediately appealed these findings and called for a new investigation.

In December 2011, a Turkish airforce aerial bombardment killed 34 Kurdish villagers, many of them young people and children, near Uludere, close to the Iraqi-Kurdistan border, as they crossed back into Turkey with smuggled goods. Concerns that there had been an official cover-up were fuelled by repeated statements by the prime minister rejecting calls by media, opposition parties, and families of victims for a full explanation of the incident, lack of a public inquiry, and a protracted criminal investigation that had not concluded at this writing.

Increasing public discussion of the past, and emerging new information on past crimes, provided new momentum for criminal investigations into human rights abuses by state actors in the 1980s and 1990s. In October, a brigadier general stood trial for the murder or disappearance of 13 villagers in Derik, in southeast Turkey, in the early 1990s. Without government-initiated reform of statutes of limitations some cases of murder and torture are likely to be deemed time-barred for prosecution under applicable laws. Fair trial standards also require strengthening. The trial of the two surviving leaders of the September 12, 1980 military coup began in April, an important opportunity to secure justice for the gross human rights violations committed after the coup.

The trial of the alleged anti-AKP coup plotters (known as the Ergenekon gang) whose defendants include senior retired military, police, mafia, journalists, and academics, continued after separate proceedings were combined in April into one trial. In a related coup plot trial of serving military personnel (known as the Sledgehammer case), 324 out of 365 defendants received sentences of 13 to 20 years. All defendants were appealing their sentences at this writing. The serious fair trial concerns in these cases and the prolonged pre-trial detention of some defendants overshadowed the important contribution of these efforts to combat impunity of the military.

Key International Actors

Turkey's European Union accession negotiations remained stalled. The election of France's President François Hollande helped to improve French-Turkish relations. In October, the European Commission in its annual progress report voiced strong criticism in most areas relating to human rights, emphasizing the importance of work on a new constitution, and stressing "the Kurdish issue remains a key challenge for Turkey's democracy."

The United States government remains an important influence on Turkey, sharing military intelligence on PKK movements in northern Iraq. In May, the State Department's annual human rights report raised deficiencies in the justice system, free speech, and inadequate protection of women, children, and lesbian, gay, bisexual, and transgender (LGBT) persons as key concerns.

In January, a groundbreaking report by the Council of Europe (CoE) commissioner for human rights focused on "long-term, systemic problems in the administration of justice," and its negative impact on human rights.

In its October review of Turkey, the UN Human Rights Committee recommended reforms including amending the National Human Rights Institution law, introducing comprehensive anti-discrimination legislation, and addressing the vagueness of the definition of terrorism in law and prolonged pretrial detention.

Turkmenistan

Following February 2012 presidential elections, President Gurbanguly Berdymukhamedov retained unchallenged power, and Turkmenistan remains one of the world's most repressive countries.

The country is virtually closed to independent scrutiny, media and religious freedoms are subject to draconian restrictions, and human rights defenders and other activists face the constant threat of government reprisal. The government continues to use imprisonment as a tool for political retaliation.

Turkmenistan continued to expand relations with foreign governments and international organizations in 2012, but without meaningful outcomes for human rights.

Cult of Personality and Presidential Elections

President Berdymukhamedov, his relatives, and associates enjoy unlimited power and total control over all aspects of public life in Turkmenistan. In official publications Berdymukhamedov, who has been power since 2007, is known as *arkadag* (patron), and his cult of personality continued to grow during the year. In April 2012, for example, he won a carefully choreographed car race.

Berdymukhamedov was reelected president on February 12, 2012. According to the Central Election Committee (CEC), he received 97 percent of the vote with a nearly 97 percent turnout. Conditions for a competitive vote were so lacking that the Office for Democratic Institutions and Human Rights, part of the Organization for Security and Co-operation in Europe (OSCE), declined to send an election observation mission.

A law on political parties adopted in January 2012 envisaged for the first time the registration of parties other than the ruling party. In August, a close associate of Berdymukhamedov founded the Party of Industrialists and Entrepreneurs, but there is no indication that it will present meaningful political alternatives.

Civil Society

Turkmenistan's repressive atmosphere makes it extremely difficult for independent nongovernmental organizations to operate. Human rights and civil society activists and journalists, including those living in exile, face a constant threat of government reprisal.

In August, state security services warned at least four activists not to attend a meeting convened by the OSCE to welcome its new ambassador. In July, a state security official warned one activist not to try to meet OSCE Representative on Freedom of the Media Dunja Mijatović when she visited Ashgabat, the capital.

In February, Natalia Shabunts—one of the few openly active human rights defenders—found a bloody sheep's head on her doorstep in Ashgabat, one day after speaking about the presidential election with Radio Free Europe's Turkmen Service.

For more than four years, the authorities have refused to reinstate the confiscated passport of Gurbandurdy Durdykuliev, a dissident, who cannot receive his pension or disability allowance, and cannot move freely inside the country without it.

Freedom of Media and Information

The state controls all print and electronic media and it is very difficult for foreign media to cover Turkmenistan because they often cannot access the country.

Internet access remains limited and heavily state-controlled. The country's only internet service provider is state-operated, and political opposition websites are blocked. Internet cafes require visitors to present their passports. The government is known to monitor electronic and telephone communications.

In the lead-up to the presidential election, the website for the Turkmen Initiative for Human Rights (TIHR)—a Vienna-based exiled human rights group—was disabled for nine days due to hacking, and the website of the exiled Turkmen political opposition endured several days of denial-of-service attacks.

Holders of Gmail accounts in Turkmenistan could not access their e-mails between February 16 and 26, and for two weeks in June, internet users could not access *Ertir.com*, a web platform popular among young adults for social contact and political discussion.

Freedom of Movement

Turkmenistan's government continues to restrict the right to travel freely internationally by means of an informal and arbitrary system of travel bans commonly imposed on civil society activists and relatives of exiled dissidents.

After twice barring Bisengul Begdesenov, a former political prisoner, from traveling abroad, migration authorities finally allowed him to travel in May 2012.

Several incidents in 2012 indicated that Turkmen authorities still bar people from traveling abroad with valid Kyrgyz visas in their passports, continuing a practice begun in late 2009. In August 2012, the migration office of the Ashgabat airport without explanation barred a dozen students from travelling to Bulgaria and Russia to commence their studies. In October, Turkmen authorities barred a number of Turkmen citizens from traveling to seek medical treatment in neighboring Iran.

The Turkmen government continues to create travel obstacles for Turkmen citizens who also hold Russian passports. In December 2011, Turkmenistan Airlines warned travelers that from July 2013 tickets for destinations abroad will only be sold to holders of the new Turkmen international passport. The authorities use various pretexts to deny issuing new international passports to persons who continue to hold Russian passports, and require that they sign documents renouncing Russian citizenship.

Freedom of Religion

The right to freedom of thought, conscience, and religion is heavily restricted in Turkmenistan, where no congregations of unregistered religious groups or communities are allowed. Religious communities have been unable to register for years.

In February 2012, Ilmurad Nurliev, a Pentecostal pastor sentenced in 2010 to four years in prison on bogus swindling charges, was freed under a general amnesty.

According to Forum 18, an independent international religious freedom group, as of August 2012 at least four Jehovah's Witnesses who are conscientious objectors were imprisoned, and five received suspended prison sentences for evading military service.

Forum 18 also reported that local officials harassed and threatened several Protestants for printing religious materials without state approval. Among them was a 77-year-old Baptist who had tried to print a book of his own Christian poetry. Police questioned him and threatened to press criminal charges but did not do so.

In three separate trials held in August 2012, courts fined at least five Protestants in Lebap province, northeast Turkmenistan, for engaging in religious activity without state approval.

Political Prisoners and Enforced Disappearances

Unknown numbers of individuals continue to languish in Turkmen prisons on what appear to be politically motivated charges. The justice system lacks transparency, trials are closed in political cases, and the overall level of repression precludes independent human rights monitoring.

In April 2012, the International Committee of the Red Cross (ICRC) made one visit to one prison. The government has persistently denied access to the country for independent human rights monitors, including international NGOs and 10 United Nations special procedures whose requests for visits remain unanswered.

In March, the Turkmen foreign minister announced that Ovezgeldy Ataev and his wife had been released from prison. Ataev was the constitutionally designated successor of dictator Saparmurad Niyazov. He and his wife were arrested one month after Niyazov's death in 2007.

However, the government ignored calls by several UN bodies to release well-known political prisoners Annakurban Amanklychev and Sapardurdy Khajiev, who had worked with human rights organizations prior to their imprisonment in 2006. Political dissident Gulgeldy Annaniazov, arrested in 2008, also remains imprisoned. He is serving an 11-year sentence.

In October 2012, the authorities arrested Geldymyrat Nurmuhammedov, a former government minister who had openly criticized the government, and sent him to a detention center to allegedly undergo six months of forced treatment for drug addiction, even though he had no history of drug use.

Two popular singers, Murad Ovezov and Maksat Kakabaev, whom courts sentenced on bogus charges in 2011 to five and seven years' imprisonment respectively, remain behind bars. The sentences were retribution for their music and their involvement in a talk show that aired on a Turkish satellite channel in 2011. Kakabaev's father, brother, and brother-in-law—also sentenced in 2011 to two-year prison terms for the broadcast—remain in custody.

Several dozen persons convicted in relation to the November 2002 alleged assassination attempt on Saparmurat Niyazov—including former Foreign Minister Boris Shikhmuradov and Turkmenistan's former ambassador to the OSCE, Batyr Berdiev—remain victims of enforced disappearances. Their fate is unknown. Human Rights Watch is aware of unconfirmed reports that several defendants in the 2002 plot case have died in detention.

Sexual Orientation and Gender Identity

Homosexual conduct between men is criminalized with a maximum prison sentence of two years. The penal code does not mention same-sex relations between women. According to one local NGO, police sometimes blackmail and extort homosexual men due to their sexual orientation.

Illegal House Evictions in Ashgabat

In 2012, authorities in Ashgabat and the surrounding area failed to provide adequate compensation or redress to residents forcibly evicted and expropriated in previous years and whose homes were demolished without a court ruling. The demolitions made way for construction as part of massive urban renewal projects initiated in the late 1990s. Further demolitions are scheduled to continue through 2020 in some areas of Ashgabat.

Key International Actors

Several international actors continue to seek to leverage Turkmenistan's energy wealth, sidelining concerns about the government's human rights record. The European Union continued to press forward with a Partnership and Cooperation Agreement (PCA) with Turkmenistan, frozen since 1998 over human rights concerns, without requiring any human rights reforms in exchange. Throughout 2012, the European Parliament continued to hold up its necessary approval of the PCA over human rights concerns. At this writing, the European Parliament's vote on the PCA remained pending.

The United Nations Human Rights Committee reviewed Turkmenistan in March 2012, and issued a highly critical assessment highlighting the government's clampdown on freedom of expression and repression of civil society activism, torture, and ill-treatment in places of detention, and the lack of an independent judiciary. It directed the Turkmen government to report back within one year on measures taken to address them.

In October, the UN Committee on the Elimination of Discrimination against Women (CEDAW) issued its observations about the state of women's human rights in Turkmenistan, expressing deep concern in particular about women's disadvantaged and unequal status in many areas, including education, public life and decision-making, and the absence of specific legislation on violence against women, including domestic and sexual violence.

While in Turkmenistan for a July conference on media, the OSCE representative on freedom of the media called upon Central Asian states to guarantee freedom of media and expression online.

After having had no active projects on Turkmenistan since 1997, the World Bank is working to reengage in the country. It was unclear at this writing whether the bank will require improvements in governance as part of reengagement.

Ukraine

Ukraine's human rights record remained poor in 2012. Candidates and supporters faced violence and harassment from authorities ahead of October parliamentary elections. Opposition leader Yulia Tymoshenko alleged ill-treatment in prison, where she is serving a seven-year sentence, and two of her former political allies were imprisoned. The government extradited two asylum seekers. Lesbian, gay, bisexual, and transgender (LGBT) activists faced violence and harassment from nationalist groups. Parliament passed an anti-discrimination law and revised laws protecting asylum seekers. The European Union, United States,, and other countries criticized the country's deteriorating human rights situation.

Parliamentary Elections

Following the October 28 parliamentary elections, President Yanukovich's Party of Regions retained a majority of seats. The ultra-nationalist Svoboda party made it into parliament for the first time, securing 9 percent of seats. The absence of leading opposition figures as candidates marred the elections. The Organization for Security and Co-operation in Europe (OSCE) reported pre-election violations, including beatings of and threats against opposition candidates and campaign workers, and pressure on state employees and students to vote for the Party of Regions. The OSCE, EU, and US criticized the elections, citing irregularities, delays in vote-counting, and lack of transparency in electoral commissions. Election results were annulled in five districts because of irregularities.

The November 2011 parliamentary elections law failed to reflect recommendations of the Council of Europe's (CoE) Venice Commission and the OSCE; the law introduced a mixed majoritarian-parliamentary system, increased the threshold to enter parliament, and banned electoral blocks.

Rule of Law

In April, former Prime Minister Yulia Tymoshenko alleged that prison authorities in Kharkiv beat and denied her adequate medical care for chronic back problems. In May, Tymoshenko was transferred to a civilian hospital for treatment. Tymoshenko was sentenced to seven years in prison in 2011 on abuse of office charges related to a natural gas contract with Russia. In August, Ukraine's Specialized High Court rejected her appeal.

At least 20 former officials from Tymoshenko's government are under investigation or have been charged with alleged crimes. In February, a Kiev court sentenced Yuri Lutsenko, minister of interior under Tymoshenko, to four years in prison on charges of embezzlement and abuse of office. In August, Lutsenko was convicted on additional charges. In July, the European Court of Human Rights (ECtHR) found that Ukraine violated Lutsenko's right to liberty and security of person, with respect to both his arrest and ongoing detention. In April, a Kiev court sentenced former acting Defense Minister Valerii Ivashenko to five years in prison for abuse of office. Ivashenko was released on appeal.

Migration and Asylum

Amendments to the criminal procedure code brought it into line with international standards by specifying protection from refoulement for asylum seekers and prohibiting extradition of recognized refugees. However, Ukraine extradited two men recognized as refugees by the United Nations High Commissioner for Refugees (UNHCR) who faced a clear risk of torture. One was extradited to Russia in August and the other to Uzbekistan in September.

In January 2012, 58 Somali asylum seekers detained in Zhuravychi, northwestern Ukraine, went on hunger strike over severe delays in, and lack of access to, asylum claim application procedures. Local police suppressed the protest using tear gas and by beating detainees with batons. Some protesters received asylum following the incident.

In a report on Ukraine's implementation of benchmarks under visa liberalization negotiations, the EU found that despite 2011 reforms, some asylum law provisions still contradict international standards, including the short appeals period and the potential for agencies other than the state migration service to revoke refugee status.

Sexual Orientation and Gender Identity

On May 19, unidentified assailants defaced photographs at a Kiev exhibition depicting lesbian, gay, bisexual, and transgender (LGBT) families in Ukraine.

At a May 20 press conference, LGBT Pride organizers cancelled the march scheduled for that day in Kiev because police claimed they could not protect participants from potential violence from neo-Nazi and nationalist groups planning a protest at the same time and location.

After the press conference, five men beat Kiev Pride organizers Svyatoslav Sheremet and Maksim Kasyanchuk. The authorities opened a criminal investigation but failed to identify the suspects despite video recordings of the attack, and failed to consider the activists' sexual orientation or activism in the investigation.

In June, an unidentified man approached Kiev Pride head Taras Karasiichuk near his home, asked his sexual orientation, and beat him, breaking his jaw and giving him concussion. Investigators were unable to identify the attacker.

On July 2 and 9, neo-Nazis and nationalists verbally attacked and tore posters belonging to LGBT activists who were protesting in Kiev against two draft laws regarding "promotion of homosexuality" in the public domain and media. The first law, which imposes up to five years' imprisonment, was passed by parliament on October 2 in a first reading. The second law, claiming to "protect children," envisions administrative fines of up to US$1,500. On July 2, police intervened and detained one individual. On July 9, police who were present at the rally did not intervene.

Hate Crimes and Discrimination

Roma, Crimean Tatars, and other ethnic minorities faced violence from neo-Nazi groups. In September, for example, a group of unidentified people threw a

Molotov cocktail into a Roma settlement in Uzhgorod, southwestern Ukraine. Police subsequently provided the settlement with 24-hour protection.

In October, the ECtHR ruled that Ukraine failed to effectively investigate a similar attack in 2001 that killed five members of a Romani family.

In September 2012, parliament passed an anti-discrimination law, which prohibits discrimination in public services, courts, employment, healthcare, education, housing, and other areas. The law does not include sexual orientation, citizenship, occupation, political affiliation, or labor union membership as protected categories. President Viktor Yanukovych signed the bill despite calls from a coalition of 34 nongovernmental organizations to veto the legislation due to insufficient parliamentary review.

In July 2012, parliament passed a controversial state language law allowing the use of 18 minority languages in regions with at least 10 percent minority language speakers. Russian became a regional language in 13 out of 27 regions. The OSCE high commissioner for national minorities called the law "deeply divisive" for disproportionately favoring Russian while "removing most incentives for learning or using Ukrainian," and criticized the law's hasty adoption.

Civil Society

On August 1, two unidentified assailants attacked and beat environmental activist Volodymyr Honcharenko from Dnipropetrivsk. Honcharenko died from his injuries three days later. A few days before the attack, Honcharenko publicized allegations about radioactive scrap metal dumped in the city of Kryviy Rig, in southeastern Ukraine. The authorities have not identified a suspect in Honcharenko's death or investigated the environmental concerns.

The OSCE's September interim election report noted the lack of political pluralism on television. In 2011, TVi television station, the only remaining national broadcaster openly criticizing the ruling party, was denied a license under the transfer to digital broadcasting, forcing it to rely on cable networks. Several cable providers excluded TVi in the 2012 pre-election campaign, apparently under pressure. In September, a Kiev court ordered TVi to pay four million hryvnas ($485,000) in back taxes, nearly forcing the station's closure.

In August, investigators identified a former Kharkiv police officer as the main suspect in the murder of *Novy Styl* newspaper editor Vasyl Klymentyev, who disappeared in August 2010 after reporting on official corruption in Kharkiv.The suspect remained at large.

The ongoing trial of Oleksy Pukach, a senior ministry of interior official charged with murdering journalist Grihory Gongadze in 2000, remained closed. Human rights groups criticized the authorities' failure to investigate alleged pressure on investigators by other suspects.

In March 2012, parliament passed a new law on public associations simplifying registration procedures and expanding the scope of approved activities for NGOs, in response to CoE recommendations from 2007.

Health

Tens of thousands of patients with advanced cancer suffer from severe pain and other symptoms every year. In order to improve access to quality palliative care services, the government took several preliminary steps to make oral morphine available. At this writing, the government was also considering adopting new drug regulations that remove many barriers to accessing strong pain medications.

Ukraine continued to slowly expand the number of people with opioid drug dependence receiving opiate substitution treatment—a key HIV prevention intervention—but remained far from meeting medical need. In prisons, which hold many injecting drug users, opiate substitution treatment remained unavailable.

Key International Actors

Ukraine's international partners repeatedly criticized Ukraine's deteriorating human rights record.

A May 2012 report by the European Commission and a September statement by Stefan Füle, the commissioner for enlargement and neighborhood policy, stressed that a proposed association agreement between the EU and Ukraine hinges upon concrete actions on human rights concerns, including politically motivated prosecutions, fair and transparent elections, judiciary reform, free-dom of media and association, and ill-treatment in detention.

The UN's Office of the High Commissioner for Human Rights (OHCHR), the EU, US, and others condemned the draft laws on propaganda of homosexuality.

Leaders from the United Kingdom, Italy, Germany, and France boycotted the Union of European Football Associations (UEFA) European Football Championship in Ukraine in July to protest Tymoshenko's imprisonment and alleged ill-treatment.

The US repeatedly criticized the cases against Tymoshenko and Lutsenko as politically motivated and called for their release. The US Embassy in Kiev criti-cized amendments to the Law on Procuracy for failing to balance law enforce-ment and the judiciary and protect the presumption of innocence.

The UN Human Rights Council's (HRC) Universal Periodic Review (UPR) in October called on Ukraine to combat racism and xenophobia, enact legislation that protects LGBT people from discrimination, and ensure fair trial rights and freedom of expression.

Uzbekistan

Uzbekistan's human rights record remains atrocious, with no meaningful improvements in 2012. Torture is endemic in the criminal justice system. Authorities intensified their crackdown on civil society activists, opposition members, and journalists, and continued to persecute religious believers who worship outside strict state controls.

Freedom of expression is severely limited. The government continues to sponsor forced child labor during the cotton harvest. Authorities still deny justice for the 2005 Andijan massacre, in which government forces shot and killed hundreds of protesters, most of them unarmed. 2012 marked 10 years since Uzbekistan allowed a United Nations special rapporteur to visit the country.

Despite the government's persistent refusal to address concerns about its abysmal human rights record, the United States and European Union continued to advance closer relations with Tashkent in 2012, seeking cooperation with the war in Afghanistan.

Human Rights Defenders and Independent Journalists

Authorities regularly threaten, imprison, and torture rights defenders and civil society activists, and block international rights groups and media outlets from operating in Uzbekistan.

In 2012, the Uzbek government continued to hold at least 10 rights defenders in prison on wrongful charges, and has brought charges against others because of their human rights work. The 10 are: Solijon Abdurakhmanov, Azam Formonov, Nosim Isakov, Gaibullo Jalilov, Rasul Khudainasarov, Ganihon Mamatkhanov, Yuldash Rasulov, Dilmurod Saidov, Akzam Turgunov, and Gulnaza Yuldasheva.

Yuldasheva was sentenced in July to seven years on trumped-up fraud charges for investigating police involvement in human trafficking. Another activist, Jamshid Karimov, was reportedly released from a psychiatric ward in 2011 but has "disappeared," prompting fears he was re-detained. Several imprisoned activists are in serious ill-health and have been tortured in prison.

Other journalists and opposition figures remain imprisoned on politically moti-vated charges. In January, days before his 13-year sentence was to expire, Muhammad Bekjanov, editor of the opposition newspaper *Erk*, was given an additional five-year sentence for allegedly violating prison rules. Bekjanov has been jailed since 1999, and along with another jailed journalist, Yusuf Ruzimuradov, has been imprisoned longer than any other reporter worldwide, according to the Committee to Protect Journalists.

On February 8, the government-controlled bar association upheld a ruling to dis-bar one of Uzbekistan's leading defense lawyers, Ruhiddin Komilov.

In separate incidents in March, authorities deported two foreign reporters, the BBC's Natalia Antelava and Viktoriya Ivleva of Russia's *Novaya Gazeta* newspa-per, when they arrived at Tashkent airport.

On March 26, journalist Viktor Krymzalov was convicted of defamation for an article published without a byline. The plaintiff "assumed" the article was writ-ten by Krymzalov, who denied he was the author.

On April 6, a Tashkent court fined journalist Elena Bondar US$3,700 on charges of "propagat[ing] ethnic or religious hatred" in connection with research she conducted on the pending closure of a university. Bondar and other journalists believed that the charges, devoid of any substance, were leveled in response to her record of independent reporting for news outlets whose websites are sys-tematically blocked by authorities, such as the independent news portal *www.ferghana.ru*.

Members of the Human Rights Alliance, an Uzbek rights group, were regularly subjected to arbitrary detention and house arrest in 2012. On February 28, activist Abdullo Tojiboi-ugli went to Tashkent's City Hall to picket authorities. Police detained him minutes after he began. He was sentenced for "minor hooli-ganism" and fined 70 times the minimum wage.

On March 2, the 20th anniversary of Uzbekistan's accession to the UN, Elena Urlaeva, head of the Human Rights Alliance; Tojiboi-ugli; and activists Shukhrat Rustamov, Nasiba Ashirmatova, Ada Kim, Gulchekhra Turopova, and Zoya Yangurazova planned to march to the residence of President Islam Karimov.

Police placed them under house arrest as they gathered in Urlaeva's home. Urlaeva and Tojiboi-ugli were able to leave but were later detained and released several hours later.

On May 5, activist Gulshan Karaeva posted on the internet that she had refused a demand by Uzbekistan's National Security Services (SNB) to cooperate as an informant. Days later, unknown assailants attacked her in the street.

In September, during the peak of the cotton harvest, authorities arrested Uktam Pardaev, a rights activist well known for reporting on police abuses, torture, and forced labor. Pardaev was beaten by several officers during the initial arrest and then held for over 15 days on minor administrative charges of "hooliganism" and "resisting arrest." Pardaev and other observers believe he was arrested to prevent him from monitoring the rights of children and adults who are mobilized and forced to pick cotton during the annual harvest.

Due to the increasing government crackdown, a branch office of Ezgulik (Goodness), the country's only registered human rights organization, was forced to close, and several rights activists and journalists were forced to flee the country.

The government also pursued activists and opposition figures living in exile.

In February, an unknown assailant shot prominent Uzbek exiled religious leader Imam Obidhon-kori Nazarov in Sweden. Nazarov was one of Uzbekistan's most popular religious figures in the 1990s until the government shut down his mosque, forcing him and thousands of his followers into exile. The assassination attempt came after years of death threats and intimidation. In July, Sweden's Chief Prosecutor Krister Petersson stated that Uzbekistan's secret services were probably behind the attack.

In April, authorities aired a 20-minute television program accusing France-based activist Nadejda Atayeva, president of the Association of Human Rights in Central Asia, of stealing millions of dollars, and calling for her extradition to Uzbekistan. The film came days after Atayeva had publicly called for an investigation into an assassination attempt on Nazarov.

The Andijan Massacre

The government continues to refuse an independent investigation into the 2005 massacre of hundreds of citizens in Andijan, who had gathered to protest socio-economic problems and civil and political grievances in the country in connection with the government's prosecution of local business leaders on charges of terrorism. The Uzbek government's persistent refusal to allow an independent international investigation has denied justice to victims and failed to bring to account those responsible. Authorities continue to persecute anyone suspected of having participated in, or witnessed, the atrocities.

The government also continues to intimidate family members of Andijan massacre survivors who have sought refuge abroad.

Criminal Justice, Torture, and Ill-Treatment

Torture remains rampant and continues to occur with near-total impunity. Detainees' rights are violated at each stage of investigations and trials, despite habeas corpus amendments passed in 2008. The government has failed to meaningfully implement recommendations to combat torture made by the UN special rapporteur in 2003 and other international bodies.

Suspects are not permitted access to lawyers, a critical safeguard against torture in pre-trial detention. Police coerce confessions from detainees using torture, including beatings with batons and plastic bottles, hanging by the wrists and ankles, rape, and sexual humiliation. Authorities routinely refuse to investigate allegations of abuse.

For example, in July, police in western Uzbekistan detained Jehovah's Witness Gulchehra Abdullayeva on suspicion of possessing "banned" literature. Abdullayeva complained that officers made her stand facing a wall for four hours with no food or water in the summer heat. They then placed a gas mask over her head and blocked the air supply.

Human Rights Watch continues to receive regular and credible reports of torture, including suspicious deaths in custody in pre-trial and post-conviction detention.

Freedom of Religion

Although Uzbekistan's Constitution ensures freedom of religion, authorities continued their multi-year campaign of arbitrary detention, arrest, and torture of Muslims who practice their faith outside state controls. Over 200 were arrested or convicted in 2012 on charges related to religious extremism.

Continuing a trend that began in 2008, followers of the late Turkish Muslim theologian Said Nursi were prosecuted for religious extremism, with dozens arrested or imprisoned in 2012.

Authorities also imprison and fine Christians who conduct peaceful religious activities for administrative offenses, such as illegal religious teaching.

Authorities extend sentences of religious prisoners for alleged violations of prison regulations. Such extensions occur without due process and add years to a prisoner's sentence, and appear aimed at keeping religious prisoners incarcerated indefinitely.

Forced Labor

Forced child and adult labor in the cotton sector remains a serious concern. The government took no meaningful steps to implement the two International Labour Organization (ILO) conventions on child labor, which it ratified in March 2008. Despite repeated requests, it continued to refuse the ILO access to monitor the harvest.

The government continues to force millions of schoolchildren, mainly aged 15 to 17 years old, but some as young as 9, to help with the cotton harvest for up to two months every year. Officials including police, municipal authorities, and school principals shut down schools, busing children to cotton fields where they are made to harvest cotton in line with established daily quotas. They live in filthy conditions, contract illnesses, miss school, and work daily from early morning until evening for little or no pay. In 2012, as in past years, authorities also forced adults, including schoolteachers, doctors, and other public sector employees, to participate.

Authorities regularly harass activists who try to document forced adult and child labor.

Key International Actors

The Uzbek government continued to refuse to cooperate with international institutions but faced virtually no consequences for its intransigence. For the past decade, it has denied access to all UN special monitors who have requested invitations—10 at this writing—and has failed to comply with recommendations that various expert bodies have made.

The EU's position on human rights remained disappointingly weak, with virtually no public expressions of concern about Uzbekistan's deteriorating record, and no policy consequences for the government's continued failure to meet the EU's reform expectations as articulated by EU foreign ministers in 2010. Bilateral meetings between the EU and Uzbekistan, including a Cooperation Committee meeting in Tashkent in July, yielded no known results for human rights. The EU did not seize the opportunity provided by the five-year anniversary of its strategy for Central Asia to engage in a critical rethinking of its approach.

The European Parliament voiced concern about Uzbekistan's poor record by adopting a highly critical resolution in December 2011, in which it rejected a proposed reduction of EU textile tariffs for Uzbekistan until conditions are met, including enabling the ILO to access the country. In September, for the second year in a row, Tashkent denied visas to a delegation from Germany's parliament that sought to meet Uzbek rights defenders.

In 2012, the US deepened its engagement with Uzbekistan. Since 2004, Congress had restricted assistance to Uzbekistan based on its deplorable rights record and further tightened restrictions following the Andijan massacre. However, on January 18, in a deeply troubling move and despite no meaningful improvements, the Obama administration exercised the authority Congress granted it to waive rights-related sanctions and restart military aid to Tashkent.

Uzbekistan is seen as a critical stop in the Northern Distribution Network (NDN) through which the US has sent non-lethal supplies to Afghanistan since 2009 as an alternative to unstable supply lines through Pakistan. US military contracts with Uzbek companies as part of this supply chain are potentially lucrative for those close to the Uzbek government.

Despite the State Department's re-designation of Uzbekistan as a "Country of Particular Concern" for violations of religious freedom, the US government retained a waiver on the sanctions outlined in the designation.

HUMAN
RIGHTS
WATCH

DEATH OF A DICTATOR

Bloody Vengeance in Sirte

WORLD REPORT
2013

MIDDLE EAST
AND NORTH AFRICA

Algeria

New laws adopted in January 2012, and the announcement in 2011 of an end to the 19-year-old state of emergency and of major constitutional and electoral reforms, did little to give Algerians more freedom to associate, form political parties, or express their opinions. Authorities relied on other repressive laws and regulations to stifle dissent and human rights activities, such as the 1991 law governing assembly that requires prior authorization for public demonstrations.

May's legislative elections gave the country's governing coalition, the National Liberation Front and the National Rally for Democracy, a majority of seats. Several parties, including a coalition of Islamist parties, accused the government of election fraud. Security forces and armed groups continued to enjoy broad impunity for atrocities committed during the civil war of the 1990s. The state offered compensation to families of persons forcibly disappeared in the 1990s, but provided no answers about their fates.

Freedom of Assembly

Throughout 2012, Algerian authorities continued to heavily restrict freedom of assembly, relying on preemptive techniques including blocking access to sites of planned demonstrations and arrests to prevent public protests even from getting under way, especially when the purpose of the demonstration was considered politically sensitive. For example, on April 20, police arrested 10 activists of the Youth Action Rally (Rassemblement Action Jeunesse, RAJ), a youth movement founded in 1992 around the themes of human rights and democratization, in front of the central post office while they were heading to a meeting with a French journalist, releasing them later the same day.

On April 26, police arrested several activists who were trying to demonstrate in front of the court of Sidi Mohamed in Algiers in solidarity with Abdelkader Kherba, a member of the National Committee to Defend the Rights of the Unemployed (Comité national pour la défense des droits des chômeurs, CNDDC) who had been arrested on April 18 and was on trial for direct incitement to unarmed gathering.

Among the groups most active in attempting to stage public demonstrations are independent professional unions, who sought better pay and work conditions. Authorities often prevented their activities in the capital by a heavy police presence and obtaining court injunctions.

Freedom of Association

The new Association Law, which parliament adopted on January 12, 2012, contains many new provisions that give sweeping powers to the government to control associations. The new law maintains the existing regime of prior approval for associations and gives authorities wide discretionary powers to refuse to grant legal status to new associations without first seeking a court order. They can, for example, reject an association whose purpose or goals are deemed "contrary to public order, public morality, and the provisions of existing laws and regulations." In addition, they can dissolve associations on broad grounds such as "interfering with the internal affairs of the country," "harming its sovereignty," receiving foreign funding without prior authorization, and exercising activities outside of those provided for in their statutes. Involvement in a non-recognized, suspended, or dissolved association can result in imprisonment.

Freedom of Speech

The new law on information eliminated prison sentences for speech offenses committed by journalists, including defaming or showing contempt for the president, state institutions, or courts. However, it raised the level of the fines imposed. It has also broadened restrictions on journalists by requiring respect for vaguely worded objectives and providing for sanctions that can be imposed by a professional ethics board in cases of infringements. Speech offenses continue to pervade the penal code, which provides for up to three years prison sentence for tracts, bulletins, or flyers that "may harm the national interest" and up to one year for defaming or insulting the president of the Republic, the parliament, the army, or state institutions.

The ordinance on the implementation of the Charter for Peace and National Reconciliation, was adopted in February 2006 and offers immunity from prosecution both for security force members and members of armed groups, with certain exceptions, for atrocities they perpetrated during the civil strife of the 1990s. The charter also seeks to muzzle continuing debate and scrutiny of the atrocities committed during that period: it provides for up to five years in prison for anyone who "exploits the wounds of the national tragedy, with a view to harming Algerian institutions, harming the honor of its agents who served it with dignity, or tarnishing the image of Algeria at the international level." No one is known to have been imprisoned under this provision.

Judicial Harassment

In 2012, authorities charged several human rights activists and union leaders with various crimes for the peaceful exercise of their right to assemble or for voicing their support for strikes or demonstrations. On April 18, authorities arrested CNDDC member Abdelkader Kherba in front of the Sidi Mohamed court-house in Algiers where he had come to show solidarity with court clerks, who had been on strike for 10 days and were staging a sit-in to demand better working conditions for court personnel. A court convicted Kherba on charges of "direct incitement to an unarmed gathering" and "interfering with the work of an institution" and handed him a one year suspended prison sentence. Kherba was arrested a second time on August 21 and charged with "insulting an official." He was later acquitted.

Yacine Zaid, trade unionist and president of the Laghouat section of the Algerian League for the Defense of Human Rights (LADDH), and three other union leaders were charged with "inciting an unarmed gathering" under article 100 of the criminal code. The police had arrested them on April 26 while they were holding a sit-in in front the Sidi Mohamed courthouse to denounce the prosecution of Kherba.

Accountability for Past Crimes

Khaled Nezzar, minister of defense from 1992 to 1994, was arrested by Swiss police in October 2011, interrogated, and later released on bail. The Swiss Federal Criminal Court (FCC) commenced investigations against him for war crimes and crimes against humanity for his role in commanding the harsh repression of armed resistance and civil unrest in Algeria during the 1990s. On

July 31, 2012, the Swiss FCC rejected his appeal to drop the case. He remains on bail pending the completion of the investigation and the commencement of the trial.

Women

Algeria adopted a new law on January 12, 2012, imposing a 30 percent quota of women on the electoral lists of parties for legislative, municipal, and communal elections. Women won 31 percent of the seats in the parliament elected on May 10. However, the Algerian code of personal status discriminates against women in matters of parental authority, divorce and inheritance.

Terrorism and Counterterrorism

Armed groups staged attacks far less frequently than during the 1990s. However, Al Qaeda in the Islamic Maghreb (AQIM) continued to launch fatal attacks, directed mostly at military and police targets.

After Bouteflika lifted the state of emergency, authorities transferred suspected terrorists who had been in "assigned residence" for several years without any judicial review to official places of detention. However, long delays tainted their trials as the judges refused to summon key witnesses and postponed their hearings repeatedly. In 2012, the trials of Hassan Hattab, Amari Saifi, and Kamel Djermane, three suspected terrorists who were held for several years under secret detention and brought to trial after the lifting of the state of emergency, were postponed several times.

Algeria strengthened its role as a regional player on counterterrorism, for example hosting the inaugural meeting of the Global Counterterrorism Forum, a multilateral group that the US created to broaden counterterrorism discussions beyond the western, industrialized countries.

Key International Actors

François Hollande, the new president of France, issued a statement on October 17, 2012, in which he recognized the responsibility of the French republic in the killing of scores of Algerian protesters in Paris on October 17, 1961.

The European Union, which already has an "association agreement" with Algeria, agreed to provide Algeria with €172 million (approximately US$234 million) in aid between 2011 and 2013. Western countries consider Algeria as a major partner in combating terrorism. With the takeover of northern Mali in April by Islamist radical groups, the US and European countries increased their counter-terrorism cooperation with Algeria.

The UN special rapporteur on torture, the UN Working Groups on Enforced or Involuntary Disappearances (WGEID) and on Arbitrary Detention (WGAD), and the special rapporteur on summary, arbitrary or extrajudicial executions continued to be denied access to Algeria.

UN High Commissioner for Human Rights Navi Pillay visited Algeria on September 18 and 19. She praised growing freedom of expression in the media but expressed concern for the continued clampdown on freedom of assembly and association. During the visit, the government said it would accept WGEID's long-standing request for a mission.

Bahrain

The Bahrain Independent Commission of Inquiry (BICI), which King Hamad bin Isa al-Khalifa appointed to investigate the government's response to pro-democracy demonstrations in February and March 2011, issued its findings in late November 2011. The BICI concluded that security forces had used excessive force against peaceful protesters, and had arbitrarily arrested, tortured, ill-treated, and denied them fair trials.

The BICI proposed recommendations to redress those violations and for the first time, the authorities investigated some low-ranking security officials in connection with torture allegations. However, the government failed to fully implement the commission's core recommendations, notably the release of protest leaders convicted for exercising their right to freedom of expression and peaceful assembly; and the investigation of high-ranking officials responsible for abuses.

Security forces used excessive force in 2012 to disperse anti-government protests. Authorities jailed human rights defenders and individuals for participating in peaceful demonstrations and criticizing officials.

In November 2011, the Ministry of Social Development cancelled the election results of the Bahrain Lawyers' Society (BLS) and reinstated the previous board and president. In July 2012, a court ruling sought by the Ministry of Justice dissolved the opposition Islamic Action Association (Amal).

Freedom of Assembly

After lifting the state of emergency on June 1, 2011, authorities permitted opposition political societies to hold several rallies, which remained peaceful, but clashes with security forces regularly broke out when protesters held demonstrations in Shia villages.

In 2012, authorities increasingly rejected permit requests from opposition groups and riot police often used force to disperse peaceful protests. On June 22, riot police fired tear gas and shot sound grenades at close range to disperse a peaceful demonstration in Manama, the capital. A tear gas canister seriously injured one protestor in the head. During protests in which demonstrators threw rocks and Molotov cocktails, police often attacked crowds indiscriminately using teargas, sound grenades, and pellet guns.

While abuse in detention appears to have declined during 2012, police routinely beat protesters, in some cases severely, at the time of arrest and during their transfer to police stations.

According to opposition groups, at least 26 protesters and bystanders died in protest-related injuries between November 1, 2011 and November 1, 2012. Many of the deaths have been attributed to excessive use of teargas. The government claimed that anti-government protesters injured 1,500 policemen in 2012.

Prosecuting Government Critics

Human Rights Watch documented serious and systematic due process violations in trials of opposition leaders and activists before Bahrain's special military courts in 2011. Violations included denying the right to counsel and failure to investigate credible allegations of torture and ill-treatment during interrogation.

The BICI reached a similar conclusion, saying that military courts convicted around 300 people solely for exercising their right to freedom of expression and assembly.

Despite authorities' promise to review military courts' sentences for speech crimes and to void convictions imposed after grossly unfair trials, the protest leaders and many others remained behind bars at this writing.

On August 2, 2012, authorities arrested rights activist Zainab al-Khawaja for allegedly tearing up a picture of the king and participating in illegal demonstrations. On September 25, a court sentenced her to two months' imprisonment for destroying government property.

On August 16, Nabeel Rajab, president of the Bahrain Center for Human Rights, was sentenced to three years' imprisonment for calling for and participating in peaceful demonstrations without permits between January and March 2012.

HUMAN
RIGHTS
WATCH

NO JUSTICE IN BAHRAIN
Unfair Trials in Military and Civilian Court

Earlier, Rajab received a three-month sentence for "tweets" that called for the prime minister to step down. On August 23, an appeals court overturned the Twitter conviction, but at this writing he remained in prison pending appeal on the illegal assembly convictions. The court's verdict gave no indication that Rajab had called for, or participated in, violence.

On September 4, 2012, a civilian appeals court upheld the military court's convictions and long sentences of 20 protest leaders.

On November 6, 2012, the Interior Ministry revoked the citizenship of the 31 people, including opposition political activists, lawyers, and rights activists, accusing them of "damaging the security of the state." The order left most of those affected stateless.

Freedom of Association

On August 12, the government approved a draft law for nongovernmental organizations. Local associations complained that authorities had not consulted them and that they were not aware of the law's adoption until media reported it.

On November 30, 2011, a few days after the Bahraini Lawyers' Society elected new board members, Minister of Social Development Fatima al-Balooshi cancelled the election results, declaring that the society had "not complied with the legal procedures." Al-Balooshi reinstated the previous board and president to manage the affairs of the society. The society challenged the order, saying it had notified the ministry of the election two weeks before holding its election as required by law.

On June 3, 2012, the Ministry of Justice filed a lawsuit accusing the opposition Islamic Action Association (Amal) of violating provisions of the 2006 political societies law, such as failing to "convene a general conference for more than four years" and "taking its decisions from a religious authority that calls openly for violence and incites hatred." An administrative court ordered the group's dissolution on July 9. At this writing, a court of appeals was reviewing the ruling.

Accountability

The BICI noted that Bahrain's security forces operated within a "culture of impunity" and concluded that the abuses "could not have happened without the knowledge of higher echelons of the command structure" of the security forces.

The authorities claimed they investigated 122 officers for alleged torture and unlawful killings documented by the BICI. However, the few prosecutions involve mainly low-ranking officers, most of them non-Bahraini. On September 27, a criminal court sentenced a Bahraini police lieutenant—the highest-ranking security official known to have been convicted for abuses—to seven years in prison for the murder of Hani Abd al-Aziz Jumaa in March 2011.

Investigations and prosecutions have so far not included any high-ranking official at the Interior Ministry or the National Security Agency. No official from the Bahrain Defense Forces is known to have been investigated, although the military played a leading role in the 2011 campaign of repression.

Migrant Workers

More than 460,000 migrant workers, primarily from Asia, work in Bahrain on temporary contracts in construction, domestic work, and other services. Human Rights Watch documented abuses against migrant workers in Bahrain such as unpaid wages, passport confiscation, unsafe housing, excessive work hours, physical abuse, and forced labor. In July, King Hamad signed a new private sector labor law that contained improved safety regulations, measures to combat human trafficking, and granted migrants greater ability to leave their employers. The law extends a few protections to domestic workers such as annual leave, but excludes them from most key provisions, including limits to hours of work, weekly days off, and ability to leave their employers. Authorities inadequately enforce existing laws against withholding wages, charging recruitment fees, and confiscating passports.

Enforcement of a 2009 law sharply reduced transport of workers in open-air trucks, previously a cause of many injuries and deaths.

Women's Rights

Unlike for Sunni Muslims, Bahrain has no codified personal status law dealing with marriage, divorce, child custody, and inheritance for Shia Muslims. Such matters are left to the judge's discretion in sharia courts. The penal code does not adequately address violence against women. There are no provisions on sexual harassment or domestic abuse. Rape can be punished with life in prison, but marital rape is not recognized as a crime.

Key International Actors

Bahrain hosts the United States Navy's Fifth Fleet. In May, the US resumed the sale of some military equipment to Bahrain, a "major non-NATO ally," after having suspended sales in the wake of the government's repression of peaceful protests. The US continued to restrict provision of arms that could be used for domestic repression, such as helicopters and armored vehicles. After the February 2011 attacks on demonstrators the United Kingdom and France announced they would cut off security and military sales and assistance. In February 2012, several news organizations reported that the UK continued to supply arms to Bahrain.

On March 15, the European Parliament adopted a resolution calling on Bahrain to respect freedom of expression and assembly, and unconditionally release peaceful protesters and political prisoners.

In May, the United Nations Human Rights Council (HRC) examined Bahrain's human rights record under the Universal Periodic Review (UPR) process. Many countries expressed concern about the human rights crisis in Bahrain, lack of accountability for abuses, and restrictions on international rights groups' access to the country. In September, Bahrain officially accepted most of the recommendations it received during the UPR, including holding security forces accountable for rights abuses and the immediate release of prisoners convicted for participating in peaceful demonstrations, but at this writing the government had not implemented these key recommendations.

HUMAN RIGHTS WATCH

For A Better Life

Migrant Worker Abuse in Bahrain and the Government Reform Agenda

On June 28, countries, including France and Germany, condemned ongoing violations in Bahrain through a joint declaration read by Switzerland during a HRC debate. The statement called on Bahrain to implement fully the recommendations of the BICI, including releasing political prisoners and holding officials responsible for abuses accountable for their actions.

Egypt

The rocky transition from autocratic and military rule continued following the 2011 ouster of President Hosni Mubarak. Egypt held democratic parliamentary and presidential elections, and ended 31 years of rule under emergency laws. However, serious human rights problems remain, including police abuse and impunity; restrictions on freedom of expression, association, and religion; and limits on the rights of women and workers.

Egypt's first post-revolution parliament, elected between November 2011 and January 2012, failed to make significant human rights reforms before it was dissolved by the Supreme Constitutional Court on June 14 because the election law was deemed unconstitutional. Three days after the dissolution of parliament, the Supreme Council of the Armed Forces (SCAF), which had taken power after Mubarak's ouster, passed an addendum to the constitutional declaration giving itself legislative powers, and a substantive role in drafting the constitution and limiting the powers of the new president.

On June 24, however, Muslim Brotherhood leader Mohamed Morsy was declared winner of the presidential elections, and on August 12 he repealed the SCAF addendum and ordered the retirement of Field Marshal Mohamed Hussein Tantawy and Lieutenant General Sami Anan, the two most senior members of the SCAF. On November 22, President Morsy issued a constitutional declaration granting his decrees and laws immunity from judicial oversight, and dismissing the sitting public prosecutor, a move greeted with uproar and strikes by the judiciary. On November 30, the 100-person assembly started voting on the draft constitution, with a referendum due to take place 15 days after the final draft is approved.

Freedom of Expression

Overall, there was an increase in prosecutions under restrictive laws from the Mubarak era that penalize defamation and "spreading false information," and security services continued to arrest and abuse journalists during protests. Security services assaulted, arrested, and tortured journalists and protesters during protests outside the Ministry of Interior in February and outside the Ministry of Defense in May.

Following President Morsy's election, the authorities ordered the closure of one TV station and censored at least three editions of newspapers. The public prosecutor filed criminal defamation charges against at least nine journalists in connection with their writing or broadcasting. In November, the minister of justice appointed an investigative judge to interrogate a number of journalists and activists on charges of "insulting the judiciary." In 2012, prosecutors interrogated or indicted at least 15 individuals on criminal charges of "insulting religion." In September, a court in Assiout sentenced Bishoy Kamel to six years' imprisonment for "insulting Islam."

In the same month, the blasphemy trial opened of Alber Saber, whose atheist beliefs led to his indictment on charges of insulting Islam and Christianity. Media freedom activists criticized the upper house of parliament, the Shura Council, for failing to include independent journalists in their appointments of the new editors of state newspapers. In August, President Morsy amended the press law to cancel pretrial detention for journalists after a judge ordered the detention of Islam Afifi, editor of *Dustoor* newpaper, after he was charged with defamation.

Police, Military Torture and Abuses

Police continued to use torture in police stations and at points of arrest, mostly during investigations in regular criminal cases, but also in some political cases, such as the torture of protesters arrested in Cairo in August and November. Police torture led to at least 11 deaths in custody cases. Police have also continued to use excessive and sometimes lethal force, both in policing demonstrations and in regular policing. Torture by the military also took place. In May, military officers arrested at least 350 protesters, including 16 women after a protest near the Ministry of Defense in Cairo turned violent. Those released over the following days gave consistent accounts of torture and beatings during arrest and in detention.

Since December 2011, police and army members have arrested and detained over 300 children who participated in protests. Children arrested at protests at the Ministry of Interior in February 2012, and in front of the American embassy in September reported beatings that in some cases amounted to torture. Despite the high numbers of juvenile detainees, including children living and working on the street, authorities consistently detained children with adults in police stations and brought them before regular prosecutors, instead of referring them to the juvenile justice system as required by law.

Impunity for Police and Military Abuses

There has been no process of transitional justice in Egypt to account for the crimes of the Mubarak era nor has there been real accountability for the violence during the January 2011 uprising, which left 846 dead. On June 2, a judge sentenced Hosni Mubarak and his former Minister of Interior Habib al-Adly to life imprisonment for failing to protect protesters from attacks by "criminal foreign elements." The judge acquitted the four other assistant ministers of interior because he was not convinced that "the police was connected with the protester deaths."

Prosecutions of the violence against protesters resulted in 35 trials of at least 200 mid- and high-level police officials around the country. At this writing, 26 trials had concluded with 21 acquittals on grounds of lack of evidence or self-defense, with five trials resulting in sentences that were mostly in absentia or suspended. At this writing, only two police officers were actually serving time for the excessive and illegal use of force against protesters. In July, Morsy established a fact-finding committee and in November, he passed a law creating a dedicated court to try cases of violence against protesters.

There has been no accountability for the military's involvement in the torture and beating of hundreds of demonstrators on February 25, March 9, April 9, May 4, and December 17, 2011. In March 2012, a military judge acquitted the only military officer on trial for the sexual assault against seven female protesters in a military prison in March 2011 under the guise of "virginity tests." In September, a military court sentenced three military officers to two years' imprisonment for driving the armored vehicles that ran over and killed 13 protesters in front of Maspero television building in October 2011. However, there was no investigation into the shooting of 14 other protesters on the same day. No other military officers have been held accountable for abuses since the January uprising.

Freedom of Association

Parliamentarians have been drafting a new law on associations which was nearing completion when a court dissolved parliament. Meanwhile, Egypt continues to apply the repressive Mubarak-era law 84 on associations. In 2011, the government launched investigations into scores of unregistered nongovernmental organizations), in many cases human rights organizations whose registration had been blocked by the security agencies. As a result, 43 NGO workers, 16 Egyptians and 27 foreign nationals, were charged with operating "unlicensed" groups under the existing law on associations. The trial started in March.

Security agencies also blocked funding for human rights projects at registered NGOs, leading to a freeze on activities and a loss of staff. The New Women Foundation, a local women's rights group, sued the government after being unable to obtain approval for incoming foreign funds for ongoing projects.

Emergency Law and Military Trials

On May 31, the state of emergency expired in Egypt and was not renewed, ending 31 years of uninterrupted emergency rule. By the end of August, the Ministry of the Interior had released all those detained under the administrative detention provisions of the emergency law. At least eight trials referred to court during the state of emergency continued before notorious Emergency State Security Courts, which do not provide the right of appeal. In September, Morsy appointed 3,649 judges to these courts, but human rights groups mounted a legal challenged to this move arguing that Morsy did not have the authority to order such mass appointments outside a state of emergency.

Military prosecutors continued to try civilians before military courts, including after President Morsy took power. In November, military police arrested 25 civilians during an attempted eviction on the island of Qursays in Cairo, and prosecutors ordered their detention pending trial before a military court. A committee set up by presidential decree to review all those convicted by military courts recommended the release of up to 700 prisoners by presidential pardon, but failed to recommend the retrial of the remaining 1,100 prisoners convicted by military courts on "security" grounds.

Freedom of Religion and Sectarian Violence

Incidents of sectarian violence between Copts and Muslims continued throughout 2012 with no new prosecutions or serious investigations, with the exception of the investigation into sectarian violence in Dahshour, Giza, where prosecutors ordered the detention of nine suspects. On February 1, police and local religious and political leaders ordered the eviction of eight Christian families after Muslim residents sacked homes and shops of Christian residents in the village of Sharbat, near Alexandria. The eviction was overturned two weeks later after parliamentarians visited the area, but by the end of the year, police had still failed to prosecute anyone for the violence despite a police report identifying suspects.

On May 21, 2012, in the southern city of Minya an Emergency State Security court, which does not meet fair trial standards, sentenced 12 Christians to life in prison and acquitted 8 Muslim defendants who had been charged in connection with clashes between Muslims and Christians in April 2011. The clashes had left two Muslims dead, several wounded from both sides, and scores of Christian shops and homes torched.

Women's and Girls' Rights

Systematic sexual harassment of women and girls in public spaces continued without serious attempts by the government to intervene and halt, or deter the practice. For example, in June, mobs attacked and sexually assaulted at least six Egyptian and foreign women in Tahrir square. Although prosecutors investigated two of those incidents, they did not refer any cases to court in 2012, and overall the government failed to prioritize addressing violence against women. After a public outcry, proposals by Islamist members of parliament to lower the minimum age of marriage, repeal the right of a woman to initiate no-fault divorce, and decriminalize female genital mutilation (FGM) were shelved. The Constituent Assembly drafted provisions on women's rights that further embedded the Sharia law exception to equality in the new draft constitution, echoing Egypt's reservations to women's rights conventions which remain in place.

Refugee, Asylum Seeker, and Migrant Rights

Police arrested hundreds of Eritreans and Ethiopians in the Sinai on their way to Israel, detained them indefinitely in local police stations, and denied them access to the Office of the United Nations High Commissioner for Refugees (UNHCR), in violation of their right to make an asylum claim. Egyptian border police shot at unarmed African migrants attempting to cross the Sinai border into Israel, reportedly killing 12 between January and November. African migrants continued to report torture and rape at the hands of traffickers operating in Sinai, but the government failed to address or acknowledge the problem. Investigations of human trafficking were rare, and focused solely on cases of foreign domestic workers or Egyptians being trafficked abroad.

Labor Rights

Strikes, sit-ins, and labor protests continued in the face of demands for economic and social rights. The new parliament refused to issue the draft trade unions law that had been drafted by former Minister of Labor Mohamed Bor'i in consultation with independent trade unions, leaving hundreds of new independent trade unions without legal protection or access to services. Military and police officers used excessive force on at least seven occasions to disperse labor protests and sit-ins. Workers faced disciplinary measures and at times, criminal investigations in connection with organizing strikes or independent trade unions.

Key International Actors

Relations between Egypt and the United States deteriorated in January when the public prosecutor indicted staff of four American NGOs, and subsequently imposed a travel ban on them. For the first time, the US government seriously

HUMAN
RIGHTS
WATCH

THE ROAD AHEAD

A Human Rights Agenda for Egypt's New Parliament

considered suspending military aid on the basis of legislation that required certification of human rights progress in Egypt as a condition for aid. In February, Secretary of State Hillary Clinton waived the human rights conditions after the Egyptian authorities lifted the travel ban on the indicted foreign nationals, even though the government continued its prosecution of Egyptian NGO workers.

Later in the year, however, the US government placed considerable pressure on the Egyptian military to respect the results of the presidential elections and allow a transfer of authority to the victorious Muslim Brotherhood candidate. In November, the European Union held a high-level task force with Egyptian officials in Cairo, where it approved a US$6.4billion aid package to Egypt, of which at least $900 million was conditioned on good governance.

Iran

In 2012, Iranian authorities prohibited opposition candidates from participating in parliamentary elections. They have held prominent opposition leaders under house arrest for more than a year-and-a-half. Executions, especially for drug-related offenses, continued at high rates. The government targeted civil society activists, especially lawyers, rights defenders, students, and journalists, and announced plans for the first phase of a *halal* (legitimate) internet. Authorities continued to block access to the United Nations special rapporteur on Iran.

Freedom of Assembly, Association, and Voting

Security forces prevented peaceful demonstrations marking the anniversary of February 2011 anti-government protests. Opposition leaders Mir Hossein Mousavi, Zahra Rahnavard, and Mehdi Karroubi remained under house arrest at this writing.

On February 21, the Guardian Council, an unelected body of 12 religious jurists, disqualified more than 2,000 candidates running for seats in Iran's March 2 parliamentary election on ill-defined criteria. The Iranian judiciary announced on December 31, 2011, that calls for an election boycott constituted "a crime."

At this writing, dozens of activists affiliated with banned opposition parties, labor unions, and student groups were in prison. The judiciary targeted independent and unregistered trade unions. In May, a revolutionary court in Tehran sentenced Reza Shahabi, a prominent labor rights activist working with the Syndicate of Workers of Tehran and Suburbs Bus Company, to six years' imprisonment for "conspiracy against the national security" and "propaganda against the regime."

In January, the Ministry of Culture ordered the dissolution of the country's largest independent film guild, the House of Cinema, allegedly because it was not properly registered.

Death Penalty

In 2011 authorities carried out more than 600 executions, second only to China, according to Amnesty International. Crimes punishable by death include murder, rape, trafficking and possessing drugs, armed robbery, espionage, sodomy, adultery, and apostasy.

The majority of those executed in recent years have been convicted of drug-related offenses following flawed trials in revolutionary courts. The number of executions increased following the entry into force in late December 2010 of an amended anti-narcotics law.

Iran leads the world in the execution of juvenile offenders (i.e. individuals under 18 when they allegedly committed the crime). Iranian law allows capital punishment for persons who have reached puberty, defined as 9 for girls and 15 for boys. In late 2012, there were more than 100 juvenile offenders on death row.

In January 2012, the Guardian Council approved the final text of an amended penal code. Children convicted for "discretionary crimes" such as drug-related offenses would no longer be sentenced to death under the amended code, but a judge may still sentence to death juveniles convicted of crimes such as rape, sodomy, and murder if he determines that the child understood the nature and consequences of the crime, a vague standard susceptible to abuse.

Authorities have executed at least 30 people since January 2010 on the charge of *moharebeh* ("enmity against God") or "sowing corruption on earth" for their alleged ties to armed groups. Since May 2011, authorities have executed at least 11 Iranian Arab men and a 16-year-old boy in Ahvaz's Karun prison for their alleged links to groups involved in attacking security forces.

As of September 2012, at least 28 Kurdish prisoners were awaiting execution on national security charges, including *moharebeh*.

Freedom of Expression and Information

According to Reporters Without Borders, 48 journalists and bloggers were in Iran's prisons as of August 2012. On April 4, a revolutionary court notified

HUMAN
RIGHTS
WATCH

Codifying Repression
An Assessment of Iran's New Penal Code

Mansoureh Behkish, a prominent blogger and supporter of the Mourning Mothers, that she had been sentenced to four-and-a half-years for "propagating against the regime" and "assembly and collusion against national security." Behkish had been active on behalf of families of victims of the 2009 post-election crackdown and 1988 prison massacres.

On September 2, 2012, authorities summoned journalist Jila Baniyaghoob to Evin prison to serve a one-year sentence for "spreading propaganda against the regime" and "insulting the president." Authorities also banned Baniyaghoob from practicing journalism for 30 years. Baniyaghoob's husband, Bahman Ahmadi-Amoui, is serving a five-year prison sentence on similar charges.

On November 6, authorities notified family members of blogger Sattar Beheshti that he had died in custody following his arrest on October 30. In response to international and domestic pressure, and allegations that Beheshti has been tortured, Iran's judiciary announced on November 11 that it would launch an investigation into what happened, and hold anyone responsible for wrongdoing accountable.

The government systematically blocked websites, slowed internet speeds, and jammed foreign satellite broadcasts. In March 2011, authorities announced that they would soon launch a *halal*—legitimate—internet to protect Iran from socially and morally corrupt content. In September, they announced that the first phase had been implemented in most provinces.

Human Rights Defenders

On March 4, prominent rights lawyer Abdolfattah Soltani learned that a revolutionary court had sentenced him to 18 years in prison, barred him from practicing law for 20 years, and ordered that he serve his sentence in Borajan, a city more than 600 kilometers south of Tehran. Prosecutors charged Soltani with "propaganda against the state," assembly and collusion against the state, and establishing the Center for Human Rights Defenders (CHRD), which Soltani co-founded with Nobel peace laureate Shirin Ebadi. An appeals court later reduced Soltani's sentence to 13 years and reversed the ban on practicing law. The same day, an appeals court issued a six-year sentence for Narges Mohammadi, a CHRD spokesperson, on similar charges.

In April, an appeals court informed defense lawyer Mohammad Ali Dadkhah that it had upheld his nine-year sentence on charges related to his interviews with foreign media and membership of CHRD. The court also sentenced Dadkhah to fines and corporal punishment (in the form of lashes) and banned him from teaching for 10 years.

Women's Rights

Iranian women face discrimination in personal status matters related to marriage, divorce, inheritance, and child custody. A woman needs her male guardian's approval for marriage regardless of her age, and cannot pass on her nationality to her foreign-born spouse or their children. A woman may not obtain a passport or travel outside the country without the written permission of a male guardian.

Several universities banned female enrollment in several academic fields, including engineering and the sciences, and set quotas limiting the number of women in university courses as well as gender segregation in several higher education facilities.

Treatment of Minorities

The government denies freedom of religion to adherents of the Baha'i faith, Iran's largest non-Muslim religious minority. Authorities conducted a campaign targeting Baha'is in the northern city of Semnan. According to the Baha'i International Community, at least 17 Baha'i-owned businesses have been shut down, and 22 Baha'is have been sentenced to prison terms ranging from 6 months to 6 years since 2009.There were 111 Baha'is detained in Iran's prisons as of September 2012.

Authorities discriminate in political participation and employment against non-Shiite Muslim minorities, including Sunnis, who account for about 10 percent of the population. They also prevent Sunnis from constructing mosques in major cities and conducting separate Eid prayers. Government targeting of Sufis, particularly members of the Nematollahi Gonabadi sect, continued unabated.

In September, authorities released Yousef Nadarkhani, the pastor of a 400-member Church of Iran congregation in northern Iran, after almost three years' imprisonment on the charge of apostasy, which carries the death penalty. Authorities reduced Nadarkhani's charge to "evangelizing to Muslims" and commuted his sentence to three years' imprisonment, which he had already served. According to Ahmed Shaheed, the special rapporteur on human rights in Iran, authorities have arbitrarily arrested and detained over 300 Christians, the majority of them evangelicals or Protestants, since June 2010.

The government restricted cultural and political activities among the country's Azeri, Kurdish, Arab, and Baluch minorities. Security forces detained, tortured, and executed dozens of Arab activists in southwestern Khuzestan province since 2011. According to Arab minority rights activists, at least six people have been tortured to death in custody in connection with anti-government demonstrations that swept Khuzestan province between April 2011 and February 2012.

Key International Actors

On August 11, President Barack Obama signed new legislation into law expanding United States sanctions in the form of asset freezes and travel bans against human rights violators in Iran.

In March, the European Union reinforced its restrictive measures adopted in response to serious human rights violations in Iran and prolonged them by 12 months. These moves came on top of expanded sanctions aimed at blocking Iran's alleged efforts to acquire nuclear weapons.

On March 7, Ahmed Shaheed released his second report, documenting a "striking pattern of violations." Later that month, the UN Human Rights Council (HRC) renewed the mandate of the special rapporteur, established in 2011. In October, UN Secretary-General Ban Ki-moon released his annual report on the situation of human rights in Iran, saying he was "deeply troubled" by continuing violations in that country. Later that month, Shaheed released his third report, which also provided a "deeply troubling picture of the overall human rights situation" in Iran.

The UN Office of Drug Control (UNODC) continued to provide financial support to law enforcement projects to combat drug trafficking in Iran despite guidelines that require it to temporarily freeze or withdraw support in cases where executions for drug-related offenses continue.

Iraq

Human rights conditions in Iraq remain poor, particularly for detainees, journalists, activists, and women and girls. Security forces continued to arbitrarily detain and torture detainees, holding some of them outside the custody of the Justice Ministry. The Justice Ministry announced a record number of executions in 2012, but provided little information about the identities of those executed.

Iraq security forces continued to respond to peaceful protest with intimidation, threats, violence, and arrests of protesters and journalists. Security forces and pro-government non-state actors harassed journalists and media organizations critical of the government.

In April, Iraq's parliament passed a law criminalizing human trafficking, but has yet to effectively implement it. The Kurdistan Regional Government (KRG) has not taken steps to implement a 2011 law banning female genital mutilation (FGM).

Hundreds of civilians and police were killed in spates of violence, including targeted assassinations, amid a political crisis that has dragged on since December 2011.

Detention, Torture, and Executions

Forces controlled by the Defense, Interior, and Justice Ministries, as well as elite forces reporting directly to the prime minister's office, continued arbitrary detentions of a broad spectrum of detainees, including in secret prisons outside the purview of the Interior and Justice ministries. Despite a Justice Ministry announcement in March 2011 that it would close the Camp Honor secret detention facility—where Human Rights Watch documented systematic torture—HRW received information from multiple sources that the prison continued to be used as late as March 2012.

Several detainees reported being tortured after mass arrest campaigns in late 2011 and March 2012, the latter in preparation for an Arab League summit in Baghdad, in what arresting officers characterized as "precautionary" measures to prevent terrorist attacks. Six detainees released in April reported that interrogators told them that they were being held to curb criminal activity during the summit and any "embarrassing" public protests.

Vice President Tariq Hashimi's former guard, whose body bore wounds suggesting torture, died in government custody in March, and poet Irfan Ahmed Mohammed died in KRG police custody in August. Authorities have not released investigation results for either case.

Government officials reported that 70 percent of prisons are over capacity, with large numbers of detainees held in lengthy pre-trial detention without judicial review. Inmates in numerous prisons, including the women's facility in Rusafa prison complex in Baghdad, suffer from overcrowding and lack of sufficient access to food and water.

The Justice Ministry announced 129 executions as of mid-November 2012, up from 68 in 2011. Under Iraqi law, 48 offenses are subject to the death penalty, including offenses recently criminalized in the Countertrafficking Law.

Freedom of Assembly

Security forces continued to respond to peaceful protests with intimidation, threats, violence, and arrests of protesters. On February 17, hundreds of security forces of the KRG surrounded a peaceful demonstration in Sulaimaniya's Sara Square. Dozens of men in civilian clothing attacked protesters and made many arrests.

In Baghdad, security forces blocked hundreds of protesters from reaching demonstrations in Tahrir Square on February 25. Up to 1,000 armed personnel amassed on side streets, informing approaching protesters that they had a long list of names of people to arrest and that they would arrest even those with names "similar" to those on the list.

Freedom of Expression

The environment for journalists remained oppressive in 2012. The Iraqi parliament was at this writing considering a number of laws restricting the media and freedom of expression and assembly, including the draft Law on the Freedom of

Expression of Opinion, Assembly, and Peaceful Demonstration, and a draft law regulating the organization of political parties that punishes expression "violating public morals" and conveying "immoral messages." In September, the Federal Supreme Court denied a petition by a local press freedom organization to repeal the Journalists Protection Law on the basis that it fails to offer meaningful protection to journalists and restricts access to information.

The Committee to Protect Journalists (CPJ) ranked Iraq at the top of its 2012 Impunity Index, which focuses on unsolved journalist murders, and reported that there have been no convictions for murders of journalists since 2003. Iraqi authorities made no arrests for the murder of Hadi al-Mahdi, a journalist critical of the government, killed in September 2011. Another journalist, Zardasht Osman, was abducted and murdered after publishing a satirical article about KRG president Massoud Barzani in 2010. The KRG never released details of the investigation into his death.

On May 8, the National Communications and Media Commission of Iraq (NCMC) asked the Interior Ministry to "take the necessary legal measures" against 44 foreign and Iraqi media outlets it stated were operating illegally. The media outlets remained open at this writing, but registration is difficult, leaving them vulnerable to closure.

A draft law on information technology crimes awaits parliamentary ratification. One article provides for life imprisonment and large fines for vaguely defined crimes, such as "intentionally" using computer devices and information networks to undermine the country's "supreme economic, political, military, or security interests."

Women's and Girls' Rights

Many Iraqi women have lost their husbands as a result of armed conflict, generalized violence, and displacement. The resulting financial hardship has made them vulnerable to trafficking for sexual exploitation and prostitution.

The parliament passed a countertrafficking law in April that outlines government obligations and provides for prosecution of traffickers. Iraqi authorities announced the arrest of a Baghdad trafficking ringleader in September, but little

HUMAN
RIGHTS
WATCH

Iraq's Information Crimes Law

Badly Written Provisions and Draconian Punishments
Violate Due Process and Free Speech

has been done to prosecute other people accused of trafficking, or to take measures to prevent it. Victims of trafficking continue to report having passports confiscated and being prevented from obtaining visas and new identification papers, leaving them vulnerable to arrest and unable to access health care.

In June 2011, the KRG parliament passed the Family Violence Bill, which includes provisions criminalizing forced and child marriages; abuse of girls and women; and a total ban on FGM. Implementation of the law is poor, and dozens of girls and practitioners said that they had either undergone or performed FGM since the law was passed. The authorities took no measures to investigate these cases.

Other Vulnerable Groups

In March, Iraq witnessed a string of attacks against young people with socially non-conforming appearances, including gender non-conforming and gay men and those who identify as "emo"—a subculture characterized by distinctive clothes and musical tastes. Local human rights groups, community activists, and media reported numerous deaths of these youths. Rather than undertaking measures to protect targeted individuals, the Interior Ministry said reports of attacks on those suspected of homosexual conduct or who appeared "emo" were "fabricated" and "groundless" and took no measure to prosecute or arrest attackers.

In January, Iraq ratified the Convention on the Rights of Persons with Disabilities (CRPD). However, Iraq's government has failed to take the necessary steps to ensure that persons with disabilities do not face discrimination, as the CRPD requires, and to ensure access to their rights to education, employment, personal mobility, health care, and comprehensive rehabilitation services and programs, among other things. Large numbers of Iraqis with disabilities—including those resulting from conflicts, disease, and non-war-related injuries—are unable to find support for integration into their local communities.

In October, a study published in the Environmental Contamination and Toxicology bulletin found "compelling evidence" to link increased rates of mis-

MIDDLE EAST AND NORTH AFRICA

carriages and developmental disabilities in children in Fallujah and Basrah to environmental toxins left by US military operations in those areas.

Refugees and Displacement

According to the United Nations high commissioner for refugees, nearly 30,000 Syrian refugees have fled to Iraq since armed conflict began in Syria in 2011. Iraq closed the al-Qaim border to Syrian refugees in August. The government reopened the crossing in September but stated that it would not admit young Syrian men.

The Iraqi government has no adequate plan for the return of Iraqis who have been displaced internally or those who have fled to neighboring countries. In July, Iraq's government assisted in returning thousands of Iraqis from Syria, providing flights and bus tickets to returnees, but the government has failed to assist them in finding housing or jobs. Thousands of displaced persons within Iraq continue to reside in squatter settlements without access to basic necessities such as clean water, electricity, and sanitation. Many are widows with few employment prospects.

In September, the UN nearly completed the transfer within Iraq of about 3,200 members of the exiled Iranian opposition organization, the Mojahedin-e Khalq (MEK). The UN Assistance Mission for Iraq (UNAMI) oversaw their transfer from Camp Ashraf, a refugee camp and former military base, where the group had resided since 1986, to Camp Liberty, another former military base. The United States secretary of state approved the removal of the group from the State Department's list of designated terrorist organizations at the end of the same month.

Key International Actors

The US government has not sufficiently pressed the Maliki government to rein in corruption and serial human rights abuses.

Accountability for abuses committed by coalition forces in Iraq remains almost non-existent. On January 24, a military court sentenced Staff Sgt. Frank Wuterich to a reduction in rank and forfeited two-thirds of his pay for three months for leading the "Haditha Massacre"—in which US forces killed 24 unarmed Iraqi civilians, including women and children, in the town of Haditha in 2005. Wuterich, who pled guilty for negligent dereliction of duty for telling his men to "shoot first, ask questions later," was originally charged with murder. He avoided jail time.

In April, the British *Guardian* newspaper reported that Australian military personnel working in Iraq in 2003 transferred 64 detainees to a secret prison where CIA and MI6 carried out interrogations that year. Two of the detainees died during the transfer and may have been beaten to death by British soldiers, the paper said.

Israel/Palestine

Serious violations of international human rights and humanitarian law continued in 2012 in Israel and in the West Bank and Gaza. Renewed armed conflict between Israel and Hamas and armed groups in Gaza from November 14-21 involved unlawful attacks on civilians by both sides. At least 103 Palestinian civilians and 4 Israeli civilians died during the fighting, which ended after a ceasefire brokered by Egypt and the United States. Israeli forces killed at least four Palestinian civilians during the year off Gaza's coast and in the "no-go" zone on the Gaza side of the boundary fence. Israeli authorities destroyed homes and other property under discriminatory practices, forcibly displacing Palestinian residents of the West Bank, as well as Bedouin citizens of Israel.

In the West Bank, including East Jerusalem, Israeli settlers injured 151 Palestinians as of November 27. Israel imposed severe restrictions on Palestinians' right to freedom of movement, continued to build unlawful settlements in occupied territory, and arbitrarily detained Palestinians, including children and peaceful protesters.

Israel, operating in conjunction with Egypt, has impeded the rebuilding of Gaza's devastated economy by blocking virtually all exports from Gaza. Israel has also barred Gaza residents from traveling to the West Bank. Israel's use of lethal force against Palestinians close to Israel's border with Gaza deprived them of access to 35 percent of Gaza's farmland and 85 percent of its fishing waters. As part of the cease-fire agreement ending November's hostilities, Israel and Hamas were to negotiate reductions in these restrictions, which remained unclear at this writing.

Hamas authorities in Gaza carried out six judicial executions in 2012, including after unfair trials, and men whom witnesses said were members of Hamas's armed wing claimed responsibility for seven extrajudicial executions in November. The authorities frequently denied detainees access to their lawyers. Security forces conducted arbitrary arrests and tortured detainees. The authorities permitted some local human rights organizations to operate, but suppressed political dissent, free association, and peaceful assembly. Palestinian armed groups in Gaza launched more than 1,400 rockets that struck inside

Israel as of November 2012, killing three civilians; a mortar shell killed a fourth civilian. The vast majority of rockets were launched indiscriminately towards populated areas.

In the West Bank, Palestinian Authority (PA) security services beat peaceful demonstrators, detained and harassed journalists and online activists, and arbitrarily detained hundreds, including during waves of arrests in May and September. Credible allegations of torture committed by the PA's security services increased.

Gaza Strip

Israel

Israel Defense Forces (IDF) conducted aerial and artillery attacks in Gaza, including in response to rocket attacks on population centers in Israel by Palestinian armed groups. They also fatally shot at least five Palestinian civilians in the "no-go" zone inside Gaza's northern and eastern borders, as of November, according to the Israeli rights group B'Tselem.

In July, Israel amended the law governing the state's civil liability for wrongdoing to bar all compensation lawsuits against Israeli forces by Palestinians from Gaza. Palestinians from Gaza with ongoing cases were barred from traveling to Israeli courts to testify.

In August, a military court accepted a soldier's plea bargain and sentenced him to 45 days in prison for shooting his weapon without authorization in January 2009. The charge was reduced from manslaughter for killing a mother and daughter on the basis of discrepancies between soldiers' and Palestinian witnesses' accounts. The military investigation failed to re-interview witnesses to reconcile the accounts. The soldier was the fourth to be convicted of wrongdoing during Operation Cast Lead, and the second to serve prison time, despite many other cases of unlawful harm to civilians and civilian property.

Hamas prosecuted no one for unlawful attacks against Israeli civilians during the 2008-2009 conflict, or since.

In August, an Israeli civil court rejected a claim for damages by the family of Rachel Corrie, an American who was fatally crushed by an IDF armored bulldozer in Gaza in 2003 while attempting to prevent it from demolishing a home. The judge held that the military investigation into Corrie's death "did not have any faults," and that Israel was immune from liability because Corrie's death occurred during a "combat operation."

Blockade

Israel's punitive closure of the Gaza Strip, particularly the near-total blocking of exports from Gaza, continued to have severe consequences for the civilian population. Egypt also blocked all regular movement of goods at the crossing it controls. The World Bank reported that the "the severity of poverty has increased" among impoverished Gazans. More than 70 percent of Gaza's population receives humanitarian assistance.

Israel and Egypt allowed imports to Gaza that amounted to less than half of pre-closure levels, the United Nations reported, including construction materials for projects undertaken by international organizations. As of September, Gaza still had an estimated shortage of some 250 schools. In a ceasefire agreement with Hamas, announced on November 21, Israel agreed to negotiate via an Egyptian intermediary, "opening the [Gaza] crossings and facilitating the movement of people and transfer of goods."

Egypt, for its part, continued to ease restrictions on the movement of Palestinians at the Rafah crossing between Gaza and Egypt's Sinai. But as of November 2012, it still did not permit regular imports or exports of goods through Rafah, although it tended to turn a blind eye to commerce through an extensive network of tunnels.

"No-Go" Zone

Israeli forces continued to impose a "no-go" zone on lands within 500 meters inside Gaza from the armistice line with Israel by regularly firing on any Gazan in the vicinity; areas up to 1.5 kilometers from the Israeli perimeter fence were considered "high-risk" due to shootings by Israeli forces. As of November 4, 2012,

Israeli forces had killed five Palestinian civilians and wounded dozens of civilians in these zones, which comprise 35 percent of Gaza's agricultural land, according to the UN.

Israeli forces also fired on and confiscated Palestinian fishing boats that sailed more than 3 nautical miles from the coast, prohibiting access to 85 percent of Gaza's maritime area under international law. The Palestinian Center for Human Rights documented 49 attacks against Palestinian fishermen as of June 30. On September 27, Israeli forces killed a fisherman and wounded his brother as they were pulling in their nets a few meters from shore, near Gaza's northern boundary.

In the November 21 ceasefire agreement, Israel agreed to refrain from restricting Palestinians' internal freedom of movement and "targeting residents in border areas."

Hamas and Palestinian Armed Groups

Hamas and Palestinian armed groups launched more than 1,800 rockets toward Israeli population centers in 2012 as of November 21, compared with 293 rockets in 2011. Israel's anti-rocket system shot down at least 400 rockets headed towards Israeli population centers. A rocket that hit a residential building in Kiryat Malachi on November 15 killed three Israeli civilians. A mortar fired from Gaza on November 20 killed a civilian in the Bedouin village of Rejwan in Israel.

Rocket attacks from Gaza seriously wounded at least four Israeli civilians in March and November. A bus bombing in Tel Aviv on November 21 injured more than 20 civilians, one seriously; no group has taken responsibility for the attack.

The Hamas Ministry of Interior carried out six judicial death sentences. On July 17, Hamas executed by hanging Na'el Doghmosh following his conviction for murder. The appeals court increased his sentence from life imprisonment to death, in violation of Palestinian law, and did not address allegations that security forces had tortured him. Courts in Gaza have repeatedly accepted coerced confessions as evidence of guilt in other capital cases.

HUMAN
RIGHTS
WATCH

Abusive System
Failures of Criminal Justice in Gaza

In November, Hamas's armed wing extrajudicially executed seven men for allegedly collaborating with Israel. At least six of them had been sentenced to death, but were appealing their sentences when armed men took them from a detention center and killed them.

The internal security agency and Hamas police tortured or ill-treated 121 people as of October 31, according to complaints received by the Independent Commission for Human Rights (ICHR), a Palestinian rights body. The ICHR received 102 such complaints in all of 2011.

Hamas security forces assaulted, arbitrarily detained, and allegedly tortured civil society activists and peaceful protesters who had called for an end to the political split between Hamas and its rival, Fatah.

Hamas continued to ban three newspapers from Gaza printed in the West Bank.

Hamas security forces destroyed scores of homes, leaving hundreds of people homeless, without due process and with inadequate or no compensation, and in some cases using excessive force against protesters. In February, the Israel Land Administration demolished dozens of homes to widen a road in the Izbet Hamamiya neighborhood. In July, it evicted 132 families from the al-Rimal neighborhood, claiming that the homes were built illegally on "state land." A court appeal was pending at the time of the demolitions.

West Bank

Israel

The IDF in the West Bank killed at least two Palestinian civilians in circumstances that suggest the killings may have been unlawful. In July, Israeli forces at the al-Zayim checkpoint near East Jerusalem shot at a vehicle attempting to take Palestinian workers without permits to their jobs inside Israel, killing the driver as he attempted to flee the checkpoint, B'Tselem reported. In November, Israeli forces fatally shot Rashdi Tamimi, 31, with rubber bullets and one round of live ammunition at a close distance during a demonstration in Nabi Saleh village.

Israeli authorities took inadequate action against Israeli settlers who injured Palestinians and destroyed or damaged Palestinian mosques, homes, olive trees, cars, and other property. As of September 31, the UN reported 247 such attacks in 2012. In a positive step, police promptly arrested Israeli suspects in two high-profile cases, including a firebomb attack on a Palestinian taxi that burned six people, including five members of one family, and the severe beating of a Palestinian youth.

Settlement Building and Discriminatory Home Demolitions

In June 2012, Israeli media reported that the number of settlers had increased by 15,579 in the previous 12 months. In April, the government officially "authorized" three previously unrecognized settlements. In July, a committee established by Prime Minister Binyamin Netanyahu concluded that Israel is not an occupying power in the West Bank and settlements do not violate international law, an opinion not shared by the International Court of Justice (ICJ) or any other government.

As of November 27, Israeli authorities had demolished 568 Palestinian homes and other buildings in the West Bank (including East Jerusalem), displacing 1,014 people.

Building permits are difficult or impossible for Palestinians to obtain in East Jerusalem or in the 60 percent of the West Bank under exclusive Israeli control (Area C), whereas a separate planning process readily granted settlers new construction permits. Israel approved donor-funded construction of 14 schools and 5 clinics for Palestinians in Area C, but threatened entire Palestinian communities with demolition, such as 8 villages in an area designated as a military training zone.

Settlers continued to take over Palestinian homes in East Jerusalem, based in part on discriminatory laws that recognize Jewish ownership claims there from before 1948, but bar Palestinian ownership claims from that period in West Jerusalem.

HUMAN RIGHTS WATCH

"FORGET ABOUT HIM, HE'S NOT HERE"

Israel's Control of Palestinian Residency in the West Bank and Gaza

Freedom of Movement

Israel maintained onerous restrictions on the movement of Palestinians in the West Bank, including checkpoints, closure obstacles, and the separation barrier. Settlement-related movement restrictions forced around 190,000 Palestinians to take time-consuming detours rather than the most direct route to nearby cities, the UN reported.

Israel continued construction of the separation barrier around East Jerusalem. Some 85 percent of the barrier's route falls within the West Bank, isolating 11,000 Palestinians who are barred from traveling to Israel and who must cross the barrier to access livelihoods and services in the West Bank, and separated Palestinian farmers and landowners in 150 communities from their lands, the UN reported.

Arbitrary Detention and Detention of Children

Israeli military authorities detained Palestinians who advocated non-violent protest against Israeli settlements and the route of the separation barrier. In May, an Israeli military court sentenced Palestinian activist Bassem Tamimi to 13 months in prison for leading demonstrations against land confiscation, in violation of his right to peaceful assembly, and for urging children to throw stones. The conviction on the latter charge was based primarily on a child's coerced statement.

Israeli authorities continued to arrest children suspected of criminal offenses, usually stone-throwing, in their homes at night, at gunpoint, question them without a family member or a lawyer present, and coerce them to sign confessions in Hebrew, which they did not understand.

Israel allowed detainees from Gaza to have family visits, which it had suspended in 2007. As of October 31 Israel held 156 Palestinian administrative detainees without charge or trial on the basis of secret evidence.

Palestinian Authority

Complaints of torture and ill-treatment by West Bank PA security services increased compared to the same period last year, with the ICHR reporting 142 complaints as of October 31, as opposed to 112 complaints for all of 2011. In May and September, PA security services arbitrarily arrested scores of men without charge in the Jenin, Nablus, and Tubas governorates, and allegedly tortured dozens on suspicion of support for Hamas or attacks against the PA. In some cases, PA military courts continued to exercise jurisdiction over civilians.

The PA security services, and men in civilian clothes identified as security employees, violently dispersed peaceful protests, and assaulted and arbitrarily detained protesters and journalists. In several cases, security officials arrested and abused Palestinians who had posted criticisms of the PA online, including on their Facebook pages.

Palestinian courts in the West Bank have not found any security officers responsible for torture, arbitrary detention, or prior cases of unlawful deaths in custody. The PA did not publish any information indicating that it took disciplinary measures against or prosecuted individual officers whom witnesses and a government-commissioned report identified as responsible for brutally beating demonstrators and journalists in Ramallah's main square on June 30 and July 1.

Palestinian civilians injured 43 settlers in the West Bank as of November 27, the UN reported.

Israel

Bedouin citizens of Israel who live in "unrecognized" villages suffered discriminatory home demolitions on the basis that their homes were built illegally. Israeli authorities refused to prepare plans for the communities and to approve construction permits, and rejected plans submitted by the communities themselves, but have retroactively legalized Jewish-owned private farms and planned new Jewish communities in the same areas. In 2012, the Israel Land Administration demolished 47 Bedouin structures as of September, , not including tents erected by villagers from al-Arakib, which Israeli authorities have demolished 39 times the Bedouin-rights group Dukium reported.

There are an estimated 200,000 migrant workers in Israel. Most are indebted to recruiting agencies, beholden to a single employer for their livelihood, and unable to change jobs without their employer's consent. Government policies restrict migrant workers from forming families. The Ministry of Interior deports migrants who marry other migrants while in Israel, or who have children there, on the basis that these events indicate an intent to settle permanently in violation of their temporary work visas.

Israel continued to deny asylum seekers who entered the country irregularly from Egypt the right to a fair asylum process. In June, the Ministry of Interior began to implement the "anti-infiltration law," which provides for the indefinite detention of all border-crossers without access to lawyers, without exception for asylum seekers, and allows the military the discretion to prosecute them for the crime of "infiltration." Israeli forces repeatedly refused to allow groups of migrants who had reached a newly constructed border fence to enter the country or present asylum claims, and detained and forcibly returned other groups to Egyptian custody without considering their asylum application. Most of the asylum-seekers come from countries other than Egypt—predominately Eritrea and Sudan—but Egypt has not proven a safe or fair venue for adjudicating their claims.

Key International Actors

Israel has been the largest overall recipient of foreign aid from the US since World War II, receiving US$3 billion in military aid in 2012. In 2012, the US provided $100 million in assistance to Palestinian security forces and $396 million in economic support to the PA.

In April 2012, the International Criminal Court (ICC) Office of the Prosecutor closed its consideration of a 2009 Palestinian declaration seeking to accept ICC jurisdiction, stating it did not have the authority to determine whether Palestine was a "state" for the purposes of the ICC treaty.

On November 29, the UN General Assembly voted to recognize Palestine as a non-member observer state. Prior to the vote, Israel and the UK pressured Palestinian leaders not to join the ICC. It is unclear at this writing what effect the observer-state determination will have on the 2009 Palestinian declaration with the ICC.

The EU allocated €300 million (about $390,000,000) to the Palestinian territory for 2012, including €100 million (about $130,000,000) of 2011 credits to be spent in 2012.

Jordan

Jordanian authorities increasingly resorted to force, arrests, and politicized charges to respond to continuing demonstrations for political and economic reform. The fifth prime minister to serve since the protests started in January 2011, Abdullah Ensour, took over in October 2012.King Abdullah II has called for early parliamentary elections in January 2013 under a 2012 electoral law that opposition groups complain favors loyalist candidates.

Freedom of Expression

Jordan criminalizes speech that is critical of the king, government officials and institutions, Islam, as well as speech deemed defamatory to other persons. In 2010, a revision of the penal code increased penalties for some speech offenses and the 2010 Law on Information System Crimes extended these provisions to online expression. In September, amendments to the Press and Publications Law broadened speech restrictions on online publications, also holding website managers responsible for user comments.

In 2012, the legal aid unit of the Amman-based Center for Defending Freedom of Journalists assisted journalists with 10 ongoing criminal cases for speech in violation of articles 5 and 7 of the Press and Publications Law requiring journalists to be "objective."

In April, military prosecutors charged Jamal al-Muhtasab, editor of *Gerasanews* website, with "subverting the system of government" for an article concerning the king's supposed intervention in a corruption investigation. Al-Muhtasab spent several weeks in detention before being released on bail. The case was pending at this writing. In February, military prosecutors also charged Ahmad Oweidi al-'Abbadi, a former member of parliament, with subverting the system of government because he had peacefully advocated making Jordan a republic. He was also released on bail with the case pending. In January, the State Security Court (SSC) sentenced protester 'Uday Abu 'Issa to two years in prison for "undermining his majesty's dignity" because he had set fire to a poster with the king's picture in Madaba. The king pardoned Abu 'Issa in February.

Freedom of Assembly and Association

Under the amended Public Gatherings Law, which took effect in March 2011, Jordanians no longer required government permission to hold public meetings or demonstrations. However, during 2012 prosecutors began resorting instead to charging protesters with "unlawful gatherings," under article 165 of the penal code.

Hundreds of protests demanding political and economic reforms occurred in urban and rural areas throughout the kingdom. Groups calling themselves the Popular Youth Movement in many towns protested against corruption, the government's economic policies, and the new election law, and called for an end to military-dominated trials of civilians in the SSC.

The government's decision to lift gas and fuel subsidies in November fueled protests, some of them violent and featuring once-rare calls for the king's ouster. Security agencies arrested an estimated 250 people within the first two weeks of the protests; 89 of them were summoned to appear before the military prosecutor on charges that included unlawful gathering. Authorities dispersed protesters using teargas and rubber bullets.

Authorities continue to try protesters in SSCs, which under the Jordanian Constitution have jurisdiction only over high treason, espionage, terrorism, and drug charges. In March, security forces arrested at least eight protesters from the southern town of Tafila in one such protest, referring them to the SSC for "unlawful gathering." At a March 31 protest in Amman for their release, police detained 13 protesters whom the military prosecutor at the SSC charged with "insulting the king," "unlawful gathering," and "subverting the system of government in the kingdom or inciting to resist it." They were released on bail in mid-April. In a series of arrests in early September, security forces arrested well over a dozen peaceful reform activists, including eight from Tafila, two from Karak, and seven from Amman. All were charged under terrorism provisions, which place them under the purview of the military-dominated State Security Court. All remained in detention at this writing.

For the first time under the amended 2008 Nongovernmental Organization Law, the Council of Ministers on June 27 denied the local NGO Tamkeen funding from foreign foundations for programs to assist migrant workers in Jordan. In August, Tamkeen challenged the decision in court, but the case remained pending at this writing.

Refugees and Migrants

Over 100,000 persons from Syria have sought refuge in Jordan. In July, the government took all newly arriving Syrian refugees to al-Za'tari camp near the Syrian border, which very few have been able to leave. The change ended the previous policy under which Syrians fleeing the conflict could move freely in Jordan if they had a Jordanian guarantor. By October, the more than 30,000 refugees in the camp had rioted several times over the closure and harsh conditions.

Since April 2012, Jordan confined Palestinians who arrived from Syria in separate facilities: Cyber City and King Abdullah Park, in Ramtha, and denied them freedom of movement. Jordanian authorities forcibly returned at least nine Palestinians from Syria and threatened others at gunpoint with deportation, in an apparent display of discriminatory treatment of refugees according to their national origin.

In May, Jordan stopped the extradition to Eritrea of nine recognized Eritrean refugees, allowing them to leave for Italy.

Hundreds of foreign migrants working in the duty-free Qualified Industrial Zones and in agriculture and domestic work complained about labor violations, including unpaid salaries, confiscation of passports, and forced labor. Government inspections and judicial redress remained lax.

In November 2011, the government ordered police stations to follow a protocol when receiving migrant domestic workers who left their employers. On the positive side, they may no longer send the worker back without her written consent. However, migrant domestic workers are not free to leave the station without a Jordanian guarantor, even if they have been a victim of abuse. In March, the government passed a regulation that would establish a shelter for victims of human trafficking, but had not yet opened one at this writing.

NGOs repeatedly referred domestic workers who had suffered a range of abuses to investigators. However, investigators rarely classified them as victims of the crime of trafficking. Instead they treated each aspect of abuse, such as non-payment of salaries, separately, sometimes even detaining workers for "escaping" employers. In September, 50 female migrant workers were in administrative detention awaiting their return home, although many had claims of abuse against their employers and were not themselves facing any charge, Tamkeen reported.

NGOs won modest judicial precedents for migrant workers. In October 2011, a court ordered, apparently for the first time, employers of a domestic worker to pay her fines for being in the country without documented residency status. The employers had failed to apply for a residency permit, a common problem, but the law holds the migrant responsible. Other court victories included verdicts against employers for confiscating workers' passports.

Women's and Girls' Rights

On August 29, parliament approved amendments to the passport law, removing a stipulation that a woman must obtain her husband's consent before she can obtain a Jordanian passport.

Jordan's personal status code remains discriminatory despite a 2010 amendment. Marriages between Muslim women and non-Muslims are not recognized. A non-Muslim mother forfeits her custodial rights after the child reaches seven years old.

Article 9 of Jordan's nationality law denies women married to foreign-born spouses the ability to pass on their nationality to their husbands and children.

Torture, Arbitrary Detention, and Administrative Detention

Perpetrators of torture enjoy near-total impunity. The redress process begins with a deficient complaint mechanism, continues with lackluster investigations and prosecutions, and ends in a police court, where two of three judges are police-appointed police officers.

In March, police officers beat close to 30 demonstrators in an anti-government rally with truncheons, kicked them, and slammed their heads into the walls at a police station; two fainted from the ill-treatment. The results of a reported internal police inquiry were not made public. Lawyers for and relatives of peaceful anti-government protesters detained and charged under terrorism laws in January and September also reported physical ill-treatment at police stations in addition to prolonged solitary confinement in pre-trial detention.

On November 16, 2011, Najm al-Din 'Azayiza, a 20-year-old man from Ramtha, died from asphyxiation on his third day in detention at the Military Intelligence offices in the Rashid suburb of Amman. The government did not adequately investigate his death.

A royally appointed commission of inquiry in May found numerous instances of ill-treatment in several state-run and private homes for the disabled, including persons being placed in a closed home in Karak under the governor's orders. An undercover video capturing scenes of cruel treatment of residents by staff had previously aired on the BBC.

The government did not submit to parliament changes it proposed in 2011 to the Crime Prevention Law that would limit provincial governors' authority to detain people administratively. The National Center for Human Rights reported that 11,345 persons were administratively detained, some for longer than one year, in 2011.

Key International Actors

The United States has a memorandum of understanding to provide Jordan with a minimum of $360 million in economic assistance, and $300 million in foreign military financing annually. In October 2010, the US Millennium Challenge Corporation committed a total of $275 million grants to Jordan over the coming five years.

The European Commission on September 18 announced €9 million (about US$11.5 million) to foster dialogue between Jordanian civil society and media and the government —one day after the king promulgated a new law censoring online media that the European Union failed to publicly criticize.

The European Bank for Reconstruction and Development Technical Assessment for Jordan concluded in 2011 that "Jordan is moving in a direction of more democratic governance within the framework of a constitutional monarchy." Despite the worsening human rights climate in 2012, the bank saw no risks to its commitment to the "fundamental principles of multiparty democracy, the rule of law, [and] respect for human rights" by operating in Jordan.

Kuwait

Recurring political disputes between the government and parliament paralyzed political institutions. In February, the Islamist-led opposition made significant gains in parliamentary elections. In June, the Constitutional Court voided the February elections and reinstated the previous parliament, originally elected in 2009. In October, Emir Sabah al-Ahmed al-Sabah dissolved the reinstated parliament and set December 1 to hold a new parliamentary election. However opposition groups, consisting of Islamists, liberals, and nationalists, boycotted the elections.

Kuwait continues to exclude thousands of stateless people, known as Bidun, from full citizenship, despite their longstanding roots in Kuwaiti territory. The government continues to violently disperse Bidun protests while promising to grant Bidun social benefits including government-issued documentation and free education and health care.

Authorities criminally prosecuted individuals for expressing nonviolent political opinions, including web commentary. Kuwaiti courts issued two landmark rulings cancelling legally-sanctioned discrimination against women in the judicial and education sectors.

Bidun

At least 106,000 Bidun live in Kuwait. After an initial registration period for citizenship ended in 1960, authorities shifted Bidun citizenship applications to a series of administrative committees that have avoided resolving their claims.

Authorities claim that most Bidun are "illegal residents" who deliberately destroyed evidence of other nationality in order to get the generous benefits that the state provides to its citizens.

In March 2011, the government granted Bidun benefits and services such as free health care and education, as well as registration of births, marriages, and deaths. However, those benefits don't provide a path to citizenship. Some

Bidun complained that bureaucratic processes prevented many from accessing those benefits.

Since February 2011, hundreds of Bidun have frequently taken to the streets to protest the government's failure to address their citizenship claims. The government issued repeated warnings that Bidun should not gather in public, despite the country's obligation under international law to protect the right to peaceful assembly. Article 12 of the 1979 Public Gatherings law bars non-Kuwaitis from participating in public gatherings.

The security forces beat Bidun protesters and detained dozens when they suppressed peaceful demonstrations. Detained Bidun reported physical abuse in detention. In one instance, on May 1, security forces violently dispersed around 300 protesters in Taima, northwest of Kuwait City, and arrested 14 of them. The Ministry of Interior said protesters had committed "shameful acts," such as trying to "burn tires and block roads." Local rights activists told Human Rights Watch that the gathering was peaceful. The detained Bidun were freed after nearly two weeks.

According to local activists and lawyers, nearly 180 Bidun and Kuwaitis were tried on charges such as "participating in an illegal gathering," "resisting, insulting, and threatening police officers," and "destroying police property," stemming from their participation in demonstrations in 2011 and 2012.

Freedom of Expression

2012 saw some gains for free expression, but authorities continued to detain and criminally prosecute individuals based on nonviolent political speech, including web commentary.

In December 2011 authorities allowed the bureau of the television news network Al Jazeera to reopen after shutting it down in late 2010 for reporting on security forces' crackdown on opposition protests.

In March 2012, a criminal court suspended *Al Dar* newspaper for three months and sentenced the editor-in-chief, Abd al-Hussain al-Sultan, to a six-month suspended jail term and fined him 1,000 Kuwaiti Dinars (US$ 3,500) for allegedly publishing articles that "raise[d] sectarian strife and incite[d] to violate public order." The charges arose after the newspaper published three articles that contained statements critical and demeaning to the Shia minority in Kuwait. On May 14, 2012, a court of appeal increased the sentence to a one-year suspended jail term.

In May 2012, parliament amended the country's penal code to authorize the death penalty or life imprisonment for religious blasphemy. However, the emir, who has the power to review legislation, rejected the amendment in June.

On June 5, 2012, a criminal court sentenced Hamad al-Naqi to 10 years' imprisonment for allegedly posting tweets "insulting" the Prophet Muhammad and criticizing the kings of Saudi Arabia and Bahrain. Al-Naqi claimed that someone had hacked his Twitter account and impersonated him. At this writing, his appeal was pending.

In July 2012, police detained Sheikh Meshaal al-Malek al-Sabah, a member of Kuwait's ruling family, for several days over comments he posted on Twitter in which he allegedly accused authorities of corruption and called for reform.

Women's Rights

On April 22, 2012, an administrative court cancelled a ministerial order that barred women from entry-level jobs at the Ministry of Justice. The case stemmed from a July 2011 job announcement in which the ministry said it would accept applications only from "male candidates" for entry level legal researcher positions—a first step to becoming a prosecutor.

In early June 2012, an administrative court ordered Kuwait University to cancel a policy requiring female students to do better in exams than male students in order to enroll in certain departments, including colleges of medicine and architecture. In its ruling the court said that the university had "treated male and female [students] differently." The Court of Appeal upheld the ruling a week later.

Despite these gains, women continue to face discrimination. Kuwait's nationality law denies Kuwaiti women married to foreign men the right to pass their nationality on to their children and spouses, a right held by Kuwaiti men married to foreign spouses. Kuwait has no laws prohibiting domestic violence, sexual harassment, or marital rape.

Households in Kuwait employ more than 600,000 domestic workers, primarily from Asia and East Africa. Kuwait's labor law excludes domestic workers and the restrictive sponsorship (*kafala*) system requires them to obtain permission from their employers to change jobs, effectively trapping many domestic workers with employers who mistreat them. Embassies report receiving thousands of complaints about confinement in the house, months or years of unpaid wages, long work hours without rest, and verbal, physical, and sexual abuse. In a rare conviction in February, a Kuwaiti court sentenced a Kuwaiti woman to death and her husband to ten years in prison for beating and killing a Filipina domestic worker.

Personal Freedoms and Privacy

In May and June 2012, the Kuwaiti police arrested hundreds of young people on spurious grounds which included "imitating the appearance of the opposite sex," practicing satanic rituals, engaging in lewd behavior and immoral activities, prostitution, and homosexuality. Many of these arrests took place during raids on private homes. A month earlier, the Justice Bloc, a Salafi parliamentary group, proposed establishing "a prosecutions office and a police force to combat crimes against public morality," which could potentially lead to an institutionalization of such crackdowns.

These crackdowns follow the arbitrary detention, ill-treatment, torture, sexual harassment, and sexual assault of scores of transgender women by the police since 2007. These arrests and abuses are a result of an amendment to article 198 of the penal code which criminalized "imitating the appearance of the opposite sex," imposing arbitrary restrictions upon individuals' rights to privacy and free expression.

Key International Actors

In April 2012, the United Nation's Committee on the Elimination of Racial Discrimination (CERD) called upon the government to provide a "just, humane and comprehensive solution to the situation" of Bidun.

The United States, in its 2012 State Department Trafficking in Persons report, classified Kuwait as Tier 3—among the most problematic countries—for the sixth year in a row. The report cited Kuwait's failure to enact comprehensive anti-trafficking legislation, weak victim protection measures, and lack of coordination between various governmental institutions focusing on anti-trafficking issues.

Lebanon

Reforms in Lebanon were stagnant in 2012 as draft laws to stop torture, improve the treatment of migrant domestic workers, and protect women from domestic violence, remained stalled in parliament. Women face discrimination under personal status laws, and vulnerable groups report being mistreated or tortured by security force members during arrest and in custody. Lebanese authorities and humanitarian organizations have provided material assistance to the influx of Syrians fleeing their country's fighting, but needs are increasing. Approximately 300,000 Palestinian refugees in Lebanon live in appalling social and economic conditions.

Torture, Ill-Treatment, and Prison Conditions

Despite repeated pledges by the Lebanese government to prevent torture and ill-treatment, accountability remains elusive. A number of former detainees, including refugees, migrants, drug users, lesbian, gay, bisexual, and transgender (LGBT) persons, and sex workers told Human Rights Watch that security force members ill-treated them during arrest or while they were in detention facilities, including the Ministry of Defense, the General Security detention facility in Adlieh, and the Hobeish police station in the capital, Beirut, which houses the Internal Security Forces' (ISF) vice squad.

In July, the ISF vice squad arrested 36 men during a raid on a theater suspected of screening pornographic movies. The men were transferred to Hobeish police station, where they were subjected to anal examinations. Forensic doctors conduct the examinations on orders of the public prosecutor to "prove" whether a person has engaged in homosexual sex. The tests violate international standards against torture, including the Convention Against Torture and the International Covenant on Civil and Political Rights (ICCPR), which Lebanon has ratified. The Lebanese Doctor's Syndicate denounced the tests as a form of torture and issued a directive in August calling on doctors not to conduct the examinations. In September, Justice Minister Shakib Qortbawi called for an end to the anal examinations.

In August, ISF arrested 14 Sudanese refugees and asylum seekers as they engaged in a sit-in in front of an entrance to the United Nations High Commissioner for Refugees (UNHCR) office in Beirut to protest the refugee agency's handling of their cases. The refugees reported that ISF officials kicked, insulted, and threatened some of them while arresting them, and that when the group arrived at the General Security detention facility in Adlieh some of them were subjected to beating, humiliation, and threats, including threats of deportation.

On August 30, unidentified armed gunmen detained Lebanese Palestinian journalist Rami Aysha while working on an arms smuggling story. They beat him and transferred him hours later to Military Intelligence, who also beat him. He was released on bail on September 26.

In September, at two separate protests in front of the Lebanese parliament, one calling for electoral reform and the other for a non-religious personal status law, security forces also beat several protesters.

In October, members of the Lebanese army beat at least 72 male migrant workers in the Beirut neighborhood of Geitawi. The soldiers did not interrogate them about any specific incident, but accused them of "harassing women." According to the Lebanese Army, they detained 11 of the migrants but did not specify the charges against them.

Lebanon has not yet established a national preventive mechanism to visit and monitor places of detention, as required under the Optional Protocol to the Convention against Torture (OPCAT), which it ratified in 2008. In October, the parliamentary Administration and Justice Committee began considering draft legislation that would establish a National Human Rights Institute, with a permanent Committee for the Prevention of Torture that would fulfill this obligation. The committee must approve the draft law before it is reviewed by parliament.

Refugees

Lebanon has witnessed an influx of Syrians escaping the crisis in their country. Most of the Syrians reside with host families or in ad hoc shelters, often in difficult circumstances, and in public accommodations, such as schools or rented apartments. At this writing, 95,452 Syrian refugees had registered with the UNHCR with an additional 34,275 waiting to be registered. Registration does not grant Syrians legal status, only a right to receive assistance. As a result, they face the risk of detention and deportation. Lebanon deported 14 Syrians back to Syria in August, four of whom said they feared persecution upon return.

Many Syrian refugees in Lebanon also report feeling insecure, particularly following the kidnappings of Syrians and other retaliatory attacks in August for the kidnapping of Lebanese by armed opposition groups in Syria.

The estimated 300,000 Palestinian refugees in Lebanon live in appalling social and economic conditions. 2012 saw no improvement in their access to the official labor market, despite a labor law amendment in 2010 that was supposed to ease such access. A survey conducted by the International Labour Organization (ILO) in 2011 found that only 2 percent of Palestinians have obtained work permits, that the majority earn less than the minimum wage, and that they are paid 20 percent less on average than Lebanese workers. Lebanese laws and decrees still bar Palestinians from working in at least 25 professions requiring syndicate membership, including law, medicine, and engineering, and from registering property.

Migrant Workers' Rights

Migrant domestic workers are excluded from the labor law and subject to restrictive immigration rules based on employer-specific sponsorship—the *kafala* system—which put workers at risk of exploitation and abuse. In January, Labor Minister Charbel Nahhas announced that he would look at abolishing the *kafala* system, but he resigned over unrelated matters a month later. The newly appointed labor minister, Salim Jreissati, has yet to put forward legislation that would protect the estimated 200,000 migrant domestic workers from excessive work hours, non-payment of wages, confinement in the workplace, and in some cases, physical and sexual abuse. Migrant domestic workers suing their employers for abuse also face legal obstacles, and risk imprisonment and deportation due to the restrictive visa system.

In March, Alem Dechasa-Desisa, an Ethiopian domestic worker, committed suicide at the Deir al-Saleeb psychiatric hospital. Six days earlier, a video aired
showing a labor recruiter physically abusing her outside the Ethiopian consulate
in Beirut. Following a public outcry, the labor and justice ministers announced
that they were opening investigations into Dechasa-Desisa's beating and ill-
treatment, but the outcome of the investigation had not been made public at
this writing.

Women's Rights

Parliament is still considering a 2010 draft bill that would protect women from
domestic violence. In August 2012, a parliamentary subcommittee put forward
an amended version of the bill limiting protections dealing with marital rape. As
of November, parliament had yet to consider the amended bill.

Discriminatory provisions that significantly harm and disadvantage women continue to exist in personal status laws, determined by an individual's religious
affiliation. Women suffer from unequal access to divorce and, in the event of
divorce, are often discriminated against when it comes to child custody.
Lebanese women, unlike Lebanese men, still cannot pass their nationality to
foreign husbands and children, and continue to be subject to discriminatory
guardianship and inheritance law.

Legacy of Past Conflicts and Wars

In 2011, as part of the UN Human Rights Council's (HRC) Universal Periodic
Review (UPR) process, the government pledged to establish a national commission to investigate the fate of those Lebanese and other nationals who "disappeared" during and after the 1975-1990 Lebanese civil war and to ratify the
International Convention for the Protection of all Persons from Enforced
Disappearances (ICCPED). In October 2012, Justice Minister Shakib Qortbawi put
forward a draft decree to the cabinet to establish the commission, which in turn
formed a ministerial committee to examine the draft. Representatives of certain
families of the disappeared and other groups proposed a draft law to set up the
committee.

In 2011 and 2012, reports continued to emerge of Syrians and Lebanese kidnapped in Lebanon being taken to Syria. Suleiman Mohammed al-Ahmad, a Lebanese man, was kidnapped in June in Hisah, Lebanon, and transferred illegally into Syrian custody. He was returned after his relatives conducted a series of retaliatory kidnappings in Lebanon. An official joint Syrian-Lebanese committee established in May 2005 to investigate cases of Lebanese who "disappeared" at the hands of Syrian security forces had not published any findings at this writing.

In February, the UN's special tribunal for Lebanon announced that it would proceed with an in absentia trial of four indicted members of Hezbollah for the killing of former Prime Minister Rafik Hariri in 2005. In July, the trial court rejected motions by the defense arguing that in absentia proceedings violate human rights. The trial is set to begin in March 2013.

Key International Actors

Multiple international and regional actors compete for influence in Lebanon. Regionally, Syria, Iran, and Saudi Arabia maintain a strong influence on Lebanese politics through their local allies.

France, the United States, and the European Union provide assistance for a wide range of programs, including military training, seminars on torture prevention, and civil society activities. However, these countries have not fully used their leverage to push Lebanon to adopt concrete measures to improve its human rights record, such as investigating specific allegations of torture or adopting laws that respect the rights of refugees or migrant workers.

As of August 2012, the UN deployed 11,360 peacekeepers at Lebanon's volatile southern border with Israel as part of its 33-year-old peacekeeping force in the country.

Libya

After 42 years of dictatorship under Muammar Gaddafi, Libya held elections for a General National Congress (GNC) in July, but a weak interim government failed to disband a myriad of armed groups around the country, end arbitrary detention and torture against detainees, or address the forced displacement of groups perceived to be pro-Gaddafi.

Throughout the year, Libyans suffered from ongoing violence, with tribal clashes, deadly attacks on foreign diplomatic missions and international organizations, the destruction of Sufi religious sites, kidnappings for financial and political reasons, and targeted killings of former Gaddafi security officers. Non-Libyans from sub-Saharan Africa faced arrests, beatings, and forced labor.

Political Transition

Libya's National Transitional Council (NTC), which governed Libya during and after the 2011 conflict to oust Gaddafi, was dissolved with the GNC's election on July 7, 2012. International observers largely viewed the elections as fair, despite some violence and attacks on polling stations. The transfer of power to the 200-member Congress marked the first step of democratic governance. The GNC is mandated to form a government, prepare a new electoral law and hold new elections. It was originally tasked to form a body to draft a constitution, but the NTC revoked that power just prior to elections in an attempt to defuse tension between eastern and western Libya. The mechanism for drafting a constitution is currently under review.

Libya's first elected government was sworn in amid tension surrounding the exclusion of four proposed ministers by the Integrity and Patriotism Commission for failing to meet set criteria for public office.

Security and Militias

Despite some positive steps, the interim authorities struggled to establish a functioning military and police that could enforce and maintain law and order. Many of the armed groups that came into existence to fight Gaddafi refused to

Unacknowledged Deaths

Civilian Casualties in NATO's Air Campaign in Libya

disarm and filled the security void. Some cooperated with the government and provided security services. Others operated without state sanction; the state proved unable to confront these well-armed groups.

The authorities' failure to demobilize the armed groups contributed to an esca-lation of violence in the Nafusa Mountains, in northwestern Libya, in the south-ern towns of Kufra and Sebah, and in the towns of Sirte and Bani Walid. As of October, an array of government and militia forces from Misrata had surrounded Bani Walid and enforced a partial siege, demanding the arrest of wanted per-sons suspected to be in the town.

Libya's national military deployed in the south after tribal clashes between Arabs and Tabu over border control, land rights, and trafficking routes. Spread thin, the army at times served as an intermediary between clashing regions and tribes.

The police force remained weak, and depended largely on the Supreme Security Committee (SSC) for ensuring law and order—a quasi-official body of former anti-Gaddafi fighters that is cooperating with the Interior Ministry—for ensuring law and order. The SSC's lack of vetting criteria and scant training contributed to abuse by its members.

Arbitrary Detention, Torture, and Deaths in Custody

As of October, roughly 8,000 people were in detention. The majority of them were held for more than a year without charge or due process rights, including judicial review and access to a lawyer. The Ministry of Justice holds around 3,000 detainees, around 2,000 are held by the Ministry of Defense or Supreme Security Committee. The rest were being held illegally by various armed groups.

Conditions in militia-run facilities varied, with detainees in some facilities reporting repeated torture and deaths in custody. Conditions in state-run facili-ties appeared to improve, although there continued to be cases of abuse and some deaths in custody.

Non-Libyans from sub-Saharan Africa, mainly migrant workers, are particularly vulnerable to abuse, facing harassment, arrests, ill-treatment in detention, forced labor and no regulated access to United Nations High Commissioner for Refugees (UNHCR).

Failure to Investigate Killings

Apparently targeted killings occurred throughout the year, particularly of former members of Gaddafi's intelligence and security services. At this writing, at least 15 former officers were killed in seemingly targeted attacks in Benghazi. The authorities did not announce any investigations into these killings, or arrest any suspects.

Judicial System and Transitional Justice

The judicial system remained weak, especially in its ability to pursue criminals affiliated with anti-Gaddafi militias. Threats and physical attacks on prosecutors and judges further inhibited the rule of law.

On May 2, the NTC passed Law 38, which granted amnesty to those who committed crimes if their actions were aimed at "promoting or protecting the revolution" against Gaddafi.

At this writing, no one has been charged or arrested for the apparent execution of 53 Gaddafi supporters in Sirte in October 2011, or for the apparent execution of Muammar Gaddafi and his son Muatassim. An NTC-formed commission to look at Gaddafi's death released no results.

In contrast, the judicial authorities began proceedings against several former Gaddafi officials. Detained officials complained that they did not have access to a lawyer and did not know the charges against them.

Abuzaid Dorda, the former prime minister and head of foreign intelligence, was injured after jumping from a two-story building while detained by a militia. Dorda said he jumped in order to avoid abuse.

International Justice and the International Criminal Court

Muammar Gaddafi's son Saif al-Islam and former intelligence chief Abdullah Sanussi—both in Libyan custody—remain subject to arrest warrants by the International Criminal Court (ICC), for crimes against humanity for their roles in attacks on civilians, including peaceful demonstrators, in Tripoli, Benghazi, Misrata, and other Libyan cities and towns after the start of anti-government protests in eastern Libya on February 15.

Libya says that Gaddafi is under domestic investigation for corruption and wartime abuses, and Sanussi is being investigated for serious crimes before and during the conflict, including his suspected involvement in the 1996 killing of about 1,200 prisons in Tripoli's Abu Salim prison. Gaddafi is being held by a militia in Zintan; Sanussi is under full state control after his extradition to Libya from Mauritania in September. The Libyan government has challenged the admissibility of the case against Gaddafi at the ICC, and that proceeding is ongoing. Pending the challenge, the ICC judges have authorized Libya to post-pone Gaddafi's surrender to the court in The Hague. However, at this writing Libya was still under an obligation to surrender Sanussi to the court pursuant to UN Security Council resolution 1970.

From June 7 to July 2, the militia in Zintan holding Gaddafi arbitrarily detained ICC staff members, who traveled to Libya to meet with Gaddafi in a visit author-ized by the ICC judges and agreed to by Libya.

Forced Displacement

Approximately 35,000 people from the town of Tawergha are still displaced around Libya and prevented from going back to their homes. The Tawerghans are accused of siding with Muammar Gaddafi's forces during the 2011 conflict and of having committed serious crimes, including rape and torture, against res-idents of nearby Misrata. Militias from Misrata have harassed, beaten, arrested, and killed Tawerghans in custody.

Other displaced groups include residents of Tamina and Kararim, also accused of having sided with pro-Gaddafi forces. Armed groups have barred the

HUMAN
RIGHTS
WATCH

Delivered Into Enemy Hands
US-Led Abuse and Rendition of Opponents to Gaddafi's Libya

Mashashiya tribe from returning to their villages in the Nafusa Mountains due to tribal and political disputes.

Freedom of Speech and Expression

In May, the NTC passed Law 37, which criminalized a variety of political speech, including "glorifying the tyrant [Muammar Gaddafi]," "damaging the February 17 Revolution," or insulting Libya's institutions. A group of Libyan lawyers challenged the law and in June the Supreme Court declared the law unconstitutional.

The fragile security environment has hindered free speech, with journalists, human rights activists, and members of the GNC facing threats by armed groups. The government's inability to implement a coherent visa-management system has made it difficult for international media and nongovernmental organizations to access the country.

Freedom of Religion

Attacks against religious minorities started in October 2011, and intensified in 2012. Armed groups motivated by their religious views attacked Sufi religious sites across the country, destroying several mosques and tombs of Sufi religious leaders. Armed groups attacked churches in at least two incidents in Tripoli in May and September. The government's security forces have failed to stop the attacks and have made no significant arrests.

Women's Rights

The 2012 elections for the GNC marked a positive step for female political participation; 33 women were elected (out of 200 seats) after the NTC adopted an electoral law requiring each party run an equal number of male and female candidates.

Libya's penal code considers sexual violence to be a crime against a woman's "honor" rather than against the individual. The code's provisions permits a reduction in sentence for a man who kills a wife, mother, daughter, or sister whom he suspects is engaged in extramarital sexual relations. The law does not specifically prohibit domestic violence and there are no voluntary shelters for victims of violence.

Key International Actors

The US, European Union, and UN all played significant roles throughout the year. The EU sought to build on migration cooperation agreements with Libya. The US expanded cooperation in the economic and security sectors particularly after the attack on its embassy in Benghazi on September 11, 2012, which resulted in the killing of the US ambassador Christopher Stevens and three other embassy staff. The UN Support Mission in Libya (UNSMIL) continued its focus on elections and transitional justice.

To date, NATO, which waged the air campaign against Gaddafi's forces, has failed to investigate properly at least 72 civilian casualties caused by its airstrikes.

Security Council members that initially championed resolution 1970 referring Libya to the ICC have been largely silent on Libya's obligation under that resolution to cooperate with the court.

The Commission of Inquiry for Libya (COI) expressed concern that human rights violations continue to be committed especially by armed militias, and recommended continued monitoring by the Human Rights Council (HRC) to ensure the implementation of its recommendations. Yet the resolution that the council adopted on March 23, 2012, at its 19th session, failed to acknowledge specific violations, to recognize the extent and gravity of ongoing rights abuses, and to include a mechanism to ensure monitoring of the human rights situation by the council.

Morocco/ Western Sahara

Human rights conditions were decidedly mixed in Morocco, as a 2011 constitution containing strong human rights provisions did not translate into improved practices. While Moroccans exercised their right to protest in the streets, the police often dispersed them violently, and protest leaders and dissidents risked imprisonment after unfair trials, sometimes based on the many laws repressing speech that have yet to be revised in light of the new constitution.

In January 2012, for the first time, an Islamist became prime minister, after the Hizb al-Adalah wal-Tanmiya (Justice and Development) party won a plurality of seats in legislative elections. Moustapha Ramid, a well-known human rights lawyer, became justice minister. On July 31, Ramid declared in a television interview that among Morocco's 65,000 prisoners there were no "prisoners of opinion," a statement contradicted by the incarceration of rapper al-Haqed and student Abdessamad Haydour for their peaceful speech.

Freedom of Assembly, Association, and Expression

Inspired by popular protests elsewhere in the region, Moroccans have since February 2011 held periodic marches and rallies to demand sweeping political reforms .The police tolerated many of these protests, spearheaded by the youthful, loosely organized February 20 Movement for Change, but on some occasions attacked and beat protesters severely.

Seddik Kebbouri, president of the Bouarfa section of the independent Moroccan Association for Human Rights, served eight months in prison following his conviction in an unfair trial for his alleged role in a May 2011 demonstration that ended in rock-throwing and property damage. A royal pardon freed Kebbouri and nine co-defendants on February 4, 2012. A Casablanca court on September 12 sentenced five protesters to between eight and ten months in prison on charges they assaulted police at a street protest on July 22, even though the court relied on confessions that the defendants claimed had been beaten out of them.

Terrorism and Counterterrorism

Hundreds of suspected Islamist extremists arrested in the aftermath of the Casablanca bombings of May 2003 remain in prison. Many were convicted in unfair trials after being held in secret detention and subjected to mistreatment and sometimes torture. Since further terrorist attacks in 2007, police have arrested hundreds more suspected militants, many of whom were convicted and imprisoned, not for having committed acts of terrorism, but for belonging to a "terrorist network" or preparing to join the *jihad* in Iraq or elsewhere.

Police Conduct, Torture, and the Criminal Justice System

Moroccan courts continue to impose the death penalty, but Morocco has not executed anyone since the early 1990s.

United Nations Special Rapporteur on Torture Juan Mendez stated he was grant-ed unimpeded access to prisons and prisoners. He noted the "political will" among authorities "to build up an institutional culture that prohibits and pre-vents torture and ill-treatment." However he also stated he had received "credi-ble reports of beatings [by police] (with fists and sticks), application of electric shocks, and cigarette burns." Mendez concluded: "In practice, the safeguards against torture do not effectively operate because 'there is no evidence' torture has happened and so the confession or declaration remains on the record and no serious effort is made to investigate, prosecute, and punish perpetrators."

Courts deprived defendants in political cases of the right to fair trials and in a number of cases ignored their requests for medical examinations following their allegations of torture, refused to summon exculpatory witnesses, and convicted defendants based on apparently coerced confessions.

Twenty-five Sahrawi civilians faced a trial before a Rabat military court for their alleged role in clashes that caused fatalities on both sides in and around El-Ayoun in November 2010 between security forces and Sahrawis. At this writing, the trial had yet to begin, even though 22 of the defendants had spent nearly 2 years in pretrial custody.

Prison conditions were reportedly harsh, due in large part to severe overcrowd-ing, a problem aggravated by the frequent resort to pretrial detention by judges, as documented by recent reports on prison conditions. Conditions for Islamist prisoners at the high-security Sale 2 prison improved compared to the inhumane and highly restrictive conditions that they faced in 2011, ex-prisoners told Human Rights Watch.

The National Council of Human Rights, a state-funded body that reports to the king, issued a pioneering report in September on mental hospitals, criticizing the inadequacies of existing facilities. In November, the council issued a report on prison conditions that cited a pattern of beatings, abusive policies on punishment and transfers, and excessive use of preventive detention by judges.

In 2012, there were several reports of police abuse of sub-Saharan migrants, many of whom live in precarious conditions along the Mediterranean coast. For example, on August 24, police reportedly raided an abandoned house inhabited by migrants on the outskirts of Nador, destroying or confiscating property, and putting migrants on buses and dumping many of them at the Algerian border without formally verifying their status. Generally, Morocco has refrained from expelling migrants who have documents proving that they have applied for or received recognition as refugees from the UN High Commission for Refugees (UNHCR).

Freedom of Association

The 2011 constitution protects for the first time the right to create an association. However, officials continued to arbitrarily impede the legalization of many associations, undermining their freedom to operate. Groups affected include some that defend the rights of Sahrawis, Amazighs (Berbers), sub-Saharan migrants, and the unemployed, as well as charitable, cultural, and educational associations whose leadership includes members of al-Adl wal-Ihsan (Justice and Spirituality), a well-entrenched, nationwide movement that advocates for an Islamic state and questions the king's spiritual authority. The government, which does not recognize Justice and Spirituality as a legal association, tolerated many of its activities, but prevented others. In Western Sahara, authorities withheld legal recognition for all local human rights organizations whose leadership supports independence for that territory, even associations that won administrative court rulings that they had wrongfully been denied recognition.

Women's Rights

The new constitution guarantees equality for women, "while respecting the provisions of the Constitution, and the laws and permanent characteristics of the Kingdom." Major reforms to the Family Code in 2004 raised the age of marriage from 15 to 18 and improved women's rights in divorce and child custody. However, the new code preserved discriminatory provisions with regards to inheritance and the right of husbands to unilaterally divorce their wives.

On March 10, 16-year-old Amina Filali apparently took her own life after enduring beatings from her husband, according to her family. Filali's parents, who live near Larache, northern Morocco, had filed a complaint in 2011 stating that their daughter's future husband had raped her; later they petitioned the court successfully to allow the two to marry. The case focused attention on article 475 of the penal code, which provides a prison term for a person who "abducts or deceives" a minor, but prevents the prosecutor from charging him if he then marries the minor. That clause, say women's rights activists, effectively allows rapists to escape prosecution.

Domestic Workers

Despite laws prohibiting the employment of children under the age of 15, thousands of children under that age—predominantly girls—are believed to work as domestic workers. According to the UN, nongovernmental organization, and government sources, the number of child domestic workers has declined in recent years, but girls as young as 8 years old continue to work in private homes for up to 12 hours a day for as little as US$11 per month. In some cases, employers beat and verbally abused the girls, denied them an education, and refused them adequate food. In 2012, an appeals court sentenced a woman to 10 years in prison for beating a 10-year-old domestic worker, leading to the child's death.

Morocco's labor law excludes domestic workers from its protections, including a minimum wage, limits to work hours, and a weekly rest day. In 2006, authorities presented a draft law to regulate domestic work and reinforce existing prohibitions on under-15 domestic workers. The draft had been modified but not adopted at this writing.

Freedom of Expression

Morocco's independent print and online media investigate and criticize government officials and policies, but face prosecution and harassment when they cross certain lines. The press law includes prison terms for "maliciously" spreading "false information" likely to disturb the public order or for speech that is defamatory, offensive to members of the royal family; or that undermines "Islam, the institution of the monarchy, or territorial integrity," that is, Morocco's claim on Western Sahara.

Moroccan state television provides some room for investigative reporting but little for direct criticism of the government or dissent on key issues. In April, Rachid Nini, a popular columnist and editor of *al-Masa'* daily, completed a one-year prison sentence on charges, based on his articles, of attempting to influence judicial decisions, showing contempt for judicial decisions, and falsely accusing public officials of crimes.

Morocco revoked the accreditation of Agence France-Presse journalist Omar Brouksy on October 5 because of an article in which he described a political party running candidates in a by-election that day as being close to the palace. In November, authorities announced that it would allow Al Jazeera television to re-open its bureau, two years after they closed it after criticizing its coverage of the Western Sahara conflict.

In May, a Casablanca court convicted and sentenced rap musician Mouad Belghouat (known as "al-Haqed"—the sullen one) to one year in prison for insulting the police in the lyrics of one of his songs. The conviction and sentence were upheld on appeal in July.

A Taza court in February sentenced Abdelsamad Haydour, 24, of Taza, to three years in prison for attacking the king by calling him a "dog," "a murderer," and "a dictator" in an online YouTube video; the penal code criminalizes "insults to the king."

Key International Actors

In 2008, the European Union gave Morocco "advanced status," placing it a notch above other members of the European Neighbourhood Policy (ENP).

Morocco is the biggest Middle Eastern beneficiary of EU aid after the Occupied Palestinian Territories, with €580 million (US$757 million) earmarked for 2011 to 2013. In its 2012 ENP report, the EU urged Morocco to protect freedom of expression by, among other things, adopting a new press code, and to "put into effect the principles contained in the new constitution, notably the adoption of organic laws ... and formulate a strategic plan for reforming the justice sector with a view toward consolidating its independence."

France is Morocco's leading trading partner and source of public development aid and private investment. France increased its Overseas Development Assistance to €600 million ($783 million) for 2010 to 2012. France rarely publicly criticized Morocco's human rights practices and openly supported its autonomy plan for Western Sahara. On March 9, then-Foreign Minister Alain Juppé hailed Morocco's "exemplary" progress toward democratization and called it "a model" during the Arab Spring. On May 24, King Mohamed VI became the first head of state to be received by François Hollande, president of France, after his election as president.

The United States provided financial aid to Morocco, a close ally, including a five-year $697 million grant beginning in 2008 from the Millennium Challenge Corporation to reduce poverty and stimulate economic growth. On human rights, the US continued to publicly praise Morocco's reform efforts. Secretary of State Hillary Clinton, in a statement about Morocco at the first bilateral "strategic dialogue" on September 13, voiced no reservations on human rights.

The 2012 UN Security Council resolution renewing the mandate of the peacekeeping force for Western Sahara (MINURSO) did not enlarge the MINURSO mandate to include human rights monitoring, an enlargement that the Polisario supports and Morocco opposes. MINURSO is one of the only peacekeeping operations created since 1990 that has no human rights monitoring component. Resolution 2044 welcomed "the steps taken by Morocco to ensure unqualified and unimpeded access [to Western Sahara] to all Special Procedures of the United Nations Human Rights Council" visiting Morocco. In September, the UN special rapporteur on torture conducted a mission to Morocco and Western Sahara (see above).

Oman

Omani authorities in 2012 restricted the right to freedom of expression through use of criminal defamation laws, sentencing over 30 pro-reform activists to between 12 and 18 months' imprisonment and substantial fines on the charge of "defaming the Sultan."

Authorities restricted the freedoms of association and assembly, both in law and in practice.

Oman's mostly elected Shura Council exercised limited legislative and oversight powers for the first time in late 2011, following royal decrees by Sultan Qabus bin Sa`id Al Sa`id, Oman's ruler, in response to large-scale street demonstrations throughout the country in early 2011.

Pro-Reform Activists

On May 31, Omani authorities launched an assault on freedoms of expression and association through mass arrests and trials of peaceful online activists and demonstrators.

The crackdown began when police detained human rights activists Isma`il al-Meqbali, Habiba al-Hana'i, and Ya`coub al-Khorousi as they were traveling to the Fohoud oil field to interview striking oil workers. All three are founding members of the independent Omani Group for Human Rights. Authorities denied the men access to their families and lawyers for several days, eventually releasing al-Hana'i and al-Khorousi while holding al-Meqbali to investigate potential charges.

Over the following two weeks, authorities detained a group of 10 pro-reform activists allegedly for Facebook and Twitter comments critical of Omani authorities, particularly the arrests of al-Meqbali, al-Hana`i, and al-Khorousi. The arrests of online activists escalated following a June 4 statement by Muscat's public prosecutor saying he would take "all appropriate legal measures" against activists who have made "inciting calls ... under the pretext of freedom of expression." He added that "the rise of rumors and incitement to engage in negative behavior eventually harms the nation, its citizens, and the national interests."

By the end of July, authorities had arrested another 22 online activists on the basis of alleged defamatory Facebook and Twitter comments. The public prosecutor charged 31 of the detained activists with "defaming the Sultan," based on article 126 of Oman's penal code, and violating provisions of Oman's Information Crimes Law. One, Hamud al-Rashidi, faced the sole charge of "defaming the Sultan." Following a series of group trials during July, August, and September, the Muscat Court of First Instance convicted 29 of the activists and sentenced them to between 6 and 18 months in prison and fines ranging from 200 to 1,000 Omani Riyals (US$520-$2,600). The court exonerated only one detainee, female activist Ameena al-Sa`adi.

Several of the detained activists, including Mukhtar al-Hana`i, Khaled al-Noufali, Sultan al-Sa`adi, and Hatem al-Maliki, challenged the charges on the basis that unknown persons had hacked their Facebook pages and posted the alleged defamatory remarks. On September 9, the lower court judge postponed their trials on the condition that each pay 500 Omani Riyals ($1,300) to hire a court-appointed technology expert to review the hacking allegations. Al-Noufai, al-Sa`adi, and al-Maliki paid for the review but were nonetheless convicted by the court on September 16. Al-Hana`i refused to pay, and the court convicted him on September 18.

Local activists told Human Rights Watch that many of the detainees reported ill-treatment in prison, including prolonged periods of solitary confinement, forced wearing of hoods whenever outside their cells (including while being escorted to the bathroom), sleep deprivation, loud music, and repeated verbal abuse from prison guards. One female detainee told Human Rights Watch that prison guards refused to grant her access to medical attention following several days on hunger strike.

Freedom of Assembly

Omani authorities require government approval for all public gatherings. In 2012, riot police quickly dispersed impromptu demonstrations and sit-ins.

On June 11, police arrested at least 20 protesters at a peaceful sit-in in front of the Special Section of the Omani Police in Muscat, where demonstrators believed authorities were holding activists detained during the first week of June. According to one participant, authorities sealed all roads leading to the station in the late afternoon, and 60 to 70 riot police officers descended in black vans and detained all the demonstrators.

Several of those participating in the sit-in, including Saeed al-Hashemi, Basma al-Kayoumi, Mukhtar al-Hana'i, and Basima al-Rajhi, had signed a public appeal earlier that day demanding the immediate release of the activists. They addressed the appeal to the president of the Shura Council; the president of the State Council, a purely consultative appointed body; the inspector general of police and customs; and the head of the quasi-official National Committee for Human Rights.

Omani police charged 11 demonstrators, including al-Rajhi, al-Hashemi, and al-Kayoumi, with "illegal gathering with the intention of provoking a riot" and "blocking the flow of traffic" under article 137 of Oman's penal code. A Muscat lower court convicted them on August 8 and sentenced them to one year in prison and fines of 1,000 Omani Riyals ($2,600). At this writing all were free on bail pending appeal.

Naming Restrictions

The Ministry of Interior's Committee for the Correction of Tribal Names and Titles continued to regulate and arbitrarily change tribal surnames, effectively assimilating members of one tribe into another. Despite numerous court decisions against ministry orders compelling members of the Al Towayyah and al-Khalifin tribes to change their surnames to names of other tribes, ministry officials continued to challenge the names of individuals when they attempted to renew identification documents.

In 2012, the Directorate General of Civil Status, a branch of the Royal Oman Police, continued its policy of restricting names permitted to newborns to those found on a civil registry database. Any newborn whose name was not found in the database and consequently rejected could not get a birth certificate until the parents submitted an acceptable name. Activists reported that the appeals process was lengthy and unclear.

Women's Rights

Article 17 of Oman's Basic Law officially bans discrimination on the basis of gender, and authorities have made efforts to ensure that women are visibly represented at the highest levels of government and society.

Oman adjudicates family law and personal status matters in religious courts in which judges base rulings on their interpretations of Islamic law. Individuals have no option to seek adjudication pursuant to a civil code. Family law as generally interpreted discriminates against women in matters of divorce, inheritance, child custody, and legal guardianship, granting men privileged status in these matters.

Key International Actors

Both the United States and the United Kingdom provide significant economic and military aid to the sultanate and both maintain a sizeable military presence there. Neither country altered its policy toward Oman in 2012 despite the ongoing protests and restrictions.

Qatar

In 2012, Qatar's population grew nearly 5 percent, to 1.95 million, primarily due to an influx of foreign labor to meet the demands of a booming construction sector. Qatar has the highest ratio of non-citizens to citizens in the world, with nationals comprising approximately 12 percent of the population. The country has some of the most restrictive sponsorship laws in the Gulf region, and forced labor and human trafficking are serious problems. The government has failed to address shortcomings in the legal and regulatory framework despite the initiation of many large-scale projects in preparation for Qatar hosting the World Cup in 2022.

In June 2012, the Shura Council passed a new draft media law with provisions on free speech that may jeopardize Qatar's reputation as a center for media freedom. While the constitution protects freedom of expression"in accordance with the conditions and circumstances set forth in the law", in practice Qatar restricts freedom of speech. Local media tend to self-censor, and the law permits criminal penalties, including prison terms, for defamation.

Migrant Workers

More than 1.2 million migrant workers—mostly from India, Pakistan, Sri Lanka, the Philippines, Nepal, and Bangladesh—live and work in Qatar, and that number is increasing rapidly. The country may recruit up to a million additional workers in the next decade to overhaul its infrastructure and build the stadiums required to host the 2022 World Cup.

Qatar's Law 14 of 2004, governing labor in the private sector, limits working hours, requires paid annual leave, sets requirements on health and safety, and requires on-time payment of wages each month. However, laws intended to protect workers are rarely enforced. Passport confiscation is customary and workers typically pay exorbitant recruitment fees, much of which end up in Qatar, according to a 2011 World Bank study on the Nepal-Qatar migration corridor. Migrant workers have no right to unionize or strike, though they make up 99 percent of the private sector workforce. In addition, the *kafala* (sponsorship) system ties a migrant worker's legal residence to his or her employer, or "spon-

HUMAN
RIGHTS
WATCH

Building a Better World Cup
Protecting Migrant Workers in Qatar Ahead of FIFA 2022

sor." Migrant workers cannot change jobs without their sponsoring employer's consent except in exceptional cases and with Interior Ministry permission. If a worker leaves his or her employer, even if fleeing abuse, the employer can report the worker as "absconding," leading to detention and deportation. In order to leave Qatar, migrants must obtain an exit visa from their sponsor, and some workers said sponsors denied them these visas. Reporting mechanisms and remedies are effectively unavailable to migrant workers. In addition, the labor law excludes domestic workers, almost all female, denying them basic protections such as limits to hours of work and weekly days off.

Migrant workers reported extensive labor law violations. Common complaints included late or unpaid wages. Some lived in overcrowded and unsanitary labor camps, and lacked access to potable water. Many workers said they received false information about their jobs and salaries before arriving and signed contracts in Qatar under coercive circumstances.

Qatar employs only 150 labor inspectors to monitor compliance with the labor law, and inspections do not include worker interviews.

The International Federation of Association Football (FIFA) pledged to raise worker rights issues with Qatari authorities. While the local organizing committee publicly said it would establish strict labor standards for contractors hired to build World Cup venues, no such standards appeared to be in place at this writing.

Freedom of Expression

In June 2012, the Shura Council approved a new draft media law with provisions on free speech that pose a threat to Qatar's reputation as a center for media freedom. The draft law still requires cabinet approval before becoming law. Al Jazeera, the international news network broadcasting in Arabic and English, is headquartered in Doha and funded by the Qatari government. While the station played an important role in reporting the pro-democracy movements in many Arab countries, it broadcasts few critical stories on Qatar, and the provisions of the draft media law may make it difficult for any media outlets in Qatar to criticize any Gulf Cooperation Council states. Article 53 of the draft law prohibits anyone from publishing or broadcasting anything that will "throw relations between the state and the Arab and friendly states into confusion," and provides for a fine of one million Qatari Riyals (US$275,000) for offenders. The law also prohibits the publication or broadcast of anything that offends the ruling family or causes serious harm to the state or its interests.

After his arrest in November 2011, Qatari poet Muhammad ibn al-Dheeb al-Ajami remained in detention a year later for a poem he recited in which he insulted the emir, Sheikh Hamad bin Khalifa Al Thani. Article 134 of the penal code provides for five years' imprisonment for criticism of the ruler. The state prosecutor charged al-Dheeb with "inciting the overthrow of the ruling regime" under article 130 of the penal code, a charge that can carry the death penalty.

Statelessness

Qatar has between 1,200 and 1,500 stateless Bidun who claim they have a right to citizenship. The 2005 Nationality Law allows individuals to apply for citizenship after living in Qatar for 25 years, but limits naturalization to 50 people per year. Bidun cannot register for education or health benefits, or legally work. The government does not register the birth of Bidun children.

In 2004 and 2005 the government stripped more than 5,000 Qataris from the al-Murra tribe of citizenship as delayed punishment for some members' participation in a 1996 coup attempt against the current emir. In 2006, the Qatari government officially reinstated the citizenship of most of this group, but an estimated 200 remain stateless.

Women's Rights

Both women and men vote in municipal elections, though elected representatives have limited power. Qatari women do not have the same rights as Qatari men to obtain nationality for their spouses and children. In 2010, Qatar appointed its first female judge.

Qatar has no law specifically criminalizing domestic violence, and the government currently publishes no data on incidents of domestic violence.

Representatives of the Qatar Foundation for the Protection of Women and Children, a government-funded charitable institution, told local media that domestic violence remained a problem, based on their work with women and children who sought assistance.

Qatar adjudicates family law and personal status matters in religious courts, in which judges base rulings on their interpretations of Islamic law. People have no option to seek adjudication pursuant to a civil code. Family law as generally interpreted discriminates against women and grants men privileged status in matters of divorce, inheritance, and child custody.

Key International Actors

The 2022 World Cup in Qatar provides an opportunity to apply international pressure on Qatar to improve conditions for migrant workers who will be working on infrastructure for the event. FIFA pledged to raise worker rights issues with Qatari authorities. However, while Qatar's World Cup organizing committee publicly said it would establish strict labor standards for contractors hired to build World Cup venues, no such standards appeared to be in place at this writing.

Saudi Arabia

Saudi Arabia in 2012 stepped up arrests and trials of peaceful dissidents, and responded with force to demonstrations by citizens. Authorities continue to suppress or fail to protect the rights of 9 million Saudi women and girls and 9 million foreign workers. As in past years, thousands of people have received unfair trials or been subject to arbitrary detention. The year has seen trials against half-a-dozen human rights defenders and several others for their peaceful expression or assembly demanding political and human rights reforms.

Women's and Girls' Rights

Under the discriminatory Saudi guardianship system, girls and women are forbidden from traveling, conducting official business, or undergoing certain medical procedures without permission from their male guardians. In July, after a car chase by religious police left the driver dead and his wife and daughter in critical condition, King Fahd hospital in Baha postponed amputating the wife's hand because she had no male legal guardian to authorize the procedure, *Okaz* newspaper reported.

In July 2012, the Ministry of Labor issued four decrees regulating women's work in clothing stores, amusement parks, food preparation, and as cashiers, for which guardian permission was no longer required. However, the decrees reinforced strict sex segregation in the workplace, mandating that female workers not interact with men. Women remain barred from certain professions. On October 8, *Al-Watan* newspaper published a directive from the Ministry of Justice that approved granting Saudi female lawyers the right to obtain practice licenses. Prior to the announcement, women who graduated from law schools were allowed to work as consultants but could not officially represent clients in court. The new directive will apply to all women who have a law degree and at least three years of experience.

At the London 2012 summer Olympic Games, Saudi women for the first time participated in an official sporting event: Sarah Attar competed in the 800 meters, and Wujdan Shahrkhani in judo. Women and girls remain effectively banned from sports within the kingdom.

HUMAN
RIGHTS
WATCH

"STEPS OF THE DEVIL"
Denial of Women's and Girls' Rights to Sport in Saudi Arabia

Women remain banned from driving. In November 2011, lawyer Abd al-Rahman al-Lahim sued the traffic department on behalf of Manal al-Sharif, who led a women's driving protest in May 2011, for gender discrimination after the department refused to issue her a driving license. The case remained pending at this writing.

Strict clothing requirements for women were publicly enforced. In July, the Mecca public prosecution department detained three women for taking off their full-body cloaks and headscarves in a shopping mall, *sabq.org* news website reported.

Al-Sharq al-Awsat newspaper in March reported that the first women-staffed police stations had opened in Jeddah and Riyadh in order to facilitate women's access to police. However, punishment for domestic violence remained lax. The government failed to enact a 2011 draft law to combat violence against women and children. In May, Jeddah's Summary Court convicted a man for physically abusing his wife to the point of hospitalization, but sentenced him to learning by heart five parts of the Quran and 100 sayings of the Prophet Muhammad.

Migrant Workers' Rights

Over 9 million migrant workers fill manual, clerical, and service jobs, constituting more than half the workforce. Many suffer multiple abuses and labor exploitation, sometimes amounting to slavery-like conditions.

The *kafala* (sponsorship) system ties migrant workers' residency permits to "sponsoring" employers, whose written consent is required for workers to change employers or exit the country. Employers abuse this power to confiscate passports, withhold wages, and force migrants to work against their will, against Saudi law.

In April, the Labor Ministry proposed to abolish the *kafala* system by transferring immigration sponsorship to newly created recruitment and placement agencies, but the change had not taken effect at this writing. To tackle *kafala*-related abuses, Saudi Arabia would also need to amend its Residency Law so that a migrant worker no longer would require a sponsor's consent to change jobs or leave the country.

Some 1.5 million migrant domestic workers remain excluded from the 2005 Labor Law. In years past, Asian embassies reported thousands of complaints from domestic workers forced to work 15 to 20 hours a day, seven days a week, and denied their salaries. Domestic workers, most of them women, frequently endure forced confinement, food deprivation, and severe psychological, physical, and sexual abuse.

In 2011 and 2012, the rampant abuse led the Philippines, Indonesia, Nepal, and Kenya to impose restrictions on their citizens from migrating to Saudi Arabia for domestic work. In October 2012, the Philippines and Saudi Arabia approved resuming migration after agreeing upon a US$400 minimum wage but few other rights.

In April, Saudi Arabia pardoned 22 Indonesian domestic workers on death row. Many migrant domestic workers still face the death penalty, often after having limited access to legal advice and translators during court proceedings. These include 32 Indonesian domestic workers whose convictions include witchcraft and "sexual offenses," and Rizana Nafeek, a Sri Lankan domestic worker who was under 18 years old when a baby died in her care.

Criminal Justice and Torture

Detainees, including children, commonly face systematic violations of due process and fair trial rights, including arbitrary arrest and torture and ill-treatment in detention. Saudi judges routinely sentence defendants to thousands of lashes.

Judges can order arrest and detention, including of children, at their discretion. Children can be tried and sentenced as adults if physical signs of puberty exist.

Authorities do not always inform suspects of the crime with which they are charged, nor of supporting evidence. Saudi Arabia has no penal code, so prosecutors and judges largely define criminal offenses at their discretion. Lawyers are not generally allowed to assist suspects during interrogation and face difficulty examining witnesses or presenting evidence at trial.

From January to September 2012, Saudi Arabia executed at least 69 persons, mostly for murder or drug offenses, but also, in the case of one Saudi man, Muri' al-'Asiri, for "sorcery."

By October 2012, The Saudi Association for Civil and Political Rights (ACPRA), an unlicensed Saudi rights organization, had filed over 60 cases over two years against the secret police for long-term detention without trial and, in some cases, torture. The court typically ruled it did not have jurisdiction, ACPRA said.

Saudi Arabia continued to sentence children to death. In March, *Okaz* reported that authorities had sentenced to death eight persons aged 16 to 19.

Freedom of Expression, Belief, and Assembly

Authorities in 2012 arrested persons for peaceful criticism or human rights activism. Muhammad al-Bajadi, a businessman and rights activist, was convicted for setting up ACPRA and Yusuf al-Ahmad, a cleric, for disobeying senior clerics by calling for release or trial of detainees. Prosecutors issued politicized charges, including being in touch with international rights organizations, against Abdullah al-Hamid, Muhammad al-Qahtani, Walid Abu al-Khair, and Fadhil al-Manasif.

Saudi Arabia does not tolerate public worship by adherents of religions other than Islam and systematically discriminates against its Muslim religious minorities, in particular Shia and Ismailis. The chief mufti in March called for the destruction of all churches in the Arabian Peninsula. In 2012, authorities made arrests for expression of religious opinion, including, in February, of Hamza Kashgari, whom Malaysia extradited to the kingdom on blasphemy charges related to his fictitious Twitter dialogue with the Prophet Muhammad. In May, authorities in the northern town of 'Ar'ar arrested two persons for apostasy because they adopted the Ahmadi interpretation of Islam.

In June, prosecutors arrested Ra'if Badawi on the charge of operating the Saudi Liberals website, deemed insulting to Islam. By August, all 35 Christian Ethiopian men and women arrested in December for "illicit mingling" during a religious service had been deported. Official discrimination against Shia encompasses religious practices, education, and the justice system. Shia protests

607

revived in October 2011 and escalated in January and again in July 2012, when the authorities arrested Shaikh Nimr al-Nimr, a prominent cleric. Security forces have killed at least 11 Shia in protests since 2011. Protesters demanded the release of Shia prisoners and an end to discrimination.

In July, activists reported that 100 Saudis in Buraida and about a dozen in a Riyadh shopping mall demonstrated for the release of long-term detainees without trial. University and public security forces in March intervened to quell a protest by female students in King Khaled University, leaving at least one woman dead. She reportedly suffered from an epileptic fit that was triggered after security guards attempted to force the students to disperse.

Saudi Arabia does not allow political or human rights associations. In December 2011, the authorities denied the Justice Center for Human Rights a license, and did not reply to requests for a license by the Saudi Human Rights Monitor, which registered in Canada in May.

In July, authorities released Nadhir al-Majid, detained since April 2011 for critical writings, and a court released Khalid al-Juhani, detained since demonstrating, alone, on the Saudi day of rage, March 11, 2011. In February, Hadi Al Mutif was freed after 18 years in prison, most of them on death row, convicted of apostasy for insulting the prophet. The chief mufti had accepted his repentance.

Key International Actors

Saudi Arabia is a key ally of the United States and European countries. The US did not publicly criticize any Saudi human rights violations except through annual reports. Some members of the US Congress have expressed skepticism about Saudi's policy priorities. The US concluded a $60 billion arms sale to Saudi Arabia, its largest anywhere to date.

The European Union also failed to publicly criticize human rights abuses in the kingdom, although the Subcommittee on Human Rights of the European Parliament in May held a rare hearing on human rights in Saudi Arabia.

United Nations High Commissioner for Human Rights Navi Pillay in January voiced alarm over the use of the death penalty and cruel sentences such as "cross-amputation" of both the right hand and left foot.

Syria

Syria's uprising turned increasingly bloody in 2012 as the government's crack-down on anti-government protests developed into an entrenched armed conflict. Government forces and pro-government militia known as *shabeeha* continue to torture detainees and commit extrajudicial killings in areas under their control. Some opposition forces have also carried out serious abuses like kidnapping, torture, and extrajudicial executions. According to opposition sources, 34,346 civilians had been killed in the conflict at this writing. The spread and intensification of fighting have led to a dire humanitarian situation with hundreds of thousands displaced internally or seeking refuge in neighboring countries.

Violations during Large-Scale Military Operations

Security forces conducted several large-scale military operations in restive towns and cities across the country, resulting in mass killings. In February, government forces killed hundreds of civilians in the Baba Amr neighborhood of Homs, western Syria, as a result of indiscriminate shelling and sniper fire. The government used similar tactics in cities across the country. Syrian forces and pro-government *shabeeha* militias also committed summary and extrajudicial executions in the governorates of Idlib, Homs, Aleppo, and in the suburbs of the capital, Damascus, following ground operations to reconquer terrain lost to the opposition. On May 25, at least 108 residents of Houla near Homs were also killed, most shot at close range. According to survivors and local activists, it was pro-government armed men who were responsible for the executions. In late August, residents from the Damascus suburbs of Daraya and Moadamiya also described finding hundreds of bodies following ground operations there. Some of the victims appeared to have been executed by government forces.

In August, the government began relying more extensively on air power, often firing indiscriminately at heavily populated areas. In an attack on August 15, a fighter jet dropped two bombs on Azaz, in Aleppo governorate, killing more than 40 civilians including many women and children. In August, Syrian government forces also dropped bombs and fired artillery at or near at least 10 bakeries in

Aleppo province, willfully killing and maiming scores of civilians who were waiting for bread.

Arbitrary Arrests, Enforced Disappearances, Torture, and Deaths in Custody

Security forces subjected tens of thousands of people to arbitrary arrests,

unlawful detentions, enforced disappearances, ill-treatment, and torture using
an extensive network of detention facilities throughout Syria. Many detainees
were young men in their 20s or 30s, but children, women, and elderly people
were also included.

Those arrested include peaceful protesters and activists involved in organizing,
filming, and reporting on protests, as well as journalists, humanitarian assistance providers, and doctors. In some instances activists reported that security
forces detained their family members, including children, to pressure them to
turn themselves in.

A large number of political activists remain in incommunicado detention. Some
have been held for over a year, while others have faced trial for exercising their
rights. In one case on February 16, Air Force intelligence forces raided the Syrian
Center for Media and Freedom of Expression (SCM) and arrested 16 people,
including seven women. In September, seven members of the SCM staff were
charged and convicted of publishing banned documents with the intent to
change the basic principles of the constitution. Five of the men arrested—
including Mazen Darwish, the group's president—remain in incommunicado
detention.

According to released detainees and defectors, the methods of torture included
prolonged beatings, often with batons and wires, holding the detainees in
painful stress positions for prolonged periods of time, electrocution, sexual
assault and humiliation, the pulling of fingernails, and mock execution. The
interrogators and guards also subjected detainees to various forms of humiliating treatment, such as making them kiss their shoes and declare that President

Bashar al-Assad was their god. All detainees described appalling detention conditions, with overcrowded cells in which detainees could only sleep in turns.

Several former detainees said they had witnessed people dying from torture in detention. At least 865 detainees died in custody in 2012, according to local activists. In cases of custodial death that Human Rights Watch reviewed, the bodies bore unmistakable marks of torture including bruises, cuts, and burns. The authorities provided the families with no information on the circumstances surrounding the deaths. In some cases, families of dead detainees had to sign statements that "armed gangs" had killed their relatives and promise not to hold public funerals as a condition to receiving the bodies.

In the vast majority of detention cases, family members could obtain no information about the fate or whereabouts of the detainees.

Displacement Crisis

Iraq, Jordan, Lebanon, and Turkey have mostly opened their borders to more than 341,000 refugees from neighboring Syria. However, in violation of Syrians' right to seek asylum, in mid to late August, Iraq and Turkey began to deny tens of thousands access to their territories, either by limiting daily numbers and the profile of those who could cross or by closing border crossings entirely and only sporadically allowing a limited number to cross. Syrians stranded as a result lived in poor conditions and were at risk of air and artillery attacks by government forces. All four countries have denied Syrians secure legal status, and after July, Jordan and the Iraqi central government forced all new arrivals to live in closed camps.

Lebanon deported 14 Syrians in August, four of whom said they feared persecution upon return.

Refugees have also been subject to attack by Syrian government forces as they attempt to flee the country. Refugees described incidents in late May and June in which the Syrian Army opened fire indiscriminately and without warning at civilians trying to flee for Jordan.

Unlawful Use of Weapons and Human Shields

According to witnesses and Syrian de-miners, Syrian forces have placed landmines— including anti-personnel and anti-vehicle mines of Soviet or Russian origin—near the borders with Lebanon and Turkey, resulting in civilian casualties.

Since July, and increasingly since October, Syrian armed forces have used cluster bombs—weapons that are considered inherently indiscriminate when used in populated areas. From October 9 to this writing, Human Rights Watch documented 35 cluster bomb strike sites across Syria in the governorates of Aleppo, Idlib, Deir al-Zor, Homs, Latakia, and Damascus.

Syrian government forces have also endangered local residents by forcing them to march in front of the army during arrest operations, troop movements, and attacks on towns and villages. Witnesses from the towns of al-Janoudyah, Kafr Nabl, Kafr Rouma, and Ayn Larouz in Idlib governorate said they saw the army and *shabeeha* force people to march in front of them during the March offensive to retake control of areas that had fallen into opposition hands.

Sexual Violence

Syrian government forces have used sexual violence to torture men, women, and boys detained during the current conflict. Witnesses and victims also said that soldiers and pro-government armed militias have sexually abused women and girls as young as 12 during home raids and military sweeps of residential areas.

Children's Rights

Syrian army and security officers have detained children under inhumane conditions and tortured them with impunity during the past year. Government forces have also shot at children in their homes and on the street. Both government and opposition forces have used schools as detention centers or barracks turning them into military targets. Government forces have also used them as sniper posts and arrested and beaten children and teachers in schools.

Armed Opposition Abuses

Armed opposition groups have committed serious human rights abuses including kidnapping, arbitrary detention, ill-treatment, and torture and carried out extrajudicial or summary executions of security force members, government supporters, and people identified as *shabeeha*.

In one case, two Free Syrian Army (FSA) fighters from the Ansar Mohammed battalion in Latakia said that their battalion executed four people after storming a police station in Haffa in June—two immediately and the others after a trial. In August, six detainees in two opposition-run detention facilities said that armed opposition fighters and officials in charge of detention facilities had tortured and mistreated them.

Key International Actors and Developments

The international community remains deeply divided on Syria. On February 4, the United Nations Security Council considered a resolution that condemned the violence in Syria and called for a political transition. The resolution was the second of three Security Council resolutions in 2011-2012 to be vetoed by Russia and China.

In December 2011, Syria accepted a plan by the League of Arab States (LAS) to end the violence against peaceful protesters, release those detained, and withdraw armed elements from cities and residential areas. The LAS sent monitors in on December 26, but suspended the monitoring mission on January 28 because of the deteriorating security situation.

On February 23, the UN secretary-general appointed Kofi Annan as the joint special envoy of the UN and LAS on Syria. In mid-March, Annan proposed a six-point peace plan to bring about a ceasefire and open political dialogue. In the following weeks, Annan negotiated the peace plan with the Syrian government and announced on April 4 that President Assad had given assurances he would "immediately" start pulling back his forces and complete a military withdrawal from urban areas by April 10. On April 21, the Security Council established a UN supervision mission in Syria (UNSMIS)—with 300 observers—tasked with monitoring the cessation of violence and implementation of Annan's plan.

Amid ceasefire violations by government and opposition forces, on June 16, the observer's monitoring activities were suspended because of escalating violence and the unwillingness of the parties to seek a peaceful transition.

The Security Council then voted on a resolution on July 17 that would have threatened non-military sanctions against the government for non-compliance with the six-point plan which China and Russia again both vetoed. In August, Annan announced his resignation as special envoy and the monitoring mission withdrew. In September, the Algerian diplomat and UN veteran Lakhdar Brahimi took over from Annan as special envoy.

Despite the stalemate in the Security Council, the General Assembly and the Human Rights Council (HRC) did pass a number of strong resolutions on Syria with overwhelming majorities. The HRC extended—until March 2013—and strengthened the international commission of inquiry mandated to investigate violations and, where possible, identify those responsible. There were also repeated calls in support of the HRC referring the situation in Syria to the International Criminal Court (ICC) by member states and by Navi Pillay, the UN high commissioner for human tights.

Efforts were also taken outside of the UN to pursue a negotiated settlement to the conflict and to put additional pressures on the Syrian government including through the establishment of a "Friends of Syria" contact group in February. In June, Annan and several foreign ministers, including the five permanent Security Council members, met to discuss how to end the violence and begin a political process leading to a transition. In November, Brahimi encouraged the Security Council to turn the Geneva agreement into a Security Council resolution.

In November, Syrian opposition factions also created a new umbrella grouping: the National Coalition of Syrian Revolutionary and Opposition Forces. At this writing, the Gulf Cooperation Council and France had recognized the coalition as the legitimate representative of the Syrian people.

In 2012, Canada, the European Union, Switzerland, Turkey, and the United States implemented sanctions against individuals and entities implicated in human rights abuses, including senior officials and the Syrian Central Bank. Imports of Syrian oil and arms sales have also been banned. Nineteen LAS member states pledged to implement sanctions, but the extent to which these have in fact been implemented remains unclear and the LAS itself has not established any effective sanctions monitoring mechanism.

The governments of China, Iran, and Russia continued to support the Syrian government either diplomatically or through financial and military support. According to Syrian opposition activists and media reports, armed opposition groups in Syria also received financial and military support from Qatar, Saudi Arabia, and Turkey. France, the United Kingdom, and the US also pledged non-lethal aid to opposition groups.

Tunisia

Following the ouster of President Zine el-Abidine Ben Ali in January 2011, Tunisians elected a National Constituent Assembly (NCA) in October 2011 and entrusted its members with drafting a new constitution, to be followed by legislative and presidential elections. The Islamist party Al-Nahdha, which won a plurality of seats in the elections for the NCA, formed a governing coalition with Al-Mu'tamar min ajl al-Jumhuriyya party (Congress for the Republic) and the leftist Ettakatol party (Democratic Forum for Labor and Liberties) to form a ruling coalition. At this writing, the NCA was debating a draft constitution, drafted by a group of six NCA committees, which upholds several key human rights and fundamental freedoms but also contains provisions that undermine women's rights, as well as freedom of expression and of thought.

Tunisians enjoy a greater degree of freedom of assembly, expression, and association, and the right to form political parties than in the past. However, the consolidation of human rights protections was hampered by the failure to adopt reforms that would lead to a more independent judiciary, attempts by the executive branch to exert control over the media, the prosecution of speech offenses, and the failure of the authorities to investigate and prosecute physical assaults against individuals attributed to fundamentalist groups.

Accountability for Past Crimes

The interim government took some positive steps to investigate crimes committed during the December 2010 to January 2011 uprising and compensate those whom the security forces injured or who lost family members. A national fact finding commission, created by the first transitional government to investigate abuses during the uprising, issued its final report in April 2012, and identified 132 people killed and 1,452 injured up to January 14, 2011, the day Ben Ali fled.

Military courts tried several groups of defendants for the killing of protesters, and sentenced Ben Ali in absentia to life in prison for complicity in murder under article 32 of the penal code. Military courts also sentenced a minister of interior who held office at the time of the uprising to a total of 27 years in prison, and sentenced 20 other senior officers to several years in prison for intentional homicide during the uprising. Although the trials appeared to respect the defendants' basic human rights and allow victims to access justice, several factors undermined their contribution to achieving accountability, including failure to identify the direct perpetrators of the killings, an inadequate legal framework for prosecuting senior officers for command responsibility for crimes that their subordinates committed, and lack of political will from the government to press for Ben Ali's extradition from Saudi Arabia.

A military court sentenced Abdallah Kallel, former interior minister under Ben Ali, and three other security officials to two years in prison, for "using violence against others either directly or through others," in a case involving 17 high-ranking military officers who were detained in 1991, and accused of plotting with Al-Nahdha against Ben Ali.

Reform of the Judiciary

Executive branch influence over the judiciary persisted due to the failure to adopt long-awaited reforms of the judiciary, including a law that would set up a temporary judicial council to supervise the judiciary pending adoption of a new constitution. In its absence, the Ministry of Justice has been directly supervising the judiciary, including the appointment, advancement, and discipline of judges.

Freedom of Expression and Media

Decree-law 115-2011 on the print media, and decree-law 116-2012 on the broadcast media had not yet been fully implemented at this writing. Decree-law 116 requires the creation of an independent high authority to regulate broadcast media. The interim government refused to implement the decree-law and continued to unilaterally appoint the heads of public media.

In June, Al-Nahdha deputies in the NCA submitted a draft bill that would amend the penal code by imposing prison terms and fines for broadly worded offenses such as insulting or mocking the "sanctity of religion." The courts made wide use of repressive provisions of the penal code inherited from the Ben Ali era, such as article 121 (3), which makes it an offense to distribute material "liable to cause harm to the public order or public morals."

In September, a public prosecutor brought charges against two sculptors for artworks deemed harmful to public order and good morals. On March 28, in the first instance of a tribunal run by the city of Mahdia, two bloggers were sentenced to prison terms of seven-and-a-half years, confirmed on appeal, for publishing writings perceived as offensive to Islam. On May 3, Nabil Karoui, the owner of the television station Nessma TV, was fined 2,300 dinars (US$1,490) for broadcasting the animated film Persepolis, denounced as blasphemous by some Islamists. On March 8, Nasreddine Ben Saida, publisher of the newspaper *Attounssia*, was fined 1,000 dinars ($623) for publishing a photo of a football star embracing his naked girlfriend.

In addition, a military tribunal sentenced Ayoub Massoudi, former advisor to interim President Moncef Marzouki, to a suspended prison term of four months for the crime of impugning the reputation of the army under article 91 of the code of military justice, and for defaming a civil servant, because he accused the army chief-of-staff and the minister of defense of dereliction of duty for failing to inform Marzouki in a timely manner of the plan to extradite former Libya Prime Minister Baghdadi Mahmoudi to Libya.

Women's Rights

Tunisia was long viewed as the most progressive Arab country with respect to women's rights. However, the NCA adopted a draft article that could erode women's rights by emphasizing "complementary" gender roles within the family, an apparent retreat from the principle of equality between men and women as required by article 2 of the Convention on the Elimination of All Forms of Discrimination against Women (CEDAW), ratified by Tunisia in 1985.

Sexual Orientation and Gender Identity

Minister of Human Rights and Transitional Justice Samir Dilou said in a TV interview that "freedom of expression has its limits," and stated that homosexuality was a "perversion" that needed to be "treated medically." However, Chakib

Darouiche, the ministry's press attaché, confirmed that Dilou acknowledged his responsibility to protect the rights of Tunisia's LGBT minority like those of any other Tunisian citizens.

Failure to Investigate and Prosecute Attacks by Fundamentalist Groups

Throughout the year, there were several physical assaults on intellectuals, artists, human rights activists, and journalists carried out by individuals or groups who appeared to be motivated by a religious agenda. In cases monitored by Human Rights Watch, the victims filed complaints at the police stations immediately after the assault. However, the police proved unwilling or unable to arrest the alleged perpetrators, and several months after the incidents no formal investigation or prosecution had been initiated against them. For example, Rajab Magri, a drama teacher and civil society activist, said that on May 25, 2012, a group of men with the long beards commonly associated with Salafis assaulted him in Le Kef, a city 170 kilometers west of Tunis, breaking five of his teeth. Zeineb Rezgui, a journalist for an economics magazine, said that on May 30, several bearded men assaulted her in a working-class neighborhood in Tunis, allegedly because she was wearing a sleeveless summer dress. Magri and Rezgui both filed complaints with local police, but never heard from the authorities about investigations into these incidents.

Abuses against Protesters

While Tunisians enjoy the right to demonstrate to a far greater degree than in the past, the security apparatus has yet to learn and implement crowd control techniques aimed at minimizing the use of force. For example, security forces attacked a mostly peaceful demonstration on April 9, injuring some protesters and in some cases causing bone fractures. The demonstrators were marching towards Habib Bourguiba Avenue, an iconic site of the Tunisian revolution, to protest against Interior Minister Ali Laarayadh's decision to ban demonstrations at the site indefinitely. The minister rescinded the decision two days later.

Key International Actors

The European Union provides assistance for a wide range of programs for institutional reforms, including for the judiciary and the security sector. In October 2012, the EU approved €25 million ($32 million) to aid strengthening the independence of the judiciary. In its 2012 European Neighborhood Policy (ENP) report, the EU urged Tunisia to ensure the effective implementation of international human rights conventions ratified by Tunisia, and to adopt the necessary legislative reforms for the consolidation of democracy, including the reforms relating to the judiciary, the security sector, and the media.

On May 22, 2012, the United Nations Human Rights Council (HRC) Universal Periodic Review (UPR) mechanism examined Tunisia's human rights record. In its official response to the debate on September 19, 2012, Tunisia upheld most of the recommendations it had received. However, it has rejected those related to the decriminalization of defamation, particularly of religion, non-discrimination against women, and on the basis of sexual orientation, and abolition of the death penalty, on the ground that these are contentious issues that need extensive discussion at the NCA.

United Arab Emirates

The human rights situation in the United Arab Emirates (UAE) worsened in 2012 as authorities arbitrarily detained and deported civil society activists, and harassed and intimidated their lawyers. In September, an independent monitor found significant problems in the treatment of migrant workers on the high-profile Saadiyat Island project in Abu Dhabi, identifying the payment of illegal recruitment fees as a key concern.

Freedom of Association and Expression

The UAE intensified its campaign to silence critics of its ruling elite. Authorities detained 61 human rights defenders and civil society activists without charge on the pretext that they aimed to harm national security. The authorities detained two prominent human rights lawyers, Mohammed al-Roken and Mohammed al-Mansoori, and arrested, deported and intimidated foreign lawyers employed by the UAE law firm that offered legal assistance to the detainees.

The detainees all had links to al-Islah, a peaceful Islamist group that has advocated for political reform in the UAE.

However, the UAE's crackdown on free expression also targeted individuals with no ties to al-Islah. On June 16, the UAE deported Ahmed Abd al-Khaleq, an advocate for the rights of stateless residents known as Bidun, to Thailand. Authorities had held him without charge since May 22 and threatened to hold him indefinitely unless he left the UAE. Abd al-Khaleq is one of a group of activists whom the government had previously jailed for several months in 2011 for peacefully advocating for reforms and posting internet statements that criticized UAE government policy and leaders.

In February, security officials called in for questioning hundreds of Syrian nationals suspected of attending a demonstration in front of the Syrian consulate in Dubai. The UAE government revoked the residency permits of about 50 of them.

In November, the UAE passed a federal decree on cyber crime that provides for prison sentences for a range of non-violent political activities carried out on or via the internet, from criticism of the UAE's rulers to calling for unlicensed demonstrations.

Torture, Inhuman Treatment, and Enforced Disappearance

In July, the UAE acceded to the United Nations Convention against Torture. However, its assumption of treaty obligations to prohibit, prevent, and criminalize torture coincided with reports of torture in State Security facilities.

Syrian national Abdulelah al-Jadani told Human Rights Watch that for 18 days in May 2011, men who identified themselves as State Security officers subjected him to regular torture due to what they claimed were his links to political violence in Syria. He said they beat and whipped him, held him in painful stress positions, and hung him from the wall by his arms and legs. A UAE court freed him in January 2012, but convicted his close acquaintance, Musab Khalil Abood, on terrorism charges. Al-Jadani said that during the time he spent with Abood in al-Wathba prison, where the authorities transferred them after each had spent three months in solitary confinement in the State Security facility, Abood told him he had been subjected to the same pattern and methods of torture.

The UAE authorities forcibly disappeared at least one political detainee, Ahmed al-Suweidi, refusing to divulge his location after initially claiming to have transferred him to al-Sader jail on April 26. Unlike other political detainees who made semi-regular calls to their families, al-Suweidi made only one call to his family during his detention, five months after his initial arrest. The whereabouts of all but a handful of the detainees remained unknown during their time in detention. They had no access to legal assistance during that time, and were permitted only intermittent, monitored phone calls to their families. On September 6, witnesses who saw six of the detainees at a Supreme Court hearing to extend their detention said they appeared disheveled, disoriented, and distressed.

On June 12, 2012, a Dubai criminal court cleared 13 Dubai police officers—a lieutenant colonel, six lieutenants, and six lower-ranking officers—of charges of torturing three Pakistani detainees during interrogation in 2010. One of the detainees claimed that the officers hit him in the groin with a metal bar, then stripped him naked and sprayed his body with WD40, an industrial lubricant harmful to human skin. The court acquitted all the officers on the torture charges. It sentenced five to one month's imprisonment for the "unlawful detention" of a man who died in custody, but did not find them responsible for the injuries that led to his death.

Migrant Workers Rights

According to 2011 government statistics, foreigners account for more than 88.5 percent of UAE residents, many of them poor migrant workers. Immigration sponsorship laws grant employers extraordinary power over the lives of these workers. They have no right to organize or bargain collectively, and face penalties for going on strike. Although the law calls for a minimum wage, the Ministry of Labor has yet to implement it.

Across the country, abuses include unsafe work environments, the withholding of travel documents, and low pay or nonpayment of wages, despite a mandatory electronic payment system introduced in 2009.

In September, PricewaterhouseCoopers (PwC), an independent monitor contracted to assess labor conditions on Saadiyat Island, the site of a major government-sponsored development run by the Abu Dhabi Tourism and Development and Investment Company (TDIC) in Abu Dhabi, reported disturbing findings verifying ongoing labor abuses on the island: 75 percent of the interviewed workers said they paid recruitment fees and 77 percent said they paid visa and travel costs—all costs that UAE law requires employers to pay and that TDIC had pledged to eliminate.

Recruiting fees, which often take months or years for workers to repay, are the single greatest factor in creating conditions of forced labor. PwC said that TDIC, which is the master developer at a project that will host branches of the Louvre and Guggenheim museums, faced "significant challenges" in adhering to UAE labor law on account of "established practices and norms in the regional construction sector."

UAE labor law excludes domestic workers, denying them basic protections such as limits to hours of work and a weekly day off. In May, a local newspaper obtained a copy of a new draft law for domestic workers. The draft reportedly provides for one weekly day off, two weeks of paid annual leave and 15 paid sick days. However, it also reportedly makes a domestic worker who reveals the "secrets" of her employers liable for prosecution and sanctions of up to six months in prison and a fine of 100,000 dirhams (US$27,000). The draft law also imposes harsh criminal sentences on those who "encourage" a domestic worker to quit her job or offer her shelter. It is unclear whether the law will exclude people who shelter domestic workers fleeing from abusive employers. Authorities have not made the draft law public.

Many female domestic workers in the UAE suffer unpaid wages, food deprivation, long working hours, forced confinement, and physical and sexual abuse. The standard contract for domestic workers introduced in April 2007 calls for "adequate breaks," but does not limit working hours or provide for a weekly rest day, overtime pay, or workers' compensation.

Women's Rights

The UAE adjudicates family law and personal status matters for Muslims pursuant to interpretations of Islamic law, with no option to seek adjudication pursuant to a civil code. The law in particular discriminates against women by granting men privileged status in matters of divorce, inheritance, and child custody. Emirati women can obtain a divorce through *khul'a* (a no-fault divorce) thereby losing their financial rights. They may only ask for a divorce in exceptional circumstances. Females can only inherit one-third of assets while men are entitled to inherit two-thirds.

The law further discriminates against women by permitting Emirati men, but not women, to have as many as four polygamous marriages and forbidding Muslim women, but not men, from marrying non-Muslims. As a result of a 2011 proposal to allow Emirati women married to foreigners to pass their citizenship to their children, the Interior Ministry granted Emirati citizenship to over 2,000 children of Emirati women in 2012 and identified a total of 5,000 individuals who may be eligible for citizenship.

جزيرة السعديات
SAADIYAT ISLAND

HUMAN
RIGHTS
WATCH

THE ISLAND OF HAPPINESS REVISITED
A progress report on institutional commitments to address abuses
of migrant workers on Abu Dhabi's Saadiyat Island

Despite the existence of shelters and hotlines to help protect women, domestic violence remains a pervasive problem. The penal code gives men the legal right to discipline their wives and children, including through the use of physical violence. The Federal Supreme Court has upheld a husband's right to "chastise" his wife and children with physical abuse.

Key International Actors

Key allies such as the United States and the United Kingdom have refrained from publicly criticizing the UAE's crackdown on freedom of expression and repression of civil society, although US officials say that they have raised these issues privately. In 2012, the US signed a $3.48 billion dollar deal with the UAE to provide a missile defence system. In June, "industry sources" in Abu Dhabi cited criticism of the UAE in the UK press as one factor in a decision not to invite British oil company BP to tender for 2014 oil concessions.

Yemen

The fragile transition government that succeeded President Ali Abdullah Saleh in 2012 following mass protests faces multiple challenges in ending human rights violations such as arbitrary detention, attacks on free speech and assembly, and child-soldier deployment. Fighting linked to the political upheaval decreased, but sectarian clashes continued in the north, and government forces fought with the Yemen branch of al Qaeda in the south. The country faces a growing humanitarian crisis, with nearly half the population lacking sufficient food.

Saleh left office in February 2012, under an exit accord brokered by the Gulf Cooperation Council (GCC) and backed in most aspects by the United Nations Security Council (Security Council), the United States, and European Union member states. As part of the accord, Yemen's parliament on January 21 granted immunity to Saleh, and those who served with him for political crimes committed during his 33-year rule. The immunity law violates Yemen's international legal obligations to prosecute serious human rights violations, including attacks by government forces and pro-government gangs that killed at least 270 protesters and bystanders during the uprising.

The accord designated Saleh's deputy, Abdu Rabu Mansour Hadi, as a two-year transition president.

Under a UN-facilitated "Implementing Mechanism" that serves as a transition blueprint, the government is to bring security forces—including those run by Saleh's relatives—under civilian command, pass a transitional justice law, draft a new constitution, reform the electoral and judicial systems, and hold general elections in 2014. It is also to convene a national dialogue conference to address grievances by groups including northern Huthi rebels and the Southern Movement, a coalition of groups seeking greater autonomy or secession for the former South Yemen.

Transition measures were resisted by loyalists of Saleh, who remains in Yemen as head of the General People's Congress. Pro-Saleh troops and tribesmen in

July and August stormed the Interior and Defense ministries, prompting gun-fights that killed 21 people.

Accountability

President Hadi on September 22 authorized the creation of an independent commission to investigate violations during the uprising, and recommend accountability for perpetrators and redress for victims. A transitional justice draft law remained stalled.

The trial began in September for 78 defendants in the deadliest attack on pro-testers of the uprising, in which pro-government gunmen killed 45 and wounded 200 on March 18, 2011. Political interference and failure to investigate evidence that implicated government officials marred the prosecution's case. Most key defendants remain fugitives.

Arbitrary Detention

All sides in the uprising have released scores of protesters, fighters, and others whom they had arbitrarily detained. However, dozens more detainees remained in the custody of government and opposition forces, and some upon release alleged torture.

Armed Conflict

Fighting ended in Sanaa, the capital, and Taizz but conflicts elsewhere among various armed groups killed dozens of civilians. Many were casualties of land-mines and improvised explosive devices.

All sides in fighting in southern Abyan governorate—Yemeni soldiers and popu-lar committees backed by US aerial drones, and the Yemen branch of al Qaeda and its local affiliate, Ansar al-Sharia—have been implicated in laws of war vio-lations.

In the north, Huthi rebels clashed with Salafi fighters seeking to stem their takeover of Sa'da governorate and nearby governorates. Fighting between gov-ernment and tribal forces in Arhab, outside Sanaa, ebbed in mid-2012.

Classrooms in the Crosshairs
Military Use of Schools in Yemen's Capital

Children and Armed Conflict

In Sanaa, government and opposition forces continued to deploy children to patrol streets, guard checkpoints, and sometimes fight, in violation of international prohibitions against the use of children in armed conflict. Human Rights Watch received credible reports of Islamist militants and pro-government popular committees deploying child soldiers in Abyan.

State security forces and opposition armed groups deployed in schools around the country, placing children at risk and undermining education. Between January and June, more than 170 schools were attacked or subjected to other military use nationwide, according to the UN Office of the High Commissioner for Human Rights (OHCHR).

Freedom of Expression, Association, and Peaceful Assembly

Freedom of expression, association and peaceful assembly improved significantly in 2012. However, scores of journalists were attacked or harassed by individuals or armed groups from across the political spectrum.

Al-Ayyam, an influential Aden-based newspaper, has been closed since an assault by government forces in 2010. Criminal cases that the former government brought against it remained pending.

The authorities continued to prosecute journalists on politically motivated charges in a specialized media court that failed to meet international standards of due process.

Abdulelah Haidar Shae of Saba news agency remained in prison on terrorism charges, despite having received a pardon from then-President Saleh in February 2011. Yemeni and international media reported that US President Barack Obama requested Shae's continued detention. The specialized media court in January 2011 sentenced Shae to a five-year term after a trial marked by procedural irregularities. Shae had alleged that the Yemeni and US governments had committed abuses in their fight against al Qaeda.

Authorities allowed several new political parties and more than 100 nongovernmental organizations to register, and lifted bans on visits by international human rights groups.

Humanitarian Crisis

More than 10 million people—nearly one-half the population—lack sufficient food, 12 million lack access to clean water, and 1 million children are malnourished, according to the World Food Program (WFP) and other UN humanitarian agencies.

The number of internally displaced nearly doubled to half a million people, largely due to fighting in Abyan. As of November, tens of thousands of people had returned to Abyan despite damaged homes, shattered infrastructure, and the presence of landmines and other unexploded ordnance.

Terrorism and Counterterrorism

Yemen-based Al Qaeda in the Arabian Peninsula (AQAP) conducted dozens of deadly bombings and other attacks on Yemeni security targets.

AQAP and Ansar al-Sharia in April released 73 government soldiers after holding them hostage for more than a month and threatening to kill them if the authorities did not exchange them for detained terrorism suspects. AQAP held foreigners for ransom, including a Saudi diplomat and a Swiss teacher.

Ansar al-Sharia reportedly committed numerous abuses against people in areas it controlled in Abyan, including amputating limbs of alleged thieves and publicly executing three alleged spies in February.

The US increased covert drone strikes and piloted air attacks on alleged AQAP militants, conducting 25 to 83 such attacks in 2012, according to the Bureau of Investigative Journalism (TBIJ), a UK-based public interest reporting service. The strikes killed at least 173 militants and civilians, TBIJ reported, but lack of access to the targeted areas prevented independent verification of the data, including the number of civilian casualties.

Crackdown on Southern Movement

In Aden, Mukallah and other southern flashpoints, state security forces used disproportionate force against largely peaceful factions of the Southern Movement, and armed factions of the Southern Movement increased attacks on security forces.

Security forces threatened health care in Aden by forcibly removing wounded alleged Southern Movement militants from hospitals, exchanging fire with gunmen seeking to block the arrests, and beating medical staff. Gunmen protecting the alleged militants fueled the violence by firing at the security forces on hospital grounds.

In December 2011, security forces released two Southern Movement leaders, Hassan Baoum and his son Fawaz, after arbitrarily detaining them for 10 months.

Women's and Girls' Rights

Women in Yemen generally are excluded from public life but played an important role in anti-Saleh protests.

The transition blueprint envisaged "adequate" representation of women in all political bodies both during and after the transition. Many Yemeni women's rights activists are seeking a quota of 30 percent.

Child marriages remain widespread, exposing girls to domestic violence and truncating their education.

Yemen has a high maternal mortality rate of 370 deaths per 100,000 live births. Seven or eight women die each day from childbirth complications.

Key International Actors

Saudi Arabia, Qatar, and other Gulf states provide substantial assistance to the Yemen government, tribal leaders, and religious institutions. The US is the largest donor outside the region. EU states also provide significant aid. The mul-

HUMAN
RIGHTS
WATCH

"NO SAFE PLACES"
Yemen's Crackdown on Protests in Taizz

tilateral Friends of Yemen donors in September pledged US$7.9 billion to aid the transition.

The US pledged $346 million in bilateral aid for 2012, of which $185 million is for humanitarian and development assistance, its largest non-security package to date. In May, President Obama issued an executive order allowing the Treasury Department to freeze the US-based assets of anyone who "obstructs" implementation of the political transition.

In October, for the third consecutive year, Obama issued a waiver allowing Yemen to receive military assistance, despite documented use of child soldiers by forces, including government troops and pro-government militias.

In June, the UN Security Council passed resolution 2051, threatening sanctions against those undermining the transition. In September, Yemen allowed the Office of the High Commissioner for Human Rights (OHCHR) to open an office in Sanaa. In March and September, the UN Human Rights Council called for the release of all those arbitrarily detained, an end to child soldier recruitment, and transparent and independent investigations into violations during the 2011 uprising.

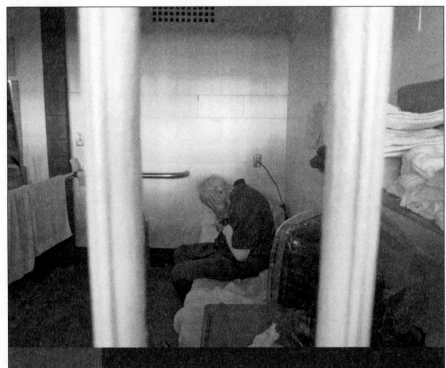

HUMAN
RIGHTS
WATCH

OLD BEHIND BARS

The Aging Prison Population in the United States

WORLD REPORT

2013

UNITED STATES

United States

The United States has a vibrant civil society and media that enjoys strong constitutional protections. The victims of abuse are typically the weakest and most vulnerable in US society: immigrants, racial and ethnic minorities, children, the elderly, the poor, and prisoners.

The US incarcerates more people than any other country. Practices contrary to human rights principles, such as the death penalty, juvenile life-without-parole sentences, and solitary confinement are common and often marked by racial disparities. Increasing numbers of non-citizens are held in immigration detention facilities although many are not dangerous or at risk of absconding. Federal prosecutions for illegal entry and reentry have escalated.

The federal government under President Barack Obama has continued some abusive counterterrorism policies, including detentions without charge at the military prison at Guantanamo Bay, and proceedings before fundamentally flawed military commissions.

Death Penalty and Excessive Punishments

In 2012, Connecticut joined 16 other states and the District of Columbia in abolishing the death penalty. Thirty-three states continue to allow its imposition. In November, California voters narrowly rejected Proposition 34, which would have abolished the death penalty in that state. At this writing, 42 people had been executed in the US in 2012. There has been a downward trend in executions since 2000.

Almost 20 years ago, California was among the first states to pass a punitive "three-strikes" law, mandating lengthy sentences for repeat offenders. In November, California voters overwhelmingly approved a ballot measure eliminating mandatory life sentences for certain nonviolent third offenses and allowing prisoners serving life for such nonviolent third strikes to seek resentencing. Massachusetts moved in the opposite direction, becoming the 27th state to enact a three-strikes law.

Growing Up Locked Down
Youth in Solitary Confinement in Jails and Prisons Across the United States

HUMAN RIGHTS WATCH

ACLU AMERICAN CIVIL LIBERTIES UNION

Long sentences have contributed to a growing number of incarcerated elderly people. Human Rights Watch's 2012 report, *Old Behind Bars*, found that, between 2007 and 2010, the number of sentenced prisoners aged 65 or older grew 94 times faster than the total sentenced prisoner population during that same period. Prisons are ill-equipped to handle this aging population.

Approximately 2,600 youth offenders are serving life-without-parole sentences, but in 2012 there was significant progress towards abolishing use of the sentence for juveniles. In 2012, Human Rights Watch found that nearly every youth offender serving life without parole reported physical violence or sexual abuse by inmates or corrections officers.

In June, the US Supreme Court held mandatory life-without-parole sentences for juvenile offenders to be unconstitutional, calling into question approximately 85 percent of all juvenile life-without-parole cases in the country. In September, California enacted a law providing for the possibility of review and parole for nearly 300 youth sentenced to life without parole in the state.

There is widespread use of solitary confinement against juveniles in adult prisons and jails, often for weeks or months. In 2011, more than 95,000 people under age 18 were held in adult prisons and jails. Solitary confinement provokes serious mental and physical health problems, and undermines teenagers' rehabilitation.

Youth convicted of sex offenses also experienced harsh treatment. The Adam Walsh Child Protection and Safety Act requires jurisdictions to register juveniles convicted of certain sexual offenses on a national, publicly accessible, online registry. Registration impacts youth offenders' access to education, housing, and employment. Many states have similar harsh laws.

Prison Conditions

As of 2010, the US maintained the world's largest incarcerated population, at 1.6 million, and the world's highest per capita incarceration rate, at 500 inmates per 100,000 residents.

Against All Odds

Prison Conditions for Youth Offenders Serving
Life without Parole Sentences in the United States

HUMAN
RIGHTS
WATCH

In May 2012, the US Department of Justice (DOJ) issued final standards under the Prison Rape Elimination Act (PREA), for the detection, prevention, reduction, and punishment of prison rape. The standards are immediately binding on all DOJ facilities. A presidential memorandum clarified that other federal agencies operating detention facilities, including the Department of Homeland Security, are also bound by PREA and must propose rules or procedures to comply with PREA.

California responded to a 2010 Supreme Court ruling that it must reduce its prison population because of inadequate medical and mental health care due to overcrowding by shifting a large number of inmates from the state prison system to county jails in a process called realignment. Realignment initially led to a sharp reduction in the state inmate population, but that drop has leveled off.

Racial Disparities in the Criminal Justice System

Racial and ethnic minorities have long been disproportionately represented in the US criminal justice system. While accounting for only 13 percent of the US population, African Americans represent 28.4 percent of all arrests. According to Bureau of Justice Statistics approximately 3.1 percent of African American men, 1.3 percent of Latino men, and 0.5 percent of white men are in prison. Because they are disproportionately likely to have criminal records, members of racial and ethnic minorities are more likely than whites to experience stigma and legal discrimination in employment, housing, education, public benefits, jury service, and the right to vote.

Whites, African Americans, and Latinos have comparable rates of drug use but are arrested and prosecuted for drug offenses at vastly different rates. African Americans are arrested for drug offenses, including possession, at three times the rate of white men.

In 2008, African American motorists were three times as likely as white motorists and twice as likely as Latino motorists to be searched during a traffic stop. In New York City, 86 percent of persons "stopped and frisked" by the police were African American or Latino, even though they represented 52 percent of the population. According to the New York Civil Liberties Union (NYCLU), 89 percent of those stopped were innocent of any wrongdoing.

Non-Citizens' Rights

There are approximately 25 million non-citizens in the US. The government estimates that 10.8 million of them are in the country without authorization.

In fiscal year 2012, US Immigration and Customs Enforcement (ICE) deported a record 396,906 non-citizens. A dramatic increase in federal prosecutions of immigration violations and in the number of immigrants in detention has fed a nationwide detention system comprised of over 250 facilities.

In 2011, prosecutions for illegal entry and reentry into the US surpassed 34,000 and 37,000 respectively. Illegal reentry is now the most prosecuted federal crime. Many of those who are prosecuted for these crimes have minor or no criminal history and have substantial ties to the US.

Secure Communities and other federal programs involving local law enforcement play a major role in the increase in deportations. The federal government has portrayed these programs as focused on dangerous criminals, but most immigrants deported through Secure Communities are categorized by the federal government as "non-criminal" or lower level offenders. These programs may exacerbate distrust of police in immigrant communities, and thus may deter crime victims from seeking protection and redress. Some local and state governments have sought to limit the reach of these programs.

In September, ICE said it would reconsider its policies on transfers of detainees between facilities. Human Rights Watch documented in 2011 how high numbers of detainees were subjected to chaotic and frequent transfers between facilities, hampering detainees' access to due process and family support.

Also in September, federal courts rejected parts of several state laws impacting the rights of unauthorized immigrants. In Alabama, a court struck down provisions authorizing the state to require immigration verification of children before they enroll in school, or to prohibit state courts from enforcing contracts in which one party is an unauthorized immigrant. In Georgia, a court ruled against a provision allowing the state to punish people who work with or transport undocumented immigrants. The US Supreme Court overturned several sections of Arizona's immigrant law, though it left intact a section requiring police to attempt to verify a person's immigration status if there is a "reasonable suspicion" the individual is in the country without authorization. This provision increases the risk that immigrant families in Arizona and other states will face abuse from local authorities.

Alabama's immigrant law, like Arizona's, denied basic rights to unauthorized immigrants and their families, including US citizen children.

In a positive step in June, federal officials suspended deportation of certain unauthorized immigrants who were brought to the US as children. To qualify for Deferred Action for Childhood Arrivals, immigrants must be under 30 years old, have lived in the country for at least 5 years, must not have been convicted of a serious criminal offense, and must be in school, have earned a high school diploma, or have served in the military.

Hundreds of thousands of immigrant woman and girl farmworkers face a high risk of sexual violence and harassment in their workplaces. Immigrant women often fail to report these crimes because of the lack of adequate workplace protections, and their fear of deportation or reprisals from employers.

Labor Rights

Hundreds of thousands of children work on American farms. The 1938 Fair Labor Standards Act exempts child farmworkers from the minimum age and maximum hour requirements that apply to all other working children, exposing them to work at far younger ages, for longer hours, and under more hazardous conditions. As a result, child farmworkers, most of them Latino, often work 10 or more hours a day and risk pesticide poisoning, heat illness, injuries, life-long disabilities, and death. Of children under age 16 who suffered fatal occupational injuries in 2010, 75 percent worked in crop production. Thousands more are injured each year. Federal protections that do exist are often not enforced.

In April, the Department of Labor withdrew new regulations proposed in 2011 that would have updated, for the first time in decades, the list of hazardous

HUMAN
RIGHTS
WATCH

Cultivating Fear
The Vulnerability of Immigrant Farmworkers in the US
to Sexual Violence and Sexual Harassment

agricultural tasks prohibited for children under age 16. (Federal law bans hazardous work for children under age 18 outside agriculture). Several members of Congress claimed, inaccurately, that the rules would hurt family farms and agricultural training, and introduced bills to block them.

Millions of US workers, including parents of infants, are harmed by weak or non-existent laws on paid leave, breastfeeding accommodation, and discrimination against workers with family responsibilities. Inadequate leave contributes to delaying babies' immunizations, postpartum depression, and other health problems, and causes mothers to stop breastfeeding early.

The Obama administration proposed a regulation to end the exclusion of certain home care workers from minimum wage and hour protections. These workers, most of whom are women, including many immigrants and minorities, provide essential services to people with disabilities and the elderly.

Health Policy

In June, the US Supreme Court upheld the Affordable Care Act, which significantly expands many citizens' access to health insurance and medical care.

HIV infections in the US continue to disproportionately affect minority communities, men who have sex with men, and transgender women. Many states continue to undermine human rights and public health with restrictions on sex education, inadequate legal protections for HIV-positive persons, resistance to harm-reduction programs such as syringe exchanges, and failure to fund HIV prevention and care. Harmful criminal justice policies include laws that target people living with HIV for enhanced penalties and the use of condoms as evidence of prostitution. This practice, which Human Rights Watch documented in four major cities, makes sex workers reluctant to carry the number of condoms they need to protect themselves from disease and pregnancy, and undermines both human rights and public health.

Persons with Disabilities

The Senate Foreign Relations Committee sent the UN Convention on the Rights of Persons with Disabilities (CRPD) to the Senate for ratification in July. The ratification package has a number of reservations, including one that says US law is already compliant with the convention. At this writing, ratification appeared stalled until at least 2013.

Women's and Girls' Rights

The Violence Against Women Act (VAWA), the primary federal law providing legal protection and services to victims of domestic and sexual violence and stalking, faced an uncertain future. At this writing, the congressional renewal process had stalled due to disagreements over protections for immigrant victims; lesbian, gay, bisexual, and transgender (LGBT) victims; and victims on tribal lands.

Department of Defense statistics indicate that out of an estimated 19,000 sexual assaults in the military each year, only 3,192 were reported in fiscal year 2011; just 240 of those resulted in military prosecution. Recently announced initiatives to address the problem include removing investigative responsibility from frontline commanders; however, cases would remain within the chain of command.

Inadequate investigations of sexual violence are a problem beyond the military. Nationally, fewer than 20 percent of sexual assaults are reported to police, and even reported cases are not always adequately investigated. For example, Human Rights Watch research indicates that between 2009 and 2011, numerous victims who reported their sexual assaults to the police in the District of Columbia saw their cases languish after being effectively closed without investigation. Human Rights Watch previously found that forensic exams for sexual assault victims in California and Illinois sat in storage for years without being tested.

Despite dozens of lawsuits from objecting employers, a healthcare reform requirement that employers cover contraception in employee health insurance plans went into effect this year, allowing an estimated 47 million women to access contraceptives without cost. State anti-abortion laws passed in 2012 included limits on insurance coverage for abortion, medical abortion restrictions, and bans on abortion after 20 weeks of pregnancy. Laws mandating ultrasounds before abortion, which exist in eight states, encountered a public backlash when debate over a Virginia bill exposed that the proposed requirement could force women to undergo the insertion of a transvaginal probe.

Sexual Orientation and Gender Identity

Public attitudes towards gay marriage appear to be shifting. During the November elections, Maryland, Maine, and Washington State passed ballot initiatives supporting gay marriage, joining six other states and the District of Columbia in permitting same-sex marriage. It was the first time anywhere that gay marriage has been approved by popular vote. Minnesota voters also rejected an effort to ban gay marriage in that state. In February, a federal appeals court declared unconstitutional a California ballot measure that banned same-sex marriage in 2008. That ruling is being appealed to the US Supreme Court.

The Defense of Marriage Act (DOMA) continues to bar recognition of same-sex marriage at the federal level. In May, North Carolina became the 30th state in the US to include a prohibition on same-sex marriage in its state constitution. And while New Jersey's legislature passed a bill permitting same-sex marriage, the governor vetoed it.

President Barack Obama has expressed his personal support for gay marriage, and senior US officials have made statements recognizing LGBT rights as human rights.

Yet federal law offers no protection against discrimination based on sexual orientation or gender identity. Only 21 US states and the District of Columbia have laws prohibiting employment discrimination based on sexual orientation.

Counterterrorism

On December 31, 2011, Obama signed the National Defense Authorization Act for Fiscal Year 2012 (NDAA). The act codified the existing executive practice of detaining terrorism suspects indefinitely without charge, and required that cer-

HUMAN
RIGHTS
WATCH

Sex Workers at Risk
Condoms as Evidence of Prostitution in Four US Cities

tain terrorism suspects be initially detained by the military if captured inside the US. A presidential policy directive issued in February reduced the reach of the mandatory military detention portion of the act, calling it rigid and a danger to US national security.

January 11 marked the tenth anniversary of detention of terrorism suspects at Guantanamo Bay. The NDAA reaffirmed congressional restrictions on transfer of detainees from Guantanamo, with minor changes. At this writing, no detainee has been transferred out of Guantanamo under that regime. Two Uighur detainees—to whom the congressional restrictions did not apply as their detention had already been ruled unlawful by a federal judge—were resettled to El Salvador in April. In July, in another exception to the restrictions, Ibrahim al-Qosi was returned to his native Sudan under the terms of a plea agreement in a military commission proceeding. In September, Adnan Latif, became the ninth detainee to die at the facility since it opened; and Omar Khadr, only 15 when captured by the US in Afghanistan, was sent back to his home country of Canada to serve out the remainder of his eight-year sentence pursuant to a plea agreement. This brought the total population of detainees in Guantanamo to 166.

A one-year deadline to establish a system of periodic review for detainees held at Guantanamo expired in March. The Defense Department did not conduct any reviews, but did issue regulations outlining the procedures. The Defense Department also sought to limit detainees' access to counsel by creating a new set of rules that would have been overseen by the military commander at Guantanamo; in September, a federal judge ruled the new counsel access rules unlawful. In November, the US filed a notice of appeal.

On August 30, the Justice Department closed without charges its investigation, led by special prosecutor John Durham, into the deaths of two detainees in secret CIA custody. The investigation had originally encompassed the cases of approximately 100 detainees who had been held in CIA custody, but in 2011 the Justice Department narrowed its focus to only two.

The US unlawfully transferred at least 15 Libyan citizens back to Muammar Gaddafi's Libya from 2003 to 2006. The US had detained, interrogated, and tortured or otherwise ill-treated several of them for years before sending them back. Two former detainees alleged they had been subjected to waterboarding or other water torture, calling into question the US assertion that only three detainees had ever been waterboarded. None had been approached by US officials in connection with Durham's investigation.

Five men accused of plotting the September 11, 2001 attacks were arraigned in a military commission in Guantanamo in June. Pre-trial proceedings before a military commission continued against Abd al-Rahim al-Nashiri, accused of plotting the bombing of the USS *Cole* in Yemen in October 2000. The Defense Department issued preliminary charges against an additional detainee.

Following exposure of the New York Police Department's (NYPD) broad surveillance of mosques, Muslim student groups, and Muslim-owned businesses, NYPD Assistant Chief Thomas Galati testified in court that no information from the program produced a lead in a terrorism investigation.

Through speeches and media reports, US officials sought to explain US policy on targeted killings in Pakistan, Somalia and elsewhere by unmanned aerial vehicles, or drones. They said the policy was to engage in targeted killings only if traditional law enforcement means were unavailable, although they relied on both the laws of war and self-defense as legal bases for targeted killings.

John Brennan, Obama's chief counterterrorism advisor, asserted that targeted killings were justified against anyone who is "part of" al Qaeda, the Taliban, or associated forces, even in situations far from a recognized battlefield. This definition, if applied, would exceed the scope of targeting permitted under the laws of war. CIA involvement in many drone strikes has meant little or no accountability for possible laws of war violations. Media reports described President Obama as personally approving each targeted killing conducted by the US military.

H U M A N
RIGHTS
WATCH

"Like a Death Sentence"

Abuses against Persons with Mental Disabilities in Ghana

WORLD REPORT
2013

2012
HUMAN RIGHTS WATCH
PUBLICATIONS

The following is a list of Human Rights Watch reports published from mid-December 2011 to December 2012. This list does not include press releases or other Human Rights Watch material released during the year.

December 2011

"By All Means Necessary": Individual and Command Responsibility for Crimes Against Humanity in Syria, 60 pp.

Tunisia's Repressive Laws: The Reform Agenda, 49 pp.

January 2012

Administrative Error: Georgia's Flawed System for Administrative Detention, 38 pp.

Against All Odds: Prison Conditions for Youth Offenders Serving Life without Parole Sentences in the United States, 47 pp.

Justice for Serious Crimes Before National Courts: Uganda's International Crimes Division, 29 pp.

Old Behind Bars: The Aging Prison Population in the United States, 104 pp.

The Road Ahead: A Human Rights Agenda for Egypt's New Parliament, 46 pp.

"The Root of Humiliation": Abusive Identity Checks in France, 55 pp.

"They Hunt Us Down for Fun": Discrimination and Police Violence Against Transgender Women in Kuwait, 63 pp.

"Waiting Here for Death": Forced Displacement and "Villagization" in Ethiopia's Gambella Region, 119 pp.

HUMAN RIGHTS WATCH

WHEN I DIE...
THEY'LL SEND ME HOME
Youth Sentenced to Life without Parole in California, An Update

February 2012

"Forget About Him, He's Not Here": Israel's Control of Palestinian Residency in the West Bank and Gaza, 90 pp.

No Justice in Bahrain: Unfair Trials in Military and Civilian Court, 94 pp.

No Place for Children: Child Recruitment, Forced Marriage, and Attacks on Schools in Somalia, 104 pp.

"No Safe Places": Yemen's Crackdown on Protests in Taizz, 75 pp.

"Steps of the Devil": Denial of Women and Girls' Right to Sport in Saudi Arabia, 58 pp.

"They Took Everything from Me": Forced Evictions, Unlawful Expropriations, and House Demolitions in Azerbaijan's Capital, 96 pp.

March 2012

"I Had To Run Away": Women and Girls Imprisoned for "Moral Crimes" in Afghanistan, 120 pp.

Justice for Atrocity Crimes: Lessons of International Support for Trials Before the State Court of Bosnia and Herzegovina, 44 pp.

The Island of Happiness Revisited: A Progress Report on Abuses of Migrant Workers on Abu Dhabi's Saadiyat Island, 85 pp.

"Untold Miseries": Wartime Abuses and Forced Displacement in Burma's Kachin State, 83 pp.

"When I Die ... They'll Send Me Home": Youth Sentenced to Life in Prison without Parole in California, An Update, 28 pp.

April 2012

In Cold Blood: Summary Executions by Syrian Security Forces and Pro-Government Militias, 23 pp.

Second Class Citizens: Discrimination again Roma, Jews and Other National Minorities in Bosnia and Herzegovina, 62 pp.

May 2012

"Beat Him, Take Everything Away": Abuses by China's Chengguan Para-Police, 55 pp.

Criminal Reprisals: Kenyan Police and Military Abuses against Ethnic Somalis, 65 pp.

Cultivating Fear: The Vulnerability of Immigrant Farmworkers in the US to Sexual Violence and Sexual Harassment, 95 pp.

"If You Come Back We Will Kill You": Sexual Violence and other Abuses against Congolese Migrants during Expulsions from Angola, 49 pp.

"I Want to be a Citizen Just like Any Other": Barriers to Political Participation for People with Disabilities in Peru, 89 pp.

"They Burned My Heart": War Crimes in Northern Idlib during Peace Plan Negotiations, 38 pp.

Unacknowledged Deaths: Civilian Casualties in NATO's Air Campaign in Libya, 76 pp.

"You Will Not Have Peace While You Are Living": The Escalation of Political Violence in Burundi, 81 pp.

June 2012

Building a Better World Cup: Protecting Migrant Workers in Qatar Ahead of FIFA 2022, 146 pp.

Isolated in Yunnan: Kachin Refugees from Burma in China's Yunnan Province, 68 pp.

Out of Control: Mining, Regulatory Failure and Human Rights in India, 70 pp.

"Prison Is Not For Me": Arbitrary Detention in South Sudan, 105 pp.

"What Will Happen if Hunger Comes?": Abuses against the Indigenous Peoples of Ethiopia's Lower Omo Valley, 85 pp.

July 2012

"Between Two Sets of Guns": Attacks on Civil Society Activists in India's Maoist Conflict, 60 pp.

Boat Ride to Detention: Adult and Child Migrants in Malta, 56 pp.

"Even a 'Big Man' Must Face Justice": Lessons from the Trial of Charles Taylor, 55 pp.

Hate on the Streets: Xenophobic Violence in Greece, 99 pp.

Iraq's Information Crimes Law: Badly Written Provisions and Draconian Punishments Violate Due Process and Free Speech, 16 pp.

Sex Workers at Risk: Condoms as Evidence of Prostitution in Four US Cities, 112 pp.

"The Fear Never Leaves Me": Torture, Custodial Deaths, and Unfair Trials after the 2009 Mutiny of the Bangladesh Rifles, 57 pp.

Tightening the Grip: Concentration and Abuse of Power in Chávez's Venezuela, 133 pp.

HUMAN
RIGHTS
WATCH

"Even a 'Big Man' Must Face Justice"
Lessons from the Trial of Charles Taylor

Torture Archipelago: Arbitrary Arrests, Torture, and Enforced Disappearances in Syria's Underground Prisons since March 2011, 81 pp.

Torture in the Name of Treatment: Human Rights Abuses in Vietnam, China, Cambodia, and Lao PDR, 23 pp.

August 2012

Angola's Upcoming Elections: Attacks on the Media, Expression, and Assembly, 13 pp.

Codifying Repression: An Assessment of Iran's New Penal Code, 48 pp.

Curtailing Criticism: Intimidation and Obstruction of Civil Society in Uganda, 53 pp.

"The Government Could Have Stopped This": Sectarian Violence and Ensuing Abuses in Burma's Arakan State, 56 pp.

September 2012

Ad Hoc and Inadequate: Thailand's Treatment of Refugees and Asylum Seekers, 143 pp.

Classrooms in the Crosshairs: Military Use of Schools in Yemen's Capital, 46 pp.

Delivered Into Enemy Hands: US-Led Abuse and Rendition of Opponents to Gaddafi's Libya, 154 pp.

Striking Oil, Striking Workers: Violations of Labor Rights in Kazakhstan's Oil Sector, 152 pp.

Time for Justice: Ending Impunity for Killings and Disappearances in 1990s Turkey, 65 pp.

"Will I Get My Dues ... Before I Die?": Harm to Women from Bangladesh's Discriminatory Laws on Marriage, Separation, and Divorce, 109 pp.

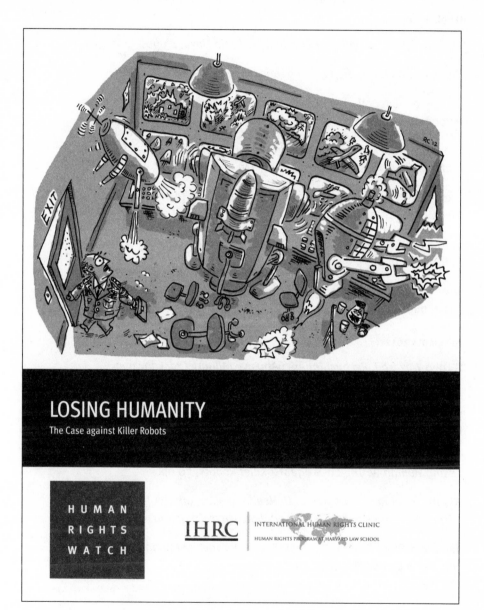

LOSING HUMANITY
The Case against Killer Robots

HUMAN
RIGHTS
WATCH

IHRC INTERNATIONAL HUMAN RIGHTS CLINIC
HUMAN RIGHTS PROGRAM AT HARVARD LAW SCHOOL

October 2012

Abusive System: Failures of Criminal Justice in Gaza, 43 pp.

Death of a Dictator: Bloody Vengeance in Sirte, 58 pp.

For a Better Life: Migrant Worker Abuse in Bahrain and the Government Reform Agenda, 123 pp.

Growing Up Locked Down: Youth in Solitary Confinement in Jails and Prisons Across the United States, 147 pp.

"Like a Death Sentence": Abuses against Persons with Mental Disabilities in Ghana, 84 pp.

Spiraling Violence: Boko Haram Attacks and Security Force Abuses in Nigeria, 98 pp.

Toxic Tanneries: The Health Repercussions of Bangladesh's Hazaribagh Leather, 101 pp.

November 2012

"A Long Way from Reconciliation": Abusive Military Crackdown in Response to Security Threats in Côte d'Ivoire, 73 pp.

A Red Herring: Marijuana Arrestees Do Not Become Violent Felons, 33 pp.

Lonely Servitude: Child Domestic Labor in Morocco, 73 pp.

Losing Humanity: The Case against Killer Robots, 50 pp.

Rights Out of Reach: Obstacles to Health, Justice, and Protection for Displaced Victims of Gender-Based Violence in Colombia, 97 pp.

"Tell Them That I Want to Kill Them": Two Decades of Impunity in Hun Sen's Cambodia, 68 pp.

"The Law Was Against Me": Migrant Women's Access to Protection for Family Violence in Belgium, 57 pp.

The Answer is No: Too Little Compassionate Release in US Federal Prisons, 128 pp.

December 2012

Waiting for Justice: Accountability before Guinea's Courts for the September 28, 2009 Stadium Massacre, Rapes, and Other Abuses, 58 pp.

Under Siege: Indiscriminate Bombing and Abuses in Sudan's Southern Kordofan and Blue Nile States, 39 pp.

Why They Left: Stories of Iranian Activists in Exile, 60 pp.

All reports are available online at www.hrw.org/en/publications.